*Strangeness and Power*

# Strangeness and Power

*Essays on the poetry of Geoffrey Hill*

edited by

# Andrew Michael Roberts

Shearsman Books

First published in the United Kingdom in 2020 by
Shearsman Books Ltd
PO Box 4239
Swindon
SN3 9FN

Shearsman Books Ltd Registered Office
30–31 St. James Place, Mangotsfield, Bristol BS16 9JB
*(this address not for correspondence)*

ISBN 978-1-84861-600-4

Copyright © 2020 by the authors.

The right of the persons listed on page 5 and 6 to be identified as the authors of this work has been asserted by them in accordance with the Copyrights, Designs and Patents Act of 1988.
All rights reserved.

ACKNOWLEDGEMENTS

I am grateful to the Arts and Humanities Research Institute, School of Humanities, University of Dundee, for assistance with permissions and indexing costs, and to Paula Clarke Bain for her work on the index.

I would like to thank Aurora Woods for her meticulous work on permissions and editing, Martin Dodsworth for his invaluable advice and Tony Frazer for his enthusiasm, patience and support in bringing this book to press.

Grateful acknowledgement is made to the following sources for permission to reproduce material previously published elsewhere:

T.S. Eliot, excerpts from *Collected Poems 1909–1962* (London: Faber, 1974), reprinted by permission of Faber & Faber.

Geoffrey Hill, poems from *Broken Hierarchies: Poems 1952-2012*, ed. Kenneth Haynes (Oxford: Oxford University Press, 2013). Excerpts reprinted by permission of Oxford University Press.

Geoffrey Hill, poems from *Collected Poems* (Harmondsworth: Penguin, 1985), excerpts reprinted by permission of Penguin Books.

David Jones, excerpts from *The Sleeping Lord, and other fragments* (London: Faber, 1974), *The Anathémata* (London: Faber, 1952), *In Parenthesis* (London: Faber, 1963), reprinted by permission of Faber & Faber.

J.H. Prynne, poems excerpts from *Poems* (Tarset: Bloodaxe Books, 2005), reprinted by permission of the author.

Denise Riley, poems from *Mop Mop Georgette* (London: Reality Street Editions, 1993), excerpts reprinted by permission of the author.

# CONTENTS

Introduction / 7
ANDREW MICHAEL ROBERTS

CHAPTER ONE / 16
'Felt Unities': Geoffrey Hill, T.S. Eliot and David Jones
STEVEN MATTHEWS

CHAPTER TWO / 39
The Nature of Hill's Later Poetry
STEPHEN JAMES

CHAPTER THREE / 64
'Poetry's a public act by long engagement':
Geoffrey Hill and the Eighteenth Century
TOM JONES

CHAPTER FOUR / 85
Geoffrey Hill and J. H. Prynne: Language, Subjectivity and Longing
EDWARD LARRISSY

CHAPTER FIVE / 98
Lyric, Awkwardness and Music in Geoffrey Hill and Denise Riley
ANDREW MICHAEL ROBERTS

CHAPTER SIX / 134
Affinities with Radical Landscape Poetry
in the Work of Geoffrey Hill
ELEANORE WIDGER

CHAPTER SEVEN / 151
'Self going spare': Geoffrey Hill and Philosophy
ALEX PESTELL

CHAPTER EIGHT / 174
Geoffrey Hill's Difficulties
MARTIN DODSWORTH

CHAPTER NINE / 203
Playing (to) the Crowd: Examining Performance
in *Speech! Speech!*
SAMIRA NADKARNI

CHAPTER TEN / 223
'Like a Mason Addressing a Block':
Materiality and Design in Geoffrey Hill's Poetry
NATALIE POLLARD

CHAPTER ELEVEN / 252
Geoffrey Hill and Publishing: 'The Recalcitrance of the World'
MATTHEW SPERLING

ABBREVIATIONS / 276

NOTES ON CONTRIBUTORS / 277

BIBLIOGRAPHY / 279

INDEX / 284

# Introduction

## Andrew Michael Roberts

In one of his final publications, a review of Grevel Lindop's biography of Charles Williams, Geoffrey Hill asserts his commitment to 'the strangeness and the power of poetry'.[1] The words accord with many readers' responses to Hill's own poetry. It is generally seen as 'powerful', in rhetorical, formal, intellectual and emotional terms, and is much concerned with issues of political and aesthetic power. Those who are most critical of Hill's work often acknowledge a certain power of language, but suspect the uses to which that power is put, especially in relation to political allegiance and intellectual authority. 'Strangeness' may here stand for the remarkable distinctiveness of his poetry, which over more than sixty years, from the mid-1950s to his death in 2016, followed a trajectory of development and innovation which engaged in unique ways with many of the crucial questions in late twentieth century and early twenty-first century poetics: the lyrical and the anti-lyrical, Romantic, Modernist and earlier inheritances; form and formal innovation; the personal and the impersonal; history and ethics. But more than that, the word suggests the way in which that poetry is somehow 'strange' and much concerned with strangeness, in both negative and positive terms: estrangement, peculiarity, revelation. Hill's writing fulfils to a high degree the Russian Futurist aim of 'making strange' the familiar, as well as bringing to the reader's attention, through its learning and allusion, aspects of history and culture which are likely to be unfamiliar to many. For some readers, Hill's late work in particular is simply *too* 'strange': too resistant to reading and understanding. Both his admirers and his detractors, and those who come somewhere between, might acknowledge qualities of strangeness, even that if judgment would carry different implications and values in each case. A number of essays in this volume pair Hill with another poet, or poets, to consider his 'strange likeness' with contemporaries and predecessors.[2]

---

[1] Geoffrey Hill, 'Mightier and Darker': review of Grevel Lindop, *Charles Williams: The Third Inkling*, *Times Literary Supplement*, 23 March 2016.

[2] The phrase is from *Mercian Hymns* XXIV, where the poet comments on the relationship of his youthful persona in to his 'outclassed forefathers': 'Not strangeness, but strange likeness' (BH 111).

The chapters in this book were written, or begun, during Geoffrey Hill's lifetime, but some minor revisions have been made since his death in June 2016. In literary studies in general, so much attention has been paid to Roland Barthes' theoretical 'death of the author' that the literal event has been somewhat neglected as a phenomenon of literary reception and interpretation. The most succinct treatment remains, perhaps, Auden's 'In Memory of W.B. Yeats'. Auden's line 'The death of the poet was kept from his poems' captures the paradoxical quality of that moment: the way in which the works, the words on the page and the books on the shelf, remain unchanged, with all their wealth of meaning and history, their 'voice' and their presence, even while the reader's relationship to them is subtly but crucially transformed.[3] For many of the contributors to this book, most of whom have read and commented on Hill's work over an extended period of time, the loss of his living presence was clearly an event of considerable significance. The experience of writing about the work of a living author is a distinctive one, introducing into critical practice possibilities for both positive dialogue and awkward relation, and placing the distinction between biographical personality and literary *oeuvre* (however necessary as a principle) under the pressure of potential collisions or interventions. The critic may believe in the necessary freedom and potential creativity of interpretation, and remain aware of the restrictive nature (for both author and reader) of 'the intentional fallacy', yet the lurking fear remains of receiving the reproof which Prufrock anticipates: 'That is not what I meant at all; / That is not it, at all'.[4] When the living presence disappears, there can be a strong sense of loss. For some critics this will have been a personal loss; for others there will have been the more diffuse but still powerful sense of an intellectual and creative force having been removed from future interventions, even while its textual embodiment remains, and its reception or 'after-life' continues to develop.

A striking feature of Hill's *oeuvre* is the extent and richness of its development: a combination of formal, technical and thematic innovation with persistent imaginative imperatives, for which Yeats' poetic development seems the obvious comparison. While the patterns of this development are multiple and complex, the shape of a set of

---

[3] W.H. Auden, 'In Memory of W.B. Yeats', *Collected Poems*, ed. Edward Mendelson (London: Faber and Faber, 1976), p. 197.

[4] T.S. Eliot, 'The Love Song of J. Alfred Prufrock', *The Poems and Plays of T.S. Eliot* (London: Faber, 1969), p. 16.

antitheses between 'early' and 'late' Hill emerges from the work and its recent reception. The work up to *Collected Poems* (1985) can be characterised by a poetic in which strong energies and tensions are contained with terse formal limits. This takes the form of highly concentrated lyrics, prose poems and short sequences (often sonnets), marked by 'impersonality' (the poetic 'self' being absent, highly mediated, or ironized) and a certain grandeur and formality of tone, but shot through with subversive strains of double meaning and colloquialism. *Canaan* (1996) marks a transition, following which a later phase with some well-defined characteristics establishes itself. The book-length sequence dominates, beginning with a mid-period series of four books (of which the first three were seen by some as a trilogy): *The Triumph of Love* (1998); *Speech! Speech!* (2000); *The Orchards of Syon* (2002) and *Scenes from Comus* (2005).[5] Of the fourteen volumes which follow *Canaan*, the only ones which are not a single sequence are *Without Title* and *A Treatise of Civil Power*. Most of the sequences are in regular sections of defined length, though *The Triumph of Love* has verse units ranging from one to fifty-seven lines in length. The poetic 'I' becomes more prominent, although still frequently treated with irony. Disputation, denunciation, self-mockery, colloquialism and scabrous humour diversify the tone, though solemnity and lyric beauty still persist. In places the poetry can have a quality of annotation, or an internal conversation notated. The subject-matter admits more of the contemporary and the autobiographical, though the poetry is still deeply informed by political and intellectual history, with the density of allusion becoming if anything more intense. Hill's work, especially from *Speech! Speech!* onwards, includes forms of performed and imagined dialogue, often adversarial (though sometimes humorously so) with imagined (and perhaps real) critics. In many ways this extended his long-standing reflexive dialogue with his own critical

---

[5] Jeffrey Wainwright suggested that '*The Orchards of Syon* completes a tentative trilogy begun with *The Triumph of Love* and *Speech! Speech!*. "Tentative" because all three-part sequences are bound to refer to the model of Dante's *La Divina Commedia* as … Hill's can be seen to do'. Jeffrey Wainwright, *Acceptable Words: Essays on the Poetry of Geoffrey Hill* (Manchester: Manchester University Press, 2006), p. 109. Alex Wylie identifies *Scenes from Comus* as 'the last (for now) of a series of book-length sequences which began with 1998's *The Triumph of Love* … Hill is now so prolific that what people were casually referring to as his "late period" … from *The Triumph of Love* on, has begun to be more cautiously labelled the "middle period".' 'Eros in Geoffrey Hill's *Scenes from Comus*', *English* (2011), 1-15 (p. 1).

and self-critical impulses. A 'touchy' response to others' criticism is evident, and widely noticed, in some of Hill's poetry, critical writing and interviews, but a generosity and scrupulosity of relation to critics was equally in evidence in other contexts: at certain conferences and readings, and in his responses to individuals. During his final years, there emerged a strong sense of his wish to shape and define his literary legacy, embodied in the two substantial, hardback Oxford University Press volumes of his prose (*Collected Critical Writings*, 2008) and poetry (*Broken Hierarchies: Poems 1952-2012*, 2013), and in his 2009 sale of his literary papers to the Special Collections at the University of Leeds, where he had held his first academic post.[6] Indeed, this careful curation of his legacy continued posthumously: *Broken Hierarchies* culminates in five sequences, *The Daybooks* (2007-2012), but has been followed by a final, posthumously-published volume, *The Book of Baruch by the Gnostic Justin*, identified by his publisher as 'his final statement'.[7]

Hill's 'place' in British and Anglophone poetry of the later 20th and early 21st centuries was a complex one, and remains in many ways to be more fully defined by the assimilation of his rich late period work, and by the perspectives which time will allow. His poetry did not fit into either of the broad (and often debatable) categories of 'mainstream' and 'alternative' which informed much discussion about British poetry in general during the second half of the twentieth century. However, the term 'late Modernist', which could be applied with some caveats to

---

[6] See https://explore.library.leeds.ac.uk/special-collections-explore/8501/geoffrey_hill_archive. In the present volume, Matthew Sperling notes that 'Before *Broken Hierarchies* had been published, Hill was comparing it to Whitman's 1892 "deathbed edition" of *Leaves of Grass*'.

[7] *The Book of Baruch by the Gnostic Justin*, ed. Kenneth Haynes (Oxford: Oxford University Press, 2019). 'At his death in 2016, Geoffrey Hill left behind *The Book of Baruch by the Gnostic Justin*, his last work, a sequence of more than 270 poems, to be published posthumously as his final statement. Written in long lines of variable length, with much off-rhyme and internal rhyme, the verse-form of the book stands at the opposite end from the ones developed in the late *Daybooks* of *Broken Hierarchies* (2013), where he explored highly taut constructions such as Sapphic meter, figure-poems, fixed rhyming strophes, and others. The looser metrical plan of the new book admits an enormous range of tones of voices. Thematically, the work is a *summa* of a lifetime's meditation on the nature of poetry.' https://global.oup.com/academic/product/the-book-of-baruch-by-the-gnostic-justin-9780198829522?q=book%20of%20baruch&lang=en&cc=gb# [accessed 29 March 2019]. The idea of *The Book of Baruch* as a '*summa*' must be balanced by the sense (and fact) that it is unfinished (though substantial). Hill's line from 'Funeral Music' – 'Crying to the end "I have not finished"' (BH 54; KL 32) seems apposite.

Hill's work, indicates some affinities with aspects of the 'alternative' or 'innovative' stream of writing. One of the aims of the present volume, and notably the chapters which compare Hill to J.H. Prynne, to Denise Riley and to 'radical landscape poetry', is to rectify a certain critical neglect of these affinities, arising perhaps from a strong sense of Hill as *sui generis*. Although some of his early work was briefly linked to 'Oxford poetry' (early pamphlets and poems in *Isis*), to the post-Movement reaction (through his inclusion in Alvarez's *The New Poetry*) and to 'Leeds poetry' (through his connections to *Stand* and to Jon Silkin), he quickly emerged as a writer unamenable to grouping. As both poet and critic Hill attracted both strong praise and some hostility. The widely-shared and often aired sense of him as a strong contender for 'greatness' was at times a mixed blessing, prompting irritation from some as well as celebration from others. Hill's interest in Englishness and its history, although sceptical and critical, and far from narrowly nationalistic, sometimes attracted praise from those whose political affiliations led to others viewing this with suspicion. The view of his work as 'difficult' (sometimes seen as praise but more usually figuring as complaint) became such a staple of reviews as to risk being what Hill himself particularly disliked, a cliché, evoked but not really scrutinized. In the present volume Martin Dodsworth addresses this issue directly and analytically, acknowledging but also subjecting to critique Hill's arguments in favour of 'difficulty'; Edward Larrissy compares Hill's difficulty to comparable elements in the work of J.H. Prynne; and Stephen James argues that the immediately appealing descriptive passages in Hill's poetry cannot be separated from the complexity of its other elements.

    The book begins with six chapters addressing in various ways the relationship of Hill's poetry to predecessors and contemporaries. In his chapter '"Felt Unities": Geoffrey Hill, T. S. Eliot and David Jones', Steven Matthews examines Hill's relationship to two modernist predecessors, as a means to articulate aspects of the development of his criticism and poetry. Focusing on the local and pastoral within modernism, ideas of *enracinement,* and common experience, Matthews argues for the importance to Hill of Jones's re-emergence via two issues of *Agenda* magazine in the late 1960s and early 1970s. He goes on to use Hill's own distinction between 'discursive intelligence' and a Bradleian 'way of apprehension' as a way of interpreting the poetic of Hill's later work.

That later work is also the focus of Stephen James's chapter, 'The Nature of Hill's Later Poetry'. Starting from the preferences of many reviewers for passages of natural description in that poetry, James shows how such descriptions are 'often modes of cultural, historical, theological or philosophical engagement'. James goes on to explore 'poetic alchemy', esoteric thought, doubleness, 'thisness' (haecceity) and musical analogies of dissonance and resolution, and a series of poetic relations (with Hopkins, Donne, Thomson, Clare and Vaughan), so as to argue for the inextricability of visual beauty and complexity of 'apperception'.

Tom Jones, in '"Poetry's a public act by long engagement": Geoffrey Hill and the Eighteenth Century', uses Hill's references to, and affinities with, eighteenth-century authors, notably Jonathan Swift, to pose some pointed questions around matters of authenticity, the control of language, and relations between the poet and readers. In particular, he asks whether Hill's project requires the existence of 'a mob for whom the "noble vernacular" ... will be forever out of reach', and whether 'sovereign authority over the language in poems is possible or even desirable', raising questions about the distance between Hill and his audience. Drawing parallels with Swift, Lord Shaftesbury and Joseph Butler, Jones argues that a 'regulatory attitude' to 'the conditions of production and reception of speech' is central to Hill's work, and yet is 'at odds with his recognition of the idea of contingency in poetic composition'. Finding a running tension in Hill's poetic between 'authority' and 'fallenness', Jones points towards a question for Hill's more secular-minded readers: whether an 'external standard' for judging poetic style is attainable.

In the first of three chapters which seek to articulate the location of Hill's poetry in relation to the traditions of contemporary 'innovative' poetry, 'Geoffrey Hill and J.H. Prynne: Language, Subjectivity and Longing', Edward Larrissy finds profound similarities between the seemingly 'ill-matched couple' of Hill and J.H. Prynne. These include a tendency to difficulty in both poets' work arising from 'similar aesthetic aims', 'a self-consciousness about the historically-conditioned nature of language and discourse', a 'political and ethical ... critique of free-market capitalism' arising from mid-twentieth-century New Left ideas and the use of 'the language of the sacred and transcendent'. More widely, he argues for a shared complexity of relationship to Romanticism, Modernism and Postmodernism, in which the poets' seriousness in ethical and spiritual matters marks them as late Modernist writers, but this is combined with a 'representation of subjective experience' derived from Romanticism, and a postmodernist sense of the 'limits of understanding'.

In my own contribution to the present volume, 'Lyric, Awkwardness and Music in Geoffrey Hill and Denise Riley', I explore another affinity across difference, connecting Hill's poetry and prose to that of Denise Riley, through reflections on awkwardness as both theme and technique in the lyric. Awkwardness, in both capacities, is closely related to effects of temporality in poetic form, conceptualised by Hill in terms of 'return' and 'resistance', and by Riley in terms of 'regression'. Focusing on one volume by each poet, along with material from essays, I address the poets' shared allegiance to forms of musicality, their ethically-motivated critiques of lyric expressiveness, and their sense of guilt in relation to language and utterance. My suggestion is that the two poets use awkwardness to negotiate such issues, and in Hill's case to define his relationship to Romantic and Modernist predecessors, so that despite marked differences in their understanding of the self, Hill and Riley are alike in deploying the power of the lyrical within a self-consciously critical late-modernist poetic.

Eleanore Widger, in her chapter 'Affinities with Radical Landscape Poetry in the Work of Geoffrey Hill', argues that Hill's use of shape on the page to create poetic meaning, notably in *Clavics*, points to an under-recognised affinity with the contemporary practice which has come to be known as 'radical landscape poetry': the work of poets such as Frances Presley, Wendy Mulford, Mark Goodwin and Peter Riley, collected in Harriet Tarlo's anthology *The Ground Aslant* (published in the same year as *Clavics*, 2011).[8] Widger begins by tracing some of Hill's earlier evocations of the idea of landscape, from *Mercian Hymns* to *The Mystery of the Charity of Charles Péguy*. Turning to *Clavics*, she acknowledges the crucial influence of Herbert and Vaughan, as well as Greek pattern poetry, but also finds an 'exploration of the ethico-politics of representing the landscape' which Hill shares with much of the work in *The Ground Aslant*. The use of shape on the page in *Clavics*, she concludes 'implicates the poet in the production of the cultural landscape', and seeks to 'bring the history of the landscape to visual perception'.

In '"Self going spare": Geoffrey Hill and Philosophy', Alex Pestell approaches Hill's thought through a disciplinary framing, considering what he terms Hill's 'agon with Philosophy', especially in relation to

---

[8] Harriet Tarlo, ed., *The Ground Aslant: An Anthology of Radical Landscape Poetry* (Exeter: Shearsman Books, 2011).

ideas of contingency, objectivity and (in)completion. Noting Hill's 'adversarial' attitude to J.L. Austin's empiricism, Pestell analyses Hill's turn to Idealism and to philosophers who 'make a virtue of incompletion', including Gillian Rose, Simone Weil and Coleridge. While Rose's 'aporetic ethics' prompt Hill to agonistic dialogue, Weil offers the poet a model of discursive drama via intersecting planes of composition and planes of experience. Coleridge, in Pestell's account, is an ambivalent influence, whose celebration of the critical power of the imagination runs the risk of complacency, and a fading from critique to consolation. Turning to Hill's later engagement with F.H. Bradley (in the 'Alienated Majesty' section of *Collected Critical Writings*), Pestell argues that philosophy can offer the poet 'the idea of truth as something struggling to come into being', but adds a note of caution in his observation that Hill is sometimes led by his passionate engagement with philosophers into 'unwarranted assertions'. These include Hill's widely-noticed value criteria for writing of 'getting within the judgement the condition of the judgement', an idea which, according to Pestell, is rejected both by Bradley and by Hill himself in his earlier essay 'Our Word is Our Bond'.

Martin Dodsworth, in 'Geoffrey Hill's Difficulties', analyses this vexed topic by first identifying three kinds of difficulty encountered by Hill's readers: allusiveness, indefiniteness of relation, and ambiguity. He goes on to approach the issue from the other direction, in terms of the difficulties encountered by Hill in the act of writing, and how these might bear on readers' difficulties. Finally, he assesses the justification for difficulty. Dodsworth is sceptical about Hill's claim that 'difficult art is truly democratic' (which he sees as an inappropriate application of a political term), and sharply critical of aspects of the poet's attitude, such as his 'tendency to adopt or endorse extreme points of view'. However, he finds justification for at least some of the challenges of the poetry in those poems which exemplify Hill's greatness as a poet.

The role (or absence) of 'self' and 'voice' within poetry has been a major debating point since Hill's early 'impersonal' work, and in 'Playing (to) the Crowd: Examining Performance in *Speech! Speech!*', Samira Nadkarni returns to the issue in the light of the prominence given to ideas of performance in Hill's 2000 volume *Speech! Speech!*, the second of his mid-period series of four book-length sequences. In an extended reading of the volume, Nadkarni argues for the centrality of ideas of performance, both as symptom of the consumerist culture which the poem critiques, and as satirical technique; the work's 'poetic persona', she suggests, aspires to authenticity, but is undercut by the poem's many 'voices'. Paradoxically the fragmentary incoherence which results 'lends it a greater strength' because it promotes readerly evaluation. Authenticity is located within a 'final silence'; 'the uneloquent [as] a form of eloquence', in Hill's words from his 2000 interview.[9]

Finally, two chapters are particularly concerned to reconnect Hill's work with questions of the materiality and conditions of production and publication. Natalie Pollard, in '"Like a Mason Addressing a Block": Materiality and Design in Geoffrey Hill's Poetry', draws attention to the importance, for Hill's poetry, of the built environment as a means to negotiating 'cultural inheritance and personal artistic legacy'. Giving detailed consideration to book jackets as well as allusions to architecture in Hill's poetry, she argues that, for Hill, architecture is not merely a metaphor for language (as critics have sometimes seemed to assume), but provides 'sites on which aesthetic relations are negotiated', with ethical and political implications. Engagement with architecture and sculpture functions as part of the poet's 'fraught attention to the politics of redeploying existing built form', both in material terms, in buildings alluded to in the poetry, and 'through literary and historical re-descriptions and reinvestments'.

In 'Geoffrey Hill and Publishing: 'The Recalcitrance of the World', Matthew Sperling takes two striking phrases from a public conversation between Hill and the publisher Andrew McNeillie as key notes for a consideration of the poet's 'thinking in and about poetry and … in and about publishing'; 'the recalcitrance of the world' and 'inescapable error'. Correspondence in the André Deutsch Collection of archive papers held at Tulsa University in Oklahoma, along with material from the memoir of Diane Athill with whom Hill principally dealt during his relationship with André Deutsch, offers insights into his distinctive approach to his own poetry and to his career as a poet. Many aspects of this approach will not surprise long-term readers of his work, but it is nevertheless revealing to see them playing out in this personal / professional context; they include: a mixture of high confidence in his own abilities with self-deprecating irony; an exceptionally strong sense of vocation; difficulties associated with anxiety and sensitivity; an 'anxious care for minute details'.

---

[9] 'The Art of Poetry LXX', Geoffrey Hill interviewed by Carl Phillips, *The Paris Review*, 154 (Spring 2000), 272-99.

CHAPTER ONE

'Felt Unities': Geoffrey Hill,
T. S. Eliot and David Jones

STEVEN MATTHEWS

Two important journal numbers, across a seven-year period, had a possibly significant impact upon the development of Geoffrey Hill's work, a development which had consequences for the critical stance, and the poetic subject-matter, which he adopted in the latter period of his writing. The Spring-Summer 1967 issue of the English modernist journal, *Agenda*, began the process of re-accommodation through which the Anglo-Welsh poet David Jones's later writing was aired, and his earlier work re-considered – a process which culminated with the publication of the later work as *The Sleeping Lord* by Faber, in 1974. Then, to mark the advent of this book, the Winter 1973-4 issue of *Agenda* constituted a tribute volume to David Jones, one which included new writing by Jones again, alongside poems written in his honour, and critical essays on the recent work. What might be called the re-emergence of Jones into the consciousness of British and Irish poets in 1967, after an absence of new work by him for nearly fifteen years, had specific consequences for Hill, which this essay will consider.

Jones's late pieces, first printed in the Spring 1967 *Agenda*, confirm the drift of his previous epics, *In Parenthesis* (1937), but, more especially, *The Anathémata* (1952). These writings review the brutal impositions, and consequent accommodations, effected between coloniser and colonised in a variety of local and particular historical contexts, especially those involving Celtic peoples. These colonial impositions form a complexity which Jones himself comments upon, when considering the make-up of the Imperial Roman army in various conflicts, in a phrase with multiple resonance, as the 'heterogeneous composition of the forces of a world-imperium'.[1] That archetypical Roman imperium is considered by Jones, in piece after late piece in *The Sleeping Lord*, to be a levelling force, one seeking to 'discipline the world-floor / to a common level', or breaking

---

[1] David Jones, 'The Fatigue', in *The Sleeping Lord and other fragments* (London: Faber, 1974), p. 24.

down 'all the sweet remembered demarcations' which have hitherto fostered local tradition, difference, and specific religious potential.[2] Heterogeneity existed in the imperium, as the army (that archetypical community for Jones) absorbed men from conquered peoples within it. But that heterogeneity is aimed towards further conquest, the assumption of new tribal spaces which must in turn yield up their distinctive inflections to the centralising power. Jones's 'common level' here is a bureaucratic, or technocratic, voiding of meaning, rather than a democratic one – a concise inflection which, as will be clear later, resonates with Geoffrey Hill's political understanding, and particularly so in his later career.

Hill's own first two poetry collections, *For the Unfallen* (1959) and *King Log* (1968), had taken their tenor from wars and conflicts. They had included work which reflected on ancient historical or mythic materials (Greek history, Arthurian legends) and, in *King Log*, more specifically upon the Holocausts of the English War of the Roses, and of the Second World War, through which Hill had lived as a child. But that more general focus on the brutalities of history was now, and perhaps in the wake of David Jones's renewed presence, to take a decisive turn. For, in terms of the development of Geoffrey Hill's career, the timing of the first *Agenda* Special Issue on David Jones, and its exposure of that poet's later thinking and modes of writing, is suggestive and revealing. The years 1967-1974 include the writing of Hill's third collection *Mercian Hymns* (1971), which, as Hill told the critic John Haffenden, took 'three years', a comparatively rapid period of creation for him – although this reflection might now need reconsidering, given the late outflow of Hill's work.[3] The widespread critical acceptance of the formally-unusual sequence of prose poems, *Mercian Hymns*, confirmed Hill's prominence amongst contemporary writers working in a late modernist mode.[4] Its decisive attention to the local, to the places and landscapes of Hill's upbringing near the border between England and Wales, however, brought a particular orientation within that modernism which it is the purpose of this essay to explore. That attention is 'decisive' in several senses, as shall also be seen, since it also marks the tenor of a turn in Hill's work towards

---

[2] David Jones, 'The Tribune's Visitation', in *The Sleeping Lord*, p. 50.
[3] John Haffenden, *Viewpoints: Poets in Conversation* (London: Faber, 1981), p. 94.
[4] Andrew Michael Roberts, *Geoffrey Hill* (Tavistock: Northcote House, 2004), p. xi.

pastoral and locale, especially in volumes which awkwardly celebrated his late awareness that he had Welsh ancestry. Both *A Treatise of Civil Power* (2007) and *Oraclau | Oracles* (2010) contain work in which Hill once more renegotiates the modernist inheritance in English poetry, but more specifically here through local Welsh perspectives.

Those perspectives are perhaps informed by the ways in which the re-emergence of David Jones's work was contextualised in the later 1960s. The 1967 *Agenda* number is suggestive not just for its airing of Jones's recent work, but for the discursive realm in which that work is placed by the eclectic range of contributors to the included essays on various aspects of Jones's writings. For instance, the archaeologist Stuart Piggott made common cause with Jones's poetic processes, noting that

> 'Deposits' are an essential part of his poetry ... It is a significant and revealing word. Deposits may imply a slow process of accretion ... or again, they are the man-made caches and hoards – hidden treasures; votive, ritual and foundational deposits, and the last great deposit of all, the body in burial.[5]

That 'process of accretion', acknowledged here as a signature within David Jones's writings, might be said directly and verbally to inform the poetics of Hill's *Mercian Hymns* particularly, and thence to form a technical process within his later career. The diggers of the 'variably-resistant soil' in Hymn XII come upon a 'hoard' (BH 94); the uncertainly-autobiographical voice in the earlier VI recalls that 'I dug and hoarded' (BH 88). Hymn IV, which recalls the same speaker's early 'investedness' in 'mother-earth', conjures a Jones-like archaeology in miniature, as 'badgers thronged the Roman flues, the / long-unlooked-for mansions of our tribe' (BH 86). As in Jones, imperium and 'our tribe' sediment as separate deposits in the same patch of familiar local ground. The whole notion of 'mother-earth', which runs across Hill's sequence, is, in itself, not remote from Jones's own figuration of 'The Tutelar of the Place', as 'mother of particular perfections / queen of

---

[5] Stuart Piggott, 'David Jones and the Past of Man,' *Agenda* Vol. 5, Nos. 1-3, Spring-Summer 1967, p. 77. Piggott's terminology here points to the importance of the two David Jones Special Issues for Seamus Heaney also, as he moved towards writing the so-called 'bog poems' in the first part of *North* (1975). Jones's fragment 'The Sleeping Lord', which appeared in this same 1967 number, opens with a description of a burial site (*The Sleeping Lord*, p. 71). Later, Heaney reviewed the volume of which this is the title piece approvingly, in 'Now and in England', *The Spectator*, 4 May 1974.

otherness / mistress of asymmetry'.⁶

Such consonance between Jones's project and Hill's across these years was immediately recognised. The Winter 1973/4 *Agenda* Special Issue on David Jones contained Nicolas Jacobs's 'David Jones and the Politics of Identity,' which takes as the key point of comparison for Jones's politics Hill's *Mercian Hymns*:

> Both [writers] are engaged in a mythopoeic re-assertion of the importance of origins, of *enracinement*, in the age of the mass culture of megalopolis and suburbia.⁷

Jacobs's intuition here is almost, in retrospect, uncanny. His enlistment of Simone Weil's late work *L'Enracinement* for guidance in understanding both Jones, and thence also Hill's then recent poetry, points towards a writer Hill had increasingly identified as the most profound influence upon his writing and thinking of any from twentieth-century European philosophy.⁸ Yet, Weil's sense of rootedness is, as she has been cited approvingly by Hill to reveal, a complex possibility and counter-assertion, one involving both political and artistic potential. Hill has praised Weil in his 'A Postscript on Modernist Poetics' for her 'uncondescending attempt to reduce ... the intractable nature of poetry to a position of moral influence,' as exemplified by the assertion in *L'Enracinement* that 'Simultaneous composition on several planes at once is the law of artistic creation' (CCW 573).

But Jones and Hill are also of course attuned, within their politics, to the spiritual dimension or plane, which Weil directed readers towards as inhering within the concept of rootedness. This is evident in statements by her such as 'The truly Christian inspiration has fortunately been preserved by mysticism.'⁹ In Hill's case, his responsiveness to *this* aspect of Jones's work was evidenced most immediately in the second, Winter 1973-4, *Agenda* David Jones Special Issue. His contribution to the issue came in the form of 'Three Mystical Songs', versions of what

---

⁶ David Jones, *The Sleeping Lord*, p. 62. 'The Tutelar of the Place' first appeared in *Poetry* in 1961.

⁷ Nicolas Jacobs, 'David Jones and the Politics of Identity', *Agenda* Vol. 11 No. 4 – Vol. 12 No. 1, Autumn-Winter 1973/4, p. 72.

⁸ As registered, for instance, by Hill in his talk at the Collège de France, 8 March 2008.

⁹ Simone Weil, *The Need for Roots: Prelude towards a Declaration of Duties Towards Mankind*, trans. Arthur Wills (London: Routledge, 2002), p. 274.

were, five years later, to become sections 7, 8, and 13 of 'The Pentecost Castle', the opening sequence of *Tenebrae* (1978) (BH 117, 119; T 10, 11, 13).[10] 'Three Mystical Songs', in the *Agenda* version, carried an epigraph from the Preface to David Jones's collection of essays, *Epoch and Artist*: 'and they call Good Friday Dydd Gwener y Groglith, Venus Day of the Lesson of the Cross'.[11] So extracted, Jones's phrase forms a nice texture of themes which underlie the eventual full sequence from *Tenebrae* (themes which resonate across the remainder of that volume); the binding of divine sacrifice and secular love, of Christianity to the ancient classical religions, and the relation of locale to utterance ('and they call') being prime amongst them.

In its original context, however, Jones's phrase, which comes from near the end of the Preface to *Epoch and Artist*, marks the culminating point of an extensive polemic against scientific positivism, technocracy, and the resultant contemporary 'cultural situation'. Jones acknowledges that, in these circumstances, 'heritage', is threatened, 'the actual land itself, its sites and its rooted communities and all that has hitherto afforded a connection, however fragmented and attenuated, with the foundational things.' What he rails most forcibly against is the modern attitude that, as he repeats, 'particular facts are no more than they are'. This attitude, he asserts, denies '*poiesis*', the human spiritual, or religious, urge to 'make radiant' all 'facts'.[12] The phrase cited by Hill in his epigraph to 'Three Mystical Songs' comes, therefore, as an example of *poiesis* for David Jones, one in which the tones of a world-religion become inflected by an intimate, and erotic, charge through local intonation and history. 'Three Mystical Songs', as a mini-sequence, intensifies these connections in ways not so directly rendered by the more abstract dramas of the complete version, 'The Pentecost Castle'.

The second of the 'Songs' (which becomes poem 8 of the eventual sequence), is the one which was most heavily revised when it came to form a part of 'The Pentecost Castle.' This second 'Song', in its original version, opens with the lines 'Jesus my poor heart's treasure / my only true

---

[10] 'The Pentecost Castle' carries two epigraphs, one from Yeats's *Letters*, the second from Weil's *Notebooks*.

[11] David Jones, 'Preface by the Author', *Epoch and Artist: Selected Writings by David Jones*, ed. Harman Grisewood (London: Faber and Faber, 1959), p. 18; quoted as epigraph to 'Three Mystical Songs', *Agenda*, David Jones Special Issue, 11.4 – 12.1 (Autumn / Winter 1973-74), 54-55 (p. 54).

[12] Jones, *Epoch and Artist*, pp. 13-14, 16, 18.

desire'.[13] These lines become modulated into the typically paradoxical and elusive 'And you my spent heart's treasure / my yet unspent desire' in the final version (BH 117; T 11). The second stanza of the *Agenda* original then mentions 'your friendship ... your wrath', before finding an analogy for its despair in an 'earthly bliss as broken / as your disfigured side.' Later, these lines are replaced by 'your solitude a token', and mention of 'sentries' at 'your side'. In their original version, in the *Agenda* Special Issue for Jones, Hill's 'Songs' offered, in other words, a significantly more antithetical and worldly picture of the correlative between religious and human loves, than the later collected sequence does.

The 'Three Mystical Songs', in their original context and form, in fact, read more like sections from the sonnet sequence 'Lachrimae', also from *Tenebrae*, in their troubling through of a direct relation between the poems' speaker, and Christ, the deceiver-redeemer. It is Christ who, at the end of this second 'Song', is responsible for saying 'the nothing' which leaves the 'fulfilment', 'forgiveness', and savage natural consonance ('the sparrowhawk the sparrow'), posited in this last stanza of the second 'Song', unresolved. To that extent, the 'Songs' do not, any more than the final version of the sequence, evince a 'pentecostal' situation. Jones describes *poiesis* in his Preface to *Epoch and Artist* as 'intimations of some otherness of some sort'. [14] Hill's tribute to Jones, which includes in the third 'Song' the line 'likening us our unlikeness' (BH 119; T 13), interprets that 'otherness' through a Christian tradition which is later evoked more subliminally through the Pre-Raphaelite world of 'The Pentecost Castle'. Jones's argument for *poiesis* in his Preface is, of course, at one with his sense of 'making ... facts ... radiant', as '"anathema", using that double-edged word in its single, primal, bright and beneficent meaning of a thing devoted.'[15] Hill's 'Three Mystical Songs' are, to this degree, more directly 'radiant' than the twisted and involuted paradoxes of 'The Pentecost Castle' – troubled, as the whole volume *Tenebrae* is, by the manneredness and potential for self-reflecting preciousness in the poetic medium itself.

It is possible then, in this light, to see Jones's thinking as potentially informing something of the complicated seeming contrasts between *Mercian Hymns* and *Tenebrae*. The '*enracinement*' of the former Hill

---

[13] *Agenda* 11.4 – 12.1 (Autumn / Winter 1973-74), 54-55.

[14] Jones, *Epoch and Artist*, p.16.

[15] Jones, *Epoch and Artist*, p.15.

collection has, to adapt Weil's words, another 'plane' of its composition teased out in the latter. This significant influence from Jones upon Hill's writing has its formal qualities across these years as well. *The Anathémata* and *The Sleeping Lord* both deploy passages of poetic prose interjected between passages of more-or-less unpunctuated verse, in which the single poetic line acts, as it does in 'The Pentecost Castle', as a unit of sense poised within and against the flow of the sentence. It is as though Hill's two extended sequences – *Mercian Hymns* and 'The Pentecost Castle' – meditate upon these two distinctive, formal, facets of Jones's writings. Both writers, for instance, surprisingly deploy their prose-poetry to create dramatic vocal effects which mimic the meaning of the passage. Jones's *The Anathémata* has this brief passage upon Christ at the Last Supper:

> In the prepared high-room
> he implements inside time and late in time under forms in-
> delibly marked by locale and incidence, deliberations made
> out of time.[16]

The enjambment 'in-/delibly' holds in suspension the positive and negative connotations of 'marked', as something '*in*side time', but also timeless. This is a notion reinforced by the hesitation in the next enjambment, 'made / out of time', as though the incident is something which time / history has been itself established to constitute, but also as an act which supersedes or transcends time. Similarly, Hill's versets in *Mercian Hymns* deploy a poet's (or artist's) eye in arranging the prose on the page, in order to retain the poetic possibilities of enjambment – 'muti-/lation' (XI), 'en-/sconced' (XV), 'en-/acted' (XXIII) being a few of the most obvious examples (BH 93, 97, 105). Both writers, therefore, are concentrated upon the fact that prose-poetry must sustain many of the tensions and foci of all verse, and that there is a mimetic and dramatic or performative energy to be obtained in running the voice against the ending of the prose, as much as of the poetic, line.

Contrarily, the suspended and unpunctuated lines of Hill's adaptations of Spanish lyrics in 'The Pentecost Castle' are consonant in some ways with the (albeit unrhymed) method of Jones's poetry, as evidenced for instance in the re-echoing lines towards the end of 'The Sleeping Lord':

---

[16] David Jones, *The Anathémata* (London: Faber, 1952), p. 53.

> Are the slumbering valleys
>         him in slumber
>         are the still undulations
> the still limbs of him sleeping?
> ...
> Does the land wait the sleeping lord
>         or is the wasted land
> that very lord who sleeps? [17]

Compare the unrhymed lines from poem 9 of Hill's sequence:

> where you dwell I
> dwell also says my lord
>
> dealing his five wounds
> so cunning and so true
> of love to rouse this death
> (BH 118; T 11)

It is perhaps inevitable that we hear behind both writers' lines the pressure of the mid-career technical methods of T.S. Eliot. Despite the 'hint' in the Jones lines just quoted, and his persistent recourse to the Grail mythology which underwrites to a degree also *The Waste Land*, it is more pertinent to see consistently behind the work of both writers the influence of the post-1922 Eliot. This is the Eliot of 'The Hollow Men', *Ash-Wednesday*, the translation from the French prose poems by St-John Perse, *Anabasis*, and of the *Ariel Poems*. Hill's method in 'The Pentecost Castle' is to split the pentameter in two, and to slightly vary the resultant line length, whilst sustaining the unpunctuated line as the unit of sense. But he also deploys a method of altering the direction of the sentence's 'logic' between lines. All these poetic methods are features perhaps most reminiscent of Eliot's mini-sequence 'The Hollow Men':

> Is it like this
> In death's other kingdom
> Waking alone
> At the hour when we are
> Trembling with tenderness

---
[17] David Jones, 'The Sleeping Lord', *The Sleeping Lord*, p. 96.

> Lips that would kiss
> Form prayers to broken stone.[18]

Jones's late poetry offers similar brief lines, whilst the example cited above, from 'The Sleeping Lord', partakes also of the unmarked or acknowledged questions, and the deployment of repeated words, characteristic of middle-period Eliot, in works including *Marina*:

> What is this face, less clear and clearer
> The pulse in the arm, less strong and stronger —
> Given or lent? more distant than stars and nearer than the eye[19]

Compare to this, for instance, the unquestioning question of Hill's poem 12 of 'The Pentecost Castle': 'lost in the dream's grasp where / shall I find you everywhere' (BH 119; T 13). The giddy switching of verbal referent establishes the same open-ended psychological and subjective paradox, between proclaimed intimacy and unbridgeable and lamented distance and difference, as Eliot's lines had.

Late Jones, and the contexts of writing which he provided, would seem then to have allowed in Hill an oblique re-negotiation of Eliot's legacy, one which enabled also consideration of a continuing local inheritance within the disjunctions of modernist composition. Martin Dodsworth has explored the importance of Eliot's translation of St-John Perse's *Anabase*, a sequence of prose-poems about the founding of a civilisation, for *Mercian Hymns*.[20] Jones saw Eliot's translation as being pivotal for him, in getting started writing again after a breakdown in the early 1930s. As Jones wrote to Auden, *Anabasis* 'made a pretty big impression on me when it was published – I see that I read it early in 1931'.[21] When Eliot wrote 'A Note of Introduction' to a new American edition of Jones's first book, *In Parenthesis*, he pointed to the 'affinity' between Jones's work and that of Joyce, Pound, and himself, seeing Jones's work as rendering the defining experience of their age from out of his own, and out of a more generally mythologized, past: 'The lives

---

[18] T.S. Eliot, *Collected Poems 1909–1962* (London: Faber, 1974), pp. 90-91.

[19] T.S. Eliot, *Collected Poems 1909–1962*, p. 115.

[20] Martin Dodsworth, '*Mercian Hymns*: Offa, Charlemagne and Geoffrey Hill', *Geoffrey Hill: Essays on His Work*, ed. Peter Robinson (Milton Keyes: Open University Press, 1985), pp. 55-7.

[21] David Jones, *Dai Greatcoat*, ed. René Hague (London: Faber, 1980), p. 153.

of all of us were altered by [the] War, but David Jones is the only one to have fought in it'.[22] Eliot here, then, rather compliantly confirms the drift of by-then already-established critical opinion about the impulses of the first generation of modernists, amongst whom he anoints Jones as but 'the youngest, and the tardiest to publish.' Yet what he grants to Jones also is a particular authenticity, because of his harrowing in the trenches. This is an authenticity to be granted by Eliot, seemingly, because of Jones's version of *enracinement*, his 'Celtic ear for the music of words,' a Celticism which, for Eliot (in a moment of almost Arnoldian racial blurring), is reminiscent of the manner of James Joyce.

In a rare critical comment made partly about Jones, Hill seems to be preoccupied by a similar concern to Eliot's about the authenticity in poetry to be gained through lived experience. But, unlike Eliot, he foregrounds also a class-inflected notion of authenticity, as it translates into the poetry of war. In 'Language, Suffering, and Silence', Hill makes a sharp distinction between the 'imbalance' of sympathy, and special-pleading, in the officer-poet Wilfred Owen, and that more direct experience of suffering, when translated into language experienced as the lot of the 'common soldier':

> Owen's sense of his own value as a 'pleader' for the inarticulate common soldier presupposes his unawareness or inability to comprehend that at least three of the finest poets of that war, Isaac Rosenberg, Ivor Gurney, and David Jones, had gone, or still were going, as 'common soldiers' through all that he describes – none of them rose above the rank of private. (CCW 399)[23]

At one level, this distinction plays alongside that continuous pressing upon the resonance of the word 'common' in Hill's late prose, 'common' in its derogatory sense as sheerly banal, but also as marker of a shared inheritance, as shared practice or artisanship. Amongst the most telling

---

[22] David Jones, *In Parenthesis*, with 'A Note of Introduction' by T.S. Eliot (London: Faber, 1963), p. viii.

[23] A similar point would seem to underlie Hill's other reference to Jones, when writing about the Second World War poet Sidney Keyes, as he notes in passing that Keyes also was not from a background which enabled him to control his own destiny in a time of national strife: 'Keyes is a war poet only by accident, or "by misadventure", as David Jones expresses it'. 'Sidney Keyes in Historical Perspective', in Tim Kendall ed., *The Oxford Handbook of British and Irish War Poetry*, Oxford: Oxford University Press, 2007, p. 401.

of Hill's later reflections on 'common' is the conclusion to his essay about another poet who sought authenticity through 'Celticness', the Welshman R.S. Thomas. Adapting a phrase used about Wittgenstein's description of the nature of language-use ('the common behaviour of mankind'), Hill draws another telling distinction:

> Where [my] view may differ from Eliot's is in its conceiving the incoherence [inhering in poetry] not as debility or bathos but as essential to the tripartite nature of creativity. ... Poetry as utterance – both genuine and fraudulent – is part of 'the common behaviour of mankind', even though people are commonly oblivious to its peculiar attractions and demands.[24]

Poetic diction, therefore, is an attempt to 'regulate incoherence' through radical shorthand, a containing of the forces of dissipation: 'Among modern instances I note "bone" and "blood" in the poetry of Yeats, Eliot, and of those strongly influenced by them.'[25]

To that extent, Hill must account himself amongst those strongly so influenced: *King Log* alone presents us with the phrases 'ancient troughs of blood' (BH 39; KL 13), 'colourful blood' (BH 40; KL 15), 'white turds of bone ... with what blood?'(BH 42; KL 1), 'Plato's blood' (BH 46; KL 21), 'meaty conduit of blood' (BH 47; KL 25), 'marriage-blood' (BH 49; KL 27), 'the waking-taste of manna or of blood ... poor bones' (BH 59; KL 39), 'the trodden bone' (BH 61; KL 41), 'far-fetched blood'. (BH 68; KL 48). In its coinages and unlikely juxtapositions, Hill's diction is a 'behaviour' also at odds, however, with later Eliot's Mallarméan urge, as expressed in *Little Gidding* II, to 'purify the dialect of the tribe'.[26] It is a 'behaviour' which has underscored the political aesthetics of Hill's recent dialogues with the shade of Milton. As one of the premises of the opening section of the book-length sequence *Scenes from Comus* has it:

---

[24] Sophie Radcliffe has some cogent things to say about Hill's dissension from later Eliot, especially around the lack of 'sensuous interest' in the latter, in her 'On Being "A Man of the World"', *Geoffrey Hill: Essays on his Later Work*, edited by John Lyon and Peter McDonald (Oxford: Oxford University Press, 2012), pp. 75-6.

[25] 'R.S. Thomas's Welsh Pastoral', *Echoes to the Amen: Essays after R.S. Thomas*, ed. Damian Walford-Davies (Cardiff: University of Wales Press, 2003), pp. 56-7.

[26] T.S. Eliot, *Collected Poems 1909–1962*, p. 218.

> That, in these latter days, language
> is the energy of decaying sense;
> that sense in this sense means *sensus communis*.
>
> That common sense bids me add: not
> all language. If power's fuelled by decay
> so be it—decay being a natural force.
> (BH 423; SC 5)

'So be it', since the inertia infecting language 'in these latter days' (as opposed, presumably, to in Milton's day), is, ironically, a 'natural force'. 'Not / all language': there are moments glimpsed in this later verse of Hill's where 'the common people' become something other than themselves, are redeemed from that 'common levelling' which David Jones, in 'The Tribune's Visitation', had seen as the inevitable consequence of any technological, centralising, or imperialising, imposition upon local community and histories.[27] Hill carries such redemptive possibility into stanza XXVI from the original, Clutag Press pamphlet's, title-poem version of 'A Treatise of Civil Power':[28]

> Tap the bookie, subpoena the judge – he lives
> one street over – whistle the boys who scrub cars,
> nab the black lady shuffling in the queue
> at the post office on pension day; heel
> the old dog with cancer; tame the Norwegian
> Forest Cat purchased in Wolverhampton:
> they are all radiant – law outshining chance –
> New Zion is a light-source to itself.[29]

---

[27] It is notable, in the late poetry by Hill, that the word 'common' seems, however, more naturally to recur in contexts which, ironically or otherwise, sustain Jones's 'levelling' pressure within the word. See *Expostulations on the Volcano* sections 2, 6; *Liber Illustrium Virorum*, section XLVIII; *Clavics*, section 26, 42; *Odi Barbare*, sections XII, XVII. (BH 630, 634, 732, 816, 832, 846, 851).

[28] Hill radically altered the wording and the form of many of these pamphlet poems when he prepared them for publication in a full book collection as the Penguin / Yale University Press's *A Treatise of Civil Power* (2007).

[29] Geoffrey Hill, *A Treatise of Civil power* (Thame: Clutag Press, 2005), unnumbered pages.

Poetry works to ironic effect, overturning the traditional order of quotidian actions, in the opening lines here. Yet enjambment maps urban and class division, as the judge 'lives / one street' (and so one separated line) 'over'. 'Radiant', so centrally used by Milton when describing God looking down at his creation ('On his right / The radiant image of his glory sat / His onely Son') (*Paradise Lost* III.63), carries also a charge here from Jones's definition of *poiesis*, as 'making ... facts ... radiant'. Such transfiguration through radiance has continued as an aspect of Hill's poetry. His reflections upon his Welsh ancestry in *Oraclau | Oracles* opens with brief hosannas at 'The World much fabled to be what it is – / Radiant mica'd creatures drawn through stress.' (BH 741; O1) [30]

Such radiance impels the culmination of 'Coda' (originally in the Clutag Press pamphlet an aftermath to the sequence 'A Treatise of Civil Power'), when Hill, in this first printing of the poem, recalls his Welsh iron-puddler great grandfather, and the 'burial hoard' of his legacy to the poet, which is like Péguy's, that of a 'defeated man':

> even so I hope —
> not believe, hope – our variously-laboured
> ways notwithstanding – we shall accountably
> launch into death on a broad arc; our dark
> abrupt spirit with fourth day constellations
> that stood assembled to its first unknowing —
>
> 8
> which is an abashed way of saying light,
> the beatific vision ... [31]

In revising 'Coda' for the Penguin / Yale University Press book *A Treatise of Civil Power*, Hill surely erred in allowing 'poetic diction' to dictate that he erase what had been a transfiguring use of common speech in the playful phrase 'saying light'. The Penguin / Yale book version has 'invoking light' (BH 600; TCP 50). For once, 'poetic utterance' subsumes, wrongly in my view, the voice of the labouring-class ancestor which the poem is concerned to claim and celebrate, 'great grandfather

---

[30] These lines are the same in both the Clutag Press edition and in BH.

[31] Geoffrey Hill, *A Treatise of Civil power* (Thame: Clutag Press, 2005), unnumbered pages.

and Dante's *Paradiso* / understanding each other straight-on' (BH 600; TCP 50). 'Saying light' carries something of the power of that liturgical use of surprising or 'impious words' which, when 'used according to established but flexible tradition', David Jones found in his fellow-soldiers' speech to confer 'dignity', 'real poetry'.[32] '[E]ven so I hope – / not believe, hope' seems, like the 'still' in Hill's line about the French poet Charles Péguy ('still Péguy said that Hope is a little child', BH 143; P10), to take its stand against the despairing stance of the opening of Eliot's *Ash-Wednesday*, 'Because I do not hope to turn again / Because I do not hope'.[33]

Hill's late encounter with the poetry and prose of Dante has enabled in part a pondering of the space, or abyss, 'Between Politics and Eternity' (to appropriate the title of Hill's essay on the *Monarchia*), and further to ponder the use of metaphor in poetry as the means by which such gaps, however radical ('great grandfather and Dante's *Paradiso*'), might be traversed. Hill favours H. Rockham's translation of the Aristotlean gloss on the meaning of metaphor, 'allotrion', as 'strange term', 'metaphor is the application of a strange term':

> a sense of striking resemblance is not to be dissociated from an awareness of strangeness; from the recognition of the abyss of proximity between, let us say, politics and eternity. In such minute particularization of judgment and alienation, Dante anticipates Shakespeare's Troilus as he struggles to comprehend the extraordinariness of the commonplace betrayal that has been inflicted upon him.[34]

The 'abyss of proximity' is that which 'we' 'launch into' along an 'arc', when dying, as 'A Coda' has it (BH 600; TCP 50). [35] Hill has added 'strange' and its variants to the modern poets' list of shorthand wards against incoherence, such as the above-mentioned 'blood' and

---

[32] David Jones, *In Parenthesis*, p. xii.

[33] Eliot, *Collected Poems 1909 – 1962*, p. 95. Christopher Ricks has some compelling things to say about late Hill's allusions to *Ash-Wednesday* in *True Friendship: Geoffrey Hill, Anthony Hecht, and Robert Lowell Under the Sign of Eliot and Pound* (New Haven, CT: Yale University Press, 2010), pp. 6-10.

[34] 'Between Politics and Eternity', in *The Poet's Dante*, eds. Peter J. Hawkins and Rachel Jacoff (New York, NY: Farrar, Straus and Giroux, 2001), p. 326-7.

[35] Also in Clutag Press edition.

'bone' of Yeats and Eliot. Amongst other possible examples, a poem published in his secondary school magazine, "Pylons", begins 'Will no one befriend these strange newcomers?'[36] The father speaking to 'my little son' in 'Funeral Music' casts himself as 'a stranger well-received in your kingdom' (BH 52; KL 30); *Mercian Hymns* offers us 'fostered a strangeness', 'strange church', 'not strangeness, but strange likeness' (BH 88, 91, 101; MH VI, IX, XXIX). Hill's version of Henrik Ibsen's play *Brand* opens with a Peasant calling after the main character 'Hey, Stranger, not so fast!'.[37] *The Mystery of the Charity of Charles Péguy* registers the 'strange Christian hope' (BH 147; P 17). *Canaan* provides 'strange / legends', 'strange salvation', 'strange beatitudes' and a 'strange homecoming / into sleep' (BH 188, 194, 206, 211; C 20, 26, 38, 43). *The Triumph of Love* proffers the idiomatic 'strange as it seems' (BH 268; TL 51); *Speech! Speech!* a 'strange virgin tribe' (BH 310; SS 22) and, in culmination, the self-assertive 'How strange it sounds' (BH 311; SS 23). *Clavics* rehearses 'strange edginess' (BH 795; CL 19), speaks of 'strange gods' (BH 811; CL 29); *Odi Barbare* sees the 'labour' that brings us into life as 'Strange to our bodies' (BH 851; OB 25), and sees the speaker resisting comparison of himself and a lover with Dante's Paolo and Francesca by asserting that they are 'Strange to each other' (BH 875; OB 49). From the prose, one late example stands in for many others; when offering praise, not criticism, of the opening of Yeats's poem 'The Statues' in 'A Postscript on Modernist Poetics', Hill remarks, that they are 'two of the strangest-sounding lines in twentieth-century poetry' (CCW 574). And there are the many synonyms for 'strange' in Hill's own poetry, such as the already-quoted line from 'Three Mystical Songs', 'likening us our unlikeness' (BH 119; T 13); or the '"kind / of otherness"' cited in 'Two Chorale-Preludes' (BH 132; T 36); or the 'alien landscape, / The dream where you are always to be found' of 'The Songbook of Sebastian Arrurruz' (BH 71; KL 55); or the bleakly enjambed 'radical / otherness' of *The Orchards of Syon* (BH 395'; OS 45)'; or the 'our alien shore' of the last line of 'Broken Hierarchies' from *Without Title* (BH 516; WT 79).

Against such transfigurations of the commonplace into what Jones loosely but scrupulously calls 'intimations of some otherness of some

---

[36] Norman Rea, '9.9.42 HILL, Geoffrey W', *Agenda*, Geoffrey Hill Sixtieth Birthday Issue, 30.1 – 30.2 (Spring-Summer 1992), 114-125 (p. 122).

[37] Henrik Ibsen, *Brand: A Version for the Stage by Geoffrey Hill* (1978; Harmondsworth: Penguin, 1996), p. 3.

sort', Hill has also established a set of markers of those 'facts' which remain untranslatable across the hermeneutic gaps traversed through metaphor. 'Stone' might be taken as one of the most significant of these. Earlier examples include from *King Log*, again, 'Fire / Flares in the pit, ghosting upon stone' (BH 47; KL 25), 'The Stone Man', 'The stones waiting in the mason's yard' (BH 62; KL 42), 'small ferns and stones ... fragments' (BH 63; KL 43), '[man's] justice / Between the stones and the void' (B 66; KL 46), 'Foxes and rain-sleeked stones and the dead – // Aliens of such a theme' (BH 67; KL 47), 'the troughed stone' (BH 77; KL 61) (this last example, from 'A Song from Armenia', bears resonance from its Mandelstamian origin). But 'stone' remains for Hill a sign of the often ludicrous, or excruciating, stubbornness, or awkwardness, of matter, as in the opening lines of 'De Jure Belli ac Pacis' from *Canaan*:

> The people moves as one spirit unfettered
> claim our assessors of stone.
> (BH 198; C 30)

If this sequence presents a middle-Europe reminiscent of *The Waste Land* ('aqueducts / where water is no longer found' (BH 198; C 30), it is possible also to feel the presence of middle-period Eliot again – the 'stone images ... prayers to broken stone' of 'The Hollow Men', or, more immediately, in relation to this last example, the 'Stone, bronze, stone, steel, stone, oakleaves, horses' heels / Over the paving' repeated from 'Triumphal March' in Eliot's abandoned work *Coriolan*.[38]

Something of the crux involving a transformative othering, and a dull intransigence of particular 'facts', informs Hill's recent re-considerations of Eliot's career. These have been consistent in their insistence upon the distinction between those works which display 'discursive intelligence' (*The Waste Land* before Pound edited it, *Four Quartets*, the plays), and those which show a Bradleian 'way of apprehension' (CCW 534) (*Sweeney Agonistes*, *Ash-Wednesday*, *Marina*, *Coriolan*):

> The very measure in which *Ash-Wednesday* and *Marina* move is the measure of becoming, the 'somehow' of coexistent appearance and reality, in which differences are a part of the 'felt unity', 'felt totality', 'internal felt core' even when they

---
[38] T.S. Eliot, *Collected Poems 1909–1962*, pp. 90, 91; 139.

elude categorization, even when no more exists between them than a sensation of belonging, of recognition. (CCW 534)

In other terms, the 'discursive intelligence' in this discussion is made by Hill to equate to an accommodation with 'the general', with the commonplace, with the 'general tone or tonelessness of things' through which the review-essay about Eliot, 'Dividing Legacies' (CCW 366-79) (along with the essays on Dante and on R.S. Thomas), indict the later Eliot. Hill's preference for *Ash-Wednesday*, *Marina*, or *Coriolan* is a preference for what, in 'Eros in F.H. Bradley and T.S. Eliot', he calls 'points of departure and of final non-resolution', a 'natural undisturbed syntax' in which 'yet' 'something' has 'intervened', 'the ambiguous existence of what has been and is about to be' (CCW 378, 552-3).

Such intensities supervene in the section of *Oraclau | Oracles* called 'T.S. Eliot in Swansea, 1944'. Hill's brief poem, indeed, imposes two key moments in Eliot's critical writing upon each other. Eliot's classical rebuke to what he calls the 'inner voice' in his essay 'The Function of Criticism' (1923) imagines football supporters travelling, 'ten in a compartment', to a match at Swansea, South Wales, and listening to that voice 'which breathes the eternal message of vanity, fear, and lust.'[39] Eliot actually travelled to Swansea late in World War Two to deliver the lecture 'What is Minor Poetry' – one of a string of such performances in Eliot's later career which Hill has dismissed as 'ingratiating', connecting 'everything with everything', however 'pragmatic' they might also have been (CCW 557). 'T.S. Eliot in Swansea, 1944' conjures the 'crammed' railway carriage carrying the workmen to the match, but, surprisingly, seems to fend off the class snobbery and disdain inherent in Eliot's so-called 'eternal message'. Having seemed to exculpate Eliot because of his having to write out of an historical context remote from Hill's own comfortable situation ('The dove descending broke upon your watch') (BH 760; O 20), Hill enacts a characteristic return upon his own offering of an olive branch: 'I am regaled past merit, past returning' (O 20).[40] He cannot accept the choice 'entertainments' which later Eliot's writing offers to him. But, on the other hand, such is Hill's place later in history to Eliot, nor can he provide a 'fair exchange' for, or go back on, what it is that Eliot offers.

---

[39] T.S. Eliot, *Selected Essays* (London: Faber, 1974), p. 27.

[40] In BH this line reads 'I am requited merit past my earning' (BH 760).

Instead, in the final line of 'T.S. Eliot in Swansea, 1944', Hill looks past 'grief' at such matters, and accepts a monastic sureness of his own emotional equilibrium, rather than being pulled away from himself to a lament for the failures of Eliot's poetic gifts. Christopher Ricks has made a persuasive case that Hill is more 'friendly' to Eliot's poetry in his own poetic meditations upon the earlier poet than he is in the often impatient comments of his recent critical prose.[41] And yet, in the complex syntactic leaps of Hill's later work, as evidenced in the three sentences closing 'T.S. Eliot in Swansea, 1944', we can see Hill adhering in his poetry to his own stricter prescription for modernist poetics. Although the sentences are 'parallel' syntactically, each taking up a single poetic line, they are unreconciled in their sense that the relation of later poet to earlier, even when acknowledging that Eliot wrote in time(s) of war, must be irresolvable, and remain so.

Syntax becomes the medium of a poetry of 'becoming', in Hill's ideal version of Eliot's mid-period poems, and his own later work proves that this is what he has learnt from Eliot's example. It might not be far from the truth to view Hill's later sequences as an attempt to reconcile the 'discursive intelligence' with this sense of a 'way of apprehension' (CCW 534): a 'becoming', as it is to be read out of the work of Eliot, 'the crucial poet and critic of the last century', as Hill calls him (CCW 561). But, unlike Eliot's unsettled, cosmopolitan, situation, Hill's attempts at reconciliation always operate under the aegis of what Jones calls 'a people, a culture already developed, already venerable and rooted' – that *enracinement* which he and Hill share with Simone Weil. It is an *enracinement*, however, which carries the traumas of twentieth-century history, for Hill as for Jones. In the latter's case, for instance, in the liturgical Queen of the Woods section ending *In Parenthesis*, the spirit of the French landscape buries the war dead: 'She carries to Aneirin-in-the-nullah a rowan sprig, for the glory of Guendota.'[42]

Partly, for Hill, the 'discursive intelligence' is that which seeks closure at a rational level of a poem. Partly, it seems to equate with a kind of static mono-tonalism, one resistant to the kinds of ambiguous address lauded by Hill in the opening line of *Marina*, one not quite an exclamation, not quite a question: 'What seas what shores what

---

[41] Christopher Ricks, *True Friendship*, p. 41.

[42] David Jones, *In Parenthesis*, pp. 49, 186.

grey rocks and what islands ... / My daughter'.⁴³ More consistently (although, of course, without the Catholic liturgical intonation of Jones), the counter to 'discursive intelligence' in Hill's poetry, the 'way of apprehension', was latterly underscored by a use of pastoral, often of pastoral moments isolated within the more discursively rhetorical flow of the poetry. There is a strange switch of direction towards this in the brief sonnet-sequence 'Discourse: for Stanley Rosen' from *Without Title*. Language, 'ours' and 'well dug-in' like the private soldier-poets, carries 'dark places', a 'fabled burden' in

> its loops and extraordinary progressions;
> its mere conundrums forms and rites of discourse;
> its bleak littoral swept by bursts of sunlight;
> its earthen genius auditing the spheres.
> (BH 500; WT 27)⁴⁴

The parallelism here amounts to an 'extraordinary' suspension also, as syntax seems to run all of the opacities, traditions and religious rhythms of language into one ('conundrums forms ... rites') whilst sustaining a sense of the separateness of the other qualities ('its ... its ... its ... its). Language is both under siege in the ongoing twentieth-century wars, 'earthen', and also open to what lies beyond, taking it into itself, as the 'extraordinary' 'auditing the spheres'. The whole on a kind of 'loop' tape, into which the vision of a 'bleak littoral' surprisingly intervenes.

The second lyric from the sequence 'In the Valley of the Arrow', also from *Without Title*, shows the speaker's resistance to the versions of pastoral sustained in Shakespeare's late plays, beginning, as the poem does, 'Not Bohemia, not Illyria', and so naming those places where 'dramatic virgins' have been granted immortality 'as common grace rhetoric's / vernacular flowers' (BH 509; WT 66). Shakespeare has presented, in this awkward concatenation by Hill's speaker, a form of

---

[43] T.S. Eliot, 'Marina', *Collected Poems 1909–1962*, p. 115. Hill usefully quotes these lines as demonstrating that a Bradleyan 'felt totality' is at play behind Eliot's poem. See CCW 552-3.

[44] Jones's army rank as a Private is foregrounded again in one of the several late mentions of him in Hill's work. Those mentions all refer specifically to Jones's works as a visual artist rather than as a poet: Private Jones's picture 'Britannia and Germania Embracing' is mentioned in *Al Tempo De' Tremuoti* section 62, again in relation to pastoral; his painting 'Petra Im Rosenhag' appears in section 7. Jones's woodcuts are referenced in section 36 of the reworked *Clavics*. BH 826, 891, 918-9.

pastoral metaphor which serves to signal transcendence. In contrast, Hill's speaker's 'dull stream' conveys a looping progression ('tight weirs / pebble-dashed with bright water') (BH 509; WT 66), which does not avoid the anthropomorphisms or the grotesqueries which can also be imposed upon nature, as in the enjambment of 'the massive briar, misshapen- / shouldered'.[45] For Perdita, read Caliban. Although the 'discursive intelligence' breaks in to Hill's poem at this point, to inform us that all of this rugged pastoralism is offered merely 'for description's sake' ('That was a way of putting it', as Eliot in *East Coker* put it), it is not possible here or elsewhere in these more recent Hill works to do other than wonder at the radiance of the pastoral moment.[46] This whole near-sonnet 'In the Valley of the Arrow' is superscribed over the phrase '*beata l'alma*', signalling that it is a re-writing of Vittoria Colonna's sonnet from *Amaro Lagrimar*, describing the blessedness of the soul which is drawn out of this world of woes. Yet Hill's poem finds in the 'earthen genius' of the 'dull stream' also a countermanding wonder, however 'variously-laboured' (to draw upon the neologism from the end of 'Coda' cited above).

In this it is typical of late Hill – and, despite his disavowals, of the Eliot of moments in *Four Quartets*, such as the sudden heave forward in *Little Gidding*:

> So, while the light fails
> On a winter's afternoon, in a secluded chapel
> History is now and England.[47]

Hill's 'Paradiso', as the cover-blurb puts it on the Penguin edition of *The Orchards of Syon*, comes close to such moments in Eliot as conveying the 'way of apprehension' amidst much play of the 'discursive intelligence':

> This is England; ah, love, you must *see* that;
> her nature sensing its continuum
> with the Beatific Vision.
> (BH 382; OS 32)

---

[45] In BH this reads: 'gross bramble, more misshapen- / shouldered' (BH 509).

[46] T.S. Eliot, *Collected Poems 1909–1962*, p. 198.

[47] T.S. Eliot, *Collected Poems 1909–1962*, p. 222.

This is a double-edged 'nature', not just an integral characteristic of the country, but also the natural world which is to be *seen*:

> This last embodiment
> indefinitely loaned, not quite
> the creator's dying gift regardless.
> Clear sky, the snow bare-bright. Loud, peat-sodden
> the swaling Hodder.
> (BH 382; OS 32)

'The creator' does not, cannot, presume absolute copyright over this mode of creation (of course not). But the poet, like the divine creator, can see no end to his being able to deploy it as occasion demands. To that extent, he is under 'regard' from the very tradition which he wishes to make his own. But he is able to differently-inflect that tradition, to bring it home through his choice of the vocabulary in which to 'embody' it. 'Swaling' is given in the *OED* as a word of dialect origin, specifically a Shropshire variant of 'sway'. As with Dante, Hill's snatch at paradise is viewed through familiar sounds – the sounds, here, of his English regional childhood. As often in this late poetic, the uncertainly-directed progression of Hill's syntax (that inflected 'regardless' swaying the possible sense of the sentence it concludes) suddenly ceases before the clarification of the immediate pastoral situation. 'Clear sky' takes us back through Hill's career to his Offa, lingering in *his* orchard, 'When the sky cleared above Malvern' (BH 96; MH XIV) – but is also identifiable with the brittle clarities of Hill's late syntax.

'Brittle', because the 'discursive intelligence' cannot be laid to rest by Hill to the extent that he felt that it could be by Eliot in his middle period. Pastoral moments in this late work are always rudely interrupted by a sense that, however much desired ('now and in memory never so / wholly awaited, the breadth of this/autumnal land') (BH 417; OS 71), they are never sufficient in and of themselves:

> This much is allowed
> us, forever tangling with England
> in her quiet ways of betrayal. Natural
> mother, good but not enough.
> (BH 417; OS 71)

The 'discursive intelligence' often works paradoxically in *The Orchards of Syon*, as elsewhere in the late work, therefore (and as it does in Eliot's *Four Quartets*): as disrupter of the settlements which the poetry might be drawn to make, moving the poetry forward through its attempts at 'categorization' or 'valuation' ('good but not enough'). Once the (local) ground upon which the poetry discovers clarity is established, it is time to shift the ground. Eliot's *Anabasis*, the constant manoeuvring-forward of civilization and understanding through time and across landscapes, springs again to mind. Partly this is a result of the threat conveyed by the anti-pathetic contemporary situation. Hill's sense of embattlement ('well dug-in') (BH 500; WT 27) is not remote from Jones's in *his* late work. The Anglo-Welsh Jones's 'The Tutelar of the Place' ends by registering the need to dig its own 'natural mother' in, against the 'technicians' who 'manipulate the dead limbs of our culture':

> Sweet Mair devise a mazy-guard
> in and out and round about
> double-dance defences
> countermure and echelon meanders round
> the holy mound.[48]

Hill's late sense of the 'extraordinary' (BH 500; WT 27), its ways of 'apprehension' (CCW 534), within the 'common behaviour' of poetry, registers similar threat to its potential 'radiance'. [49] This happens from section to section of the late sequences, where the mystical-pastoral jerks back into the discursive, in the blank space between the bursts of poetry, as in the resonant clarity of the initial image here from *The Triumph of Love*:

> that all-gathering general English light
> in which each separate bead
> of drizzle at its own thorn-tip stands
> as revelation.

---

[48] David Jones, *The Sleeping Lord*, p. 64.

[49] 'Common behaviour' is from Hill's essay, 'R.S. Thomas's Welsh Pastoral', p. 57; 'radiant' occurs in Geoffrey Hill, *A Treatise of Civil power* (Thame: Clutag Press, 2005), unnumbered pages.

> LIV
> Entertainment overkill: that amplifier
> acts as the brain of the putsch.
> (BH 253; TL 27)

    To this extent the shifting ground of Hill's work carries forward the kinds of understanding potentially evidenced by Hill's direct encounter with the lyric intensities and descriptive prose passages in Jones's work of the late 1960s and early 1970s, and, behind it, by his abiding encounter with the changing poetic strategies of T.S. Eliot. *Oraclau | Oracles*, the concerted late encounter by Hill with Celtic-ness-as-Welsh-ness shows a proper unease with such ready identifications with the regional as antidotes to the often rancorous rhetoric of (Eliotic) modernism (*'not a drop of Welsh blood in him!'*) (O 36). [50] Yet nor does Hill reject the uncommonness of a poetic which might pay and repay such attunements:

> Extraordinary the common lot
> We here project, collateral or not.
> (BH 747; O 7)

---

[50] This line is not included in *Broken Hierarchies*.

CHAPTER TWO

# The Nature of Hill's Later Poetry [1]

## STEPHEN JAMES

Geoffrey Hill has been dubbed 'the most glorious poet of the English countryside since the first romantic started gushing about flowers'; 'few readers', William Logan claims, 'would trade the drenched phrasings of Hill's backlit scenery for his brooding on obscure theologians. Hang the cost in moral uplift'.[2] These are curious observations; as Henry King has noted in response, topography and theology are not so glibly to be distinguished:

> Logan either misunderstands or does a deliberate injustice to Hill's poetry in thinking of these two aspects as discrete alternatives. For one whose theological broodings have been as thoroughgoing as Hill's, descriptions of nature (such an inadequate label!) are not divagations – the Professor of Divinity escaping to his watercolours class – but an intrinsic part of a complex whole.[3]

King's anxiety about the inadequacy of his own phrase 'descriptions of nature' is telling, not just for signalling a fear that the phrase risks

---

[1] This article draws on material held in the Geoffrey Hill Archive in the Brotherton Library at the University of Leeds. I wish to thank the staff of the Special Collections for their friendly, expert assistance and the British Academy for providing the Small Research Grant that enabled my archival studies.

[2] William Logan, 'Living with Ghosts', review of *A Treatise of Civil Power* (2007), *New York Times*, 20 January 2008 <www.nytimes.com/2008/01/20/books/review/Logan-t.html?pagewanted=all> [accessed April 2012]. In interview, Logan has said, 'I think that Hill's passages on nature – the flora of England – are the most accessible of all of his work and I certainly know readers who feel that no book of his is complete without a little natural history and perhaps even no book of his is interesting where it strays beyond nature'. Sam Tanenhaus and William Logan, 'Book Review Podcast', *New York Times*, 20 January 2008, <http://graphics8.nytimes.com/podcasts/2008/01/18/19bookupdate.mp3> [accessed April 2012].

[3] Henry King, 'Fraught Celebration', review of *Oraclau | Oracles* (2010), *PN Review* 199, 37.5 (May-June 2011), pp. 73-75 (p. 74).

devaluing the complexity of Hill's work (compare Logan's 'backlit scenery') but also for conveying an implicit sensitivity to wider concerns about the relative value of different kinds of poetic accomplishment. The issue at stake here is the one Geoffrey Grigson touches on when he refers, in the introduction to *The Faber Book of Poems and Places*, to 'lines which earn the sneer of being only "descriptive"', and that Robert Langbaum notes when, in his essay on 'The New Nature Poetry', he suggests that 'the term *nature poetry* has fallen into such disrepute that no one wants to apply it to poems he likes'.[4] It is worth dwelling on this point of anxiety, both as a means of considering how sustained responsiveness to the natural world defines Hill's achievement and for taking stock of what has now become a dominant tendency in the critical reception of the poet's work.

Logan's position, though *sui generis* in its formulation, is not entirely uncharacteristic of the responses of other reviewers of Hill's later volumes (from *The Triumph of Love* (1998) onwards), as a brief collocation of comments from journals indicates:

> Few poets can match Hill when he is writing out of … a tradition focused and dependent upon a certain exactitude of natural description. … Despite the *gravitas* of his poems of historical witness, I am not sure that it isn't as a poet of landscape – in the rich Wordsworthian or Coleridgean sense of its being mysteriously cognate with the mind's own processes of self-realization – that Hill chiefly excels.[5]

> The most accessible and perhaps the finest poems in *Without Title* are vehicles for Hill's profoundly lyrical responses to the natural and physical world. There are a generous number of these. Their luminous particularity of imagery serves as a counter to the book's sometimes unrelentingly cerebral tendencies.[6]

---

[4] Geoffrey Grigson, *The Faber Book of Poems and Places* (London: Faber and Faber, 1980), p. 32; Robert Langbaum, *The Modern Spirit: Essays on the Continuity of Nineteenth- and Twentieth-Century Literature* (London: Chatto & Windus, 1970), p. 102.

[5] Stephen Romer, 'Writing for the Dead', review of *The Triumph of Love*, *Poetry Review* 89.2 (Summer 1999), pp. 68-71 (p. 70).

[6] Douglas Houston, 'Passionate Profundities', review of *Without Title* (2006), *Poetry Review* 96.2 (Summer 2006), pp. 107-110 (p. 109).

> Hill ... can dash off a soggy English landscape in the blink of an eye. ... Hill's landscapes always come as passages of much-needed respite amid the more querulous, questioning, quarrelsome poems that otherwise set the tone of his collections.[7]
>
> Always the most visual of poets, and with 50 years' practice behind him, he now writes about England and the English countryside with a poise and vigour that would be enough by itself to set him among the great poets of the modern age.[8]
>
> There are autobiographical glimpses of childhood in Worcestershire and old age in Suffolk, and these paeans to the English landscape which has nourished Hill's work from the start are of such intensity that they allow no rival attraction. All the talk of Hill as a forbidding poet is fatally deaf to the countless breath-catching instances of beauty threaded through his work. He is especially good – that Englishness again – at writing about the weather.[9]

Such observations are symptomatic of prevalent views that currently help to shape Hill's reputation. They present a series of broadly apt and understandable yet also question-begging, argument-silencing, and up to a point mutually complicating characterizations of the poet's work. Three salient quandaries arising from the collocation may be summarized as follows:

1. The insistence that Hill's pre-eminence is founded on, or most securely achieved by, his poetic landscapes presupposes that qualities and concerns which might risk defining another writer's work (even

---

[7] Alan Marshall, 'An Uncompromising Genius at his Peak', review of *Without Title*, *Telegraph*, 12 February 2006, <www.telegraph.co.uk/culture/books/3650084/An-uncompromising-genius-at-his-peak.html> [accessed April 2012].

[8] Tim Martin, 'O Hendrix, Player of Neumes', review of *Without Title*, *Independent*, 15 March 2006, <http://enjoyment.independent.co.uk/books/reviews/article343665.ece> [accessed April 2012].

[9] Tim Kendall, 'Hire Houses', review of *A Treatise of Civil power*, *Times Literary Supplement*, 12 October 2007, p. 25.

if accomplished) as 'minor' are, curiously, in Hill's case central to the plea for 'major' status. (In this respect, it is tempting to speculate how Hill's reputation would currently stand if the work of his last two decades had been bereft of, or less frequently characterized by, as Wordsworth has it, a 'sense / Of exquisite regard for common things' in the natural world.)[10]

2. The obvious rejoinder to point 1 is that, as Romer has put it, 'landscape ... provides more than stretches of freedom, of untrammelled vision', that 'Hill's huge ambition ... could never allow him to rest content with being a "mere" poet of landscape'.[11] Not only are Hill's depictions of nature also often modes of cultural, historical, theological or philosophical engagement; they also usually function as parts of larger poems or sequences (hence King seeing them as 'an intrinsic part of a complex whole'), and their significance needs to be read in relation to the wider preoccupations and rhetorical and formal qualities of these works. Nonetheless, the proposal that the 'particularity', 'exactitude' and appealing immediacy with which Hill records his responses to the natural world provides a welcome 'counter' to or 'respite' from the more recondite, densely referential and at times rebarbative stretches of the surrounding poetry conveys a sense (not lightly to be dismissed) that his richly realized nature studies serve as appealing interludes, to be relished as much for their own sake as for their articulations of the concerns of the volume in which they appear. Indeed, such is the disjunction that often occurs between Hill's field observations and the material immediately preceding and following them, and such, by contrast, are the continuities of concern and descriptive style, in Hill's later volumes, between the poet's various evocations of tree and flower, sky and weather, that it sometimes seems at least as illuminating to take Hill's numerous notations from nature as each other's context (despite the insistent particularity and local attachments of each passage in turn) as it is to attempt to read them in relation to immediately adjacent lines.

3. As John Lyon has observed, the tendency of reviewers of Hill's later works to brandish 'a gobbet from the volume under consideration sacrificed in celebration of Hill as an English nature poet' reveals

---

[10] William Wordsworth, *The Prelude, or Growth of a Poet's Mind* (1805) ed. Ernest de Selincourt (Oxford: Oxford University Press, 1970), p. 235 (Book XIII, ll. 234-5).

[11] Romer, p. 70.

partial-sightedness, for the idea of Hill as a 'supposed laureate of English landscape' is significantly complicated by the international range of his imagined territories – including, notably, Wales and France.[12] Moreover, to conceive of Hill as a great English poet because of his concern with English locales is to imply a contentious (and potentially unexamined) conflation; to what extent does attentiveness to nature and the elements define Englishness? And is Hill any less accomplished (or English) when training his eye, as he often does, on other parts of the world?

The significance of all three of these quandaries persisted, and in certain respects intensified, in the final phase of work published before Hill's death. For all their formal, rhetorical and thematic complexities, the volumes of *The Daybooks* retain, as their collective title suggests, something of the quality of journal notations, with sketches from nature set down on the page alongside the poet's frequently oblique ruminations (as if in self-addressed short-hand) on various historical, political and religious concerns as well as the works of numerous writers and artists.[13] Many of Hill's attempts to record environmental details in these diurnal notebooks achieve the crisp immediacy, keen sense of atmosphere and distinctive word-choice that his admirers have long prized, as in section 43 of *Oraclau | Oracles*:

> Among rough-spreeing gorse, now heather
> Gives new life to the colours of mourning;
>   Expansive its dense sojourning
>   Illuminates the drab weather

---

[12] John Lyon, 'Self and Love', review of *Without Title*, *PN Review* 170, 32 no. 6 (July-August 2006), p. 66. Lyon also challenges a simplistic notion of Hill as a 'nature poet' by observing that the poet's landscapes are often subject to 'the encroachment – would Hill's self-proclaimed admirers say "contamination"? – of artifice ("More than ever I see through painters' eyes"), of *human* nature and, pre-eminently, of the poet's idiosyncratic, provocative, unpredictable self' (p. 66). The bracketed quotation is from 'In Ipsley Church Lane 1' (BH 486; WT 6).

[13] During a poetry reading for the '*Economist* Books of the Year Festival' at the South Bank Centre in London on 11 December 2011 (hereafter referenced as 'London Reading'), Hill revealed, 'I used to feel lucky if I wrote seven poems a year. Since June 2007 I've written eight books and feel that I'm flagging if I fail to write seven poems a week.' A podcast of the reading is available at <www.economist.com/blogs/prospero/2011/12/economist-books-year-festival-geoffrey-hill> [accessed April 2012].

>    That sags in off the sea,
>    Snags on the headland's thorny armoury.
>    (BH 755; O 15)[14]

A few passages, though, are somewhat closer to the nature of a conventional 'saw this, did that' diary-entry, even when the language is – as above – held taut across lines of pre-determined metre and rhyme (or occasional slant-rhyme):

> A gale from out of Ireland ploughs up rough
> Cardigan Bay; a following splendid rain
>   Beats us indoors to self-sustain
>   With radio and *Telegraph*
> (BH 778; O 38)

Hill's alertness to the elemental, to 'light's buffeting' (BH 756; O 16) over a stretch of land or water, to 'the conflagration of rain and wind' (BH 761; O 21), has found expression in vivid fragment-form across book-length poem-sequences since *The Triumph of Love*. His propensity to work such passages into his volumes has for some time now given the impression of a poet attempting to bring striking notebook observations, drawn from nature, into works often marked by seemingly disparate and discontinuous concerns. A sense of the provisionality and arbitrariness arising from numerous abrupt shifts of focus is reflected in several reviews of the first volume in the *Daybooks* series to be published; responses to *Oraclau | Oracles* perpetuated the reader's impulse to seek refuge from interpretative bewilderment (and in some cases from evaluative disappointment), and to gain reassurance regarding Hill's continued accomplishment, by turning in particular to his visions of nature.[15]

---

[14] Quotations from Hill's *The Daybooks* are as they appear in *Broken Hierarchies* (where the extent of line indentations sometimes differs from that presented in the original volumes).

[15] The particular virtues of Hill's landscape visions are extolled by several reviewers of *Oraclau | Oracles*: see Jeremy Hooker, 'Other Land', *Notre Dame Review* 32 (Summer-Fall 2011), pp. 248-52 <http://ndreview.nd.edu/assets/47784/hooker_review.pdf> [accessed April 2012]; King, 'Fraught Celebration'; William Logan, 'Blah Blah Blah', *New Criterion*, June 2011, <www.newcriterion.com/articles.cfm/Blah-blah-blah-7068> [accessed April 2012]; George Potts, '*Oraclau | Oracles* by Geoffrey Hill', *Literateur* (March 20, 2011), <http://literateur.com/oraclauoracles-by-geoffrey-hill/> [accessed April 2012].

However, the concerns of the volume have made it impossible to retain the simplistic conflation of Hill's landscapes with a sense of Englishness – a conflation that, in any case, has seemed questionable since the publication in 1983 of *The Mystery of the Charity of Charles Péguy*, in which the 'landscape and inner domain' (BH 147; TM 16) of Péguy's 'militant-pastoral' (BH 145; TM 13) vision of France is exquisitely rendered (if also tested against the battlefields of the Marne). As its bilingual title implies, *Oraclau | Oracles* is a sequence of poems imaginatively engaged with the country on the far side of Offa's Dyke from Hill's Mercian 'home' ground. The volume reflects the poet's self-professed 'historical, theological, sociological and economic interest in what has happened to Wales', an interest quickened by his discovery that his great-grandfather was one Pryce Jukes of Llanllwchaiarn: as Hill has revealed in interview, Jukes (born 1826) 'uprooted and moved east into the Mercian Black Country, where he worked as a puddler in an iron foundry'.[16] Something of a kindred spirit to Hill's 'grandmother, whose / childhood and prime womanhood were spent in the / nailer's darg' (BH 107; MH XXV), Jukes – the dedicatee of *Oraclau | Oracles* – seems to emblematize for Hill the dignity, self-sacrifice and quiet suffering of the industrial worker. He also provides Hill with an ancestral point of access to an 'intimate Welsh landscape of disquiet' (BH 769; O 29). The 'disquiet' of the sequence arises at once from Hill's uneasy purchase on his subject, given his double sense of affiliation with and alienation from the homeland of a forebear ('This is a strange country, the words foreign' (BH 757; O 17), as he puts it in section 51), and from the physical, political and economic upheavals to which the Cambrian terrain has been subjected.[17] When he writes in section 108 of 'Novembering Wales, the flooded meadows / Pewter, lead-sheeting, briefly highlighted' (BH 776; O 36), Hill himself appears to be highlighting, in abbreviated form, the extensive metal-mining to which the ground below the meadows has been subjected. This connects to a more general awareness, running through the sequence, of the fact that the Welsh landscape has, along

---

[16] Damian Walford Davies and Richard Marggraf Turley, 'Cambrian Readjustments: An Interview with Geoffrey Hill', *Poetry Wales* 46.1 (Summer 2010), pp. 10-13 (pp. 12, 11). As Davies and Turley observe, 'puddling ... involves heating and stirring molten pig iron with oxide in a furnace' (p. 12). Jukes is also a subject of contemplation in the poem 'Coda' (BH 599-600; TCP 49-50).

[17] King suggests that 'the disquiet is the quiet of a pastoral scene, broken by the intrusion of the same historically burdened language through which it is evoked' ('Fraught Celebration', p. 74).

with many Welsh citizens, been well-worked, if not exploited; Hill writes in section 51 of the coal- and iron-masters' 'blood-intrigued Capital' (BH 757; O 17), and his work reads intermittently as a sad and angry lament for the 'misprised coalfields' (BH 744; O 4). At the same time, however, the sun's brief highlighting of 'flooded meadows', so that they take on the momentary appearance of 'pewter' or 'lead sheeting', is one of Hill's numerous epiphanies, a glint of brightened and transformative vision (BH 776; O 36). It is clear, too, that Hill sees benign continuity, not merely conflict, in the relationship between the mineral world and man-made objects; in writing of a 'stone house' with a 'slate shimmer' (BH 776; O 36), of 'distant rain-draped slate flanks' that 'gleam like late snow', and of 'field walls that are quartz-spangled' (BH 745; O 5), Hill conveys a sense of mutual enrichment in the interplay of built and natural environments.

The illuminations of the world to which he responds are characteristically fleeting – as is evident from the very outset of the volume:

> The rain passes, briefly the flags are lit
> Blue-grey wimpling in the stolid puddles;
>   And one's mind meddles and muddles
>   Briefly also for joy of it.
> (BH 741; O 1)

Like the 'briefly highlighted' (BH 776; O 36) waterlogged grassland glimpsed in section 108, the wet flagstones here are kindled both by the quality of the light that colours them and by the quality of attention brought to bear upon them. Jeremy Hooker is alert to several implications in Hill's opening lines:

> The word 'wimpling' invokes Gerard Manley Hopkins, the other great English poet renewed by his experience of Wales and an exemplary figure for Hill. One may also suspect a pun on the great-grandfather's occupation in 'stolid puddles'. Certainly, what we have here is more than a neutral landscape. The puddles conjoined to the 'lit' flagstones 'wimpling' reveal at once brute existence and a fluid, visionary world. The mind meddling and muddling is part of the life it perceives.[18]

---
[18] Hooker, p. 249.

One aspect of the muddling implicit in Hill's lines derives from the momentary sense, before the first line-turn, of a reference to flag-burning ('briefly the flags are lit') – and this in a sequence that returns to issues of national identity via a contemplation of flags in section 92 (BH 771; O 31). This short-lived flicker of an interpretative possibility, along with the potential allusion to Hill's ancestral 'puddler', leaves it unclear whether the phrase 'for joy of it' reflects merely Hill's delighted response to the physical world in all its vivid particularity or, in addition to this, the pleasure his meddlesome, muddlesome mind takes in complicating visual perception with the cross-currents of cultural thinking that arise from the choice and placing of words.

Perhaps the most conspicuously deliberated word in the opening lines is 'wimpling', an adjective which, as Hooker notes, has evident Hopkinsian associations. To 'wimple' is, among other things, to ripple, an effect one can observe both when a breeze tugs the water of a puddle and when the wings of a 'Windhover' undulate on thermal currents.[19] Hill's acuity in perceiving how it is a shift in the quality of light, after the rain, that reveals the 'wimpling' in a puddle is reminiscent of descriptive capacities in Hopkins that Hill commends when he discusses the poet's work in 'A Postscript on Modernist Poetics'. Reflecting on the poem 'That Nature is a Heraclitean Fire and of the comfort of the Resurrection', Hill makes the following observations:

> The first fourteen lines delineate aspects of the Heraclitean world, of infinite change, its eternal round of creation and destruction, which is all intricately and beautifully detailed as Hopkins imitates its wondrous thisness:
>
> Down roughcast, down dazzling whitewash, | wherever an elm arches,
> Shivelights and shadowtackle ín long | lashes lace, lance, and pair.
>
> Roughcast and whitewash are indigenous ways of walling buildings, perhaps a memory of Wales where Hopkins would have seen the shadows and reflections cast by the sun and absorbed or cast back by the dazzling white of barn-sides or farmhouse walls. A 'shivelight' is a splinter of light; 'tackle' is a

---

[19] See Gerard Manley Hopkins, 'The Windhover' ('How he rung upon the rein of a wimpling wing / In his ecstasy'), in *Poems and Prose*, ed. W. H. Gardner (Harmondsworth: Penguin, 1985), p. 30.

word for bits of ships' rigging, so 'shadowtackle' is the patterns of branch and twig-work from the nearby trees and bushes rigging the bright walls in the light of the sun. (CCW 570)

Hill's own evocations of Wales are attentive to Heraclitean flux. They apprehend the numinous in the natural with a verbal inventiveness that seems at once to strive for physical exactitude and to strain beyond verisimilitude towards the visionary. His sense that in 'natural Wales / Supernature's light steadily prevails' (BH 748; O 8) is recurrently (and often riddlingly) expressed via a notion of alchemical transformation of the known world:

> Alchemic-carnal, such the earth remains
> In winter even while snow asperges
>   From shaken branches, shows the ridges
>   Fresh-configured, swept by shadow-vanes;
>     And transience transpires
> Intensely focused crowing atop spires
> To what light is, a glaze between great flares;
> The sun arraying in the brittle llyn
> A limbeck of itself or of the moon.
> (BH 750; O 10) [20]

Just as 'shadowtackle' in the Hopkins poem describes 'the patterns of branch and twig-work from the nearby trees and bushes rigging the bright walls in the light of the sun' (CCW 570), so perhaps Hill's 'shadow-vanes' are the patterns cast on the snow-whitened, sun-brightened ground by the shadows of 'shaken branches'; as 'vanes', the shadows illustrate the direction from which the wind is blowing. Signalling a debt to Hopkins, Hill captures their 'thisness' with phrasing that is, like the ridges of snow on the landscape, '[f]resh-configured'. Yet, for all Hill's attempts to hold fast in language, syntax and metre the intricacy and delicacy of what he observes, the figurative sense of a 'vane' as 'an unstable or constantly changing ... thing' (*OED*) is also pertinent, highlighting as it does the sense of the poetry's insecure purchase on the ever-shifting physical and elemental qualities it witnesses in this 'Heraclitean world, of infinite change' (CCW 570).

---

[20] In the third line quoted, O 10 has 'shews'; BH 750 has 'shows'.

The insecurity is clearly the reader's also as there is much in Hill's description that challenges imaginative visualization and strains comprehension. The stanza reads in part as a philosophy of perception, rather than merely an exercise in it, but it is not a philosophy founded on rational premises. Here, as at other moments in his later work, Hill appears to be engaging with the spiritual side of alchemy and perhaps even to be reviving and extending the tradition of English alchemical verse in which he was clearly interested. A file in the archive of the poet's papers in the Brotherton Library at the University of Leeds contains an offprint of a 1953 article entitled 'Alchemy and English Literature' by Harold Fisch which considers 'how vitally important the insights of the alchemist were [f]or the metaphysical poets of the seventeenth century'.[21] Hill has put double vertical pencil marks in the margin next to Fisch's observation that, 'For the alchemists ..., Matter and Spirit were inextricably mixed. To them, ... the external world was real and solid, ... but it was also mysterious'.[22] Hill's attention was also detained by the following claim:

> It is arguable that all Nature-poetry, insofar as it ceases to be merely descriptive or rationalistic but involves a real *meeting* between the poet and the outer world of nature, implies some ... doctrine of Immanence; but certain it is that, in the seventeenth century at least, the notions of the Hermetical School passed into the imaginations of many different poets.[23]

The notions seem also to have passed into Hill's imagination. In conceiving of the earth as 'alchemic-carnal', Hill appears to fuse, as Fisch puts it, the 'real and solid' and the 'mysterious'. As he does so, his phrasing itself partakes of the esoteric. The word 'carnal' in this context seems to extend beyond the 'corporeal' or 'sensual', but

---

[21] Geoffrey Hill Archive, Brotherton Library, University of Leeds, BC MS 20c Hill/5/1/223: Vaughan (1953-1994). See the offprint of Harold Fisch, 'Alchemy and English Literature', *The Proceedings of the Leeds Philosophical Society*, rpt. in *Literary and Historical Section*, Vol. VII, Part II (Leeds: Chorley and Pickersgill Ltd, October 1953), pp. 123-36 (p. 135); the missing 'f', a typo, is added in blue ink. Reproduced with the permission of Special Collections, Leeds University Library.

[22] Fisch, p. 124.

[23] Fisch, p. 127. Hill's double vertical pencil marks in the margin run from the words 'of nature' to the end of Fisch's sentence.

it is hard to tell whether Hill has in mind the *OED* definition 'not spiritual' or 'unsanctified', which is illustrated by an example of usage from the theologian J. B. Mozley's *Eight Lectures on Miracles* (1865): 'To a carnal imagination an invisible world is a contradiction in terms – another world besides the whole world'. To Hill's imagination, drawn to the possibility of Immanence, a clear distinction between the visible, material world and a sense of the spiritual is unavailable – hence, perhaps, the hyphen that fuses the 'carnal' to the transformative promise of the 'alchemic'. In any 'real *meeting* between the poet and the outer world of nature', the latter is susceptible to being transmuted into something beyond itself, into qualities that are invisible and immaterial. Like the Metaphysical poets who were drawn to the Hermetic and Neoplatonic aspects of alchemical thought (notably John Donne and Henry Vaughan, to whom Hill intermittently alludes in *Oraclau | Oracles*), Hill seems to invest in the idea that the natural world can reveal hidden truths and in doing so enable the process (or at least gesture towards the possibility) of spiritual regeneration – a kind of self-transmutation – for those responsive to what is being shown. The struggle towards enlightenment is aided if one perceives 'Supernature's light' (BH 748; O 8) illuminating the natural world. And such effects in turn prompt in Hill, as in his Metaphysical exemplars, the processes of poetic alchemy, whereby new configurations of phrasing are a means of transforming one's perceptions.

Hill's attraction towards (or peculiar variation upon) a tradition of Hermetic thought is liable at once to incite and to confound the critic's hermeneutic impulse. In reading the 'alchemic-carnal' stanza (BH 750; O 10), one may wish for the 'logic' of a paraphrase while also sensing the inappropriateness of this impulse. To attempt a single interpretation would be to work against the spirit of the writing, which inclines towards doubleness, if not multiplicity, of response, and which defies reductive rationality. The notion that 'the earth remains' 'alchemic-carnal' 'in winter', 'even while snow asperges / From shaken branches', is not easily glossed. There is the oddity of Hill gently twisting the verb 'to asperge' out of its standard transitive application so that it functions intransitively: asperging is sprinkling, and chiefly denotes a priest's blessing of a congregation with holy water; here, the snow does not asperge anything, but simply asperges. The implication of a sacramental glimmer in the winter scene is clear enough, but it is the grammatical twist which retains a sense of the unaccountable intrinsic to Hill's vision.

It is also ambiguous whether the earth, 'even while snow asperges', retains its intractable, unregenerate materiality or shows itself transformed. The dilemma is as irreducible as the compound adjective 'alchemic-carnal' is paradoxical, and it is akin to the contradiction of ideas present in the image, or perhaps the anti-image, of 'intensely focused crowing atop spires', in which it is unclear if one is to visualize a crow perched on a spire or, since the bird is only evoked by an aural property, if the intense focus of this line is not visual but somehow trained beyond the discernible world. A sense of complexity prevails, too, in Hill's account of 'what light is'. In describing it as 'a glaze between great flares', he hovers between an empirical account of the phenomenon of electromagnetic radiation coming in light-waves from the sun and a metaphysical awareness that the light of existence is intrinsically fleeting and ineffable, a 'transience' that 'transpires' and soon expires, a glazed condition – 'we see through a glass, darkly' (1 Corinthians 13:12) – lived out in a world whose own existence is framed by those two 'great flares': the radiance of Creation and the blaze of Judgment Day. Finally, there are the conundrums of perception at the stanza's end when Hill furthers his preoccupation with alchemy and writes of 'the sun arraying in the brittle llyn / A limbeck of itself or of the moon': here, the reflection of sunlight in the 'llyn' (the Welsh word for lake) seems to have been drawn into occult conjunction with the moon, as if the light has been distilled and transformed in a 'limbeck', or alembic – an alchemist's still. Given that the stanza form deployed throughout *Oraclau | Oracles* is derived from Donne's 'A Nocturnal Upon S. Lucy's Day, being the shortest day', one is tempted to seek a connection between Hill's vision of nature and Donne's talk of a 'new alchemy', of a mind transformed in 'love's limbeck'.[24] Yet Donne's is a poem of grief and regret, and its alchemical imagery distills a state of degradation, rather than regeneration. One cannot turn to 'A Nocturnal' to find the 'key' to Hill's engagement with, or literary exercise in, alchemy. The very idea of hunting for a philosopher's stone that will reveal the meaning of his stanza, or of his poetry more generally, is just one more version of the hunt for fool's gold.

---

[24] John Donne, *The Complete English Poems*, ed. A. J. Smith (Harmondsworth: Penguin, 1996), p. 72. It is possible that Hill's contemplation of the transmission of light is in some kind of negotiation with the cosmology of Donne's poem, in which 'the sun is spent, and now his flasks [the stars] / Send forth light squibs [weak flashes], no constant rays'. It is possible, too, that Hill's use of 'shews' and 'arraying' (O 10), which read as self-consciously contrived archaisms, imply a debt to the earlier poet: both 'shew' and 'array' are words in Donne's poetic lexicon.

Hill's 'alchemic-carnal' stanza (BH 750; O 10) is not atypical; an interest in esoteric thinking permeates *Oraclau | Oracles*. Five stanza-sections of the volume (sections 31-5, BH 751-2; O 11-12) are dedicated to the Welsh alchemist, mystic and natural philosopher Thomas Vaughan, from whose *Lumen de Lumine, or, a New Magicall Light* (1651) Hill cites in a note to 'A Pharisee to Pharisees', his essay on Thomas's brother Henry: 'When I seriously consider the system or fabric of this world I find it to be a certain series, a link or chain which is extended ... from that which is beneath all apprehension to that which is above all apprehension' (CCW 687). Hill offers this quotation for comparison to Walter J. Ong's suggestion, in the essay 'Wit and Mystery' (1947), that 'theology and poetry ... both operate on the periphery of human intellection. A poem dips below the range of the human process of understanding-by-reason as the subject of theology sweeps above it' (CCW 327). With reference to Henry Vaughan's 'The Night', Hill concludes 'A Pharisee to Pharisees' by commending an ideal of poetry which captures 'an awareness of such extremes', whereby 'that which is above understanding-by-reason (theology) and that which dips below the process of understanding-by-reason (the contingent nature of sensory material) are briefly made to chime' (CCW 327). Although such observations do not resolve, or even reduce, any of the perplexities arising from Hill's own manner of responding to 'the system or fabric of this world', they do at least intimate a cast of thought that might be felt to inform his poetic practice; especially telling is Hill's recourse to the adverb 'briefly', a word that is fundamental to his reflections on 'the contingent nature of sensory material' in *Oraclau | Oracles*: 'briefly highlighted' (BH 776; O 36); 'briefly the flags are lit'; 'briefly also for joy of it' (BH 741; O 1). One of the most significant, but also most complicated, aspects of Hill's responsiveness to transient illuminations of perception is the sense that the 'thisness' of the world is simultaneously instinct with a sense of 'otherness'. In this connection, it might be helpful to consider some observations that Hill makes in the essay 'R. S. Thomas's Welsh Pastoral'. In commending the Welsh poet for capturing 'the *haecceitas* of the Llŷn peninsula – "a branch of rock suspended between the sea and the heavens" (*Autobiographies*, 133)'[25] Hill implicitly aligns Thomas with Hopkins as a writer capable of imitating the 'wondrous thisness' of the 'Heraclitean world' (CCW

---

[25] Hill, 'R. S. Thomas's Welsh Pastoral', in *Echoes to the Amen: Essays after R .S. Thomas*, ed. Damian Walford Davies (Cardiff: University of Wales Press, 2003), pp. 44-59 (pp. 52-3).

570). But exactitude of observation of the kind Hill considers Thomas to have achieved is not to be confused with an unambiguous or unalterable grasp on the empirical; as Hill immediately goes on to observe, 'if one is determined to invest one's art in elemental things, both language and contingency must be understood to be as elemental as one's favourite rock and unharmonious (unlike the Llŷn seasons), perpetually out of kilter with our potentialities and desires'.[26] For Hill, whose own art is frequently attuned to the elemental, the idea that language can secure one's hold on the contingent world with a quasi-lapidary solidity and sureness is in perpetual tension with his recognition that language is ever-shifting in its implications. The particularity that defines 'the contingent nature of sensory material' (CCW 327), and that finds its correlative in Hill's attempts at exactitude of phrasing and cadence, is also exposed to provisionality, to the 'eternal round of creation and destruction' (CCW 570) to which Hopkins bears witness even while 'he achieves the "this" (the finished poem)' (CCW 391). Hence Hill's accordance with Ong's view: it is not that poetry passeth understanding; rather, it should ideally be responsive to, and humbled by, that which is beyond it.[27]

Another notable tension that Hill's work exhibits, and a challenge that it presents to its readers, arises from the sense that, on the one hand, 'intricately and beautifully detailed' (CCW 570) observations (of the kind Hill celebrates in Hopkins) are 'briefly made to chime' (CCW 327) in elegantly crafted phrases, held within carefully shaped forms,

---

[26] Hill, 'R. S. Thomas's Welsh Pastoral', p. 53.

[27] Hopkins is, for Hill, 'the supreme poet of "haecceitas"' (CCW 570). In the teaching notes related to Hopkins in the Hill Archive is a sheet of pasted entries from Hopkins's *Sermons*, including the observation 'Is not this pitch or whatever we call it then the same as Scotus's *ecceitas?*', along with the definition of 'haecceity' provided in the Glossary to John Duns Scotus, *God and Creatures: The Quodlibetal Questions*, tr. Felix Alluntis OFM and Allan B. Wolter OFM (Princeton, NJ: Princeton University Press, 1975), pp. 493-540 (p. 511): '*haecceity* (*haecceitas*, from the Latin *haec*, this): The term means literally "thisness." It designates the unique formal principle of individuation that makes the nature, which all individuals of the same species have in common, to be just this or that individual and no other. Scotus regards it as a distinct positive formality over and above the common nature of the individual (*natura communis*). Petrinity, for instance, would represent the "haecceity" of Peter; Paulinity, that of Paul, and so on'. See the final page of 'AS KINGFISHERS CATCH FIRE: Notes for Class (22/10/86)', headed 'BUCKLE' in red ink in Hill's hand, in the Geoffrey Hill Archive, BC MS 20c Hill/5/1/106: Hopkins: Class Notes (1986). Reproduced with the permission of Special Collections, Leeds University Library.

and, on the other, that the poetry of his later volumes is often self-consciously 'unharmonious', that lines and clauses are 'perpetually out of kilter' with each other, difficult to bring into interpretative alignment and sometimes difficult even to comprehend on the level of coherent syntax.[28] Such considerations clearly have a bearing on the quotations considered thus far in this article; but they became even more pressing with the publication of *Clavics* in 2011. Here, Hill posits that 'the grace of music is its dissonance / Unresolved beneath resolution / Of flow and stance' (BH 793; CL 14).[29] His words seem at once to refer to the subject of the volume, William Lawes, a musician in the court of Charles I, and to Hill's poetic method. There is a strong sense of 'resolution' in the predetermined forms of his stanzas; as he has stated, 'the poems in *Clavics* are ostentatiously, even aggressively, shaped, adopting patterns of rhyme and metre from Henry Vaughan's poem "The Morning-Watch" and George Herbert's shape-poem "Easter Wings"'.[30] But for all the deliberated shaping, and despite the promise of musical regularity within repeated forms, a sense of the dissonant and irresolute prevails. As several reviewers have noted, this sense is primarily generated by what Steven Matthews terms 'Hill's elaborate wringing of the language' so that it frequently functions as a curious 'variant of telegraphese'.[31] There has been some agreement that 'the syntax is, as is increasingly the case with Hill, very hard to follow', that it 'strains against meaning', that it 'does not so much unfold as infold' (another distinctly Hopkinsian turn).[32]

---

[28] Hill, 'R. S. Thomas's Welsh Pastoral', p. 53.

[29] These lines are from Section 3 of the sequence in *Broken Hierarchies*, which is section 4 in the original publication of *Clavics* (London: Enitharmon, 2011).

[30] Hill, London Reading. There is contrivance, too, in the fact that Hill designed thirty-two of these emblematic pattern poems for the original sequence; as one reviewer has noted, this is 'the number of paths of wisdom in the Cabbala' – the esoteric thought-system to which Hill makes reference in the first line of his numerologically 'keyed' volume. See Bill Coyle, 'A Difficult Poet', *Oxonian Review* 18 no. 2, <www.oxonianreview.org/wp/a-difficult-poet/> [accessed April 2012].

[31] Steven Matthews, 'About Suffering They Were Never Wrong', review of *Clavics* and Derek Mahon, *New Collected Poems* (2011), *Poetry Review* 101 no. 3 (Autumn 2011), <https://www.poetrysociety.org.uk/lib/tmp/cmsfiles/File/review/1013%20Matthews.pdf> [accessed April 2012].

[32] See, respectively, Lachlan Mackinnon, 'Discords and Distractions', *Independent*, 3 June 2011, <www.independent.co.uk/arts-entertainment/books/reviews/clavics-by-geoffrey-hill-2292235.html> [accessed April 2012]; Benjamin Myers, '*Clavics* by Geoffrey Hill', *World Literature Today* 86 no. 1 (January-February 2012), <https://www.worldliteraturetoday.org/2012/january/clavics-geoffrey-hill> [accessed April

In an attempt to account for this, one might consider the relationship between syntactical confusion and regularized patterns of metre and rhyme, stanza length and line length, in the light of Hill's suggestion that the 'grace of music' arises from the impression of dissonant and irresolute effects held within a structure intimating a 'resolution / Of flow and stance' (BH 793; CL 14). Yet so persistent is the beguiling sense that successive clauses are entangled with preceding ones, and so startling and frequent are the shifts in tone, that the 'flow' and 'stance' of *Clavics* seem anything but resolved.

However, when it comes to Hill's visions of nature, the notion of 'grace' (as both blessing and graciousness) apparently remains available. Once more, reviewers have commended Hill's evocations of an environment as of a higher order of poetic achievement – an intriguing position, given that the syntactical indeterminacy and referential complexity that so alienate these same readers are often as conspicuous in the 'nature passages' as in any other part of the sequence:

> *Making of mere brightness the air to tremble*
> So the sun's aurora in deep winter
>     Spiders' bramble
>     Blazing white floss
> (BH 794; CL 15)[33]

> Hullo, thistle,
> Silver-silk head,
> Gashed green-blue woad,
>   Buoyant in old fallow,
>     Watch by your dead.
> (BH 804; CL 25)

>     Chaste, all weathers.
>     The journal ends

2012]; Jeffrey Hippolito, 'Give Me the Key', *Critical Flame* 15 (September 2011), <http://criticalflame.org/verse/0911_hippolito.htm> [accessed April 2012].

[33] Hill's italicized words may be a translation of line 2 (which has conflicting manuscript variants) of Guido Cavalcanti's sonnet 'Chi è questa che vien, ch'ogni uom la mira' ('Who is she coming, whom all gaze upon'); see David Anderson, ed., *Pound's Cavalcanti: An Edition of the Translations, Notes, and Essays* (Princeton, NJ: Princeton University Press, 1983), pp. 42-3, 255-6. In his essay 'Envoi (1919)' Hill praises 'the sensuous intellect of Cavalcanti's "Donna mi prega"' (CCW 248).

> Here in its fronds;
> Oblivious the calm
> Jolt of a wave.
> (BH 811; CL 29)

The elliptical, clause-by-clause gathering of physical observations and thoughts (or perhaps physical observations *as* thoughts) is as hard to parse in these examples as it is in the 'alchemic-carnal' stanza (BH 750; O 10) and in numerous other notations from nature in Hill's later work. Yet if one looks beyond the local difficulties a more general understanding of the implications of the poet's technique could be developed by recourse to some of the guiding concerns of John Barrell's *The Idea of Landscape and the Sense of Place* (1972). Writing of James Thomson's *The Seasons* (1726-30), Barrell contends that 'the crux of Thomson's method was ... the energy of his syntax, arising as it does from the sense he communicates to us, that the landscapes he is trying to organise can challenge and to some extent resist his desire to organise them'. 'Thomson', he argues, 'manages to incorporate the recalcitrant energy of nature into the structure he uses to subdue her'; in Thomson's poetic, 'the form of the syntax was the form of the place as he perceived it'.[34] Yet, with his impulse towards generalized description, and towards order and containment in his vision of the natural world, Thomson represents for Barrell a limited model of the kind of poetic achievement under consideration. It is John Clare who provides a more thoroughgoing exemplar of expressive syntactic particularity; Clare's syntax, according to Barrell, records images 'as parts not so much of a continuum of successive impressions as of one complex manifold of simultaneous impressions'; the result is a poetic mode which conveys a felicitous 'aesthetic of disorder'.[35] The applicability of such ideas to the recalcitrant and energetic syntax with which Hill strives to express his response to the environment and the elements is broadly sustainable. His notion, too, that the achievement of musical grace is not incompatible with dissonance and irresolution might be said to reverberate within Barrell's understanding of Clare's aesthetic. Yet in pursuing such interpretative analogies, one would do well to remember that the peculiarities of Hill's syntax are not confined

---

[34] John Barrell, *The Idea of Landscape and the Sense of Place 1730-1840: An Approach to the Poetry of John Clare* (Cambridge: Cambridge University Press, 1972), pp. 36-7, 44, 159.

[35] Barrell, pp. 157, 160.

to his sense of place; since the same complications of clause-arrangement define the language of his later volumes more generally, it is important to recognize that the syntax and idiom of a landscape (or seascape or skyscape) as Hill renders it on the page has not necessarily or exclusively been generated out of the poet's responsiveness to the particular qualities of the locale. Nonetheless, to concede this would not be to deny that Hill's syntactical disorder may be especially well-suited to conveying 'the complex manifold of simultaneous impressions' derived from the natural world.

The hazed grammar of perception also seems appropriate to Hill's impression that the physical realm is instinct with the numinous. It is this animistic sense of nature that defines the most significant influence on Hill of Henry Vaughan, whose poem 'The Morning-Watch' provides one of the formal models for *Clavics*:

>                    hark! In what rings,
>    And *hymning circulations* the quick world
>                    Awakes, and sings;
>                    The rising winds,
>                    And falling springs,
>                    Birds, beasts, all things
>                 Adore him in their kinds.
>                    Thus all is hurled
>    In sacred *hymns*, and *order*, the great *chime*
>    And *symphony* of nature.[36]

There may be a paradigm for Hill's poetic method in these lines: attentive to what Vaughan defines as 'the great *chime* / And *symphony* of nature', his poetry can be seen as a medium in which all that Hill perceives, though 'hurled' together, is nonetheless held in formal '*order*' in such a way as to express the sense that, as he says of Vaughan's 'The Night', spiritual apprehension and 'the contingent nature of sensory material' are 'briefly made to chime' (CCW 327). The notion that this is a compositional ideal towards which Hill's poetry aspires is supported by recurrent tendencies of thought in his critical prose. Hill's affinity with the seventeenth-century poet seems to derive from what Chris Fitter describes as Vaughan's 'Neoplatonic concern with a pervasive, invisible

---

[36] Henry Vaughan, 'The Morning-Watch', *The Complete Poems*, ed. Alan Rudrum (New Haven and London: Yale University Press, 1976), p. 179.

spirituality', a concern which results in 'a deeply unempiric landscaping, a transcendental imprecision', a 'blurring of fact into radiance'.[37] Hill's work, for all its sensuous particularity and its alertness to language itself as 'sensory material', is also drawn towards an 'unempiric', imprecise mode of expression as a means of conveying perplexity when it attempts to register both the mystery of divine Immanence and the muddle of material existence:[38]

> The day cuts a chill swath,
>     Dark hunkers down.
> I think we are past Epiphany now.
> Earth billows on, its everlasting
>     Shadow in tow
> And we with it, fake shadows onward casting.
> (BH 794; CL 15)

While the syntax of this extract is not strikingly irregular, nonetheless the layout of the poem on the page, with its impression at once of nebulously floating skeins and of lines held taut in an inherited verse-structure, as in an ancient vessel ordained for the reception of transcendent intuitions, could be read as part of the grammar of the numinous. And the final line is dense with an indeterminacy that is at once semantic and Neoplatonic: in the post-Epiphanic state to which Hill refers, are we 'in tow' with the Earth itself or with 'its everlasting / Shadow', the night that underwrites each day? And do we make false forward projections ('onward casting'), as if in defiance of our mortality and the surrounding darkness, or are we ourselves 'fake shadows', as Plato's analogy of the cave suggests?[39]

It is hard to know how far to take an attempt to paraphrase, or to itemize interpretative possibilities, in response to a poetic method

---

[37] Chris Fitter, *Poetry, Space, Landscape: Toward a New Theory* (Cambridge: Cambridge University Press, 1995), pp. 307-8.

[38] See, for example, 'A Pharisee to Pharisees', in which Hill claims that 'language is a vital factor of experience, and, as "sensory material", may be religiously apprehended' (CCW 327) and argues for an 'understanding both of Vaughan's vision and his perplexities and of his way of "bringing into use formally, or by authority" the envisioning of perplexity itself' (CCW 325). (The quoted words are from an *OED* definition of the verb 'to compose'.)

[39] See Plato, *The Republic*, trans. Desmond Lee, 2nd edn (Harmondsworth: Penguin, 1974), pp. 316-25.

that seems intent on retaining a sense of the ineffable. Hill's admission in 'A Pharisee to Pharisees' that he is 'far from convinced that the relationship between vision and language in poetry ... works according to theorems, particularly hermetic ones' (CCW 326), threatens to serve as an admonition against imposing too intellectualized or intricate a framework of reading upon lines that seem resistant to such an approach. Given that Hill himself writes of 'the swarm- / ing mass, the dense / Fluctuations of the materia / Out from which' he feels he 'shall be lucky to twitch / Creative fire' (BH 791; CL 11), it would seem impertinent to assume an understanding of a poetic process that the author himself considers to be unaccountable and unstable. Professions of uncertainty in the face of his 'materia' – both the physical world he contemplates and the linguistic medium in which he works – are a conspicuous hallmark of *The Daybooks*, and are all the more pronounced in the third of them that Hill published as separate volumes. *Odi Barbare* (2012) is frequently self-reflexive regarding the fragility (and at times the seemingly unavoidable obliquity) of the poetry's own observations and operations. Hill refers to a method of writing that seems to yield only 'the merest memo' (BH 879; OB 53) or 'a token fragment' (BH 886; OB 60), and he reflects, with an attitude that seems to hover between self-criticism and self-justification, upon 'a process / Metric makes gnomic' (BH 854; OB 28) and upon 'proven things not salvageable like collage' (BH 886; OB 60).[40] The phrase 'into scrap language unpredicted landscape' (BH 869; OB 43), which arrives unexpectedly at one point in the sequence, might serve as an apt (and typically shard-like) motto for the ways in which the poetry of the volume records its perceptions of nature. Once more, Hill's visions combine a sense of the clarified and the ungraspable as they achieve (or perhaps receive) a 'glancing / Apotheosis':

> As of bare hedges as of fields awash, light
> Clouds I call grey-coppery early mornings
> Fused with sun-shot fog and the grassblades crispy
>     Barely-heard tinsel.
> (BH 846; OB 20)

The self-conscious inclusion of the words 'I call' is characteristic of Hill's tendency in his later work to retain an impression of the notepad (or

---

[40] For 'not' in BH, Hill has 'made' in OB.

'daybook') jotting in the finished – or perhaps the insistently unfinishable – poem. His reference elsewhere in the sequence to 'Goldengrove notebooks ripped for late bequeathing' (BH 874; OB 48) also captures the feeling that Hill either wishes to insist upon, or cannot but admit to, the sketchy and provisional nature of his descriptions. In its sensitivity to a posthumous state ('late bequeathing'), and in its nod to the Hopkinsian locus of grief (Goldengrove has compelled Hill's attention repeatedly from *The Orchards of Syon* (2002) onwards), Hill's wording is in touch, too, with the melancholy sense of evanescence that is another dominant element in his apprehensions of (and beyond) the natural world.[41]

The forty-fourth section of *Odi Barbare* pictures a winter scene with a combination of simple optical impressions and enigmatic interpretative implications that is indicative of the qualities of the volume more generally:

> Undisclosed clairvoyance of apperception
> All around: church towers and silos catching
>     Shafts of the broad day;
>
> Mistletoe's globules and conglomerations
> Sealing boughs waxen with rich-cupped meniscus;
> Gilding bare orchards by the moon's endowment
>     Even at sunrise.
> (BH 878; OB 52)

The form of clear-sightedness that clairvoyance represents is one which accesses insights 'undisclosed' through mere observation – and yet the implication of the first stanza may be that it is only via the actual, phenomenal world that one may discern that which is beyond perception by the eye alone. To achieve this vision, Hill seems to suggest, one needs to enter an apperceptive state of mind. Perhaps the most richly suggestive definition of 'apperception' provided in the *Oxford English Dictionary* is the one derived from psychology: 'the action or fact of becoming conscious by subsequent reflection of a perception already experienced; any act or process by which the mind unites and assimilates a particular idea (esp. one newly presented) to a larger set or mass of ideas (already possessed), so as to comprehend it as part of the whole'. Apperception, as an extension of, or extrapolation from, perception, is a means of

---

[41] See Hopkins, 'Spring and Fall', *Poems and Prose*, p. 50.

converting sense-impression into sense-making, and of discerning meaning in the combinations of what one observes. It sounds like a figure for poetry itself. In the context of these lines from *Odi Barbare*, the implication seems to be that the radiance of things beheld in the physical environment glimmers with the possibility of metaphysical meaning because of the uniting and assimilating impulses of the perceiving mind (and, by extension, of the mind that organizes them into poetic form) – although, once more, such is the semantic indeterminacy of the phrase 'Undisclosed clairvoyance of apperception / All around' that the possibility of full assimilation of what is being conveyed here eludes the reader. Hill's interest in the partly unaccountable processes of psychology shades once more into alchemical notions in the following stanza, with the strange conjunction of sun and moon in the 'bare orchards' and the 'gilding' process through which light appears to effect a transmutation of trees. The mistletoe that hangs clustered in these trees is oddly figured too. Hill's choice of the term 'conglomerations' diverts (and perhaps seeks to redeem) it from its dominant contemporary use in business contexts. Here, Hill invites consideration of its original sense: 'to conglomerate' is, at its root, 'to roll or wind (thread) into a ball', and thus a conglomeration is 'a collection of things joined in a compact body; a cluster, coherent mass' (*OED*). In this sense, the process of apperception as the relating of an idea to 'a larger set or mass of ideas (already possessed), so as to comprehend it as part of the whole' finds analogies for itself in the clustering of the mistletoe balls in the trees, and in the clustering of Hill's phrases and their densely compacted implications. Whether coherence or tangle is the sum of perception here remains an open question – but if the reader feels compelled to pose it, a recognition that the poetry also asks it of itself seems fundamental to an understanding of Hill's methods and concerns.

'The poetry is always playing oblique games with me', Hill said in relation to the composition of *Odi Barbare*.[42] His claim complicates – though it by no means invalidates – the impression many have conveyed that his poems play oblique games with their readers. The very titles of the *Daybooks* carry the risk of enhancing such an impression; yet they also point towards dilemmas with which the poetry itself contends. *Oraclau | Oracles* offers a word that seems to promise enlightenment, but the bilingual presentation, along with the Hopkinsian upright slash that perhaps stands as a typographical signifier of the Anglo-Welsh border,

---

[42] Hill, London reading.

seems to insist upon barriers to comprehension.⁴³ Also, oracles are often 'obscure or ambiguous' messages, gesturing at truths not readily grasped (*OED*). Nor is it clear whether the poems of the volume are meant to be taken as oracular in themselves or as responses (and potentially baffled ones at that) to things which Hill considers to be oracular in the culture, literature and landscape of Wales to which he responds (an oracle can be a physical site, not merely a medium, of revelation). *Clavics*, too, is a riddling title. The nonce-word invites associations with clavichord music, but a red herring epigraph provides a fake definition: 'The science or alchemy of keys – *OED*, 2012' (CL 9) (and this in a publication of 2011).⁴⁴ With perverse ingenuity, and more than a hint of irony, Hill meddles with and muddles the implications of his title, forging vaguely key-shaped emblem poems tuned to the inherited music of Vaughan's and Herbert's poetic forms. The verse alchemy of Hill's sequence (a pseudo-'science', if ever there was one) purports to transmute musical and physical keys into each other. In the process, Hill appears to be searching for the interpretative keys to his intuitions and perceptions while simultaneously admitting to the risks of delusion and deception that are intrinsic to the alchemist's craft. *Odi Barbare* works by means of decoy also: '*I / Hate barbarians*' (BH 836; OB 10) is a phrase proffered in the second section of the sequence, as if in translation of the volume's title, but in fact Hill's work takes its name, and some of its guiding concerns, from the so-called *Barbarous Odes* (1877-89) of the Italian poet Giosuè Carducci. Carducci expressed his patriotic politics in part through a pastoral vision of ancient Italy and, as David H. Higgins has noted, saw his odes as representing 'an imperfect, "barbarous" adaptation of a Romance tongue to the prosodic features of classical Latin and its poetic forms'.⁴⁵ Hill's odes – which in turn constitute a self-consciously 'barbarous' adaptation of an adaptation – eschew nostalgia in their glimpses of the natural world, offering instead perceptions (and would-be apperceptions) that seem to articulate a desire

---

⁴³ Henry King associates the 'bar running through the collection's title' with 'the English / Welsh border' and suggests that it 'divides and yet conjoins, an emblem of the poems' language'. King, 'Fraught Celebration', p. 74.

⁴⁴ In section 42 of *Oraclau | Oracles*, Hill writes of 'Clavics, the alchemy of keys' (BH 754; O 14).

⁴⁵ Giosuè Carducci, *Selected Verse*, ed. and trans. David H. Higgins (Warminster: Aris & Phillips, 1994), p. 10. The Sapphic form that Hill employs in the volume is similar to the version used by Carducci in his *Odi Barbare* and to that used by Philip Sidney in *The Arcadia*, from which one of the epigraphs to Hill's volume is derived.

for a clarity and unity of vision that they nonetheless recognize is, for the most part, beyond them.

As such, the poems of *Odi Barbare*, as of Hill's other *Daybooks*, are in accord with observations he made in an interview in 2011: to the proposal that his poetry is difficult because the reader 'cannot grasp a coherent point of view', Hill said that his reply would be 'well, neither can I' and that his poetry 'is partly a dramatization of that'. 'A lot of my poems', he then observed, 'are about failing to get something or failing to be able to clear one's meaning finally'; this, he claimed, is 'a perfectly legitimate area to write in, … provided one is technically efficient and ends up with something beautiful. … I think poems should be beautiful'.[46] In the reception of Hill's work, and in particular of the later volumes, a strong body of opinion has formed that the beauty of his work chiefly resides in his responses to nature. The impulse to make such a direct claim is understandable, but, when considered in the light of the poetry itself, its implications are far from simple. For, as Hill's work abundantly illustrates, visual beauty is indistinguishable not only from the beauty of the cadences through which a sense of the visual is conveyed but also from the intricacy, even the delicacy, of contemplation brought to bear upon one's surroundings. Coleridge's observations on this point might provide a useful, and suitably graceful, measure of Hill's achievement:

> [I]mages, however beautiful, though faithfully copied from nature, and as accurately represented in words, do not of themselves characterize the poet. They become proofs of original genius only as far as they are modified by a predominant passion; or by associated thoughts or images awakened by that passion; or when they have the effect of reducing multitude to unity, or succession to an instant; or lastly, when a human and intellectual life is transferred to them from the poet's own spirit,
>
>     Which shoots its being through earth, sea and air.[47]

---

[46] Hill, 'Poems Should be Beautiful', podcast of interview excerpts, *The Economist Online*, 2 December 2011, <www.economist.com/blogs/prospero/2011/12/economist-books-year-festival-geoffrey-hill> [accessed April 2012].

[47] Samuel Taylor Coleridge, *Biographia Literaria, or Biographical Sketches of My Literary Life and Opinions* (1817), ed. George Watson (London: Dent, 1984), p. 177. (The line of poetry is from Coleridge's 'France, An Ode' (1798).)

CHAPTER THREE

'Poetry's a public act by long engagement':
Geoffrey Hill and the Eighteenth Century

TOM JONES

> Style is a seamless contexture of energy and order which, time after time, the effete and the crass somehow contrive to part between them; either paying tremulous lip-service to the 'incomparable' and the 'incommunicable' or else toadying to some current notion of the demotic. (CCW 241)

Geoffrey Hill's poetry might be taken as an effort to rebut the dilemma of style set out above, to make a poetry of energy and order that resists the mysticism of the incommunicable and the vulgarity of the demotic. His own stylistic predicament is more complex than a dilemma: it concerns the degree to which authority, and indeed whose authority, might be invoked to determine the kind or extent of the labour required to make and understand poems, a labour that takes place in language. Hill's work, poetic and critical, calls upon poets and readers to clear away the contingencies that beset language, yet acknowledges that they can never be entirely cleared away. It invokes authority (religious, civic, and literary) as a proper determinant of action, as opposed to a dangerously anarchic reliance upon mere inclination, and yet forcefully depicts the inaccessibility of God, the corruption of the state, and the egotistical delusions of authorship. The problem Hill is confronting (I presume other readers find his work has the character of a confrontation with a real problem) is not just the question of the degree to which an author is responsible for giving in to contingency in her choice of words (such as Hill's decision to use the denigrating term 'effete', with at least shades of its current sense 'effeminate', and thereby to imply a gendered distribution of characteristics); but also whether there might be any meaningful standard for such labour beyond people saying what they like.

The terms around which these problems orient themselves in Hill's criticism include contingency and judgement, conscience and taste, and the problems might be gathered under the heading 'imbecility', the term

Hill uses to capture three defining features of being human – fallenness, sociability, language. Hill laments the way that John Locke's rationalist account of words referring to clear and distinct ideas in the minds of their users would 'disconnect language from the consequences of our common imbecility' (CCW 341). He cites Joseph Butler's interest in incarnated grace as an untimely weapon for combating common human imbecility (CCW 475). Imbecility, then, is the problem that nothing in human speech is clear, simple or correct, and Hill finds in at least one eighteenth-century author an exemplary struggle to correct this condition as far as, and in that manner that, is humanly possible. Hill recommends that poets and critics minimise their imbecility by attending to the contexture of speech, catching its drift, and registering the distribution of values through speech that is effected in syntax and rhythm (not just in the long-term shifts in meaning identified by lexicographers and literary historians of ideas). These activities, Hill claims, will clear the ground of language from the influence of extraneous contingency, and allow judgement to take place (CCW 201). Such activities distinguish the right-thinking poet or moralist from those who have simply given in to subjective taste as a ground for judgement, a capitulation that Hill suggests will lead to anarchy, and which he associates with David Hume, in specific contradistinction to Butler (CCW 468-9, 475).

The contingent, however, is not entirely to be cleared away: humans are fallen after all. Hill recognises positively the work of poets whose language is an expression of the labour of clearing the contingent out of ordinary language, but also the impossibility of doing so completely:

> Quotidian language, both casual and curial, is itself highly charged, but charged with the enormous power of the contingent and circumstantial, a 'confused mass of thoughts', a multitudinous meaning amid which the creative judgement must labour to choose and reject. There are 'meanings' which are self-evidently wrong ('reserate' is not Latin for 'shut the door') but the 'meaning' of a poem, its constitution, the composition of its elements, is not so readily abstractable from the constituted opinions and solecisms of the age; and though the grading and measuring of words presupposes the ability to recognize ambiguities, there are some ambiguities so deeply impacted with habit, custom, procedure, that the 'recognition' is in effect the acknowledgement of irreducible bafflement.

Dryden and Pound are alike in their feeling for a language that is as expressive of the labour and bafflement as it is of the perfected judgement.
(CCW 228)

And Wordsworth, despite his hatred for Hume, is identified as sharing with the philosopher, critic and historian a sense of 'the nature and power of contingent circumstance' in matters of taste (CCW 385).[1] How much, then, of the contingent has to be cleared out before one might be said to have judged well in or of language? Hill's oeuvre in verse and prose is an answer to that question, and, for those without a belief in a transcendent standard by which such questions could be answered, probably the only kind of answer possible. Hill often has recourse to kinds of intra-textual guidance to reading, pointing out the labour at work against contingency, and what has been left to stand: notes on how to read an effect (such as coincidence of phonological material across words), as in *The Mystery of the Charity of Charles Péguy*: '"Encore plus douloureux et doux." Note how / sweetness devours sorrow' (BH 153; TM 28); the insertion of stress markings that seek to direct intonation in the performance of a line (as in *Speech! Speech!*); the editorial asides and insertions of *The Triumph of Love*. These are phatic claims that the poems do the right work, clear contingency just enough. Hill contends there is a desirable level of purification of the language, falling short of which is to have committed immorality, having given in to the anarchy of taste. In asserting that a degree of linguistic and social order is required to prevent anarchy, and that the author himself, by virtue of his own linguistic performance, is the person entitled to establish that degree and its modes, Hill is very like some of the eighteenth-century authors to whom he alludes, including Jonathan Swift, Lord Shaftesbury, Joseph Butler, John and Charles Wesley, and William Cowper, in relation to whom I shall now discuss Hill's critical and creative work.

In the course of my reading of Hill I will be explicating some of his characteristic attitudes, some of which could be called Swiftian, or, more generally, Scriblerian: speech, including poetic speech, is a public act; memory, as embodied in a scholarly approach to composition, and a creative attitude to the imitation of excellent models, is vital to the

---

[1] The long eighteenth century considered in this essay begins and ends with the careers of Dryden and Wordsworth respectively.

transmission of culture; the present and the recent past have witnessed an irreversible decline in the practices that preserve cultural traditions. There is a further set of attitudes, involving advocacy of rational faith and a popular poetry which would carry some of the burden of public cultural memory. These attitudes and this poetry might be associated with religious reformist Anglicanism, and called Wesleyan or hymnal. In defending the direct, accessible religious lyric that Donald Davie wants to claim the eighteenth-century hymn is, Hill demonstrates a similarity to Davie that extends into their thinking about the interpenetration of social and linguistic order, and the necessity of regulation in both social and linguistic spheres. Hill's desire to regulate poetic speech according to (conservative) social and religious motives shares some substance with that of Davie, but is more qualified, and admits a more open encounter between the poet and the sometimes intractable language of poems. My discussion will begin with memory and move on to public speech, before considering the hymn and direct religious language. It will conclude with a discussion of William Cowper's appearance in *Speech! Speech!*. The running tension in Hill's work that I want to capture in this discussion is that between authority and fallenness: the poet, like every other poor pilgrim, is mired in human imbecility, yet the very fact of his poetic labours is a claim to authority in the matter of avoiding or amending this imbecility. Hill knows very well that language is not the private, sole possession of its manipulator, the poet, and that poets have to live with what the language, in its long public life, can give them. But certain roles and attitudes the poetic persona takes on in Hill's work suggest a desire to maintain an authoritative role for the writer, mastering the contingencies of the language.

In *The Triumph of Love* Hill makes clear his dedication to memory, he is aggressively satirical, and he frequently refers to the only eighteenth-century poet to whom he has dedicated an essay, Jonathan Swift. The book warns of the dangers of losing memory, particularly memories of the Second World War. Hill responds to an interpolated critical voice in the poem that berates him for taking on the role of the memorialiser of a war in which he did not fight (he was too young):

> My cowardice
> is not contested. I am saying (simply)
> what is to become of memory?
> (BH 281; TL 75)

Earlier in the sequence, in sections CXIX and CXXII, memory has been a loan-shark, as it demands impossible repayments of the debt of scholarship owed to the dead (BH 274-5, 275; TL 63, 65). The contemporary Britain that appears in the poem is 'A nation / with so many memorials but no memory' (BH 261; TL 40). Hill, then, places himself in a position similar to that of Swift: an ancient in the battle of the ancients and moderns, that division of intellectual terrain in the late seventeenth and early eighteenth centuries which tended, in the literary sphere, to divide those who saw literature and scholarship as attempts to imitate the great achievements of the past, and those who thought literary modernism had surpassed or would surpass its models, just as the other disciplines had. Swift's denigration of the moderns in his *A Tale of a Tub* is achieved through a narrative persona, a modern author and projector, who admires the writers of his epoch precisely because of their freedom from memory. '*Memory*', he says,

> being an Employment of the Mind upon things past, is a Faculty, for which the Learned, in our Illustrious Age, have no manner of Occasion, who deal entirely with *Invention*, and strike all Things out of themselves, or at least, by Collision, from each other: Upon which Account, we think it highly Reasonable to produce our great Forgetfulness, as an Argument unanswerable for our great Wit.[2]

Swift, then, is present in Hill's sequence as an antecedent for the association of memory-loss and cultural decline; he is also present in the poem as the poet who wrote his own epitaph, and alluded to his own *saeva indignatio*, savage indignation. There are further associations. Swift often wrote against the corruption-inducing financial innovations of his time, a target Hill seems to share when writing on Trimalchio, a representative of the finance-advertising-entertainment complex who takes his name from a character in Petronius's *Satyricon* (BH 252, 256; TL 25, 32). In Hill's sequence, however, the savage indignation of Swift has become an unattainable ideal, a fancy, in a designation recalling Blake's memorable fancies in *The Marriage of Heaven and Hell* (BH 271; TL 58). The savagery of indignation is alloyed with self-hate: 'Savage indignations / plighted with self-disgust become one flesh' (BH 269;

---

[2] Jonathan Swift, *A Tale of a Tub. Written for the Universal Improvement of Mankind*, 2nd edn (London: J. Nutt, 1704), p. 126.

TL 53). Savagery of satirical attack should not be reserved for other people, even if Hill in other parts of the poem does seem successfully to have externalised his disgust. The author here makes no claim to be outside imbecility: he is not in the business of Lockeian disconnection.

In his essay on Swift, Hill characterises him as one in whom 'a sense of tradition and community is challenged by a strong feeling for the anarchic and the predatory' (CCW 72). Swift is said to have taken some creative delight in anarchy, one of whose modes of expression was his scatological verse in which the excretory functions of women in particular are subjects of close poetical scrutiny (CCW 80, 82). One could see an increased tolerance for and creative interest in anarchy in *The Triumph of Love* (in comparison with Hill's work up to that point), and also identify a scatological aspect to it, as when the masters of the entertainment industry are attended 'like kings at stool' (BH 254; TL 27). Hill as a memorialist and scholar who at the same time knows his own proximity to the anarchy he satirically represents is very much Hill the Swiftian.[3] Indeed, Jeffrey Wainwright acknowledges that *The Triumph of Love* takes its satirical mode to Swiftian extremes, and raises similar difficulties to those Hill himself finds in Swift:

> The satirist's voice in the poem is adjacent to that of *vituperatio*, and indeed the 'splenetics' to which it returns. This is a mode that has engaged Hill before, notably in his essay on Swift … As he wryly notes there, 'invective is a touchy subject' … Aside from invoking the long tradition of raillery and invective which includes the vituperative character of Milton's tracts, Dryden, Pope and Swift, the issue is the one Hill poses with regard to Swift: is the invective 'poetically convincing' [CCW 81] The departure from moderation usually – as in the case of Swift – brings charges of being out of control, though as Hill suggests, the art of invective might include 'deft simulation' of such a condition.[4]

---

[3] This is a point also made by Henry Hart, *The Poetry of Geoffrey Hill* (Carbondale and Edwardsville, IL: Southern Illinois University Press, 1986), pp. 17, 58. For Hill and Swift see also E. M. Knottenbelt, *Passionate Intelligence: The Poetry of Geoffrey Hill* (Amsterdam and Atlanta, GA: Rodopi, 1990), p. 101.

[4] Jeffrey Wainwright, *Acceptable Words: Essays on the Poetry of Geoffrey Hill* (Manchester: Manchester University Press, 2005), pp. 84-5.

Hill (and Swift) might be deftly simulating their proximity to a scatological anarchy, or they may be full participants in it. On the other side of this divide between tradition and anarchy, however, is a claim to the role of a (rare) living connection to that which is to be cherished and preserved of a culture. Such a claim to a peculiar knowledge of and connection to a set of values that other people (other poets, a readership) cannot attain and preserve, relegates those others to membership of Hill's 'mob' (BH 257; TL 32). Here Hill veers towards one of Swift's risks: egotistical misanthropy. Could Hill's attitudes, the valuations he makes in his rhythms, syntax, allusions, and the total construction of his verse, endure a general triumph over imbecility? Or do these distinctions of his project require that there be a mob for whom the 'noble vernacular' (BH 259; TL 36) will forever be out of reach? I shall return to the distance between Hill and his audience later in this piece, and also to the degree to which sovereign authority over the language in poems is possible or even desirable.

For the little that they resemble each other as authors, Swift's work is identified by Hill as embodying some of the bantering spirit recommended by the Third Earl of Shaftesbury in his famous essay, published as part of *Characteristics of Men, Manners, Opinions, Times*, 'Soliloquy, or Advice to an Author' (CCW 86-7). Whilst Swift may not have had much to do with the particular version of politeness it was the aim of Shaftesbury's work to cultivate, he certainly followed the advice contained in Shaftesbury's idiosyncratic reading of the inscription at Delphi ('"Recognize yourself!", which was as much as to say, "Divide thyself!" or "Be two!"').[5] Many of Swift's prose works are narrated by more or less plausible figures who oppose, or demonstrate themselves to be culpably ignorant of, precisely those views a reader takes Swift to be promoting, thereby generating a divided authorial self. Shaftesbury also wrote on *sensus communis*, common sense, which he defines as a sense of what is common to all people, a species consciousness whose existence (evident to simple introspection) demonstrates that humans are fundamentally sociable animals. In 'The Argument of the Masque' of *Scenes from Comus*, Hill's concern for language that is publicly efficacious (to which also I shall return), is related to a Shaftesburyian understanding of common sense, and to the axis of cultural decline and conservation of the past just discussed. The argument of the mask will

---

[5] Lord Shaftesbury, *Characteristics of Men, Manners, Opinions, Times*, ed. Lawrence E. Klein (Cambridge: Cambridge University Press, 1999), p. 77.

be, amongst other things:

> That, in these latter days, language
> is the energy of decaying sense;
> that sense in this sense means *sensus communis*.
>
> That common sense bids me add: not
> all language. If power's fuelled by decay,
> so be it—decay being a natural force.
> (BH 423; SC 5)

Language is restricted as soon as it is mentioned: it is identified as the bearer of the energy of a common sense, but it is obvious (common sense) that only some language (that which has passed authorial muster) bears such sense. Only a certain kind of utterance can be this energy of the decaying sense of participation in community. Here, then, Hill at once claims a connection to the public life of words, and also restricts access to the peculiar kinds of language that can be considered truly public, to indicate truly what it is in humanity that is common, shared by all. This dilemma of the language that is at once public and yet exclusive (fallen and restored, imbecile and eloquent) is the characteristic way in which problems of Hill's poetry and poetics are brought into focus by his association with eighteenth-century writers.

Hill's interest in poetry as a form of public speech and civic action is connected to these eighteenth-century attitudes to community and publicity. Poetic composition is a civic, public act, according to Hill: 'I'm convinced that shaping, / voicing, are types of civic action' (BH 259; TL 36); 'Poetry's a public act by long engagement' (WT 41). Speech is capable of being a public or civic act because it is, first of all, an act, a realisation that much of Hill's critical and poetic work articulates. What Hill looks for in poetry is not something such as a 'poetic intelligence' beyond the poem itself, because the poem, the speech itself, is the act: '"utterance" and "act" are not distinct entities' (CCW 13). Hill is thinking through J. L. Austin's work on performative utterances or speech acts, identifying a question for the poet: how does poetic language make its performances efficacious? The question is located in the means by which more formal or 'typically' public performatives, such as shop signs, legitimise themselves, make themselves happy acts (to use Austin's terminology). Austin notes that signs such as 'customers are warned ...' contain an implied 'hereby', indicating that the warning is done by the sign itself. Hill comments that 'Romantic and modern poetry ... yearns for this sense of identity between saying and doing ... but to Pound's embarrassment and ours it discovers itself to possess no equivalent for "hereby"' (CCW 163). The poem cannot insist on its own efficacy, its own happiness, as does the shop sign: as Hill notes, there is no legislative force in the words of the poet as there is in the words of the shopkeeper's sign.

If poets and readers are to be happy (in Austin's sense), Hill would have them be pragmatic, sensitive and hard working. They need to be pragmatic in the manner indicated by Thomas Hobbes, in a passage Hill refers to frequently, by attending to the drift and contexture of speech (CCW 194): understanding is not just a matter of knowing the words somebody uses, nor the rules for the combinations of words, but additionally how the words are being used, to what kinds of ends, for what argumentative purposes, pursuing what kinds of contrastive evaluation within the body of speech. One way in which this understanding of drift can be developed, the literary critical way, is to attend particularly to the shape of sentences in a discourse. The distinction between terms in a complex lexicon, such as that of the language of religious experience in the eighteenth century, as Hill says in a review of a book on that subject, 'may be the breath of a syllable, dissolved in an instant, rather than that slow-motion relay race of trend and tendency depicted by literary historians of ideas' (CCW 356). The drift of a discourse may only be accessible to those readers who sensitise themselves to the distribution of values across a sentence effected by syntax, rhythm and so on. The labour that poet and reader engage in to sensitise themselves in this way is the same labour as that which clears away the contingency closing in on all uses of language, and this kind of labour is obvious in poets such as Dryden, Wordsworth and Pound, as has already been noted. In the absence of a 'hereby' to guarantee the happiness of literary speech, these forms of attention and labour must do.

But Hill does not give up altogether on the desire for a rule to emerge out of speech, a public, common, civic, binding rule. More generally, he is interested in the possibility of 'an "ought" somehow imposing itself upon us out of the matter of the actual' (CCW 16).[6] One might well

---

[6] It may be this desire to see moral obligations emerging from the nature of things organically, as it were, that makes Tory radicalism appealing to Hill, as described by Vincent Sherry: 'The structures of poetic alchemy studied in *Mercian Hymns* resonate

question the desirability, even the possibility of an 'ought' emerging from an 'is', in the case of poetry.[7] Not all utterances are rule-forming utterances in the strong sense; not all of them form institutional facts of the same kind; not all behaviour is regulated in the same way. Poems don't issue commands, nor do they have the contextual resources of proprietorship or authority that are required to legitimate such utterances as sovereign or military commands. Their modes of speech might be no less be happy, felicitous, efficacious, in making people think things, forming their attitudes to objects, social relations, emotions and so on. But these kinds of speech do not have 'hereby' to make them strong, and must rely instead on some other, much more tentative, unspoken formulation such as 'entertain along with me, if you are willing, the possibility that...' to do their work.[8] That Hill retains the ideal of a means of legitimation for poetic utterance is an indication of his desire to regulate the conditions of production and reception of speech, a desire that is at odds with his recognition of the role of contingency in poetic composition.[9] Ultimately, it is this regulatory attitude, an attitude central to Hill's work, and its shortcomings, acknowledged or unacknowledged, that eighteenth-century presences in Hill's writing illuminate most fully.

---

with the patterns of a traditional, hierarchical, "organic" society. Images of such an antique state linger elsewhere in Hill's work, and he has openly expressed an attraction to the political tradition of Tory Radicalism. That has been a pluralist tradition, articulated variously by Samuel Johnson, John Ruskin, Donald Davie, C.H. Sisson.' Vincent Sherry, *The Uncommon Tongue: The Poetry and Criticism of Geoffrey Hill* (Ann Arbor, MI: The University of Michigan Press, 1987), p. 156. Sherry's references to Edmund Burke, pp. 11, 70, 129, 161, are also made in this connection.

[7] For the assertion that no conclusion containing an 'ought' may be generated from premises containing only 'is', see David Hume, *A Treatise of Human Nature*, ed. L. A. Selby-Bigge, 2nd edn, rev. by P.H. Nidditch (Oxford: Clarendon Press, 1975), p. 469.

[8] Samuel Levin proposed '*I imagine myself in and invite you to conceive a world in which ...*' as the sentence implied by poems to legitimate the kind of act they perform, Samuel R. Levin, 'Concerning What Kind of Speech Act a Poem Is', in *Pragmatics of Language and Literature*, ed. Teun A. van Dijk (Amsterdam and Oxford; North-Holland; New York: Elsevier, 1976), p. 150.

[9] Peter Robinson considers the possibility that the poet might be the instituter of her own facts: 'Searle's distinction [between formal and informal institutional facts] is important for the study of poetry and art because, though writers have exercised and sometimes tortured themselves with the fact that poetry cannot make things happen by way of issuing official performatives, literary texts can and do (through the performance of pretended acts) invite and establish promissory relationships with a reader.' Peter Robinson, *Poetry, Poets, Readers: Making Things Happen* (Oxford: Clarendon Press, 2002), p. 2. He proposes ways in which pretended acts are real institutional facts.

The manner in which a poetic act is a public act is sketched by Hill with reference to Joseph Butler, the celebrated Anglican moralist. Hill has been considering the tendency in writers of the seventeenth century to associate excrescence in government with excrescence in language. He reflects upon the parallel between civil government and the government of the tongue in poetry – a parallel that is a perennial concern of English poetry and poetics:

> If I am constrained to choose not to be a part of the 'public riot' and if I abide by Ben Jonson's analogy (health of the State : sickness of the State :: health of language : sickness of language) or if I propose to push the issue deeper than analogy into interrelationship or even interpenetration (State-into-language / language-into-State), then Butler's argument offers more serrations and striations, more toe-hold and hand-hold for the resistant conscience of our imagination, than can be found in the arguments of any other eighteenth-century author – not excluding such a triumph of the moral imagination as Samuel Johnson's *Life of Richard Savage*. My language is in me and is me; even as I, inescapably, am a minuscule part of the general semantics of the nation; and as the nature of the State has involved itself in the nature that is most intimately mine. The nature that is most intimately mine may by some be taken to represent my intrinsic value. If it is so understood, it follows that intrinsic value, thus defined, bears the extrinsic at its heart. (CCW 477)

Hill begins with a desire to maintain civic order, and to make one's speech a contribution to a national civic order. He refers principally to two features of Joseph Butler's argument in *Fifteen Sermons*: firstly, conscience, or reflection upon the various reasons we have for acting in one way rather than another, is the definitive human characteristic, an obligation to scrutinise actions that comes from within the human constitution itself; secondly, there is an ultimate responsibility not to speak untruths of others, and indeed not to speak any more than is necessary.[10] Butler makes a parallel between the operation of conscience and the operation of the sovereign power in any state: for there to be

---

[10] Joseph Butler, *Fifteen Sermons Preached at the Rolls Chapel*, in *The Works of Bishop Butler*, ed. David E. White (Rochester, NY: University of Rochester Press, 2006), pp. 49, 70.

civil society it is not sufficient that there be various groups of people – they must all be subordinate to the sovereign power. So too it is insufficient for humanity that there be different faculties – they must all be subordinate to conscience for us to be human.[11] Butler also presents speech as a form of social action, partly intended for the conduct of all forms of business, partly for the greater social cohesion that is made possible by speech when people try to please one another in its exercise.[12] And, again with close relevance to the passage from Hill just cited, Butler distinguishes between two senses of nature, one that refers simply to following our inclinations, the other to acting in accordance with what our constitution is adapted for – following conscience.[13] Butler offers Hill a model of speech as a form of social action regulated by the conscience, with an implicit yet unbreachable subordination to absolute sovereignty (God), of a variety unavoidable, even desired, in theocratic approaches to civic life.

Given, then, that to speak poetically is an act, and a public, civic act, whatsoever its authority might be, that publicity generates conditions for the nature of poetic speech. As Butler says, not all people in a state are sages or skilled interpreters, and so 'morality and religion must be somewhat plain and easy to be understood'.[14] Hill does indeed specify conditions for public speech, for the standards of clarity it should achieve, and for the demands it is allowed to make on its audience. He does not do so in any simple or concerted way, but in a complex and pervasive manner. Here too there are eighteenth-century echoes. Peter Robinson notes that Hill finds in Swift the attempt 'to compose a transition between public and private'.[15] Robinson relates this transitional quality to those identified and valorised by Donald Davie, such as urbanity and familiarity, qualities that assure a certain amount of recognizable common order in poetic language, and so act as guarantors of civil life, of civilisation. Hart contrasts Davie and Hill on the subject of grammar as a guarantor of civilised life:

---

[11] Butler, p. 61.

[12] Butler, p. 67.

[13] Butler, p. 57.

[14] Butler, p. 76.

[15] Peter Robinson, 'Reading Geoffrey Hill', in *Geoffrey Hill: Essays on His Work*, ed. Peter Robinson (Milton Keynes: Open University Press, 1985), pp. 196-218 (p. 197).

Davie early on identified grammatical with civilized orders and therefore rejected the modernists. Hill made room for Simone Weil's definition of syntax as a 'simultaneous composition on several planes at once,' which suggests that the modernists were not simply voicing the mind's confusions and biases but its multifaceted complexity.[16]

Davie's suggestion that 'it is impossible not to trace a connection between the laws of syntax and the laws of society, between bodies of use in speech and in social life ... to dislocate syntax in poetry is to threaten the rule of law in the civilized community' has been a provocation to various forms of writing, and Hill's sense of the interpenetration of state and language just cited admits far more nuance.[17] Davie, whose work of the 1950s was important in shaping the post-war British reception of Pound, can be presented as a contrast to Hill on the question of accessibility (or familiarity, urbanity) in poetic language, and how it relates to truly public life; he is also particularly relevant to Hill's religious concerns. In Isaac Watts, the eighteenth-century Independent / Congregationalist minister, educationalist, theologian and hymn-writer, Davie finds a wit that has been 'deliberately subdued' which makes Watts comparable to Dryden and Pope.[18] (Here there is no sense of the scabrous, anarchic Pope, the Pope of *The Dunciad* who is assuredly closer to Swift as Hill sees him than he is to Watts as Davie sees him.) Davie finds Watts admirable for a paradoxical reason. Watts has chosen to address a public, to be a public poet, and in doing so has identified a distance between himself and his audience that he must stoop to conquer:

> Watts as we have seen availed himself of his indeed great sophistication only so far as his mostly *un*sophisticated public, his Dissenting congregations, would permit. And this I think is what we should mean when we say that British poetry is social: not that it is situated by society and social usage, nor that it is inescapably restricted by society and its usages, but that it

---

[16] Hart, p. 28.

[17] Donald Davie, *Purity of Diction in English Verse and Articulate Energy* (Manchester: Carcanet, 2006), p. 86.

[18] Donald Davie, *A Travelling Man: Eighteenth-Century Bearings*, ed. Doreen Davie (Manchester: Carcanet, 2003), p. 189.

is addressed to society, or rather to some identifiable group within society.[19]

Davie is here attempting to identify a characteristic of British, as opposed to American, poetry. This Watts is not merely of Davie's creation, as a citation of the hymnodist, upon which Davie then comments, demonstrates:

> "It was hard to restrain my verse always within the bounds of my design; it was hard to sink every line to the level of a whole congregation, and yet to keep it above contempt." This was a poet who, if he practised what Pope and the Scriblerus Club called "the art of sinking", did so deliberately, after counting the cost, his eyes open to the risk he was running. [20]

Hill too acknowledges a distance between ordinary readers and those in the business of producing public, poetic speech (whether as writers or publishers), but his interest is more in allowing the distance to stand and challenge the reader with material that is complex and demanding. In comments relating to the Everyman editions of prayer books, issued in original spelling, Hill suggests that the publisher Dent 'showed respect for the intelligence of "ordinary" people by occasionally making demands upon it', noting that 'irreparable damage' had been done to 'the common life of the nation' by promoting accessibility above diligence (CCW 293).[21] Hill remains sceptical of any dubious 'philosophy of authorial responsibility to the "reader"' that might unjustifiably separate them (CCW 12). The sinking such philosophies necessitate is itself debilitating, and the variety of accessibility for which Hill praises hymn writers is, by contrast, a form of religious sublimity: the 'great hymns of Watts and Charles Wesley' offer 'a sense of things inaccessible suddenly made accessible' (CCW 349).

There are some perceptible harmonies between Davie's description of Watts as an internal emigré within the church, as a tribal poet, in contrast to the less combative Wesley, and Hill's self-presentation as a partisan

---

[19] Davie, *Travelling Man*, p. 195.

[20] Davie, *Travelling Man*, p. 202.

[21] See also Peter McDonald, *Serious Poetry: Form and Authority from Yeats to Hill* (Oxford: Clarendon Press, 2002), p. 215.

of the faith.[22] Hill also echoes Watts' version of Psalm 90, probably still known most widely as the hymn 'Our God, our Help in Ages Past', which, in its second stanza, adverts to the power of God as 'sufficient':

> Under the Shadow of thy Throne
> Thy Saints have dwelt secure;
> Sufficient is thine Arm alone,
> And our Defence is sure.[23]

The striking line-initial use of 'sufficient' is notedly ambivalent in Hill's 'September Song': 'As estimated, you died. Things marched, / sufficient, to that end' (BH 44; KL 19).[24] The sufficiency of things (they are both efficacious in achieving the end, and parsimonious in offering nothing more), inverts the providential role it has in Watts. Likewise, in the second of 'Two Formal Elegies: *For the Jews in Europe*', human sufficiency is presented as a perversion of the divine security: '(To put up stones ensures some sacrifice.) / (Sufficient men confer, carry their weight.)' (BH 16; FTU 32).[25] Beyond this very local allusion, one might point to the way in which the stanza movement of Hill's 'plain style' draws on the hymnic tradition so strongly characterised by eighteenth-century reforming and dissenting movements. In a note to the poems of 'Pentecost Castle', Hill acknowledges a debt to *The Penguin Book of Spanish Verse*, which suggests that the suspended nature of the lines within the stanzas of that sequence might derive from the indeterminacy of translation, the impossibility of reproducing a word order and lineation from the source poem resulting in a diffidence in the construction of relations between the parts of the new poem (line, sentence, image) in the target language:

> I went out early
> to the far field
> ermine and lily
> and yet a child

---

[22] Davie, *Travelling Man*, pp. 187, 205, 222.

[23] Isaac Watts, *The Psalms of David, Imitated in the Language of the New Testament, and Apply'd to the Christian State and Worship* (London: J. Clark, R. Ford and R. Cruttenden, 1719), p. 229.

[24] See Wainwright, p. 22 on the connotations of 'sufficient'.

[25] The brackets are not in FTU.

> Love stood before me
> in that place
> prayers could not lure me
> to Christ's house
>
> Christ the deceiver
> took all I had
> his darkness forever
> my fair reward
> (BH 117; T 10)[26]

The skeleton of the ballad stanza, the second and fourth lines briefer and more concentrated that the first and third, combines with the plainest possible statement of the grandest theological principles to rest somewhere between the mystical and the ingenuous. The disturbing ingenuity of Smart's hymns for children (Hymn 33, 'For Saturday', for example) or Blake's *Songs* ('A Poison Tree') are a presence in the movement of these stanzas, the bold lyric transition substituting an unknowing directness for the sophistical air of an earlier poet such as Abraham Cowley.[27]

But if Hill is like eighteenth-century hymnodists, he is not to be understood to approve or embody all that Davie found in them. Davie's remarks on what is offered and what should be resisted in forming the literature of a language provide an informative contrast to Hill, who builds a recognition of what is given into his sense of the necessary labour of the poet. Davie is emphatic on the degree to which Calvinistic aesthetics and morality are focused on exclusion:

> The aesthetic *and* the moral perceptions have, built into them and near to the heart of them, the perception of licence, of abandonment, of superfluity, foreseen, even invited, and yet in the end denied, fended off. Art is measure, *is* exclusion; is therefore simplicity (hard-earned), is sobriety, tense with all the

---

[26] The word 'forever', in the penultimate line quoted, is replaced by 'ever' in BH.

[27] Christopher Smart, 'For Saturday', in *Hymns for the Amusement of Children* (Oxford: Printed for the Luttrel Society by Basil Blackwell, 1775), p. 76; William Blake, 'A Poison Tree', in *Songs of Experience*, *The Poems of William Blake*, ed. W.H. Stevenson, text by David V. Erdman (London: Longman, 1971), pp. 212-3; Hart notes, p. 33, that Hill's 'Genesis', the first poem in *Collected Poems*, was dedicated to Smart on its first publication in an Oxford poetry journal.

extravagances that it has been tempted by and has denied itself.²⁸

There is much that echoes with Hill's work in this assessment, and with his perception of Dryden being at his best when at his most laboured, when he does not just take what is offered (CCW 180-82). Hill emphasises resistance to what is offered by language, or the value of labour in poetic composition, and a recognition of 'the viciousness of virtue when virtue is not called forth to action in the *negotium* of language itself' (CCW 183). But such restraint in the face of what language offers is not a total aesthetic and moral principle as it becomes for Davie, but a recognition of the need for work on the part of both poet and reader, work directed against imbecility. At the same time, Hill knows this work is never done. Hill's allusions to John Wesley suggest concerns close to Hill's own poetic and religious practice. Hill notes that the Wesleys' interest in communicating to the body of their congregation might have been a sinking, but was not a giving in to taste, as they 'so feared and resisted the anarchic in all its religious and political manifestations' (CCW 364). When looking for a figure of the loss of religious community, Hill cites a term, and provides one of the self-mocking pseudo-editorial glosses common in his collections of the 2000s: '*Lost / estate* (WESLEY?)' (BH 347; SS 59). The sense of lost estate is the sense of fallenness that becomes evident to someone who hears the call of Christ.²⁹ And again, when Hill is characterising the church with which he identifies, and which he fears is held in contempt, he talks of

> the protracted, indeterminate,
> passion-through-history of the English Church,
> the Church of Wesley, Newman, and George Bell.
> (BH 269; TL 56).

Hill recognises the opponents of some of the most loudly, and vulgarly, trumpeted qualities of 'the enlightenment', Wainwright notes, as

---

[28] Davie, *Travelling Man*, p. 203.

[29] John Wesley, 'The Necessity and Benefit of Attending to the Gospel Call', in *Sermons on Several Occasions* (Leeds: Edward Baines, 1799), pp. 22, 26. For a balanced assessment of the place of Wesley in his context, see Jeremy Gregory, 'The Long Eighteenth Century', in *The Cambridge Companion to John Wesley*, ed. Randy L. Maddox and Jason E. Vickers (Cambridge: Cambridge University Press, 2009), pp. 13-39, esp. pp. 34-9 for the relationship between dissent, the established church and enlightenment, where Wesley is said to represent a balance of enthusiasm and reason.

"'dogged self-marginalizers like Swift, Wesley and Blake". It is a company that would readily recognise Hill, and one I think he would have been proud to own.'[30] Hill's interest in eighteenth-century religious figures is an interest in public, civic speech, but not in a version of such speech that is debased and openly servile. It is a poetry of restraint and labour, but also of reform, inclusion, change and openness. Clearing away all the contingencies to leave nothing but hardened judgement is not the objective.

In section 58 of *Speech! Speech!*, the themes of public, committed speech, poetic contingency (and resistance to it), and the fatalistic aspects of eighteenth-century dissent are brought together in reference to another writer of hymns, William Cowper, whom Hill compares to John Wesley, 'standing on opposite sides of the same central flaw or fault' between bathos and the sudden access of religious sublimity (Hill is making a local comparison between two passages rather than a general assessment), 'strikingly complementary in their felicity and wretchedness' (CCW 362):

> Better | than that I should hópe, assign me
> to bond with some other fatedness
> coveted as free will. I can read
> dry-eyed—C. Brontë cleared it with a word—
> Olney's own castaway *en famille*. Manic
> depressive, wrote about hares. PERFORCE
> hís word. Better than that I should hope: my
> word is my bond, my surety, my entail.
> Twelve press-ups at a time; such heaviness
> increased like due allowance. *Entre-nous*
> the mad are predators. Forgive me. Cry CHILD
> OVERBOARD—the self-righting hull shears on.
> (BH 317; SS 29) [31]

Cowper was prone to bouts of debilitating depressive illness and his imagination was strong enough to convince him of his own damnation, and make Milton appear to him in visions. In the 1760s he lodged with the Unwin family, with whom, particularly Mary Unwin, he shared

---

[30] Wainwright, p. 16, quoting from Roy Porter, *Enlightenment: Britain and the Creation of the Modern World* (London: Allen Lane, 2000), p. 482.

[31] The vertical line after 'Better' in the first line quoted is omitted in BH.

religious conversation, moving with them to Olney, where he met John Newton. His poem 'The Castaway' reports the death of a seaman, recorded in a prose narrative to which Cowper alludes in the poem. The final stanza of the poem switches from an implicit to an explicit relation between the castaway's condition and the moral and spiritual abandonment of the poet:

> No voice divine the storm allay'd,
>     No light propitious shone,
> When, snatch'd from all effectual aid,
>     We perish'd, each alone;
> But I, beneath a rougher sea,
> And whelm'd in deeper gulfs than he.[32]

Hill's section identifies with Cowper the depressive and fatalist: he is bonding with a person who hesitates to think his will could alter his fate. Indeed, the echo of an earlier poem – 'the mad are predators' is a citation of *Mercian Hymns* section VIII (BH 90) – suggests the indignation is turned as much against Hill himself as against Cowper. But Hill is also thinking of his standing towards his language, a relationship he sees as a coming to terms with the contingent, an understanding what to do with the given, and only free in as much as it can manage such a reconciliation. The section is partly a rejection of the pathos of Cowper: he can be read dry-eyed. He is a trivial poet ('wrote about hares', and, one might add, about sofas). But the section also lets Cowper back in, seeing in his use of a humble-seeming conjunction an understanding of free action as obliged or determined action, forced action. 'PERFORCE' is said to be Cowper's word: he uses it of those left on the boat after the man is cast away. They are 'pitiless perforce' (line 22) because they cannot go back for him, on account of the conditions at sea.[33] The paradox Cowper seems to embrace is that an action can be pitiless even if it was forced upon one by circumstance, rather than being the result of an emotional state or disposition. The ambiguity of sense controlled by Hill's stress markings emerges here: the assertion that the speaker hopes to be better than the poet who wrote about hares, and whose word was 'perforce', must be weighed against the alternative distribution of

---

[32] *The Poems of William Cowper 3: 1785-1800*, ed. John Baird and Charles Ryskamp (Oxford: Clarendon Press, 1995), p. 216 (lines 61-6).

[33] *The Poems of William Cowper*, p. 215 (line 22).

stress along the sentence, which suggests there is something better for the speaker to do than hope (and that must be not to hope, to give in). Readers are guided in their weighting of these two readings of the phrase, determining the counterpoint of poetic ambition and despair in the breath of a syllable. Hill then alludes to the title of one of his best-known essays, 'Our Word is Our Bond' (CCW 146-69), recognising that his speech, even if free, becomes a constraint. The poem is self-mockingly presented as an exercise (each line of the section a press-up) before being figured as the hull of the boat that ignores the child overboard: it is self-righting as it mechanically keeps its course, just as the poem is self-writing, pressing on with what it is given to work with.

The interaction with Cowper in this poem demonstrates Hill's interest in the kind of action that poetic speech is, and the ways in which it is constrained by the nature of language, and of human mental and moral tendencies. To be a poet of agonised conscience is to be cast away, but also to be bound by circumstances, such that one's ethical character is determined by them, even when acting with all the freedom of which people are capable. Hill's response to this situation is a grim comedy, a tightly allusive section that dramatizes his earlier career and concerns, detached and scholarly, yet confessional, seeing in the freedom of what one can say the constraints of what has been said. The section works by embracing what is given (what Cowper has left Hill to work with), at the same time as asserting control over those *data* by means of poetic labour (the developed ironies, plays on intonation, puns and so on). It illuminates the tension that I have argued is important in Hill's work, particularly when he is seen to touch on characteristic eighteenth-century themes.

In this study of Hill's connections to the eighteenth century, I have tried to describe his tendency to derive authority at some moments from his position as a representative of common, public life, at others from being distinguished from it: the poet's social role is that of claiming linguistic sovereignty whilst being the supreme student of linguistic imbecility, including his own. Hill's embrace of difficulty (if his economy, allusiveness, scholarliness and so on deserve that name) represents a different response to the challenge of making a public language of poetry after Pound from that recommended by Donald Davie, one that respects an audience by challenging it rather than by sinking to it, but one that, like Davie's, is inflected by eighteenth-century writers and ideas. But for Hill, as for any seriously Christian poet, the source of the conscience or judgement that should be applied in making and receiving public, poetic speech is ultimately God, even if God makes the law of conscience a law of human nature. Hill, just like Butler, has an ultimate resource in God, but must live in the human era, in which human imbecility attempts to reconcile itself to a perfect sovereignty that can never be adequately known. For those who do not have God, there may well be nothing but what Hill calls taste: the development over the course of human history of distinctive institutions with their own objective values that may nonetheless be found in the most serious states of tension or contradiction (the obligation to regard people as unique and the obligation to regard people as of equal value; the obligation to be aware of and preserve culture and the obligation to be original). The refusal to see taste as productive of anything other than anarchy, whilst continuing to promote the possibility of a source of civil and linguistic authority beyond the human, is a resistance to certain strands of enlightenment thinking. These were strands in which conceding a role to taste did not mean abandoning conscience, but giving it the grounds it requires if it is not to regress into that talk of the incomparable or incommunicable for which Hill denigrates certain kinds of discourse about style. The question Hill's connections to the eighteenth century leave for his readers, readers who may feel they are the heirs of a secular rather than a Christian enlightenment, is whether there might be any external standard by which to judge the appropriate combination of energy and order in poetic style, or if such judgements are a matter of conscientious taste.

Chapter Four

# Geoffrey Hill and J.H. Prynne: Language, Subjectivity and Longing

## Edward Larrissy

At first sight, Geoffrey Hill and J.H. Prynne would appear to many readers like the most starkly ill-matched couple, and there are indeed profound aesthetic and philosophical differences between them. Yet the similarities are, in fact, also profound. Indeed, when properly considered, it is the most obvious and oft-remarked aspects of the two that are in fact the most revealing and instructive. Both of these poets are known for their difficulty, and on encountering a comparison between them, the reader might be tempted to satirise the endeavour as resting solely on this characteristic. Yet this difficulty, this resistance to easy naturalisation, does reveal similar aesthetic aims in each poet. It also makes connections with the themes held in common between them. For instance, at the level of expression itself, there is a self-consciousness about the historically-conditioned nature of language and discourse. This connects to an ethically-concerned impetus to draw the reader into a challenging engagement with the use of words in the midst of the process of reading and sense-making. A simpler aim, which perhaps overlaps with this, is to prevent the poem from becoming an object of easy consumption and appreciation. A political and ethical concern, which also relates to the linguistic one, is constituted by the fairly explicit critique of free-market capitalism. In both poets, this critique can be related to the intellectual contexts in which new-Left ideas about economy and society were a subject of discussion in the mid- to late twentieth century, even if Hill's own conclusions align him with a form of organicist Toryism which now lacks political representation or significant advocacy. And both poets frequently couch their pressing ethical concerns in the language of the sacred and transcendent.

Romana Huk identified Hill's intellectual context in the Leeds of the 1950s and 60s in her essay 'Poetry of the Committed Individual: Jon Silkin, Tony Harrison, Geoffrey Hill, and the Poets of Postwar

Leeds'. She refers to *Stand* and the colour it took from the 'charged leftist spirit of its industrial, working class backdrop, as well as from the international perspective that animated the campus and certain modes of revisionist socialist thought and literary criticism at that point in time'.[1] The consciousness of the ideal of commitment, which Huk understandably relates to the influence of Sartre, bore poetic fruit in the influential anthology, *Poetry of the Committed Individual: A Stand Anthology of Poetry* (1973), edited by Silkin, and including poems by Hill and Harrison, as well as by himself.[2] One of the themes involved in the idea of commitment for these poets is that of compassion as an essential component in political action to redress injustice and institutionalised cruelty. This point might be illustrated by considering the implied connection, in Silkin's thinking, between his poems about war and his poems about the daily exercise of compassion, poems such as 'Furnished Lives' (about the 'children of London's poor') or 'Death of a Bird'.[3] His 'A Daisy' from his 'Flower Poems' takes this humble flower and makes it part of an allegory of the role of compassionate attention in human life. Daisies 'look unoriginal / Being numerous. They ask for attention' (63). And attention is what they receive from Silkin, who anthropomorphises them ('The eye-lashes grow wide') (63) and thus makes it clear that they represent the humanity we may be tempted to ignore. Yet they offer themselves 'For the mind / And its invisible organ, / That feeling thing' (64). It is illuminating to juxtapose this kind of poem with Hill's 'Funeral Music' or 'September Song'. If there is a point in the way that 'Funeral Music' shifts the focus of attention away from the politics of the Wars of the Roses, and towards the experience of death on the battlefield, it is to force us to pay attention. 'Among carnage the most delicate souls / Tup in their marriage blood, gasping "Jesus"' (BH 49; KL 27). By the same token, the whole point of the intense concentration of 'September Song' on the youth and innocence of the deportee to the extermination camp is to force hardened and complacent minds to comprehend the

---

[1] Romana Huk, 'Poetry of the Committed Individual: Jon Silkin, Tony Harrison, Geoffrey Hill, and the Poets of Postwar Leeds', in *Contemporary British Poetry: Essays in Theory and Criticism*, ed. James Acheson and Romana Huk (Albany NY: State University of New York Press, 1996), pp. 175-220 (p. 175).

[2] Huk, pp. 176-77; *Poetry of the Committed Individual: A Stand Anthology of Poetry*, ed. Jon Silkin (London: Victor Gollanz, 1973).

[3] Jon Silkin, *Selected Poems* (New Edition, London and New York: Routledge, 1988), p. 17. Further references to this volume are given after quotations in the text.

enormity of this act, and the terrible suffering it entailed. But the poem invites us to concentrate and meditate upon the incommensurable meanings that may radiate from the same word as employed in different discourses: 'undesirable' and 'untouchable' as applied to a pre-pubertal child or a member of an inferior race; 'harmless' as the root meaning of 'innocent'. Hill's poetry enacts a conviction that the most effective way in which poetry can compel us to be ethically serious is to draw us into a meditation on the way in which words are adapted to a range of different discourses whose motives may be more or less mixed. So the compassion in Hill, unlike in Silkin, is self-consciously filtered through the medium of a sceptical and unsparingly reflective mind, one that we are aware is suspicious even of the most justified expression of compassion as in 'September Song': 'I have made / an elegy for myself' (BH 44; KL 19). Such compassion cannot therefore be fittingly described in terms of the exploitation of pathos, even of pathos in the worthy cause of opening readers' eyes: Hill would open eyes with more demanding instruments than that.

Attending to others is also to attend to their own words, and that includes the words of poets. This is a fundamental clause in the contract of humankind with its fellows. It is an obligation the reader must extend to the poet. It is something that Hill feels he can insist upon: the diacritics in *Speech! Speech!*, considered alongside its title, enact the poet's attempt to possess and take responsibility for his meanings, and his exhortation to readers and auditors to pay him this courtesy. Hill's work as a whole, though, demonstrates the difficulty of asking for such attention when the poet cannot in reality impeccably fulfil this ethical imperative, even though he must try to. In the spirit of this realisation, the very insistence of *Speech! Speech!* is self-parodic. The poet, however, also bears a like responsibility to his precursors, to their complex meanings, and to the address rendered to him or her by the moral and spiritual traditions of a culture.

This is one way in which to approach that well-known *tour-de-force* of ambiguity, 'Annunciations' (BH 40; KL 14-15). That poem embodies in its multiple meanings the suspect uses to which the same terms of high value may be harnessed in a world full of self-interest, lust and violence. Indeed, a mordant meditation on the idea of the just war is only one aspect of the harsh glitter of this multi-aspected poem: 'Our God scatters corruption' (BH 40; KL 15). Repelling it, or spreading it? A reader attuned to the English poetic tradition will rapidly become aware of the figure of Empson in the background to this poem, and behind him of the intellectual conceit of the age of Shakespeare and Donne, to which Empson was so clearly indebted. But unlike Cleanth Brooks, Hill does not develop ambiguity and contradiction towards the ideal of reconciliation and harmony symbolised by a well-wrought urn. Rather, he renders discursive discord painfully obtrusive. In this he is influenced by another mentor of his, Blake, learning from the sly ambiguity with which Blake may bring together in one poem the language of innocence and that of experience: 'So if all do their duty they need not fear harm.'[4] There are overlapping aims: to situate the poet's own craft both cannily and seriously in historical relation to the tradition as it has developed; to make that situatedness as significant as possible, by integrating it with a radical questioning of the moral and spiritual assumptions of the age; and to make the language of the poem do this work not as if the poet were a coercive force, situated outside his choice of words, but in such a way that it seems like the organic, if indeed highly wrought, expression of a thinking and speaking self. There are many signs of this situatedness of the poet within language, and they comprise quite direct signifiers of the movement of the mind on the spot: in 'September Song', 'I have made / an elegy for myself / it is true' (BH 44; KL 19), or, almost forty years later in 'Discourse for Stanley Rosen: 2', 'No, put it this way' (BH 499; WT 26). This last point introduces an element of self-reflexivity that has implications at the thematic level: the poet is ensnared in the ambiguities he unfolds, and indeed, 'I have made / an elegy for myself' offers a neat encapsulation of this double effect, being both a parenthetical interjection and a self-conscious perception of the corruption of pathos in lyric poetry.

If one turns to Prynne, one can lay out some similar points in a similar order. It is sometimes said that there is a congruence between Prynne's concerns about consumerism and the language of advertising and like concerns to be found in the cultural criticism of Raymond Williams, active in Cambridge in the period when the first poems in the Prynne canon were being composed.[5] Prynne offers a discovery of 'the intangible

---

[4] William Blake, 'The Chimney Sweeper', in *Songs of Innocence*, *The Poems of William Blake*, ed. W.H. Stevenson, text by David V. Erdman (London: Longman, 1971), p. 69.

[5] Consider the ambience sketched in Edd Mustill, 'Student Activism Then And Now: An Interview with Ian Patterson', in *The Great Unrest* <http://thegreatunrest.wordpress.com/tag/raymond-williams/> [accessed 26 March 2013] Patterson chats with Williams

consumer / networks' which he critically analyses in terms of 'the waste produced by mass conversion of *want* (sectional) into / *need* (social & then total)'.[6] In this poem, he also offers a potted pre-history of consumer society:

> Imperialism was just
> an old, very old name for that
> idea, that what you want, you by
> historic process or just readiness
> to travel, also "need". (13)

The repeated idea of want being converted into need appears to be that whereby a mere appetite (associated with a sense of lack by the ambiguity of 'want') is somehow given the spurious authority of being a determinate need. By implication, the corollary is that one may feel justified in pursuing need even at the expense of others (the sly identification of imperialism with 'readiness to travel').

This kind of slyness is a persistent feature of early Prynne. Its subsuming term is irony, a frequently irate irony about the way the dominant discourses describe things. Related to this irony is a more direct tone of indignant contempt:

> society is "predictably" as we know "in
> a state of ferment" – as if that could ever turn
> to *wine* or raise *bread,* from the sad shit it
> is, to that crispy crunchy loaf we shall all
> eat only in heaven. (15)

This is one of a number of places where Prynne unfolds the painful contrast between vacuous materialism and the vaunting overtones in which it conceals its vacuity: overtones in which he discerns the echo of sacred language. The result reveals the poverty and inappropriateness of the language of ethics in contemporary society: 'the weakness, now, / of names' (16). The 'names' are terms that fully and without reductionism embody right values: 'The purity is a question of / names. We are

---

and Prynne and recalls Prynne's drafting a letter to the Home Secretary arguing that the German student activist, Rudi Dutschke, should be allowed to enter Britain.

[6] J.H. Prynne, 'Die a Millionaire', in *Poems* (Tarset: Bloodaxe, 2005), pp. 13-16 (pp.14, 15). Further references to this volume are given after quotations in the text.

here to utter them. This is / a prayer' (16). These lines reveal that the persistence of sacred language in Prynne is not only a matter of things being misdescribed. It is also the sign of his belief in the need for a language of ethical idealism, and his acceptance that the language of transcendence still provides a natural expression of that need. Yet the point is rendered more subtle by his very obvious recognition of the fact that the idea of the transcendent, being still alive for all, is necessarily a site of contention and is notably vulnerable to perversion. The title of 'Die a Millionaire', which refers to the poem's theme of forward planning for self-enrichment, is followed by a sub-title: '(pronounced "diamonds in the air")' (13). The idea of mispronunciation symbolises the misuse of names, while the content of the phrase is about the notion of enrichment projected into the sky, and thus taking the place of the traditional heaven. Indeed, the diamonds are the stars, a recurring image in Prynne, and one that frequently symbolises those ideals that have traditionally been aligned with a belief in the transcendent.

The same group of ideas is explored in 'Sketch for a Financial Theory of the Self':

> The qualities as they continue are the silk
> under the hand; because the celestial
> progress, across the sky, is so hopeless & so
> to be hoped for. (19)

Silk – and riches – possess a numinous quality akin to that which has been associated with the 'celestial'. Prynne's 'prayer' (16) is for the reassertion of some genuinely ethical discourse, and for the vanquishing of the cruel and empty lies of consumerism.

This prayer finds correlatives in other poems, though not always in such ambitious public form as is to be found in 'Die a Millionaire' or 'Sketch for a Financial Theory of the Self': 'The Holy City' (43) makes evident its relationship to questions about ethical and spiritual idealism in its very title, yet it is no essay in Christian iconography. It places itself unabashedly in what appear to be the stray thoughts of the mind in motion. This is part of the central point. The Holy City is built on 'the good moment', as Browning called it. But Prynne explicitly denies that this moment possesses a literally sacred or religious character: 'There's no mystic moment involved'(43). The beauty of the moment is 'just / that we are', and in this case, apparently, derives from the experience of love. Prynne modestly concedes that 'you / could call it Ierusalem or feel it / as you walk, even quite jauntily, over the grass' (43). This kind of modest good moment is a recurring theme of Prynne's work, and, as in 'The Holy City', it is represented in terms of the mind's movement on the spot, or, as I've suggested elsewhere, by means of 'another variant on the stream of consciousness'.[7] The meditation that constitutes 'Thoughts on the Esterházy Court Uniform' (99-100), for instance, is represented as occurring while the speaker walks up and down a hill. But it is also a self-reflexive meditation on meditation itself as an expansive movement of discovery followed by a return with tentative conclusions. The poem begins 'I walk on up the hill in the warm / sun and we do not return' (99) and ends 'once more falling into the hour of my birth, going / down the hill and then in at the back door' (100). It is this process of meditation – mundane in its availability to all, though seriousness is enjoined – that gives rise to notions of the sacred which can still be authentic, and be entertained as such, in our era: 'we make / sacred what we cannot see without coming / back to where we were' (99). Such meditations are the source of knowledge and understanding. The opening lines of 'Die a Millionaire' are: 'The first essential is to take knowledge / back to the springs' (13). And despite the facetious way in which this poem parodies modern perversions of the idea of origins, Prynne does believe that there is a worthwhile way of understanding this dictum: 'From one point of view this is a desideratum about capturing the process of the formation of knowledge in the individual mind; from another, it enjoins an archaeology of the dominant social forms of knowledge.'[8] But ultimately these two aspects are closely related, which is why they are summed up in the same phrase. And when read alongside Prynne's practice, the phrase can be seen to give priority to what happens in the individual mind. It is the process of reflection traced in his poems which represents, so to speak, the cutting edge of knowledge-formation. This is also the process where those authentic values, the true 'names' (16), are discovered, leading to the building of 'Ierusalem' (43), the longing for which can be compared to our longing for 'the stars'.

A circular process of meditation, represented as spontaneous; the discovery of new knowledge and the recognition of true values

---

[7] Edward Larrissy, 'Poets of a Various Art: J.H. Prynne, Veronica Forrest-Thomson, Andrew Crozier', in *Contemporary British Poetry*, ed. Acheson and Huk, pp. 63-79 (p. 66).

[8] Larrissy, p. 66.

in the process; and the identification of true values with ideas of the transcendent: brought together in one project these are distinctly reminiscent of the Romanticism of Wordsworth and Coleridge in *The Prelude* and the 'Conversation Poems'. Prynne's is a late modernist project, conscious of indeterminacy and antithetical to the expressive ego of Romantic lyric poetry. Yet it implicitly suggests that, like the Romantics, we are constrained to find and recognise the higher values in individual experience or not at all, even as it shows that individual experience cannot be innocent of social determination.

My argument has pushed further with Prynne than with Hill: it has taken the step of identifying a postmodernist Romanticism in Prynne's late modernist thought. Yet a parallel argument could be mounted in relation to Hill. At an earlier point I referred to the 'corruption of pathos' in lyric poetry as one of his themes. Yet pathos there undoubtedly is in Hill's own language. David Trotter identifies in him a concern with 'the pathos of origins', and goes so far as to refer to the array of powerful poetic effects to be found in some of the poems as 'the pathos-machine'.[9] He particularly has in mind some of the sections of 'Funeral Music' as well as a work which has been often accused in the same terms, namely 'An Apology for the Revival of Christian Architecture in England'.[10] The case of 'Funeral Music' is rewarding to consider, since it brings together in one work not only the moments of pathos, but also characteristically dense networks of ambiguous words and a typical concern with the extremity of suffering brought about by human corruption: a corruption reflected in the language of the poem alongside the cries of those who endure the suffering. Trotter concedes that, for Hill, the pathos of the 'fragments of subjectivity must not be allowed an easy victory over the process which has quelled them,' presumably the brutality of the war and of the culture that nurtures it.[11] And indeed, Hill's descriptions are pitiless. Yet according to Trotter, 'the conclusion of the sequence announces that pathos has, after all, triumphed.'[12] He refers to the lines where the speaker contemplates the

---

[9] David Trotter, *The Making of the Reader: Language and Subjectivity in Modern American, English and Irish Poetry* (Basingstoke: Macmillan, 1984), pp. 209, 211, 216.

[10] Trotter, pp. 212, 216.

[11] Trotter, p. 211.

[12] Trotter, p. 212.

comfortlessness of those who depart this world, 'Crying to the end "I have not finished"' (BH 54; KL 32). Hill has done himself no favours in his own commentary on this poem, where he states that he had intended an 'ornate and heartless music punctuated by mutterings, blasphemies and cries for help' (KL 67). But in fact 'Funeral Music' bears only a partial resemblance to the dark expressionist chaos evoked by this analogy. In reality, it consists of a series of meditations, separate, dense indeed, but internally ordered and tonally congruent with each other. They revolve around the question of how far faith can provide a plausible consolation to those who suffer *in extremis,* and around the related topic of the painful discord between the serene image of the empyrean and the horrifying facts of human warfare. An objection such as Trotter's requires the poem to resemble Hill's description very closely. If all the features of the poem are kinetic gestures, then the final gesture must be one of unalloyed pathos. Yet it can also be read as a rational conclusion: section 2 of the poem questions the religious justification of suffering, suggesting that 'we are dying / To satisfy fat Caritas' (BH 48; KL 26); section 4 contrasts the powerful hold of the soul to the potentially barren rule of Intellect (BH 50; KL 28); and section 5 asserts that religious imagery may be only a projection of our desires and self-pity (BH 51; KL 29). Hill concludes by questioning what comfort we may glean from a universe that seems equally cold whether one believes it possesses a meaning or not. The question in fact takes its place in a series of meditations on the way faith both exerts a powerful draw and seems to do so in chillingly impersonal terms.

Nor is it a straightforward matter to determine what the element of pathos might relate to. The poem has already suggested that the soul possesses a visceral hold akin to the physical, a power to which Intellect cannot aspire. In this it is at one with the view embodied in Hill's earlier poem 'Genesis'. Bizarrely, given the historical references it invokes, 'Funeral Music' also, like 'Annunciations', exploits an ambiguity as to whether the deaths it surveys are literal or sexual: 'blindly we lie down, blindly / Among carnage the most delicate souls / Tup in their marriage-blood, gasping "Jesus"' (BH 49; KL 27). This lying down could be for sexual congress, since the literal meaning of 'tup' is at least as salient as any figurative one – and indeed, what is the figurative meaning here? The 'marriage-blood' (a locution not found in the *OED*) could well be the hymeneal blood, and the cry of 'Jesus' a vulgar expletive. If this is a moment of pathos, it is one where pathos is distanced because it arises out of a world in which our feelings inhere in a complex, unstable and violent amalgam of flesh and spirit to which we respond 'blindly'. One is conscious of Hopkins in the physicality of the evocation of Nature as embodying spirit, and of Blake in the thoroughness with which Hill includes the most violent aspects of life in the sense of what can be deemed spiritual. The terms of this amalgam, as the poetry itself demonstrates, are not clearly-enough defined to be summed up in a *cri-de-coeur*. The last lines of the poem can therefore be read as implying that, whatever it is that the quoted 'us – or anyone' have 'not finished' (BH 54; KL 32) (and it could even suggest a sexual act), they are not in a position to understand what is at stake in not finishing. This realisation qualifies the sense of pathos, since the sense of tragic loss and terror has no clear referent. In this respect, since we are dealing with the aesthetics of what Lyotard would call the 'unpresentable', the poem provokes the question whether or not we should see it in terms of a Modernist or a postmodern sublime, a question that has been asked by Andrew Michael Roberts in respect of 'The Songbook of Sebastian Arrurruz'.[13] He concludes that 'the case seems strong for seeing it as a working-through of Modernism and as an instance of the postmodern sublime in its playfulness, self-consciousness, double-coding and strategic anachronism'.[14] A similar case can surely be made for 'Funeral Music': the craft of the poem is steeped in a sense of the English poetic tradition, but this is heavily inflected by the way in which it has been understood and transmitted by Eliot and Empson. As with a number of Hill's poems, one might occasionally be tempted to see it as a parody of Empson in particular. In this light the poem looks like an imitation of a very particular kind of modernism, namely the metaphysical strain of Anglo-American poetry inaugurated by Eliot. Yet both Eliot's sense of possible salvation and Empson's sense of the rational value of scrutinising ambiguity are undercut by the profound sense of ignorance which informs the poem as meditation ('blindly we lie down' (BH 49; KL 27)), as well as by the rich, troubling and unreconcilable confusion which characterises its picture of experience. At the same time, the Romantic ancestry of the postmodern sublime is

---

[13] Andrew Michael Roberts, 'Romantic Irony and the Postmodern Sublime: Geoffrey Hill and "Sebastian Arrurruz"', in *Romanticism and Postmodernism*, ed. Edward Larrissy (Cambridge: Cambridge University Press, 1999), pp. 141-56.

[14] Roberts, p. 154. The 'working-through' is a reference to Lyotard's application of a Freudian concept to the workings of avant-garde art.

very evident in Hill, for moments of emphatically plangent lyric affect are particularly associated with a sense of the unpresentable.

Both Prynne and Hill present their speakers in terms which are identifiably related to the aesthetic of Romantic lyric poetry: the tendency is to present them reflecting and feeling in the living stream of experience. Thought and feeling must seem unique and particular both to the speaker and the moment. Yet in accordance with the Romantic legacy, chance thoughts must be so organised as to gesture at wider significance: sometimes at the widest possible significance, the very core of meaning. These points can be illustrated by reference to two poems which broach the possibility of seeing into the heart of things, in a glimpse of the earthly paradise: Prynne's 'The Holy City' (43), which we have already glanced at, and Hill's book-length sequence, *The Orchards of Syon*.

In the former poem, 'the mind's movement on the spot' (as I phrased it above) comprises an experience so humble, framed in such simple terms, that it can only be understood as a very ordinary slice of life:

> Come up to it, as you stand there
> that the wind is quite warm on the sides
> of the face.

The speaker and another are walking 'over the rough grass', and continue to do so, as we are informed by the last line of the poem. They are going to 'a loved side of the temple', so a place with sacred associations, but it is the 'side' that is important, not the edifice, and this importance is that it is 'a place for repose, / a concrete path.' Nothing vaunting there, then, and 'There's no mystic moment: just that we are.' The capacity of certain mundane moments to shadow the sacred while being a viable replacement for it is repeated in the final lines: 'you / could call it Ierusalem or feel it / as you walk, even quite jauntily, over the grass' (43). Thematically, then, the poem implies that our ordinary lives can reach privileged moments (in this case informed, we are told, by love) that are all of paradise we can know. Formally, the poem flits from moment to moment, a process in which even a certain awkward simplicity plays its cunning part:

> and love is
> when, how &
> because we
> do

The result is a minimalist lyricism that strongly recalls the vaunting ambition of the high Romantic mode, but with the definite aim of qualifying it almost, but not quite, to the extent of negation.

Hill's poem, in analogous fashion, is 'about hanging in there, about my self, / my mind as it is' (BH 408; OS 58). And as with Prynne, the mind's perceptions are shown responding to the changing phenomenal world:

> Abruptly the sun's out, striking a new
> cleave; skidding the ridge-grass, down steep hangers;
> buddleia in dark bloom; a wayward covey
> of cabbage-whites this instant
> (BH 413; OS 65)

Within this ever-changing flow of experience one may ask 'where is my fixed home? / City of God unlikely.' (BH 380; OS 30). Yet the variety and depth of reference to Christian thinkers and structures of feeling imply that 'City of God' is, at least sporadically, to be desired. The moments when the speaker is seized by a perception of beauty are summarised as 'The Orchards of Syon' or in the Hopkinsian borrowing 'Goldengrove.'

> In Goldengrove the full
> trees trumpet their colours: earth-casualties
> majestic
> (BH 417; OS 71)

'Earth-casualties': the golden beauty of the autumn is also a reminder of death. And indeed, 'Syon's Orchards' are 'uncannily of the earth' (BH 463; OS 13). Uncannily, because their earthly appearance, as with the temple experience in Prynne's 'The Holy City', is shadowed by a spiritual one. In Hill, that spiritual appearance is a rich compound of memories and echoes derived from the Christian tradition. But no traditional linear path to salvation beckons to him or to his readers. The accent remains on a subjectivity granted sporadic respite from tormenting regret and guilt. Yet even that respite is a subjective construct:

> Here are the Orchards of Syon, neither wisdom
> nor illusion of wisdom, not
> compensation, not recompense: the Orchards
> of Syon whatever harvests we bring them.
> (BH 418; OS 72)

This perception is like a God-given grace, not to be purchased, not even to be earned, and only present to a particular consciousness in a particular way.

Prynne and Hill are both profoundly convinced that we are formed in traditions and their discourses, but write from the spirit of our times, which still equates authenticity with the representation of subjective experience. In accordance with these convictions, both poets self-consciously present their personae as speaking in terms that exceed what they can know and possess, and foreground this fact in their poetic language. Both poets find in the language of the sacred the most compelling means of representing a longing for incorruptible value, and both incorporate a sense of the predictable corruption of that language into the very fabric of their use of it. Both can be seen as late modernist in the seriousness of their ethical and spiritual quests, but as postmodernist in the depth of their sense of the limits of understanding, and in the way this sense dominates the unfolding of meaning in their poems.

CHAPTER FIVE

# Lyric, Awkwardness and Music in Geoffrey Hill and Denise Riley

## Andrew Michael Roberts

In the second section of Geoffrey Hill's poem 'A Précis or Memorandum of Civil Power' we find the sentence 'How awkward this must sound' (BH 582; TCP 28). We don't expect the lyric to be awkward, still less awkwardly to tell us that it is so. What does it mean to write an awkward lyric, or to write awkwardly in the lyric? Awkwardness can serve as a form of resistance, to expectations (social or aesthetic), to accepted norms and habits. It can reflect uncertainty or self-consciousness. It hovers between the willed and the imposed: we may accuse someone of being 'deliberately awkward', whereas social or physical awkwardness is seen as an affliction. Since writing poetry is always a deliberate act, it might seem that awkward poetry is either bad poetry (if the awkwardness is not willed) or aggressive poetry (if it is). But the act of writing, even when most skilfully controlled, involves allowing effects to become manifest, voices to be heard, language and intertextuality to exert their energies. So writing, like awkwardness, lies somewhere between the willed and the non-willed; Hill has described verse as 'both absolute will and contingency'.[1]

A sense of Hill as an 'awkward' poet may seem to echo the familiar trope of his alleged 'difficulty'. However, where 'difficulty' suggests a challenge to the reader, 'awkward' suggests also self-challenge. The element of the awkward in Hill's work co-exists with remarkable technical accomplishment, and to that extent is clearly a willed, even a tactical awkwardness. Nevertheless, it proceeds from strains of profound self-questioning, doubt and resistance. Awkwardness figures as a theme in his critical writing too. His essay on 'Eros in F.H. Bradley and T. S. Eliot' begins 'Poetry is one of the multifarious forms of self-consciousness. It is a consciousness of self, and consciousness to, and in, itself; and an embarrassment to itself and others'. The next sentence

---

[1] Preface to Henrik Ibsen, *Brand: A Version for the Stage by Geoffrey Hill* (1978; London: Penguin 1996), p. x.

registers the interaction of such awkwardness with technique: 'When a radical embarrassment is overcome by the fascination of technique we have various forms of the baroque' (CCW 548). Over the course of his writing life, the technique of awkwardness evolves in a complex play with rhetorical power, lyrical beauty and technical experiment. Here I will concentrate on poems from a single mid-to-late period volume, *A Treatise of Civil Power* (2007). I want to consider the awkward in Hill's poetry alongside the work of another poet, Denise Riley, in her collection *Mop Mop Georgette* (1993). This is in part because I feel that parallels between Hill's poetry and that of his contemporaries have been insufficiently noticed. More specifically, awkwardness is one of the techniques deployed by a number of late modernist poets to explore their complex relationship to the lyric tradition, involving questioning, and often resistance to, musicality, voice and subjectivity. Hill's work is rarely discussed in relation to what is (awkwardly) termed the 'British Poetry Revival' and its successor 'Linguistically Innovative Poetry', because many of his intellectual affiliations seem so different.[2] While poets such as Tom Raworth, J.H. Prynne, Veronica Forrest-Thomson, Allen Fisher, Geraldine Monk or Andrew Crozier (to mention only a few names) are likely to draw on post-structuralism, 60s political radicalism and American movements such as Beat, Objectivism and Black Mountain, Hill's key influences and points of reference, though very diverse, centre on the English and European poetic traditions and theological or mystical thinkers (although some American influences were found from the start, and new ones emerged in the later work).[3] Nevertheless, Hill does share with many of these poets a complex, highly-engaged relationship to both Romantic and Modernist predecessors, and a critical or interrogative engagement with the lyric as form and tradition. They also have in common a persistent and

---

[2] For the history of the poetry which has come to be known by these two terms, see Robert Sheppard, *The Poetry of Saying: British Poetry and Its Discontents, 1950-2000* (Liverpool: Liverpool University Press, 2005).

[3] Affinities have sometimes been suggested (or resisted) between Hill and Roy Fisher (including by the poets themselves): see James Keery, '"Menacing Works in My Isolation": Early Pieces', in *The Thing about Roy Fisher: Critical Studies*, ed. John Kerrigan and Peter Robinson (Liverpool: Liverpool University Press, 2000), pp. 47-85 (pp. 63-4). I have previously considered Hill in relation to Tom Raworth, although with a considerable degree of contrast ('Error and Mistakes in Poetry: Geoffrey Hill and Tom Raworth', *English*, 56 (2007), pp. 339-61). Hill has also responded to American models but rather different ones; Eberhardt and Tate in his early work; more recently O'Hara and Berryman.

insistent reflexivity, reflecting an understanding of language informed by Heidegger, Wittgenstein and other philosophers of the 'linguistic turn'.[4] Rather than attempt further generalisations, I want in this essay to consider affinities between Hill and Riley, in terms of awkwardness as both theme and technique. I will discuss their critical engagement with lyric traditions, in particular the roles of 'self' and 'voice', and their linking of awkwardness to temporality.[5]

To set the stage, some awkward moments in Hill's *A Treatise of Civil Power*: misremembering ('something about dancing / or not dancing. No, *weeping*', BH 559; TCP 1); uncertainty awkwardly phrased ('This not quite knowing what the earth requires', BH 560; TCP 2); the tactless personal question ('people keep asking why your lyric mojo / atrophied at around ninety', BH 561; TCP 3); the ponderous pun ('H. Mirren's super', BH 562; TCP 5), later acknowledged as such ('insuperable jokes'; BH 599; TCP 49); the diffident beginning ('Could so have managed not to be flinging / down this challenge', BH 581; TCP 27); the imagined gauche gesture ('I did not blunder into your room with flowers', BH 588; TCP 35); the desperate moment ('Somehow, with a near-helpless cry, I shall / wrench out of this'; BH 601; TCP 51); the impulse to embarrassing entropy ('Urge to unmake / all wrought finality, become a babbler / in the crowd's face', BH 610; TCP 51).[6] And some awkward moments in Riley's poetry: a tricky conversation ('A confession or two before dusk / flings open the fridge with loud relief / Listen honey I ....', from 'Song'); the poet's sense of self-alienating

---

[4] See Jerome Rothenberg and Pierre Joris, Introduction to *Poems for the Millennium: the University of California Book of Modern and Postmodern Poetry, Vol. 2: From Postwar to Millennium* (Berkeley, Los Angeles, CA and London: University of California Press, 1998): 'a point of reference, often, in poet-directed discussions of poetics – was the sense that the poet, like all humans, is a vehicle through which or by which language speaks. Outside the immediate poetry nexus, the point revealed itself in Heidegger's insistence ... that it is language that thinks, rather than man, in Wittgenstein's related meditations ("the limits of my language mean the limits of my world"), or in Lacan's formulation that "the unconscious is structured like a language".' (p. 10).

[5] Anthony Rowland has developed the idea of a 'poetics of awkwardness', but almost entirely in relation to the treatment of the holocaust in poetry. See Anthony Rowland, *Holocaust Poetry: Awkward Poetics in the Work of Sylvia Plath, Geoffrey Hill, Tony Harrison and Ted Hughes* (Edinburgh: Edinburgh University Press, 2005).

[6] At a conference on his work at Keble College, Oxford in July 2008, Hill explained that the line 'H. Mirren's super' in TCP (amended to 'Mirren is super' in BH), is a punning allusion to Helen Mirren's role in the British TV drama *Prime Suspect* (1991–2006) as a Detective Chief Inspector, and later a Detective Superintendent ('Super').

routine ('No this isn't me, it's just my motor running', from 'When It's Time to Go'); nervous tension ('The day is nervous buff – the shakiness, is it inside the day or me?', from 'Rayon'); the nag of memory ('Well all right, things happened it would / be pleasanter not to recall' and the comedy of embarrassment ('as a deeply embarrassed dog / looks studiedly at a sofa for just anything to do instead') (both from 'Well All Right'); the pressures of self-presentation as a woman poet ('The writer / properly should be the last person that the reader of listener need think about / yet the poet with her signature stands up trembling, grateful, mortally embarrassed / and especially embarrassing to herself, patting her hair and twittering', from 'Dark Looks').[7] In each of these examples, psychological or social forms of awkwardness are mimetically conveyed via small but noticeable awkwardness of language, syntax or lineation. Yet the word 'awkward' itself can appear in a purely lyrical context and as part of a regular iambic pentameter, as in Hill's poignant line from *The Triumph of Love*: 'My dear and awkward love, we may not need' (BH 255; TL 30). Critics have noticed the incidence or prominence of related terms or concepts in Hill's work; in the present volume Steven Matthews lists the frequent occurrence of the word 'strange' in the poetry, commenting that 'Hill has added "strange" and its variants to the modern poets' lists of shorthand wards against incoherence'; Stephen James has discussed the role of 'eccentricity' in Hill's work, commenting that as '[a]n astronomical term in origin, "eccentricity" offers a suggestive analogy for Hill's peculiarities of voice and stance, including his strangely mannered prophetic, or mock-prophetic, gestures'.[8]

Hill's sentence 'How awkward this must sound' (BH 582; TCP 28) specifically conjoins awkwardness with *sound*, evoking the aural dimension of poetry, often associated in lyric with the 'musical'. In this association the lyric's historical links to actual music combine with the metaphorical sense of 'the music of poetry'. The term 'lyric', as David Lindley observes, is used both generically (meaning a form of poetry) and modally (meaning a quality within poetry, but also within film, music,

---

[7] Denise Riley, *Mop Mop Georgette: New and Selected Poems 1986-1993* (London: Reality Street, 1993), pp. 38, 39, 41, 46, 54. Further references are given in the text as MMG.
[8] Stephen James, *Shades of Authority: The Poetry of Lowell, Hill and Heaney* (Liverpool: Liverpool University Press, 2007), p. 66.

even art).⁹ The lyric has come to be seen as the dominant poetic form, a rise variously located in the post-Romantic era, in Modernism, and in the mid twentieth century.¹⁰ However, definitions of lyric are various. M.H. Abrams gives a relatively neutral definition while stressing the key idea of consciousness rendered into a text which is understood as speech: 'any fairly short poem, consisting of the utterance by a single speaker, who expresses a state of mind or a process of perception, thought, and feeling'.¹¹ Helen Vendler adds more specific formal demands: 'extreme compression, the appearance of spontaneity, an intense and expressive structure which enacts the experience represented, an abstraction from the heterogeneity of life'.¹² Hill has been notoriously averse to the concept of 'self-expression' in poetry, commenting early in his career that 'although a poet must put a great deal of himself into his work I have never been able to agree with those who say that poetry is "self-expression"'; 'my true feelings coincide with the American poet Allen Tate's beleaguered minority opinion that "self-expression" is a word that "should be tarred and feathered"'.¹³ Similarly, the idea of poetry as 'expressive' is widely dismissed by advocates of the 'alternative' tradition in poetry. Linda Kinnahan notes 'the thematically informed rejection of the lyric speaker commonly cited as a major distinguishing point between "expressive" and "experimental" poetries'.¹⁴ Whether this constitutes a rejection of the lyric as such depends on one's definition

---

⁹ David Lindley, *Lyric* (London and New York, NY: Methuen, 1985), p. 1.

¹⁰ John Stuart Mill was already claiming it as 'the poetry most natural to a really poetic temperament' in 1833; 'The Two Kinds of Poetry', quoted in Scott Brewster, *Lyric* (London and New York, NY: Routledge, 2009), p. 4. Graham Hough identifies the emergence of modernist lyric as the 'archetype of poetry' with the post-Romantic retreat of drama into prose and the appropriation of epic function by the novel, so that '[p]oetry finds its fullest expression … in the exquisitely restricted form'. *Modernism: A Guide to European Literature 1890-1930*, ed. Malcolm Bradbury & James MacFarlane (Harmondsworth: Penguin 1976, 1991), p. 313. Scott Brewster describes it as 'the dominant mode of modern poetry' (Brewster, 4).

¹¹ Quoted Brewster, p. 2.

¹² Quoted Brewster, p. 5.

¹³ 'Geoffrey Hill writes:' (about *Tenebrae*), *Poetry Book Society Bulletin*, 98 (1978), unpaginated; *A Sermon Delivered at Great St Mary's University Church, Cambridge, 8 May 1983*, 1.

¹⁴ Linda Kinnahan, 'Experimental Poetics and the Lyric in British Women Poets: Geraldine Monk, Wendy Mulford and Denise Riley', *Contemporary Literature*, 37.4 (Winter 1996), 620-670 (p. 622).

of 'lyric'. At all events, the alleged dominance of the lyric is sharply challenged by the advocates of experimental and postmodern poetry. Marjorie Perloff, in 'Postmodernism and the Impasse of the Lyric', champions a collage-based poetics derived from Pound's *Cantos* (via William Carlos Williams and Charles Olson), in which 'such normal syntactical relations as subordination or implication are suppressed in favor of relations of similarity, equivalence, or identity'. Such poetry can incorporate diverse forms of discourse (prose, letters, documents, and so on) and 'the lyric voice gives way to multiple voices or voice fragments'.[15] The relations of form and lyric 'voice' have a specific inflection in the work of certain innovative British women poets. Linda Kinnahan observes that Riley and other 'experimental' women poets who are 'interested in questions of language and radical form have been faced with the task of rethinking the lyric self while retaining the potential for subject constitution that the speaking "I" opens'.[16] This rethinking Kinnahan sees as a response to 'a general milieu of "I aversion" ... [in] the alternative scene in Britain'.[17] The rationale for such an aversion is stated in Andrew Crozier's classic critique of the Movement and of a mainstream poetry (Hughes, Heaney) seen as its successor:

> In the poetic tradition now dominant the authoritative self, discoursing in a world of banal, empirically derived objects and relations, depends on its employment of metaphor and simile for poetic vitality ... Our sense that the details bind together into a more complex meaning derives not from the figures but from the attenuated presence of autobiographical anecdote.[18]

This is akin to Hill's dismissal of some poems as resembling 'home movies'.[19] Crozier's suspicion of the autobiographical is presumably not an objection to autobiographical material in itself, but to its use as a

---

[15] Marjorie Perloff, *The Dance of the Intellect: Studies in the Poetry of the Pound Tradition* (Evanston, IL: Northwestern University Press, 1996), p. 183.

[16] Kinnahan, p. 626.

[17] Kinnahan, p. 626, quoting chris cheek.

[18] Andrew Crozier, 'Thrills and Frills: Poetry as Figures of Empirical Lyricism', in *Society and Literature 1945-1970* (London: Methuen and Co, 1983, pp. 199-233 (pp. 229-30).

[19] 'I think a lot of the poems one sees in magazines could very well be described as stills from home movies' (Interview with Hermione Lee, *Book Four*, 2 Oct 1985, Channel Four television).

substitute for more strenuous forms of poetic thought. The 'I aversion' of 'innovative' poetry was in part a reaction to the commodification and trivialisation of identity and personality which has been a prominent feature of consumer culture over the last fifty years, and to which Hill responded when he sought to distinguish between 'creative expression of personality' and 'commodity exploitation of personality' (here 'expression' is allowed a positive meaning).[20]

Though pervasive in contemporary 'mainstream' poetry, the lyric is, for that very reason, liable to be a source of embarrassment; even a mainstream critical work aimed at a popular audience, such as Fiona Sampson's *Beyond the Lyric*, claims to go 'beyond' it, and includes chapters on the 'expanded' and 'exploded' lyric (the latter concerned with late modernist work).[21] Critical negotiation with 'the lyric tradition' (of some degree of sophistication) is bound to be a negotiation with competing and historically developing conceptions of the form. As Lindley writes, 'it is possible, with a historically sharpened generic sense, to see how competing schools ... attempt to pursue some, but not all, of the historical possibilities that lyric has entertained'.[22] He cites the use of stanza form, the expressive 'speaking self' and the musical dimension as examples. The two main axes of definition of the lyric are, first, its association with music, musicality and sound more generally and, second, its association with the private, the self, expressiveness, 'voice', and 'the poet talking to himself – or to nobody' (Eliot's 'first voice of poetry').[23] The interactions between these two axes (each of which is internally complex and divided) are partly a matter of historical contingency, and partly of the individual poet's disposition. Where does Hill's work stand in relation to a division between a 'mainstream' lyric of voice and expression and a poetics of collage or postmodern dispersal? As regards syntax, his poetry has always tended to apposition and parataxis; syntactical structure remains crucial, but it is rarely 'normal'. Multiple voices and diverse embedded discourses have

---

[20] Interview with John Haffenden, Quarto, 15 (March 1981), pp. 19-22, reprinted in *Viewpoints: Poets in Conversation with John Haffenden* (London: Faber and Faber, 1981), 76-99 (p. 87).

[21] Fiona Sampson, *Beyond the Lyric: A Map of Contemporary British Poetry* (London: Chatto & Windus, 2012).

[22] Lindley, p. 14.

[23] T.S. Eliot, 'The Three Voices of Poetry' (1953), in *On Poetry and Poets* (London: Faber and Faber, 1957), pp. 89-102.

become progressively more important, from the early double voices of *Mercian Hymns* and 'The Songbook', but especially since *Speech! Speech!*. Nevertheless, a strong sense of distinctive voice and poetic or intellectual personality is pervasive. Colin Burrow notes that the later work 'moves away from Eliot' and 'draws cautiously closer to the political intensity and associative methods of Pound's *Cantos*', but crucially complicates this model by noting both Hill's political divergences from Pound and Hill's response to seventeenth-century influences which mean that his development cannot be articulated simply as a dialogue with alternative forms of modernism.[24]

'Spontaneity', as description of the process of writing poetry, was another object of Hill's scorn: 'that facile self-expression which debases much modern acceptance of spontaneity' (CCW 23); 'a mountebank spontaneity of self-expression' (CCW 199); 'the domain of the supposedly "spontaneous" Romantic lyric' (CCW 420). Hill argues that Wordsworth's 'spontaneous overflow of powerful feelings' has been 'popularly misconstrued' (CCW 114). It is worth noting that Hill's objections to 'expressive' and 'spontaneous', like those of the 'innovative' poetry tradition, are based on the terms' strong connection to ideas of self and self-expression. 'Expression', literally 'the action of pressing or squeezing out' (OED), implies material exuded from the self (rather than collated or constructed from language), while 'spontaneous' ('arising or proceeding entirely from natural impulse, without any external stimulus or constraint; voluntary and of one's own accord', OED) similarly implies an internal origin, as reflected in Hill's linking of the term to that of 'self-expression'. However, Hill's objection to 'spontaneity' is related to OED sense (c): 'Of utterances, etc.: Coming freely and without premeditation or effort': the idea that composing poetry is a matter of easy inspiration rather than hard labour. For example, he argues, in reaction to the poet's own use of the term, against any idea of Whitman as a 'spontaneous' poet by using the evidence of his laborious composition methods (CCW 507). It might be, then, that Hill would not have objected to 'the *appearance* of spontaneity', in Vendler's cautious phrase, provided the reader did not take the finished appearance for evidence of the process of composition; although he does write, in *Speech! Speech!*, almost as if in response to Vendler, 'I disclaim spontaneity / the appearance of which is power' (BH 334; SS46). Vendler's is a curious as well as a cautious phrase, however,

---

[24] Colin Burrow, 'Rancorous Old Sod', review of *Broken Hierarchies*, *London Review of Books*, 36.4 (20 February 2014), 11-13 (p. 11).

when one reflects upon it. Does it imply that the reader is fooled by a deceptive appearance of spontaneity in what is in fact highly crafted? Or rather that both crafting and effect are evident, so that what the lyric really presents is the *appearance* of an appearance of spontaneity which fools no-one? Hill's later work, in particular, manages somehow to seem both evidently long-considered and yet also, in one sense, 'spontaneous' – it has the feeling of a mind in thought, leaping and turning from idea to association to image to sense-impression. Awkwardness – as when he interrupts himself, stops to explain, changes gear (sometimes omitting to engage the clutch) – is part of this feeling of spontaneity, and is in contrast to much of the early work, which overtly presents itself to the reader as highly-wrought and polished. It may be the association of the lyric form with ideas of spontaneity and the centrality of the quasi-autobiographical poet that have led him to allude to the lyric with some irony:

> Incantation or incontinence—the lyric cry?
> Believe me, he's not
> told you the half of it *(All who are able may stand.)*
> (BH 284, TL 79)

Another factor, though, would seem to be an irritation at readers or reviewers who complain of insufficient lyrical intensity:

> Lyric cry lyric cry lyric cry, I'll
> give them lyric cry!
> (BH 380; OS 30)

In (dis)obedient response, Simon Jenner complains that *The Orchards of Syon* (in which these lines appear) is an 'iron lung of a book' made problematic by Hill's 'cussed refusal to give us lyric cry'.[25] This comment rather ignores the volume's moments of descriptive beauty, as in section XIV:

> The full moon, now, rears with unhastening speed,
> sketches the black ridge-end, slides thin lustre
> downward aslant its gouged and watered scree.
> (BH 364; OS 14).

---

[25] Simon Jenner, 'I'll Give Them Lyric Cry', review of OS, *Poetry Express*, 19 (Spring 2004), pp. 4-5 (p. 5).

A further reason for Hill's caution in relation to the lyric (and perhaps a reason for the decisive move to book-length sequences in his later work) may lie in his wish to reclaim a public role for poetry. Graham Hough sees the post-Romantic dominance of the lyric as a retreat from such a role; from poetry which sought to express 'a shared public experience, the expression of a culture, a nation, or a ruling class'.[26] Here lies another ground for awkwardness: Hill's ethical convictions (for example the importance which he gives to memorialising the dead) demand a role for poetry as expressing 'shared public experience', but he is certainly aware of the risks and vicissitudes of such an ambition, not least that of being accused of expressing the perspective of a 'ruling class'.[27] Also at issue here is the extent to which Hill's critical perspicacity, and the self-consciousness about his own poetic practice which it informs, generate a duality inimical to 'innocent' lyricism. This is very evident in Hill's comment that 'Lyric utterance stands as witness to a faith in "sheer perfection" even while it is standing scrutiny as a piece of evidence in the natural history of such belief' (CCW 258). While a drive to 'sheer perfection' is powerfully present in Hill's earlier work, and still in evidence in the formal structures of *The Daybooks*, his development as a poet has been towards the formal integration of critical self-scrutiny. Presumably this reflects, and informs, his sense that lyricism is always at potential risk of impeding critical thought or fidelity to experience; a sense conveyed in some of his comments on the work of other poets: 'in Belloc's work the lyric metre and diction rebuff the rhythms and inflexions of the otherwise independent mind' (CCW 439); [Ivor Gurney's] discovery that the lyric voice does not necessarily square with the facts of experience' (CCW 441).

Hill's relation to the lyric might be described as allegiance to the first of the axes which I have identified (that of musicality), and resistance to the second (that of expressiveness and 'voice'), though that resistance has modified its terms since around 2000. In these respects he is in accord with LANGUAGE poetry, which, as Paul Hoover comments, 'see[s] lyricism in poetry, not as a means of expressing emotion but rather in its

---

[26] Bradbury and MacFarlane, p. 312.

[27] This was, in effect, one of the accusations in Tom Paulin's 1985 review in *The London Review of Books* ('a shabby and reactionary hegemony'). Tom Paulin, 'The Case for Geoffrey Hill', review of Robinson, *London Review of Books*, 4 April 1985, pp. 13-14 (p. 14).

original context as the musical use of words'.²⁸ Hill's poetry is far from consistently lyrical in what Lindley terms the modal sense but it is, I think, consistently musical (after all, music itself is not always lyrical in the modal sense). Hill has a strong musical ear, even if he uses it in ways some readers may sometimes dislike. Those hoping for *Kindertotenlieder* or even Elgar may encounter something more akin to Webern, Thelonious Monk or even (locally) Rap.²⁹ His tactical awkwardness is as musical in its way as his tactical smoothness. As widely noted (including by Hill himself), his resistance to the representation of the self (and to biographical allusions) in poetry has been modified in the last fifteen years, from something like avoidance to a process of negotiation (always implicit in his use of masks and personae in early works such as *Mercian Hymns* and 'The Songbook of Sebastian Arrurruz'). Irony has long been an aspect of this negotiation (as in the Eliotic or Laforguian ironies of the 'The Songbook'), but an aspect of the recent greater hospitality to the figuring of the self in Hill's poetry is a revealing irony of awkwardness, rather than a distancing irony of control.³⁰ This change has brought his use of the lyric closer to that of Riley, also definable in terms of complex and ambivalent relations to musicality and the self.

Riley's awkwardness in relation to the lyric is likely to be seen in the context of a shared suspicion, amongst 'innovative' poets, of 'voice' and 'self-expression' as aesthetically or politically regressive effects. However, she has sometimes been criticised for alleged backsliding in this respect; far more than some other poets of that grouping or designation, she is interested in a direct, if highly ironized, engagement with ideas of lyric self.³¹

The lyric, as literary form and as idea, is an explicit topic of discussion in Riley's poetry, and in critical discussion of it (by herself and others). Riley's worrying at the ethics of art's appropriative

---

²⁸ Paul Hoover, Introduction to *Postmodern American Poetry*, p. xxxv.

²⁹ I have in mind not only Hill's allusions to Rap in *Speech! Speech!*, but also his deployment of insistent and hard voice rhythms.

³⁰ 'I no longer think that the answer to this [naïve trust in the unchallengeable authority of the authentic self] lies in the suppressing of self: it requires a degree of self-knowledge and self-criticism.' Geoffrey Hill, 'The Art of Poetry LXXX' (Interview with Carl Phillips), *Paris Review*, 154 (2000), 272-299 (p. 283).

³¹ An analytical (rather than negative) argument that Riley's poetry is in some ways in conflict with her theory (concerning 'impersonality' in poetry) is presented in Andrea Brady, 'Echo, Irony, and Repetition in the Writings of Denise Riley', *Contemporary Women's Writing*, 7.2 (July 2013), 138-56.

tendencies focuses in particular on the lyric. She has commented on her own 'obstinate attachment to musicality' in response to an interviewer's suggestion that her poetry 'recuperate[s] lyrical sounds and form' for 'post-modern sensibilities'.[32] The interviewer pursues the question of Riley's ambivalent or self-critical use of lyric in relation to the familiar critical debating points (in the field of 'innovative' poetry) of voice and the 'unified "I"-view'. Another source of Riley's ambivalence, though, may be the seductive power of lyric musicality, its seeming aesthetic reconciliation of harsh suffering through harmonious sound and form. This is hinted at by Riley's allusion, in the same interview, to the 'harsh musicality' and 'piercing violence' of border ballads, in contrast to the Swinburnian or Tennysonnian lyric: the former a type of musicality which (like Riley's own) puts up resistance to aesthetic consolation. Like Hill, Riley is given to referring to the lyric explicitly in her poetry. A poem entitled simply 'Lyric' begins with the awkwardness of stammering, as it apostrophizes the lyric impulse itself, using a deliberately awkward disposition of the words 'to get held', initially across an enjambed line break, and then repeated within a line:

> Stammering it fights to get
> held and never to get held
> ('Lyric', MMG 36)

As well as referring to the lyric impulse, 'it' here may be the harshness or suffering which 'fights' to be heard within (or be voiced by) the lyric, yet not to be 'held' in the sense of reduced, enclosed, reconciled. The poem continues with the image of the motor, which Riley has used elsewhere for the ambiguous relationship between self and poetic language ('No, this isn't me, it's just my motor running'):

> as whatever motors it swells
> to hammer itself out on me
> ('Lyric', MMG 36)

Here the lyric uses the poet for its own expressive purposes (rather than vice versa). Like Hill, Riley invokes the notion of the lyric cry, with more positivity but also with distancing; the cry is that of the poem at

---

[32] Denise Riley in conversation with Romana Huk, *PN Review*, 21, no. 5 (May - June 1995), pp. 17-22 (p. 19).

a distance from the author: [33]

> then it can call out high
> and rounded as a night-
> bird's falling clean
> down out of a black tree
> ('Lyric', MMG 36)

Like Hill, Riley expresses a suspicion of the lure of the lyrical:

>              Now
> steady me against inaccuracy, a lyric urge
> to showing off
> ('A Shortened Set', MMG 16)

We might compare this to Hill's line 'the pitiless wrench between / truth and metre' ('Citations II', BH 561; TCP 3). Often Riley references lyric in the other main sense of the word: song lyrics. Phrases from pop song lyrics appear frequently in her poetry, displaced into a new context. For example, 'A Misremembered Lyric' embeds and amends (as Riley states in her Acknowledgements) lines from two pop songs of the sixties: 'Rhythm of the Rain' (sung by The Cascades) and 'Something's Gotta Hold of My Heart' (sung by Gene Pitney). The poem reflects ironically on ideas of (lyrical or musical) beauty as consolation for loss:

> you get no consolation anyway until your memory's
> dead
> ...
> There is no beauty out of loss; can't do it –
> (Riley, 'A Misremembered Lyric', MMG 31)

One might also observe an 'appearance of spontaneity' in Riley's twists, turns and digressions; indeed, divorced from an idea of self-expression, spontaneity is quite amenable to the improvisatory quality of some 'experimental poetry'; the work of Tom Raworth would be

---

[33] One might think of the idea of 'alienated majesty' which Hill explores in his three essays whose titles begin with that phrase (CCW 493–531); he begins by quoting Ralph W. Emerson: 'In every work of genius we recognize our own rejected thoughts: they come back to us with a certain alienated majesty' (CCW 493).

an obvious example. What Carol Watts, writing about Riley, terms the 'nomadism of the "I"', is understood by Riley in psychoanalytical, phenomenological and political terms, and by Hill in philosophical, theological and ethical terms. [34] Returning to Vendler's description of the lyric, we might observe that both Hill's poetry and Riley's poetry are strongly characterised by compression and expressive / enactive structure (if one removes the assumption that what is expressed is 'the self'). On the other hand, the assumption that what is enacted by the poem is a representation of 'an experience' seems too limited. Neither poet's work shows 'an abstraction from the heterogeneity of life': their respective poetries are, in different ways, deeply immersed in the 'heterogeneity of life' and this is one of the ways in which Hill and Riley might be identified as authors of 'postmodern' lyrics.

Compare the following two critical quotations:

> The difficulty of Riley's poetry resides in a passage of thought and allusion of which the critical work is also, differently, an index. What is offered in the latter as a meditation on the limitations of identity politics emerges more extensively in her poems as a scrupulously reflective and yet abandoned encounter of the self with, and by means of, the constitutive force of language.[35]

> Hill, whose work had often been read as a development and refinement of the impersonality recommended to modernism by T. S. Eliot ... has caused confusion by his embrace of elements that appear confessional in their personal frankness, at the same time making these part of a new kind of poetry in which the transparency generally accorded to autobiographical confession is a problematic business.[36]

The terms are different, reflecting the two poets' respective intellectual contexts, though the suspicion of the self in 'linguistically innovative'

---

[34] Carol Watts, 'Beyond Interpellation? Affect, Embodiment and the Poetics of Denise Riley', in *Contemporary Women's Poetry: Reading/Writing/Practice*, ed. Alison Mark and Deryn Rees-Jones (Houndmills and London: Macmillan, 2000), pp. 157-72 (p. 162).

[35] Watts, pp. 157-58.

[36] Peter McDonald, *Serious Poetry: Form and Authority from Yeats to Hill* (Oxford; Oxford University Press, 2007), p. 191.

poetry, likely to be linked to Derrida by its practitioners, is surely also indirectly indebted to Eliot. But in each case a complex renegotiation of the relationship between self and language is at issue; and both poets engage in this negotiation in the form of both poetic reflection and critical or theoretical writing. Hill, who had his own phase of 'I aversion', is surely responding to the same degrading and commercial appropriation of identity and personality as poets of the 'British Poetry Revival'. In the comments of 'linguistically innovative' poets and in Hill's early comments, the suspicion of the speaking 'I' presents itself primarily in aesthetic and literary terms: in the former case as a critique of the Movement and of a 'mainstream' which is held to continue Movement tendencies; in the latter as a dismissal of confessional modes (thus the 'linguistically innovative' poets and Hill appear to be reacting against the positions of *New Lines* and *The New Poetry* respectively).[37] Both reactions are informed by Modernist affiliations ('innovative' poets to Modernist aesthetics more widely, but with a Poundian emphasis, and often refracted through US Projectivist and Black Mountain; Hill to Eliot's poetics of impersonality).[38] But both have a source in the view that poetry which assumes too readily the possibility of a direct, communicative speech addressed by poet to reader can offer little real resistance to the commodification or trivialization of identity and

---

[37] Critics who champion the 'innovative' school, such as Crozier and Sheppard, tend to see Al Alvarez's anthology *The New Poetry* (Harmondsworth: Penguin,1962) as part of a continuing tradition (albeit with modifications), initiated by the Movement as typified by Robert Conquest's *New Lines* (London: Macmillan, 1956): see Andrew Crozier, 'Thrills and Frills: Poetry and Figures of Empirical Lyricism', in *Society and Literature 1945-1970*, ed. Alan Sinfield (London: Methuen, 1983), pp. 216-7 and Sheppard, pp. 30-32. *The New Poetry* purported to react against the Movement, and championed the so-called confessionalism of poets such as Sexton, Plath and Lowell which Hill criticized in early interviews.

[38] Andrew Crozier defines the LIPS inheritance as 'not that of Pound and Eliot but of Pound and Williams'. Introduction to *A Various Art*, ed. Andrew Crozier and Tim Longville (Manchester: Carcanet, 1987), p. 12. Robert Hampson cites as a key influence on earlier generations of 'alternative' British poets the 'radical modernism' of Williams, Pound, Zukofsky, Olson and Oppen. *New British Poetries: The Scope of the Possible*, ed. Robert Hampson and Peter Barry (Manchester: Manchester University Press, 1995), pp. 144, 154-5. Marjorie Perloff prefers to see innovative (postmodern) poetry in terms of a reaction *against* modernist poetics, but her postmodern alternative is nevertheless given a similar aetiology, deriving from Pound: 'In the English-speaking world, the pivotal figure in the transformation of the Romantic (and Modernistic) lyric into what we now think of as postmodern poetry is surely Ezra Pound'. 'Postmodernism and the Impasse of Lyric', in *The Dance of the Intellect*, pp. 172-200 (p. 181).

personality. The affinities between these positions is partly concealed by differences of language: whereas 'innovative' poets tend to use the language of critical theory and politics, Hill uses the language of ethics, Christian theology and Idealist philosophy. The difference is, of course, more than a matter of terminology. Hill's fundamentally religious understanding of experience and culture means that he is happier with the idea of a true or deep self (informed by the concept of the soul), whereas some 'linguistically innovative' poets would be inclined to claim the self as entirely a construct of language, or power, of social practices and discourses. Nevertheless, there is a significant congruence in what they are reacting *against*, and in a response which insists on language as a medium of construction and exploration, rather than 'expression'.

Awkwardness can be a poetic technique, a form of resistance to what Veronica Forrest-Thomson called 'bad naturalization' ('swift and linear sense making in terms of "external" context').[39] Both Hill and Riley are skilled deployers of awkwardness, together with what (following Schlegel's 'the irony of irony') one might term 'the awkwardness of awkwardness' (the awkwardness of being seen to be awkward with a purpose).[40] Both Hill and Riley are also inclined to associate language and utterance with embarrassment or guilt. The *locus classicus* for this idea in Hill's prose writing is 'Poetry as "Menace" and "Atonement"', where he writes of being 'possessed by a sense of language itself as a manifestation of empirical guilt' (CCW 9), and of 'the shocking encounter with "empirical guilt", not as a manageable hypothesis, but a irredeemable error in the very substance and texture of one's craft and pride' (CCW 19). Embarrassment in various forms is a theme of many of Riley's essays in both *The Words of Selves* and *Impersonal Passion*, but 'Linguistic Unease' from the former volume is particularly concerned with guilt and awkwardness in relation to language, the self and the lyric:[41]

---

[39] Edward Larrissy, 'Poets of A Various Art: J.H. Prynne, Veronica Forrest-Thomson, Andrew Crozier', *Contemporary British Poetry: Essays in Theory and Criticism*, ed. James Acheson and Romana Huk (Albany, NY: SUNY Press, 1996), pp. 63-80 (p. 70).

[40] Friedrich Schlegel, 'On Incomprehensibility' (1800), in *German Aesthetic and Literary Criticism: The Romantic Ironists and Goethe* (Cambridge: Cambridge University Press, 1984), p. 37.

[41] Denise Riley, *The Words of Selves: Identification, Solidarity, Irony* (Stanford, CA: Stanford University Pres, 2000); *Impersonal Passion: Language as Affect* (Durham, NC: Duke University Press, 2005). 'Linguistic Unease', in *Impersonal Passion*, pp. 56-92, is cited hereafter as LU.

> I've long been nursing a shapeless suspicion that there's a particular guilt, associated with both writing and with taking on an identification, which is itself *partly* generated and fed by the workings of language. (LU 56)

> there's a lyrical guilt as well as a linguistic unease, the two knotted into each other through the curious temporal effects common to both. (LU 57)

Both poets seek to draw fine distinctions concerning such feelings:

> this feeling [of inauthenticity under certain linguistic circumstances] is not purely idiosyncratic; this chapter will offer suggestions as to why it is not purely psychological. (LU 57)

> It is crucial ... to draw a distinction between ... a formal acknowledgment of the human condition of anxiety or guilt and ... 'the empirical guilty conscience'. (CCW 8)

In 'Linguistic Unease', Riley considers the intersections of three processes. These are: first, formations and interrogations of self; second, effects and anxieties of borrowing or intertextuality; third, what she terms 'lyrical guilt', which links the first two in that it is closely 'associated both with writing and with taking on an identification' (LU 56). Her essay, in its vision of language as both cause and treatment of guilt, virtually echoes the duality which Hill proposes in 'Poetry as "Menace" and "Atonement"': 'one may continue to write and to publish in a vain and self-defeating effort to appease one's own sense of empirical guilt' (CCW 9). Riley writes 'Might not language itself arouse an anxiety which it must also try, through its other circuits, to assuage' (LU 56). One explanation of the link would be that both writers inherit what Hill calls 'that obsessive self-critical Romantic monologue in which eloquence and guilt are intertwined' (CCW 5) – though Hill also associates his dual view of poetry with Modernism, when he suggests that his title, with its allusions to 'menace' and 'atonement', 'presents little more than a conflation of two modernist clichés' (CCW 3). The introduction to Riley's book offers irony as 'some effective therapy' (LU 2) in response to the trials of interpellation, and Hill's essay is heavy with ironies of tone and reflections on ironies from the outset: 'My title may well strike you as exemplary in a fashion, being at once assertive and non-committal. The quotation-marks around "menace" and "atonement" look a bit like raised eyebrows' (LL1; CCW 3 omits the first sentence). Both Hill and Riley make explicit association between language and guilt, not merely in principle, but at the level of experience, and at the level of form. For Hill, such guilt seems to be primarily associated with error, and this because he sees error in quasi-theological terms, as a form of (or at least symbolic of) original sin. For Riley 'linguistic guilt' is associated with the place of the self in writing, with 'taking on an identification' (LU 56). Riley does allude to original sin early in her essay, although in a humorous and distancing manner; evoking the possibility of authorial guilt over '[u]nwilled plagiarism' she quotes a 'brisk half-consolation' from Fran Lebowitz: 'Original thought is like original sin: both happened before you were born to people you could not possibly have met' (LU 57). In one way this clearly measures her distance from Hill, for whom original sin by definition 'happens' to everyone (though he is capable of humorous self-critique of his own sense of guilt). In another way, though, the fact that both writers make the connections between authorship, self, origin and guilt shows an affinity.

For both poets, these configurations of awkwardness and guilt are realised and confronted in the temporal processes of poetic form. In 'Linguistic Unease', Riley writes that 'There's a strange *time* of rhyme … You anticipate the rhyme's arrival, but you can hear it in retrospect; aurally, it works forwards and backwards', adding that, in the case of writing, 'sound-anticipation runs in the ear well before the eye gets to track and to pull-back what's typed', so that '[t]his eccentric temporality, this time of rhyme in its strange undecidability, is an instance of retrospective knowledge' (LU 71). Here she seems to suggest an awkwardness, in the sense of a tricky regression, at the heart of a formal feature (rhyme) strongly associated with lyric musicality and 'smoothness'. Riley instances a verbal slip made by an announcer, caused by the 'regressive assimilative influence' [Jakobson] of one word on another (LU 71): so fluency of rhyme is here linked to the awkwardness of a mistake. The awkwardness lies in the potentially conflictual interaction of human faculties: 'the ear instructs the eye, while reason must intervene later' (LU 71). In 'Poetry as "Menace" and "Atonement"', Hill attributes both ethical and political value to a process of 'return' involving self-experience, self-criticism and poetic form, instancing Coleridge's advocacy of resistance to 'common assumption and mechanical categorization', Burke's capacity to 'return

... upon himself', and Keats's verbal echo as revocation in 'Ode to a Nightingale' (CCW 7). 'Poetry as "Menace" and "Atonement"' was a 1978 lecture; returning to the theme five years later in his *Agenda* essay 'Our Word is Our Bond', Hill made a distinction between reflexive 'recoil' and purposive 'return', using the distinction to criticise Pound for asserting undue poetic power and failing to live up to his own standards of precision, leading to 'a disjunction of the aesthetic and the ethical' (CCW 165). In an essay on 'Hill's Conversions', Kathryn Murphy interprets this structure of return or recoil in Hill's thought in largely Christian and theological terms, as a figure of penitence or religious conversion.[42] It has that dimension, certainly, but is not limited to a discourse of piety: the 'returns' of Keats and Pound are aesthetic and socio-political. The 'return' for Hill is particularly associated with (though not limited to) Romanticism. The nature of the strain in Romanticism with which Hill seeks to associate himself emerges clearly from his prose writings. He identifies it, in Arnoldian terms, as self-criticism expressed in the movement of return or recoil of a line of thought upon its own assumptions, limitations, blindness, fallibility. This is a movement which he praises in the prose writings of Coleridge and in the poetry of Hopkins, Wordsworth, Yeats and Keats, and detects here and there in the work of Edmund Burke, Cardinal Newman and T.H. Green. He conceives of it as a 'recognition of the force of the contemptible, in oneself and in others', and hence as a form of resistance, both to the dangerous tendencies of one's own mind, and to those of one's times.[43] He writes that 'Romantic art is thoroughly familiar with the reproaches of life. Accusation, self-accusation, are the very life-blood of its most assured rhetoric' (CCW 5). It is in relation to the topic of self-expression and his own experience of writing poetry that he speaks of 'the euphoria of self-assertion and the recoil into self-reproach and humiliation', acknowledging that the egotism which he disdains in others is present in himself, and exemplifying the process of the return.[44] Thus the self-critical return is both implicated

---

[42] Kathryn Murphy, 'Geoffrey Hill and Confession', in *Geoffrey Hill: Essays on his Later Work*, ed. John Lyon and Peter McDonald (Oxford: Oxford University Press, 2012), pp. 127-42.

[43] '"The Conscious Mind's Intelligible Structure": A Debate', *Agenda* 9.4-10.1 (Autumn / Winter 1971-72), 14-23 (p. 18).

[44] Geoffrey Hill, 'Thus my noblest capacity becomes my deepest perplexity', *A Sermon preached at Great St Mary's, the University Church, Cambridge*, 8 May 1983, duplicated sheets, p. 1.

with self-expression and a reaction against it – a combination of responses which has its own awkwardness.

'Resistance' is a key word for Hill, and he invariably uses it as a term of praise. Often it is oneself, or at least a force felt within one's own pattern of thought, which is resisted, so that what Wordsworth evinces is 'the capacity to go against one's own apparent drift' (CCW 114). Such resistance draws on self-criticism and uses the strength thus gained to oppose various drifts: the drift of complacency, of insufficiently controlled language, above all, of the assumptions and prejudices of an age and a society. So Wordsworth's 'Immortality Ode' 'thrusts up against the arrangement' of its own rhythm, resisting 'custom's pressure' (CCW 91), as 'the immediate, abrupt surge with which the "joy" of [stanza] nine's opening lines resists, pulls away from, the gravitational field of the closing lines of stanza eight' (CCW 92). Swift's creative intelligence is described as 'at once resistant and reciprocal' (CCW 71); both poetry and scepticism may function as 'a kind of marginal resistance' to 'the drift of the age'.[45] The link between self-criticism and resistance is made explicit in discussion of Coleridge: 'Coleridge's concern is not so much with thought as with "the mind's self-experience in the act of thinking" and ... this "self-experience" is most clearly realized by the process of "*win*[*ning* one's] way up against the stream"' (CCW 7). So in 'Redeeming the Time' Hill writes of 'making a burnt offering of a powerful and decent desire, the desire to be immediately understood by "a common well-educated thoughtful man, of ordinary talents"'. This sacrifice takes the form of the return: 'its structure is a recognition and a resistance; it is parenthetical, antiphonal, it turns upon itself' (CCW 98). He goes on to make it clear that what is being resisted is 'the detrition of general taste' (CCW 99). Although Hill borrows the phrase concerning 'a common well-educated thoughtful man' from a letter of Coleridge's (CCW 97), I take it that Hill also alludes here to Wordsworth's wish to use the 'real language of men'. A passage in 'Poetry as "Menace" and "Atonement"' brings together Coleridge, Burke and Keats as writers employing a valuable movement of return, and notes that, in Keats's 'Ode to a Nightingale', 'what is revoked is an attitude towards art and within art' (CCW 7); according to this reading of Keats's poem a reflexive position is revoked by a corrective reflexive gesture. Hill's interest in the constellation of associated ideas which the return represents persists in the second of his 1986 Clark lectures

---

[45] *Viewpoints*, p. 88.

at Cambridge, where he cites Bacon's description of words as like the Tartar's Bow, turning back on the person who uses them.[46]

Of especial relevance to the style of Hill's own poetry is his emphasis on the return as a linguistic and stylistic manoeuvre, as well as a conceptual shift. This emphasis on language and the discipline of technique, crucial to Hill's ideas of self-creation and self-discovery, is a frequent theme of his critical writing. In his sermon of 1983, Hill refers to 'examples of self-discovery and self-rebuke' (again the movement of assertion and recoil) as 'inseparable from the technical process itself, when the most accomplished maker turns upon his own mastery', and his own instances of the return operating in poetry pay attention to shifts in meaning at a high level of particularity. For example, the revocation which he identifies in the 'Ode to a Nightingale' is concentrated in the shift on the word 'forlorn'. Hill's comments on the return are full of phrases such as 'in the form and texture'; 'our attention is forcibly drawn to "the very word"', 'the very recalcitrance of language'.[47] He sees the process of return as emerging from the writer's engagement with language. The technical concentration of poetry perhaps makes this more true of the poet than the prose writer: 'In Yeats's case [as opposed to that of Burke], however, one does not refer so much to the conceptual intelligence operating through language-as-medium, as to the intelligence activated by the pitch of words'.[48] In Hill's poetry the processes of recoil, return, revocation may operate with a high degree of simultaneity, by means of puns and syntactical ambiguity, when the self-assertion and the recoil, the obtuseness and the insight, are manifest at the same moment as two alternative readings of the same lines. This is distinct from, though related to, Riley's 'strange time of rhyme' which works 'forwards and backwards'. Christopher Ricks has explored in detail the 'drama of reason' which Hill creates by the use of parentheses, relating this to the 'rhythmical triumphs' by means of which the return is articulated in the work of Wordsworth and

---

[46] Bacon's phrase also provided part of the title of the lecture, 'The Tartar's Bow and the Bow of Ulysses', the second of the four 1986 Clark Lectures given by Hill in the University of Cambridge, 4 February 1986; published as *The Enemy's Country: Words, Contexture, and other Circumstances of Language* (Oxford: Clarendon Press, 1991) and collected in CCW 171-259.

[47] Sermon 2; 'The Conscious Mind', p. 21.

[48] 'The Conscious Mind', p. 21.

others.⁴⁹ Brackets, Ricks argues, can create two worlds within a single sentence: 'a simple bracket may establish a co-existing zone which is only a contained breath away and yet which breathes the pure serene of another planet. "(There is nothing, over the white fields, amiss)"'.⁵⁰ Hill's puns are yet more compact, bringing two worlds into collision in one word so that, for example, 'superb graft' ('A Pastoral'; BH 32; FTU 56) alludes both to a triumph of organic continuity and to the shameless corruption of 'graft'.⁵¹ Hill has also borrowed Keats's effect of enharmonic shift (on 'forlorn') for the transition between sonnets 4 and 5 of 'Funeral Music':

>                  ... an unpeopled region
> Of ever new-fallen snow, a palace blazing
> With perpetual silence as with torches.
>
> As with torches we go, at wild Christmas,
> When we revel in our atonement
> Through thirty feasts of unction and slaughter,
> (BH 50-1; KL 28-9)

Here the repetition draws attention to the shift or revocation.

The main thrust of Hill's own thinking about Romanticism would seem to be that what was, in the best work of the Romantic poets, a discovery and expansion of self and self-consciousness, a process involving transcendence of the contingent self through self-criticism, declined, in some twentieth-century poetry, into an habitual reliance on a less critical and more complacent conception of self-expression as a value-criterion in poetry. In this he can be seen to be valuing a feature of Romanticism related to that rejected by Eliot when establishing his doctrine of impersonality. Eliot asserts that: 'Romanticism is a short

---

⁴⁹ Christopher Ricks, *The Force of Poetry* (1984; rpt. Oxford: Oxford University Press, 1987), pp. 309-18.

⁵⁰ Ricks, p. 312.

⁵¹ The line '(There is nothing, over the white fields, amiss)' is from the early uncollected poem 'Summer Night' (*The Isis*, 19 November 1952, p. 33). In addition to discussing Hill's use of brackets, Ricks also mentions his use of paradoxical puns, of words which simultaneously assert and revoke, instancing the word 'scatters' from 'Annunciations' (Ricks, p. 301). In his article on Tenebrae he examines the paradoxical consequences of Hill's use of hyphens ('Tenebrae and at-one-ment', Ricks, pp. 319-55). All of these effects in Hill's poetry may be related to the 'return' operating in a highly condensed manner.

cut to the strangeness without the reality, and it leads its disciples only back upon themselves'.[52] Hill sees a similar movement, but reads it as a redemptive self-criticism rather than a symptom of solipsism: the return or 'self-accusation' of Romantic rhetoric. Hill and Riley, then, share a certain structure of thought and feeling, in which self-criticism, guilt and awkwardness are registered as both imposition and technique. This structure is imposed upon the poet by the process of writing within, through, and against his or her social context. In turn the poet deploys it creatively to generate late modernist forms of eloquence, involving specific temporal and formal movements, realised in poetic technique.

'A Précis or Memorandum of Civil Power' (BH 581-84; TCP 27-31) seems, by its awkward title (described as 'deadly' by Peter McDonald and 'unmusical' by Hugh Haughton), to announce itself as concerned with politics. [53] The title chimes with the term 'civil polity' which Hill adopts in his 'Alienated Majesty' set of essays on the grounds that 'the word "politics" has been rendered so suspect' (CCW 518). The Miltonic echo, more explicit in the volume title (*A Treatise of Civil Power*), suggests a concern with the relationship between 'worldly' power and (ideas of) spiritual or transcendent power, since Milton's work is concerned with power relations between state and church. [54] The opening lines suggest a certain reluctance to engage with the topic – 'Could so have managed not to be flinging / down this challenge' (BH 581; TCP 27) – and deploy a conversational informality of tone which sounds awkward rather than relaxed. McDonald hears this as an 'opening gambit ... of weary obligation', but there is an insouciance and energy in the abrupt colloquial start, and the word 'flinging'. [55] Can one fling down a challenge wearily? Possibly – if anyone can, then Hill can. The challenge may be to readers, to potentially hostile critics, or even

---

[52] T.S. Eliot, 'Imperfect Critics', in *The Sacred Wood: Essays on Poetry and Criticism* (1920; 4th edn, London: Methuen, 1934), pp. 17-46 (p. 31).

[53] Peter McDonald, '"But to my Task": Work, Truth, and Metre in Later Hill', in *Geoffrey Hill: Essays on his Later Work*, ed. John Lyon and Peter McDonald (Oxford: Oxford University Press, 2012), pp. 143-69 (p. 154); Hugh Haughton, 'Music's Invocation: Music and History in Geoffrey Hill', in *Geoffrey Hill and his Contexts*, ed. Piers Pennington and Matthew Sperling (Oxford, Bern, Berlin, etc: Peter Lang, 2011), pp. 187-211 (p. 209).

[54] John Milton, *A Treatise of Civil Power in Ecclesiastical Causes* (1659).

[55] McDonald, p. 154.

to the poet himself, and the reluctance implies a countervailing sense of obligation. As the first line omitted the pronoun, the third omits the definite article, continuing the note-like yet almost jaunty feel. 'True way is homeless' suggests it might be better to evade worldly allegiances, but this is partially revoked by 'but the better gods / go with the house'. This instance of Hill's not infrequent use of plural 'gods' to suggest quasi-pagan embodiments of qualities (as in 'the gods of coin and salt' from 'Of Commerce and Society', BH 28; FTU 48), uses a gambling metaphor ('the house') picked up later in 'a telling run of worldly luck' and 'breaking every bank'. The implication is a Casino-like realm of worldly power, with perhaps a glance at 'casino banking'. Although the poem does refer at various points to overtly political matters – the role of the judiciary (V), the Spanish Civil War (II) – the approach to politics is characteristically oblique. McDonald suggests that the word 'mischance' in section V (BH 583; TCP 30) 'links the workings of power with … "botched loves"' (two lines later), so as to shunt the term 'Civil Power' from 'the realm of abstract legal meaning … into the register of love', placing '[e]ros in the same room as politics'.[56] However, no analysis of the role of power in erotic relations is forthcoming in the poem, which returns promptly to public life, referencing politicians' expedient apologies (they might, I suppose, be apologising for their own 'botched loves'). In the next section (VI), the lines 'Money's not civil power in itself: / more the enforcer' (BH 583; TCP 30), suggest that the poem is delineating civil power by differentiating it from contiguous but distinct phenomena: love, money, history, rumour, beauty. The effect is rather akin to artillery range-finding: seeking to locate the precise position of 'civil power' by aiming around it. Politics and the 'personal' are, on one view, opposites: a political poetry concerned to address public issues, a personal poetry introspective. On other views they are inseparable, as in the 1970s feminist slogan 'the personal is political'. They have in common that they are both 'awkward' subjects, their treatment prone to misunderstanding (such as reductive, purely biographical readings of 'personal' poetry), liable to give offence (as in the reactions to Tony Harrison's *V*, one of the more overtly political poems of the last fifty years).[57] Hill's early criticisms of 'confessional' poetry perhaps implied that that particular form of the 'personal' was not *sufficiently* awkward:

---

[56] McDonald, p. 156.

[57] Tony Harrison, *V*, first published *London Review of Books*. 7.1 (24 January 1985), pp. 12-13.

too much at ease with the display of its own angst. He seemed to be suggesting that confessional poetry demeaned the personal, packaged it for a ready market.[58] Arguably politics and the personal are awkward, less in themselves, than at their intersection, as when a friendly conversation suddenly turns awkward because political differences emerge. Frequently their intersection is also the intersection of the public and the private, as when the would-be statesmanlike politician has their public stance suddenly undermined by the revelation of their personal life.

After the opening reflexive observation, the first section of 'A Précis' continues by counterposing Gabriel Marcel's Christian existentialism and Messiaen's prison-camp composition *Quartet for the End of Time* to the '*doctrine of the moment*' (BH 581; TCP 27) in Gide's *Les Nourritures Terrestres*.[59] The function of music here is a complex one. Music itself may be abrasive, shocking, dislocated, but can it be (successfully) awkward? It may deploy awkwardness as an aesthetic strategy, but the salience of form in music, and what Hill has referred to in interview as its qualities of 'direct, sensuous communication' may make one inclined to see that awkwardness as subsumed by forms of order and pleasure.[60] One aspect of music's role in the poem is an evocation, or reference to, the melopoeia which the poetry itself has largely abandoned. Hill's observations on melopoeia in Pound are relevant here:

> Pound's 'book', the twelve poems of the sequence which precede 'Envoi (1919)', is 'dumb-born' because the tradition of 'motz el son', the art of perfectly matching words and melody … has in its passing left lyric speech bereft of its truest *melopoeia*. Men like Gautier and Larforgue and Landor have reintroduced other virtues, 'hardness' and '*logopoeia*', and much may be done with these … even so 'Envoi (1919)' recognizes in its opening phrase that the music of its own unfolding will be the only *melopoeia* the 'book' will have. (CCW 249)

---

[58] As implied by his already-cited comparison of some poems to 'stills from home movies' (Interview with Hermione Lee).

[59] 'Seize from every moment its unique novelty, and do not prepare your joys.' André Gide, *Fruits of the Earth* (*Les Nourritures Terrestres* 1897), translator not identified (1949; Harmondsworth: Penguin, 1970), p. 33.

[60] *Viewpoints*, p. 91.

Hill here identifies Pound's sense of belatedness in respect of a lyric tradition. The awkward self-consciousness of 'A Précis', its allusions to a musicality which it cannot simply attain, is a belated engagement with lyric melopoeia via logopoeia paralleling Pound's:

> Pound's melopoeia is itself drawn into 'a dance of the intelligence among words and ideas and modifications of ideas and characters' since what is 'modified' in 'Envoi (1919)' is by implication the question 'What is his own voice, his own style, his own individuality?' (CCW 258)

This implies the role of awkwardness as a form of engagement with, and modification of, the understanding of self. While 'dance of the intelligence' claims that logopoeia can be deft, this is a deftness which co-exists with awkwardness to raise awkward questions about style and self. Hill's belated ('postmodern') self-conscious logopoeia in 'A Précis', like that of Pound in *Hugh Selwyn Mauberley*, can occasionally clear a space for something like the 'sheer perfection' of melopoeia, as in section III of Hill's poem:

> Not to skip detail, such as finches brisking
> on stripped haw-bush;
> the watered gold that February drains
> out of the overcast; nomadic aconites
> that in their trek recover beautifully
> our sense of place,
> the snowdrop fettled on its hinge, waxwings
> becoming *sportif* in the grimy air.
> (BH 582; TCP 29)

The pull towards the iambic pentameter which is detectable here recalls Hill's noting the presence of 'six regular pentameters in disguise' in Pound's 'Envoi (1919)' (CCW 257). The allusions in 'A Précis' to Messiaen (and later to Arvo Pärt, who I take to be the 'grand / minimalist' mentioned in section VI) introduce a non-discursive form (music) into a seemingly discursive process, creating a deliberate incommensurability within the form of Hill's reflections on power. [61] In this way the range-finding approach extends, not only to the discursive senses of the

---

[61] In particular 'the off-key sweetness of a single bell' (BH 583; TCP 30) suggests Pärt.

word 'power' (power in politics, the power in or of love, the power of beauty, the power of art) but to the extra-discursive powers of music, which are both present (by allusion and imitation) and necessarily absent within the discursive field of the poem. Hugh Haughton, in a chapter on 'Music and History in Geoffrey Hill', argues that Hill's '"love of music" and "envy of the composer" lie at the heart of [his] work, though always in tension with his interest in ethical and political contestation'. [62] Here 'tension' might suggest an awkward juxtaposition, or, alternatively, a creative tension, even a movement between tension and resolution such as may be found in music itself. Poetry, of course, has its own non-discursive power, of which the 'musicality' of lyricism is a principle manifestation. But the implications of 'musicality' depend on what music one has in mind. Vendler's 'appearance of spontaneity' guarantees some form of authenticity, but one which Hill explicitly rejects in favour of the non-discursive, and perhaps musical, quality of movement (and the power to move the reader) in poetry:

> Either the thing moves, RAPMASTER, or it
> does not. I disclaim spontaneity,
> the appearance of which is power.
> (BH 334; SS 46)

Both appearance and spontaneity recur in section I of 'A Précis'

> Grace
> appears hardly spontaneous in that sense;
> and in no sense whatever of the mere
> veto or grab
> of reality to our self-desires
> (BH 581; TCP 27)

Spontaneous ('without effort of premeditation') with reference to 'Grace', invokes the Christian doctrine of grace as a free gift from God, unearned by human works or endeavour, which is here contrasted with the sense of spontaneity that Gide asserts. Gide's existentialist celebration of the moment is denigrated as inadequate ('mere / veto or grab') and perhaps tending to subjective self-indulgence. Gide's 'doctrine', as expounded in *Les Nourritures Terrestres*, is to '[s]eize from every moment its unique

---
[62] Haughton, p. 188.

novelty and never prepare your joys', and to '[w]elcome everything that comes to you ... Long only for what you have. Understand that at every moment of the day God in his entirety may be yours'.[63] Gide's ideas are a curious mixture of asceticism, spiritual language and hedonism and, given his comments in the Preface of 1927, it is doubtful whether they constitute a 'doctrine' so much as a form of provocation and imaginative projection.[64] Nevertheless, in their rejection of the ties of family and even human society, and their equation of God with happiness, they may well have struck Hill as ethically superficial; André Maurois associates them with adolescent or youthful spirit.[65] The contrast with Messiaen centres on conceptions of time as spiritual and ethical form. *Quatuor pour la Fin du Temps* evokes the end of time at the Apocalypse whilst experimenting with the 'cessation' or transformation of musical time. The composer's programme notes place eternity in opposition to the 'weariness' of time, and associate eternity with the angel of the Revelation in *St John* chapter 10, and with the Word, but also with birdsong, which figures 'the opposite to time ... our desire for light, for stars, and for jubilant song'.[66] Given the famous circumstances of the composition and first performance of Messiaen's work (in a German prisoner-of-war camp), one implication of Hill's contrast may be that Gide's spiritualised hedonism, the project of immersion in the joy of each moment's pleasure, would hardly stand up to the challenge of prison-camp life.[67] Roger Nichols comments of *Quatuor* that it is tempting to interpret the title as 'Quartet for the end of metre', in the light of the very limited importance of the bar lines in the score; Robert Sherlaw Johnson describes how, in the first movement,

---

[63] Gide, pp. 33, 25.

[64] 'I am usually judged by this book of my youth as if the ethics of *Fruits of the Earth* were the ethics of my whole life, as if I myself had not been the first to follow the advice I give my young reader: "Throw away my book and leave me"'. Gide, 'Preface to the French Edition of 1927' (July 1926), *Fruits of the Earth*, p.12.

[65] Gide p. 34; André Maurois, 'André Gide', in *From Proust to Camus: Profiles of Modern French Writers*, trans. Carl Morse and Renaud Bruce (1966; London: Weidenfeld and Nicolson, 1967), pp. 71-95: 'Gide's character ... having been retarded in natural development ... young people are beholden to a retarded and unregenerate adolescent for having so well expressed what they feel' (p. 88).

[66] See Rebecca Rischin, *For The End of Time: The Story of the Messiaen Quartet* (Ithaca, NY: Cornell University Press, 2003), p. 52.

[67] However, Hill has expressed resistance to what he terms 'the elitism of the man-of-the-moment' (CCW 403) in relation to Czesław Miłosz's claims that moments of mortal danger '*judge* all poets and philosophers' (CCW 402).

the composer uses two independent rhythmic pedals (cello and piano) superimposed on two independent birdsongs (violin and clarinet), with the shape of the movement determined by the free course of the 'birdsong' elements, and the rhythmic pedals cut short arbitrarily at the end of the movement.[68] 'The end of metre' would apply equally to the forms of free-verse used by Hill, reminding us of the possibility of a lyricism inspired by innovative or experimental music.

Marcel's philosophy seems to stand also in implicit contract with Gide's, with time again being significant: Gide's focus on the moment contrasts with Marcel's invocation of eternity. The opposition also concerns the self: Marcel affirms the (non-Cartesian), mysterious, but inescapable reality of the self. As Gallagher summarizes his position, '[t]he existential indubitable is the self as incarnate in the body and as manifest in the world'.[69] Lines 4-7 of Hill's poem refers directly to Marcel's theory of self:

> *Cogito a bare*
> *threshold*, as G. Marcel sagely declares,
> of what's valid.

Marcel distinguishes the existential self or 'incarnate consciousness' from the Cartesian cogito:

> Descartes discovered not the existential subject, but himself as a thinking being, a universal subject: the *cogito* ... is a purely formal *a priori* which guards the threshold of the valid.[70]

Gide, in contrast, advocates an escape from self:

> it is a doctrine in which the Self (which is essentially continuity, memory of, and submission to the past) fades out and disappears in order that the individual may lose himself, dissolve himself into each perfect moment.[71]

---

[68] Roger Nichols, *Messiaen* (Oxford & New York, NY: Oxford University Press, 1986), pp. 29-30; Robert Sherlaw Johnson, *Messiaen* (London: Dent, 1975), pp. 61-3.

[69] Kenneth T. Gallagher, *The Philosophy of Gabriel Marcel* (New York, NY: Fordham University Press, 1962), p. 16. Gallagher is drawing on Marcel's works *Metaphysical Journal* (1952), *Being and Having* (1949), and *The Mystery of Being* (1951).

[70] Gallagher, pp. 16; 14-15.

[71] Maurois, 'André Gide', p. 85.

In a manner familiar to Hill's readers, the opening of the poem asks us to research or recall disparate sources, and bring them into play within the field of the poem's reflections. The obliquity of approach to the poem's theme is acknowledged and defended later in the poem:

> Why *Quatuor pour la Fin du Temps*, this has
> nothing to do
> surely with civil power? But it strikes chords
> direct and angular:
> (BH 584; TCP 31)

Section VII (the final section) continues with an evocation of the fall of France in 1940 and the subsequent Vichy regime. Messiaen's work is named in both first and last sections, giving it a framing importance for Hill's poem. Music is a significant presence in the poem, in the allusions to Messiaen, but also as a formal model: the phrase 'it strikes chords' suggests that Hill's technique here is to use allusion, juxtaposition and reference to 'strike chords' or take ethical and conceptual bearings on questions of power. Here 'angular' chords serve as model or metaphor for the poem's technical and poetic procedures. Hugh Haughton is ambivalent about the success of music's role here. Hill, he comments, evokes Messiaen's quartet 'in a grating, prosaic idiom', unlike the music itself; the poem is 'closer to a poetic commentary on music than a "musical" poem'. This returns us to the issues of musicality and awkwardness in the lyric. Haughton refers to 'the Baroque music of [Hill's] precisely pitched and paced verse', quoting Hill's 'reflection on "Baroque" as implying "nothing broken"', but Hill's allusions to twentieth-century music may offer a model in which tension and irresolution are themselves musical qualities.[72] Such a form of musicality may be illuminated by a pair of poems from *A Treatise of Civil Power*, 'Citations' (I) and (II)', poems which strongly exemplify the triad of self, intertextuality and guilt which Riley explores in 'Linguistic Unease'. The title 'Citations' seems to announce intertextual debts, but (II) reflects rather directly on the relationships between lyric, poetic power, and musicality. The poems cite, rather unexpectedly in what seems to be a defence of poetry, the war diary of a British military leader (thereby invoking also the military sense of 'citation', as in a citation for bravery). The quotation from Alanbrooke's war diary focuses on the maintenance of the self – 'a work

---

[72] Haughton, pp. 210, 211, 199, 199 (quoting OS).

done / to gain, or regain, *possession of himself* ' – for ethical purposes – '*a mode of moral life*' (BH 560; TCP 2). Like much of Hill's work, these poems are pervaded by forms of what Riley terms 'linguistic unease'. This can involve expressions of uncertainty ('this not quite knowing …'), concessions ('No decent modicum, agreed'), moral anxiety ('bad faith … defraudings') (BH 560; TCP 2), self-mocking ('why your lyric mojo / atrophied') (BH 561; TCP 3), inwoven tortuous formulations ('call writing nothing / but self-indemnity for what is denied it?') (BH 561; TCP 3). Awkwardness is apparent in these, and in the poem's self-modifications: 'For yes read possibly' (BH 561; TCP 3). The poems have a self-consciously oblique relation to the lyric. The opening question of 'Citations' II, for example, ('whether power rides on arias or recitatives') seems to figure expressive lyric as aria, with recitative standing in for the proximate but distinguishable forms of dramatic monologue or dialogue.[73] So the stanza mounts a defence of Hill's own progressive shift from the lyric intensity of his earlier work to the dialogic, more diffuse, fragmented (yet still dense) later work, claiming that this is not 'atrophy' but 'invention [which] reinvents itself' (BH 561; TCP 3). Recitative would suggest the 'spoken' (personal) voice, as opposed to the 'sung' voice of epic or prophecy (as in *Paradise Lost*), even if, in opera, it is aria that is most intensely associated with personal emotion. In 'A Précis or Memorandum of Civil Power', the awkwardness is in part that of a poetic style that seems to need to explain itself, even while remaining in places enigmatic, as in the lines: 'I cannot work much closer to the slub / or perhaps it's / diffused like rumour, meaning diffused power' (BH 582; TCP 28). Hill's poetry is often enigmatic because of ambiguous deictics such as 'it's': these lines seem to help by telling us that 'it's' refers to 'power' – it is power that is 'diffused like rumour'. But the lines remain a little elusive: a somewhat Foucauldian-sounding diffusion of power distances it, the implication seems to be, from the poet, in contrast to the proximity of working close 'to the slub'. The poem several times tells the reader what it does or doesn't mean: '(When I said / grand minimalist I'd someone else in mind – / just to avoid confusion on that score.)' (BH 584; TCP 31) (with a pun on 'score'). It also tells us what it is doing, or trying not to do, or would rather not do if it didn't have to: 'I would forgo / this chant and others if I were not / more than a shade distressed' (BH 581; TCP 27); 'Not to skip detail' (BH 582; TCP 29). Hill's poetry is frequently definable in

---

[73] See Brewster, p. 35.

terms of the creative tension between contrasting elements. One such pair could be described as musicality and annotation; and another, in parallel, as the lyrical and the awkward.

I now turn to a close reading of Riley's 'A Shortened Set' (MMG 16-24), to consider parallels and differences in how ideas of awkwardness and lyricism play out in Riley's poetry. The title of Riley's poem or sequence 'A Shortened Set' suggests a set of poems (but also perhaps a set of tennis, a mathematical set, and various other possibilities), with an emphasis on cutting (one of the themes of the poems), since 'Shortened' implies a process – not just a short set (the poem is actually on the long side for Riley) but one that has been written and then cut down. Carol Watts sees this as 'a sequence about return ... the demand for and melancholic cost of retrospection', and also as a work which 'deals with a process of "becoming other", in which the reader is also brought to participate'. [74] Beginning with the physical images of a scarred wound (a pregnancy termination, literal or metaphorical, is also implied), the poem surrounds this strong image with psychological and literary implications. In the memory and the self 'the connectives of right recall / have grown askew' (MMG 16) so that 'nothing's aligned properly' (16) and the resolve to attempt realignment through a poetic form of cutting risks the 'inaccuracy' associated with a 'lyric urge / to showing-off' (16). Ambivalence and awkwardness, animated by a stoical, self-critical awareness, seem to be the key note. The poem is heavily marked by Riley's characteristic self-consciousness, in both the main senses of that term. Literary reflexivity is manifest, for example, in the lines:

> I'd thought
> To ask around, what's lyric poetry?
> Its bee noise starts before I can.
> ('A Shortened Set', MMG 22)

Social or psychological awkwardness appears in lines which disavow the coercive 'we' of complacent coupledom or glib journalistic generalisation:

---
[74] Watts, p. 166.

> Don't quote the 'we'
> Of pairs nor worse, of sentient
> Humanity, thanks.
> (MMG 22)

The addition of the word 'thanks', as well as making the tone more conversational, introduces the characteristic social note of Riley's poetry. This is followed by self-mocking reflexivity:

> That's attitudinising, in those
> three lines. That's what I do.
> Help me out of it, you
> sentient humanity.
> (MMG 23)

Reflexivity in respect of literary form and awkward, ironical, 'personal' self-consciousness are united: 'attitudinising' refers to both a more-or-less fictional poetic 'self' and to a literary style. In the lines 'I'd thought / to ask around, what's lyric poetry?', reflexive interrogation of the traditions of the lyric form is routed, in a somewhat tongue-in-cheek manner, via the social discourse of 'ask around', rather as if the poet's quest for a poetic were akin to a search for a good restaurant or a reliable plumber. Although this might seem to measure Riley's distance from Hill's high seriousness, the tone is not so different from 'Could so have managed not to be flinging / down this challenge' (BH 581; TCP 27) or 'The power-and-beauty mob has my bequest' (BH 582; TCP 28). In Riley's poem, the always-already present 'bee noise' of the lyric is both its imposing weight of tradition, and its embroilment in the language of contemporary culture (a less affirmative version of Wordsworth's 'real language of men in a state of vivid sensation'), including the problematic discourses around the self.[75] Like the image of the motor which 'swells / to hammer itself out on me' (MMG 36), these lines convey Riley's sense of being spoken (or written) *by* language – and, more specifically, by the lyric. In these passages, a sense of awkwardness – of tone, social relations, literary positioning – is the means by which Riley articulates

---

[75] William Wordsworth, 'Preface [to *Lyrical Ballads* (1802)]', in William Wordsworth and Samuel Taylor Coleridge, *Lyrical Ballads and Related Writings*, ed. William Richey and Daniel Robinson (Boston, MA and New York, NY: Houghton Mifflin Company, 2002), pp. 390-411 (p. 390).

and negotiates complex and ambivalent relations of alienation and connection (in respect of other people, social and political collectivities, and literary-aesthetic positions). Like Hill's poem, Riley's modulates between the deliberately 'unlyrical' or 'unmusical' and passages of lyrical atmospheric evocation. Some lines for 'A Shortened Set' could be drawn from an interview or prose piece:

> to escape
> both well-oiled grief and an escaper's
> cheery whistling. Tedious. This
> representing yourself, desperate to get it right
> as if you could, is that the aim of the writing?
> (MMG 17)

Other lines belong to a more evidently lyrical register:

> The last sun on dark red brick burns violet-black where
> I wait to get back something in the narrows of the city
> under its great sides, whose brick or painted walls
> glow into the paler light above them, a hugely quiet halo
> formed from the internal heat of rooftops. These seep
> their day off to the sky cupped very coolly distant
> over this tight rim.
> (MMG 17)

Another passage, beginning 'How can black paint be warm?' (MMG 18), reflects the influence of visual art through a sustained immersion in painterly colours. However, both of these relatively descriptive passages end with a return to the poem's persistent concern with inter-human relations, and their inherent emotional and / or conceptual awkwardness: 'Your feelings, I mean mine, are common to us all' (17); 'A twist / of thought is pinned there. A sexual black. And I / can't find my way home' (18). Riley's awkwardness ('the thought of it makes me mortified', 23), resolves itself in the final section of fourteen three-line stanzas, into indifference ('Then after years, so-whattish'), and then, via a moment of near-euphoria ('Unanxious, today. A feeling of rain / and dark happiness') to something like satisfied desire and appeasement of constraint ('In a rush / the glide of the heart / out on a flood of ease', 24).

Hill and Riley share certain forms of relation to the lyric tradition and certain concerns about guilt and the self as they emerge from the poet's engagement with that tradition. Both poets use awkwardness as a technique for negotiating central technical and philosophical issues for late modernist poetry: the role of musicality, the presence or absence of 'voice', the construction or elision of subjectivity and the ethical responsibility of writing. Resisting aspects of the lyric tradition, each nevertheless finds space for the lyrical in their poetry. Awkwardness is both the price paid for maintaining the lyrical within a self-consciously late modernist poetic, and a means critically to frame melopoeia within logopoeia. Forms of philosophical and literary self-consciousness are figured by social or discursive awkwardness. In his essay on 'Envoi (1919)', Hill considers the complex interplay of melopoeia and logopoeia in Pound's poetry of this period, finding a crux in self-consciousness, which he tentatively reads as Prufrockian awkwardness:

> It is as much the strength as the weakness of 'Envoi (1919)' that its melopoeic certitude does not annul the numerous uncertainties ... this poem emerges from circumstances of derision ... into its defiant, self-conscious *melopoeia*: 'poetry which moves by its music, whether it be a music in the words or an aptitude for, or suggestions of, accompanying music'.
>
> This 'self-consciousness' is a crux which I have, perhaps contentiously, introduced. Though one is not obliged to think of it as a Prufrockian nervous inhibition, it undeniably implies a sharp apprehension, a shade more vulnerable than self-awareness, of the circumstances in which the self speaks and acts. (CCW 257)

For both poets, awkwardness serves in part as a resistant response to the potential degradation and appropriation of selfhood by the commodification of identity. As a poetic technique and effect, awkwardness is closely connected to temporality. We find in Riley's poetics a link between time and self, explored through her sense of the retrospective time of rhyme. Hill's concept of the redemptive, self-critical return gives ethical value to a temporal movement of self-critique. The difference between awkwardness and smoothness can often be a matter of time and timing – not just what is said, but when it is said – and this is as true of poetic as of social discourse.

There are, however, key differences between the two poets. Moments of lyric intensity in Riley's poetry are always implicitly in inverted commas, always subject to a surrounding pressure of irony. This is not true of Hill's work, where the intensity of lyric moments does indeed emerge from a surrounding context, often tinged with irony, but nevertheless emerges with a sense of purity, even if under pressure from critical self-scrutiny, and even if sustained melopoeia is no longer a possibility. When Hill writes that '"Envoi (1919)" recognizes in its opening phrase that the music of its own unfolding will be the only *melopoeia* the "book" will have' (CCW 249), Pound provides a means of reflection on his own situation and practice. If the 'sheer perfection' of *melopoeia* is scarcely attainable by Pound in 1919, that constraint can only have been greater for Hill in 1986.[76] In relation to ideas of the self, the major difference between Hill and Riley is that, for Hill, the soul is an ultimate form of 'true' self, however resistant to capture or representation, whereas it is not a category one imagines Riley using readily, or without irony.[77] Her thought is more amenable to the idea of a wholly fabricated or unstable self, although her poetry does not necessarily support or endorse such an idea. Nevertheless, they share both a profound commitment to musicality informed by a critical awareness of its risks, and ethical concerns about the act of writing: each has a remarkable technical mastery in their respective styles, and awkwardness both enables and restrains that mastery, working across technique and ethics.

---

[76] 1986 was the year in which Hill delivered the Clark lectures at Cambridge, including 'Envoi (1919)'; see note 46 above.

[77] I take it that the importance that Hill gave to the idea of original sin necessarily implied a belief in the soul as the ultimate foundation of selfhood.

CHAPTER SIX

## Affinities with Radical Landscape Poetry in the Work of Geoffrey Hill

ELEANORE WIDGER

The critical reception of Geoffrey Hill's poetry has tended to focus on the influence of earlier poetics, from sixteenth-century devotional works to Modernist language experiments. His own use of quotation (or paraphrase, or deliberate misquotation), reference and allusion would seem to support such comparisons, as would his political and aesthetic views, which have often been identified as traditional or even conservative. This is arguably a misrepresentation, and belies the innovative aspects of Hill's work, in which his use of space, visual patterning and linguistic experiment combine in ways that in other poets' work might be described as 'radical'. *Clavics*, Hill's most obviously visual work pays homage to the pattern poetry of George Herbert and Henry Vaughan (which was itself preceded by ancient Greek pattern poetry), in which shape is symbolic of religious harmony, order, and also provides an iconographic aid to contemplation.[1] There is also a case to be made, however, that his use of shape engages with the concept of visuality itself, the poems presenting themselves as visual objects to be looked at more explicitly than Herbert or Vaughan. This is linked to his evident attention to the details of nature and of the landscape. One would not describe Hill as a 'landscape poet', yet landscape is a recurrent and crucial presence in his work, underpinning its rootedness in particular times and places, and its exploration of visual perception: for example, the landscape of the West Midlands in the 40s and 50s in *Mercian Hymns*; and of France before and during the First World War in *The Mystery of the Charity of Charles Péguy*. It is interesting in this context

---

[1] *Clavics* differs substantially between the Enitharmon Press press edition of 2011 (which has 32 sections), and the version included in BH, where the sequence is expanded to 42 sections, with both re-ordering (section 3 in CL is revised as section 2 in BH; section 2 in CL becomes section 33 in BH, for example), and numerous internal revisions. Quotations in this chapter are based on BH, as representing Hill's final intentions, with significant variations from CL noted. Where a reference is given for BH only, the lines quoted are not in CL.

to note his use of the word 'landscape', often with a metaphorical sense: 'A deeper landscape lit by distant / Flashings' ('Soliloquies', BH 62; KL 42); 'an alien landscape, / The dream where you are always to be found' ('The Songbook of Sebastian Arrurruz' 3, BH 71; KL 55); 'the radical soul … its landscape and inner domain' (*The Mystery of the Charity of Charles Péguy,* BH 147; TM 16). He comments most explicitly on the nature of landscape in lines from *Péguy*:

> Landscape is like revelation; it is both
> singular crystal and the remotest things.
> (BH 147; TM 17)

The inner landscape and the 'scape' generated by the poems themselves, both connect in Hill's work with the physical landscape, blurring the boundaries between the natural and the cultural. This is similarly an important and pervasive feature of the work gathered by Harriet Tarlo in an anthology entitled *The Ground Aslant*, which tackles the dense framework of ideas attached to the idea of landscape.[2] Hill's affinities with the work of these 'radical landscape poets' have not been explored. With reference mainly to *Clavics*, but additionally to poems from *Canaan, Mercian Hymns,* and from 'Four Poems Regarding the Endurance of Poets', which appears in *King Log*, this chapter aims to begin such an exploration.

It goes without saying that the relation of the form of *Clavics* to Herbert's 'Easter-Wings' is clear. Similarities in the language confirm this, as when Herbert's juxtaposition of the 'fall' with 'flight' is echoed in Hill's evocation of depth and height in the 'mire' and 'cliff' of the first section of *Clavics* (BH 791; CL 11).[3] Similar too is the shared emphasis on 'sicknesses' and 'Affliction', which Hill renders as '[Distress]' and alludes to in the phrase, 'intensive care'. In both cases, such suffering can be converted into what Herbert calls a 'victory', by pious or joyful acceptance; by 'combin[ing]' with the 'Lord', Herbert's 'Affliction shall advance the flight in [him]'. In other words, both suggest that descending to the depths of despair and misery, as is proper for a fallen race, offers the chance to transcend pain and sin. Hill's 'intensive care'

---

[2] *The Ground Aslant: An Anthology of Radical Landscape Poetry*, ed. Harriet Tarlo (Exeter: Shearsman Books, 2011), Further references are given in the text as GA.

[3] George Herbert, *The Complete English Poems*, ed. John Tobin (London: Penguin, 1991), p. 38.

transforms its common meaning as hospital department or state of critical ill-health in his line, 'Intensive prayer ís intensive care'. The stress on the mediating 'is' denotes an exact equivalence between the two parts; the intensity of the prayer is both violent enough to warrant a stint in intensive care and is itself a form of self-care, the ultimate healing. Yet Hill also hints at a divergence from Herbert, and this 'Augustinian' 'theology of healing' (CCW 310). Following the line, 'Intensive prayer ís intensive care', comes, 'Herbert says. I take it …'. The full stop between what Herbert reportedly 'says' and what Hill 'takes' to be the case sets up a possible opposition. Where Hill writes, 'I take it stress marks / Convey less care than flair', he suggests that the 'attire' of visual patterning 'Be mere affect'. As such the devotional pattern poem is cast less as a prayer and more as a demonstration of compositional virtuosity. It is nothing more than 'garb and phrase' (CCW 356). Hill's poem is a warning, or self-admonishment, that 'if' this is the sum of '[his] clavic books', they should be 'Dump[ed]' in 'the mire', and he should 'strut [him]self off a cliff'. Only if his poems prove more substantially worthy or meaningful, only if they provide spiritual wings as well as a mere picture of wings will they save him from the fall.

Yet ultimately this insistence on the morality or social responsibility incumbent on poets is a major point of convergence with traditional devotional modes. Where Hill goes further than Herbert is in lines such as, 'Shewing the works / As here' (BH 791; CL 11), which participate in a self-reflexivity only implicit in 'Easter-Wings' (in which, for example, the lines 'Most poor' and 'Most thin' occur as the narrowest points). For Hill, the presentation of the work involves not only a focus on how style and content reflect each other, but explicit reference to this feature within the poems themselves. Readers are forcefully reminded that these are visual objects, occurring in a 'here'. That they may be dumped in a mire means that they exist as solid things; that anyone might wish to dispose of them in such a way implies Hill's recognition of their confrontational tone. In declaring their 'here'-ness, the poems point to the moment at which they are encountered by the reader. Just as in Frances Presley's 'April', from *Myne* (GA 73-74) and Wendy Mulford's 'Salthouse, 1986' (GA 56), any given historical moment or geographical situation brings with it a weight of association. The more explicit the moment given – 'In a rusty shed' in Salthouse, in 1986 – the more the poem 'touch[es] through centuries'. Similarly, in 'April' Presley walks 'from Greenaleigh to Porlock Bay' on 'Friday. Good', 'black shards / scattered on the field' triggering thoughts of the 'semtex' manufactured in the Czech Republic, and the degradation of 'Site[s] of Special Scientific Interest' into 'grey grass' and 'bleached trees'.

Of course, Hill's version of 'Easter-Wings' is only one half of the form of *Clavics*. The wing-shaped portion is always preceded by a key-shaped one, adapted from the forms of various works by Herbert and Vaughan. *Clavics* 1 bears some formal and several thematic similarities with Vaughan's 'The Evening-Watch: A Dialogue', in which the body and soul take turns as the dominant aspect of human existence according to the cycle of day and night, wakefulness and sleep. [4] This circularity or oscillation is echoed in Hill's line, 'Fluctuations of the materia' – materia suggesting both matter and a more ethereal metaphysical substance. And indeed fluctuation between long and short line length is what generates the image of a key in *Clavics*. Hill's 'low threshold of contemplation' is like the 'sleepy' interim state of Vaughan's body and soul, in which the 'two stray' together. The 'Protean ditch' and 'swarming mass' of *Clavics* 1 resonates with Vaughan's 'Unnumber'd' bodies lying in the 'dust', both evoking a state of Heraclitean flux. All matter will inevitably 'conform / To [this] immense / Lore' (BH 791; CL 11). In the sense of Vaughan's 'take this with thee. The last gasp of time / Is thy first breath', Hill has before him the knowledge that all will die, will '[Attach] to the swarm- / ing mass'. To have this idea of the relationship between life and death constantly in mind is again a question of morality and Christian eschatology: Hill is 'still pursuing ethics perhaps' (BH 791; CL 11).

Nevertheless, this 'perhaps' carries with it a certain irony, flippantly undercutting the pursuit of ethics by treating it as something optional. Once again Hill creates a certain ironic distance in relation to the spiritual, Christian morality of his models. As we read *Clavics*, the tension between Hill, Herbert and Vaughan variously strains and relaxes, putting the identification of Hill's morality and aesthetics as traditionally Anglican and conservative in question. Hill has written, in his essay, 'A Postscript on Modernist Poetics', that '[w]hat I find myself opposing is the whole confrontation – commitment versus caprice' (CCW 569). We are unable to disentangle the two in Hill's work, for he is both committed to and sceptical about the ethical responsibility, and indeed power of poetry.

---

[4] Henry Vaughan, 'The Evening-Watch: A Dialogue', in *Henry Vaughan*, ed. Louis L. Martz (Oxford: Oxford University Press, 1995), p. 34.

In his essay, 'Keeping to the Middle Way', Hill numbers John Donne among the 'memorialists' of the post-Reformation period (CCW 298). Perhaps as a gesture of 'grateful indebtedness', *Clavics* 'revive[s]' the 'spirit of Donne' (BH 802; CL 32), along with William Lawes, to whom the daybook is dedicated, Ben Jonson, Thomas Carew, Robert Herrick and others, as well as Herbert and Vaughan. He recycles and adds to what he claims such artists already recognized as the 'resonances' of an 'accumulating memory' in English language and history (CCW 298). Referring to Hill's drawing from sixteenth-century Spanish music, but equally applicable in this case, Andrew Roberts has observed that Hill's 'procedure of composing through the works of others is based on the practices of those earlier artists'.[5] English places whose connotations have changed since the sixteenth and seventeenth centuries, but might still through poetic endeavour be remembered, are named throughout *Clavics*, with the effect that the sequence seems layered in evocation of the sedimentation of history. For instance, the poems range from Wotton, Surrey (BH 814; CL 39), to 'Catholic Lancashire' (BH 819; CL 38), to Rowton Heath (BH 818; CL 36), in Cheshire, where William Lawes was shot by a Parliamentarian in 1645. This is perhaps partly in celebration of English history, of a time when England began to define itself as a democracy. *Clavics* 8 (10 in CL) (BH 798; CL 20) references Carew's influential *Coelum Britannicum*, which appropriated the image of Heaven as peculiar to Britain. Yet it is also in remembrance that this 'crosspatched nation' (crosspatched in its geological heterogeneity, local colour, topography and so on, as well as in the sense of being angry or disgruntled) has a violent history in which Lawes

> ups with his troop to Chester
> Unmerrily
> To register,
> To be felled, *slain*,
> Etcetera;
> In what corpse-rift unknown
> (BH 805; CL23)

Hill goes on in 'Keeping to the Middle Way', to suggest that roughly a hundred years previous to Lawes's death, 'the small grammatical shift

---

[5] Andrew Michael Roberts, *Geoffrey Hill* (Tavistock, Devon: Northcote, 2004), p. 42.

from the Church in England to the Church of England' resulted in 'the apparently slight difference of grammatical opinion which, between 1555 and 1558, had sent members of the reforming party (or schismatic faction) to their excruciating deaths' (CCW 302). The reference to Pendle in *Clavics* 29 (28 in CL) (BH 819; CL 38) intimates similar atrocities.[6] Here, England's history is remembered not because forgetting means the loss of 'some mystical private possession', but because it would mean 'losing some vital dimension of intelligence'.[7] Reusing the poetic forms of this time is, for Hill, a way of bodying forth this intelligence for contemporary readers at the same time as 'retain[ing] a firm hold on the reality of suffering and the priority of the ethical'.[8]

By composing music for the court of Charles I, 'Lawes makes his way in grinding the textures / Of harmony' (BH 805; CL 23). Unsettled in a 'corpse-rift unknown', it is his bones that now grind underneath hundreds of years of sedimented earth, or perhaps grind in earth churned by modern building machinery. Although alluding to a different period of history, Mark Goodwin's 'Borrowdale Details', which appears in *The Ground Aslant*, similarly identifies the 'calcium atoms' of buried 'teeth' as the 'jumbl[ing]' physical matter constituting the English landscape (GA 148). Whilst different in tone – Goodwin's speaker feels unified, at the atomic level, with the romantic landscape, whereas Hill calls attention to the murdered bodies that fertilize English soil – both share a sense that culture is literally embedded in the land, that all matter, including poetry, contributes to the physical and cultural existence of humanity; in 'Borrowdale Details', the local 'Herdwick meat' is 'digest[ed]', just as romantic poetry is internalized in the production of the Lake District's landscape. Hill applies this idea to the English landscape more widely, suggesting that our relationship with particular places is essentially historical, and exploring 'the *psychological* experience of a society and of an ancient and troubled nation' by poetically digging up its earth.[9] In the same way that 'Borrowdale's infinite / tiny details' penetrate Goodwin's 'soul', the cultural landscape reaches into Hill's 'inner domain', as he phrases it in the lines from *Péguy*, quoted earlier.

---

[6] In reference to the execution of the Pendle witches in 1612

[7] Hill, 'Under Judgment', interview with Blake Morrison, *New Statesman*, 8 Feb 1980, pp. 212-14 (p. 213).

[8] Roberts, *Geoffrey Hill*, p. 61.

[9] Hill, 'Under Judgement', p. 213, emphasis in original.

Goodwin

>     peer[s]   at a twig's knuckles   a needle's green edge   a tiny globe

and 'gasps' at

>     a vastness of miniscule   high   resolution beauty   immense
>     (GA 148)

Likewise, for Hill, the visual experience of the landscape is a 'revelation' of 'both / singular crystal and the remotest things' (*Péguy* 5). Goodwin and Hill share a sense of the 'vastness of miniscule' ('Borrowdale Details'), of the contrasting scales of the British landscape, and the almost imperceptible interactions between inner and outer territories; of the relationship between poetry's revelatory potential and the perceptual experience of the minutiae of the poetic text.

Hill is, though, unable to escape the 'woes' of 'Britannia' (BH 808; CL 27), or the anxiety that 'England's toxic' (BH 801). Just as Lawes was 'ruined in Cheshire', Hill claims, 'I too strut thus amid ruins' (BH 825). These are evidently the ruins of the 'Democracy', which has proved itself a 'Potemkin fiction', and a 'Phantom-chasing Natocracy' (BH 813; CL 21). In such an 'Anarchical Plutocracy' (BH 813; CL 21), Hill warns,

>     Things narrow thus
>        C h a o s
>     (BH 819; CL 38)

Hill positions modernity as a second antediluvian period of corruption. The '*Chester Play of the Deluge*' is to be 'played again'; its music is 'Ripe now to play' (BH 826). 'Dai Jones'' 'pretty' 'woodcuts' of 'Before the Flood' '[Strike]' contemporary audiences with renewed force (BH 826). Indeed, not only modernity, but all human history is implicated in this failure, for Hill writes, 'When have we ever not been in a mess? / I inquire of the winds and waters' (BH 826).

The innovation made by many of Tarlo's radical landscape poets is precisely this intertwining of human with natural crisis. The chaos of democracy, the narrowing of the political class to represent and include only the wealthiest, is identified as part of the same problem as environmental destruction. But once again Hill ostensibly severs alliance with other poetic modes in his pessimistic statement,

> I think we are past Epiphany now.
> Earth billows on, its everlasting
>     Shadow in tow
> And we with it, fake shadows onward casting.
> (BH 794; CL 15)

It is as if he is arguing that no further poetic endeavour will save an earth that 'billows on' regardless; that a poetic aimed at saving the earth will merely cast 'fake shadows' of impotent earnestness. *Clavics* as a whole is, however, expressive of a more genuine belief in the communicative power of poetry. Hill predicts the apathetic or dismissive response so often elicited by doom-laden environmental discourse: 'Trust you to be a comic poet manqué / … Taking the piss' (BH 794; CL 15). *Clavics* might enumerate the fatalistic fears of a self-'Confess[ed]' 'Melanchol[ic]' (BH 794; CL 15), but ultimately, 'Those so barely moved by such a recital' are 'not to [be] pit[ied]' (BH 832; CL 42).

These are in a sense poems of 'countdown' (BH 792), to a crisis point in the future of both the individual and the earth. Just as 'flesh dies' (BH 816; CL 34), subject inevitably to 'maggotry' (BH 814), so the 'World [is] in its rot' (BH 817; CL 37). And where 'The Vaughan brothers, Lawes presumably' had the 'good habit' of 'Faith', Hill finds himself unable to reconcile his 'world's regret' (BH 817; CL 37). The circularity of life and death which ultimately reassures in Vaughan's 'Evening-Watch' is rejected in *Clavics*. This is less a prophecy of apocalypse than an acknowledgement of 'the problems of a late twentieth-century [or early twenty-first] prophetic voice', which cannot help but have absorbed the postmodern scepticism as to historical teleology.[10] On this point, Hill has said that 'it is not entirely unreasonable to take a fairly gloomy view of both short-term and long-term prospects'.[11] A poetic which creates such 'dis-ease' (BH 826) is doubly disturbing when presented in the ordered patterns of those poets whose faith was so secure. The iconography of the wings and the key promise a way into spiritual ascendency, promise to provide a methodology for faith,

---

[10] Roberts, *Geoffrey Hill*, p. 66

[11] 'Under Judgment', p. 213.

but let us down. Yet this is even more reason for Hill to bring back these forms: in the absence of grand historical narratives, his poems suggest, we must work to create the culture we need. History will not automatically be remembered; Hill therefore attempts to do some of the work of remembering himself.

Just as Hill reaches centuries into the past for his inspiration, so he reaches into the future. What he writes now might be for future readers that 'vital intelligence' required in the remembrance of history. Poetry can extend a 'memorial theme' into the 'countdown' (BH 792). Here the visual form of the work becomes particularly important. Visual patterning has the effect of 'Shewing the works / As here' (BH 791; CL 11), of pointing to the material existence of the poems themselves. This is crucially different from 'The drummer's deathly trill' (BH 792) – deathly because it dies as soon as it ceases to be played. 'Marking time is not beating time' (BH 792): the graphic properties of writing, of marks on a page, are materially different from the properties of music or sound, in that they last significantly longer.[12] In this, two key similarities with the contemporary innovative landscape poetry in *The Ground Aslant* are united. First, the idea that innovations away from regular verse forms have a particular ability to stress poetry's objecthood; secondly the sense that this is inherently an act of epitaphic inscription. Basing his discussion on Geoffrey Hartman's reading of Wordsworth, Jonathan Bate details how the epitaph, in pointing to or designating a particular place as meaningful in some way, comes to be an 'independent nature poem'.[13] He claims that 'the history of the poetic genre of "inscription", … exemplifies the self-consciously learned and literary relationship with place'.[14] Epitaph therefore always has a relationship with the earth, and with its own poetic existence as 'a kind of self-performing text'.[15]

In Hill's most formally experimental and thus graphically present poems there is a dual emphasis on the physical matter of earth and the human instinct to memorialize which supports the comparison with radical landscape poetics. In the thirtieth and final poem of *Mercian Hymns* (BH 112; MH XXX), which is composed of four lines of sparse,

---

[12] In CL the line reads 'Marking time is not bearing time' (CL 13)

[13] Jonathan Bate, *Romantic Ecology: Wordsworth and the Environmental Tradition* (London: Routledge, 1991), p. 90.

[14] Bate, pp. 89–90.

[15] Bate, p. 90.

irregular, 'rhythmical prose' (as Hill has described them in an interview with John Haffenden), a feeling of loss – 'he vanished / he left behind coins' – is heightened by the 'traces of red mud' which attest to the earlier presence of the one lost.[16] The lines which break suddenly (and are experienced as a kind of prose enjambment) evoke the feeling of grief for a loved-one in its common colloquial expression as the 'loss of a limb'. The memorial points specifically to the 'red' mud, which in addition to its biblical allusion to the name Adam, is particular to the historic Mercian region, tying earth and death together in the gesture of self-presentation. In 'Sorrel', from *Canaan* (BH 208; C 20), we begin to see the key form emerge, the extreme indentation of certain lines causing a rupture in pace and marking emphasis. In this instance, the disrupted form mirrors the 'ill-weathering stone', whose 'carved shapes crumble'. The uncredited quote with which Hill begins the poem informs us that sorrel is 'Very common and widely distributed … It is called Sorrow … in some parts of Worcestershire'; botanical and geographical specificity ameliorates a 'Memory worsening'. The poem performs both the signposting (the local sorrel) and the sorrow of the epitaph. 'A Prayer to the Sun,' from a short sequence called, 'Four Poems Regarding the Endurance of Poets', which appears in *King Log* (BH 56; KL 36), memorializes twentieth-century Spanish poet, Miguel Hernández. In one of Hernández's best-known works, an elegy for Ramón Sijé, he writes:

> I want to be the grieving gardener
> of the earth you fill and fertilize,
>     my dearest friend, so soon.[17]

Hill's poem to Hernández recycles again the matter that fertilized the elder poet's imagination. This chain of written memorials is what ensures the endurance of poets. Hill's contribution to this chain is itself a sequence of miniature shape poems, each rather like Herbert's 'The Altar' which, however, in this context, resemble crosses or headstones:[18]

---

[16] Interview with John Haffenden, Quarto, 15 (March 1981), pp. 19-22, reprinted in *Viewpoints: Poets in Conversation with John Haffenden* (London: Faber and Faber, 1981), pp. 76-99 (p. 93).

[17] Miguel Hernández, 'Elegy', in *I Have Lots of Heart: Selected Poems*, trans. by Don Share (Newcastle upon Tyne: Bloodaxe, 1997), pp. 46-49 (lines 1-3).

[18] Herbert, p. 23.

>           i
> Darkness
> above all things
>     the sun
>      makes
>       rise
>
>
>           ii
>        Vultures
>  salute their meat
>        at noon
>       (Hell is
>        Silent)
>
>
>           iii
>        Blind Sun
>      our ravager
>        bless us
>         so that
>        we sleep

In the particular concern for the remembrance of poets, we might detect a certain 'Narciss[ism]', certain 'Flexures of styles' and a demonstration of Hill's own 'Extravagant command' of 'frills' (BH 792; CL 13). That these 'frills', or formal experiments, are 'Purposeful', however, implies that 'What comes of the upthrust and downthrust pen' is meaningful in itself (BH 792; CL 13). In Hill's poetry, shape creates meaning. Eye-tracking experiments carried out as part of the UK Arts and Humanities Research Council projects, 'The Effects of Form and Technique on Cognition, Aesthetic Response and Evaluation in Reading Poetry' (2002-3), and 'Poetry Beyond Text: Vision, Text and Cognition' (2009-11), used an example of Hill's work to suggest that readers encounter formally innovative poetry differently from 'linear' poetry, and that 'use of space may serve to articulate syntactical structures' and to 'promote richer interpretation by encouraging cross-linear semantic connections'.[19] In 'Space and Pattern in Linear and Postlinear Poetry', Roberts et al. discuss

---

[19] Andrew Michael Roberts, Jane Stabler, Martin H. Fischer and Lisa Otty, 'Space and Pattern in Linear and Postlinear Poetry', *European Journal of English Studies*, 17.2, 2013, pp. 23-40 (p. 23).

various reader responses to Hill's, 'To the Nieuport Scout', from *Canaan*, which they argue show 'evidence of a shift from reading to "scanning", where scanning can be defined as the relative predominance of vertical and/or diagonal eye movements, compared to the standard horizontal saccades'.[20] Hill's evident fascination with musical notation in *Clavics* section 2 (section 3 in CL) would seem to stem from this understanding of pattern as a stimulus for more complex eye movements. In order to create meaning from musical notation, a musician must visually follow the pattern made on the staves. The position of each note has a meaning, in that it refers to a particular pitch. Yet, as I observed earlier, in relation to the 'drummer's deathly trill' (BH 792), music has a limited temporal capacity; Hill also seems to suggest that its visual dimension as notation is 'constrained by [its] own strings', or by the notes that a particular instrument is able to play (BH 792; CL 13). Poetry would appear to offer greater potential for formal experimentation because it retains the possibility of meaning even where its grammatical, syntactical and verse structures are broken. This urges an understanding of Hill's poetry, not only as memorial – as reviving old forms – but as an innovation in the practice of writing.

It is apt therefore that *Clavics* should make use of the work of Stéphane Mallarmé, in order to show how visual patterning in poetry has been reinvigorated several times on its journey into present usage, and that it continues to yield possibilities for experimentation. The sixth section (BH 796; CL 16) references '*Pli selon pli*', a 1962 orchestral composition by Pierre Boulez, which was based on Mallarmé's poetry. The title of the work translates as 'fold by fold', and points to the importance of the linear unfolding of a sequence such as *Clavics*, where meaning accumulates and the process of reading continually lends new significance to what has been previously read. In other words, the fold by fold action of materially progressing through the poems is an important part of the imaginative and intellectual process of reading. This too can work across texts, with material currently being read resonating with previously encountered works. Hill puts this potential to extensive use, as critics and readers of his work have often noticed. Of Mallarmé he acknowledges, 'Together we shall enrich the cortège' (BH 796; CL 16); the ongoing process of reading is invested with meanings derived from affinities between their respective work. That the word 'cortège' is selected here inflects the 'countdown' of the second section with overtones of

---

[20] Roberts et al, p. 31.

a funeral procession, reinforcing not only the epitaphic significance of *Clavics*, but also the sense of the uncontrollable march of time.

In contrast with this is an allusion to the wedding ceremony, in which Hill's inclination towards order rears its head. He personifies, and genders, his own work as 'wife to Mallarmé' (BH 796; CL 16). The unification of the feminine and masculine personae produces 'Mathematicall Roses'. Themselves symbols of natural order and Euclidean symmetry, the two syntactic elements of these conceptual flowers unite what might be considered the masculine and the feminine: the geometric and the organic; the scientific and the artistic or beautiful. In spite of his recognition of 'epistemological scepticism', and his aversion to simplification, Hill's 'regard / For decorum' (BH 796; CL 16) at times proves irresistible. [21]

As if in recognition of this tendency, in the 'wing' section of *Clavics* 6, Hill undercuts the notion that the mathematical rose 'Could be an emblem of some consequence' with an outburst which seems as much self-directed as it is intended as an insult: 'you dunce'. His question to himself is, 'How to derive / Virtue from ponce' (BH 796; CL 16); is order virtuous, can authority be anything other than 'ponce'? Perhaps, this poem suggests, virtue lies in the hard work of poetic composition, of offering the idea of order for critical appraisal. The poem is 'the recusant / At [his] fingertips', which through 'ritual' and 'toll' Hill subdues in a gesture which he then offers up for scrutiny. To this end he 'write[s] well / Into [his] scant- / Extended age'. The poet is identified as a kind of labourer – one working both with a material substance and with something more subtle, something approximate to ideas, symbols, or beauty. Perhaps he is a Renaissance alchemist, or more appropriately a physicist or mathematician. Better still, a gardener, coaxing mathematical roses into life, creating beauty out of the compost of language. In extension of this gardening metaphor, Hill admits the difficulties of poetic composition, which are 'Much like the saxifrage / Breaking a wall', unintended meanings infiltrating the work like wildflowers growing through cracks in stone (BH 796; CL 16).

The unintended growth of saxifrage, which is 'smelt[ed] up' by 'limestone subsoil' and not by any human hand, is also remarked by Peter Riley in his poem, 'Vertigo', collected in *The Ground Aslant* (GA 33). Hill shares a keenness of sight with poets of landscape such as Riley. His description of 'the sun's aurora in deep winter / Spider's bramble

---

[21] Roberts, *Geoffrey Hill*, p. 61.

/ Blazing white floss', or his observation that 'The day cuts a chill swath, / Dark hunkers down' (BH 794; CL 15), demonstrate the same attentiveness to the sensuous and perceptual effects of light, atmosphere, even temperature, as poets who are understood to have made landscape their primary focus. That the line, 'A watery sun squats on the mud flats', appears as the last line of the 'key' portion of *Clavics* 36 (BH 826) is not arbitrary but signals Hill's visual attunement to his material. The horizontal line of text (which comes at the end of the section and is therefore longer than the preceding lines) itself represents the flat horizon on which the sun squats. The treatment of this line is subtle enough that it is easily overlooked; it does not announce its presence as it might. Rather it demonstrates the fact that the visual qualities of language exert a certain amount of force over their arrangement, so that the presentation of the line seems unconscious. Hill allows language to control his composition at the same time as he controls it.

The grouping of certain poets as radical, or as poets of landscape is perhaps a misnomer. Riley's poem addresses 'political hatred' and 'human wrong' too ('Vertigo', GA 33). What Hill shares with such writers is a feeling that 'landscape', as an assemblage of human and non-human processes and meanings, is indivisible from and indispensible to any discussion of poetry or culture more widely. The exploration of the ethico-politics of representing the landscape is therefore prioritized in radical landscape poetics as it is in *Clavics*. Riley's 'statement' is situated in the text of the poem in-between 'small black ants on my arm butterflies in pairs in the grass', and 'black / flies gentle breeze' (GA 33), just as all political, cultural and artistic endeavour takes place in the context of a material world. In Riley's poem, an over-inflated sense of the importance of the human results in a feeling of mismatched scale, or vertigo. Scientific advancement offers a view of the earth, perhaps from space, but leaves us 'clinging' to it: 'This is the earth, and this is us here very close to it, / watching the great valley below, everything clinging to the ground' (GA 33). Just as he might be precipitated 'off a cliff' while the sun carries on its 'hefty climb', Hill also evokes the precariousness of the human situation in distortions of scale and the vertiginous contrast of height and depth in both the language of *Clavics* and in the narrowing and widening of the wing sections:

> The sun
> In hefty climb
> Has but barely begun
> To spade its memorial theme.
> No last retort from zero to countdown.
> (BH 792)[22]

In particular, both Riley and Hill urge consideration of the impermanence of 'regimes and rebellions' ('Vertigo', GA 33). In their indictment of regimes that allowed 'earth' to be 'hidden under the fuel', to be 'endlessly concealed' by the 'black ink' of 'oil' ('Vertigo', GA 33), or which persecuted innocent women for witchcraft (BH 819; CL 38), there is however an optimism in the possibility that 'people survive' ('Vertigo', GA 33). Political oppression of any kind is transient; 'people' as a collective of the individuals who make up humanity, outlive regimes in the act of memorialization. 'People', including poets, are here opposed to those regimes which attempt to distance them from their world, which destabilize their sense of attachment to the 'small black ants' through the vertiginous domination of nature. Those people have an opportunity to empower themselves against such regimes by submitting them to rigorous analysis and critique. What Hill is so taken by in Herbert's work, he explains in 'The Weight of the Word', is his acute 'self-scrutiny' (CCW 357). Likewise, Riley claims that he is 'Seeking in this thronging / vocabulary to think a clear thought about human wrong', which could equally be a statement of Hill's intent.

It is vital to Hill's work that this 'thronging vocabulary' also be subject to examination in so far as human language is always as much an instrument of political power as it can be a tool for its destabil-ization. In 'Vertigo', language is subsumed by 'the great void of images, / the thought pit' (GA, 33). It is the poet's task to spot and to make use of the 'fires glowing in it', or in other words to imbue images which are themselves 'void' with new power. Similarly, Hill's work is to 'twitch' 'Creative fire' out of 'the swarm- / ing mass, the dense / Fluctuations of the materia' (BH 791; CL 11). The difficulties posed by Hill's use of language can in this way be read as the rehabilitation or reinvigoration of poetic language through defamiliarizing techniques such as juxtaposition and syntactical ambiguity. Such 'intensive care' over the work of poetry equates to

---

[22] In CL the equivalent lines read: 'No sun / no dying climb / Statute's oxymoron / Impassionate lost thistle-rhomb / No intercept from zero friskly drawn' (CL 13)

'self-heal' in Riley's poem. Self-heal being also a herb used medicinally, Riley links plant growth with the healing of human culture. Like the saxifrage that breaks through Hill's wall, the 'limestone subsoil' succeeds in 'smelt[ing] up' self-heal even where the earth is 'written in black ink, or 'hidden under the fuel' ('Vertigo', GA 33). *Clavics* and 'Vertigo' share a prophetic foreboding and a pessimism that are occasionally relieved by hope. But like his reluctance to come down clearly on the side of either commitment or caprice, Hill's moments of optimism are always qualified so that we teeter between a sense of disaster and salvation. For instance, in the last poem of *Clavics*, any clear indication that he is 'Wishing to end well?' is complicated by the question mark that accompanies the phrase (BH 832; CL 42).

The resolution of this problem is perhaps best looked for in the structure rather than the syntax of *Clavics*. 'Fulfill[ment]' is found 'in a thrusting / Forward of rhyme / Upon a theme' (BH 832; CL 42), in homage to the 'sense of theological discovery that Herbert's poem awakens line by line' ('The Weight of the Word', CCW 358). The enjambment of this line in the last of the *Clavics* poems thrusts forward the word 'Forward', reinforcing the importance of process and progress that was set up by the reference to Boulez's *Pli selon pli*. The particular significance of *Clavics* is therefore realised in the materiality of the poems as shapes and as a sequence. Furthermore, *Clavics* 33 (section 2 in CL) urges us to put 'Views before vows' (BH 823; CL 12) . Here, 'views' are both opinions, 'best' expressed in 'dialogue', and also perceptions, or things viewed. Both senses of the word are to be prioritized above 'vows', or empty, merely symbolic statements symptomatic of what Hill calls 'idle enthusiasm' in 'The Weight of the Word' (CCW 355). In making a poetic statement, Hill implies, something real must materialize, something which can be viewed – or perceived, and analysed through dialogue. This, according to Hill, in 'The Weight of the Word', marks 'the ethical line between … enthusiasm and meditative attention' (CCW 359), which requires the exercise of a conscious and critical perceptive faculty, in all encounters with the world and its linguistic representation.

In *Clavics* Hill emulates the work of sixteenth- and seventeenth-century artists who were 'memorialists as well as innovators' (CCW 298). The fact that the historical moments of his models are understood and represented in their full violence belies the notion that Hill is merely a nostalgic reactionary, as Tom Paulin designated him in 'The

Case for Geoffrey Hill'.[23] That he values ethics and believes in a poet's responsibility toward his or her readers and indeed material, seems to have been conflated with a reactionary nostalgia, but his use of historical modes is more complex and his reasons for employing them clear. Visually pleasant and harmonious, they undermine their own seeming order with a vertiginous political and teleological scepticism. Crucially, his implication of nature in all this is shared by poets of landscape who have been designated 'radical', and should prompt reconsideration of Hill's work by those who see it as obsessed with the past. Hill clearly engages with contemporary themes through innovative practice; attending to the connections he makes between landscape and the poetic scape will make this explicit. The way he plays with and recycles form implicates the poet in the production of the cultural landscape, at the same time as it memorializes earlier contributions to poetic innovation. His negotiation of visuality points to the existence of a perceptual world in which poetry occurs, and in which 'the poet is a maker' with certain burdens and responsibilities.[24] A tenderness for the British, and particularly the English landscape, evident in his curiously distilled descriptions of natural phenomena, is counterbalanced by a troubled insight into its historical significance. Indeed, that landscape is buried within an expansive poetic discourse, just as the landscape is buried within the psychological experience of a nation. Just as it might be said, for example, that Turner transposed the discursive significance of history painting onto that of landscape, all these elements combine in *Clavics*, to bring the history of the landscape to visual perception.

---

[23] Tom Paulin, 'The Case for Geoffrey Hill', review of *Geoffrey Hill: Essays on his Work*, ed. Peter Robinson, in *London Review of Books*, 7.6, 4 April 1985, pp. 13-14.

[24] 'Under Judgment', p. 212.

CHAPTER SEVEN

# 'Self going spare': Geoffrey Hill and Philosophy

## ALEX PESTELL

'What a wonder's / man the philosopher set on his throne', Geoffrey Hill observes in his poem 'Discourse: For Stanley Rosen': 'What a wonder he is, and how / abysmal' (BH 499; WT 25). Adversarial in tone, the poem appears at the start to be quite sure of its ground; yet as it progresses this confidence undergoes a startling series of modulations. 'I would not have you say ... that there's self / going spare in our unsparing tribute', Hill writes. But there is, in the irony of 'I would not have you say', ample evidence of a self 'going spare' (BH 499; WT 25). Under the cover of a display of gratitude and magnanimity, Hill's 'I would not have you say' betrays an imperious sensibility anxious to censor his counterpart in this discourse. Hill's tone is erratic, by turns disdainful and self-effacing, modest and judgemental. He is an '*Arbeitsknecht*' (perhaps a reference to the *knecht* or serf in Hegel's dialectic), unwilling to 'hurl down advice': unlike the philosopher, he is not tempted by the magisterial heights of judgement; tellingly, though, he takes pride in observing this humility. A self is indeed 'going spare', both in the sense of a surplus, and in the sense of a derangement or disordering of selfhood.

What is it about philosophy that precipitates this anxiety of self-regard? In a 2008 interview, Hill observed that he had been 'completely moved by philosophy only two times in my life: by Simone Weil when I was young; more recently, by F. H. Bradley'.[1] This suggests Hill's involvement with philosophy is a process laden with pathos, in which philosophy's worth is recognised by its ability to 'completely move' its reader. It is represented as an inundation of the self, marking (in the form of Weil and Bradley) two limits of Hill's emotional and intellectual life. But his remark also tacitly hints at another strategy of self-definition: it silently withdraws recognition of the many philosophers that contributed to his critical and poetic thinking over

---

[1] Anne Mounic, 'Le poème, "moulin mystique": Entretien avec Geoffrey Hill', *Temporel* 6 (2008) http://temporel.fr/Le-poeme-moulin-mystique-Entretien [accessed 4 November 2017].

the past few decades. One of the purposes of this chapter is to show that philosophy occupies an important place in Hill's writing, one that is more central than might be indicated by the quote above. As important as Weil and Bradley undoubtedly are to Hill's late work, his poetry and criticism reveal an interest in a wide range of philosophers, including, I will argue, a series of philosophers, notably Coleridge, T.H. Green, and Bradley himself, who owe a debt to German Idealism. So, as well as considering the career-long argument with philosophy of which 'Discourse' is merely a recent example, this chapter will attempt to reconstitute a submerged fascination on Hill's part with the British recipients of German Idealism.

Hill's adversarial attitude is evident even in the epigraphs to his first collection of essays, *The Lords of Limit*. Under a passage from J. L. Austin's *How to Do Things with Words* that advertises 'the doctrine of *the things that can be and go wrong*' in a performative utterance, Hill provocatively adds a question asked by Iris Murdoch in *On 'God' and 'Good'*: 'It is always a significant question to ask about any philosopher: what is he afraid of?' (CCW 1). The implication is that where Austin believes he is acknowledging the existence of a fallibility that can be consciously identified and thereby managed, he is in fact confessing a fear of the very thing that can undermine his system. Juxtaposed in this way, the two epigraphs reinscribe philosophy's identification and management of contingency as ungovernable emotion, subverting its claims to objectivity. This is the ethical and aesthetic problem I will address in this chapter, for Hill's agon with philosophy partly arises from the fact that poetry, for him, is also haunted by the spectre of completion. In the first paragraphs of Hill's essay, 'Poetry as "Menace" and "Atonement"', for example, he simultaneously confesses the 'shapelessness' of verse and its occasional 'technical perfect[ion]', which he calls 'atonement' (CCW 4). Hill, as I will show, is sympathetic with Austin's synoptic appetite, and with the discomfort it produces when faced with the unassimilable. But the thinkers to whom Hill turns to alleviate this discomfort are those whose philosophies make a virtue of incompletion, those for whom thought is precisely that which mistrusts its own finality.

For many critics of Austin's theory, its central problem is the exclusion of the literary: if the speech-act occurs in a poem 'it would not be seriously meant and we shall not be able to say that we seriously performed the act concerned'.² Hill's own attitude to this exclusion, in the essay 'Our Word Is Our Bond', highlights his ambivalence about the constitutive and transformative powers of language: to what degree can we master language, and to what degree are we mastered by it? Hill addresses these questions by means of a confrontation of Austin's philosophy with a range of philosophical systems. Hill admires Austin's 'formidable' empiricism (CCW 147), and the '"poetic" quality' of his writing (CCW 157). But he argues that Austin's inability to account for his own relationship to what he observes hobbles his thought: there is a cruel, almost belligerent quality to the philosopher's writing which betrays a particular social position. His own mannered style reflects the 'ideals and expectations' of Austin's circle of Oxford intellectuals (CCW 156). It is not that Austin should have tried to formulate a mode of address that eschews this diction: rather, the point is that the presuppositions embodied in a writer's language cannot but have an effect upon his manner of apprehending the world. There cannot be, Hill suggests, an 'Archimedean ec-stasis, ... a place of serenely measured hypotheses' (CCW 153). And this has ramifications for Austin's philosophy. How is it possible to define the context of an utterance with the detail required to guarantee an accurate picture of its felicity, when the observer is a constitutive part of that context?

Although Hill agrees that poetry occupies a different world from that in which 'things (and people) regularly "get done"' (CCW 147), and that there is an area proper to poetry beyond which it cannot stray (CCW 152), he argues that it is also able to mobilise a domain of thinking experience unavailable to Austin's theory. Interestingly, Hill turns to Idealist philosophy both to offer a corrective to Austin's synoptic disposition and to delineate the limited domain of poetry's own performative virtues. Where empiricism presumes to be able to take a position outside of that occupied by its objects of scrutiny, Idealism recognises that we remain 'within the process': at the mercy of those objects (whose historicised presence in language exerts a constitutive force over our speech) as much as we try to legislate over them (CCW 162, quoting T. H. Green). I will return to this notion later in this chapter, just noting here that for Hill, poetry, too, makes a virtue of this immersive quality, in its 'troth-plight of denotation and connotation' (CCW 152), its ability so to arrange the relationships

---

² J.L. Austin, *Philosophical Papers*, ed. J.O. Urmson and G.J. Warnock (Oxford: Oxford University Press, 1979), p. 241. Quoted in CCW 147.

between words as to establish a formal arena in which thought can test its boundaries against the histories sedimented in language. Such experiments, Hill asserts, would be viewed as fantastical by Austin. For example, Hill ventures Austin would view certain lines from Hopkins's 'The Wreck of the Deutschland' ('O Deutschland, double a desperate name!', 'Double-naturèd name') as 'self-stultifying' (CCW 160), most likely because those lines invoke both particular objects and general concepts ('Deutschland': the ship and the nation; 'name': Christ the historical figure and Christ the saviour of mankind).[3] But Hill asserts that it is at these points of stultification 'that poetry encounters its own possibilities'. The material of poetry is the no-man's-land created by the clash of the historical and the conceptual. To encounter this 'self-stultifying' moment, Hill says, 'is like encountering a blank in one's own thinking' (CCW 161), but precisely where definition becomes difficult is where poetry is able to realise its diagnostic ambitions.

Metaphors of blindness and blankness occupy a poem written in the same period as 'Our Word Is Our Bond', *The Mystery of the Charity of Charles Péguy*. In this poem blindness carries connotations with the world 'where things (and people) regularly "get done"'. The 'mediocre' statue of Péguy is in 'blank-eyed bronze', 'Jaurès was killed blindly', 'blind Vigil' is 'helpless and obdurate' (BH 144, 146, 150; TM 12, 15, 23). One passage in particular gives shape to the various connotations associated with blankness and blindness in 'Our Word Is Our Bond'. In section 9, the dream-like atmosphere of 'l'ancienne France' achieves particularly intense expression: 'this is the heart / of the mystère' (BH 152; TM 25). Among the furnishings of the natural and domestic landscape, Hill inserts one of the most famous *données* of modernist literature:

'*Je* est un autre', that fatal telegram,

floats past you in the darkness, unreceived.
Connoisseurs of obligation, history
stands, a blank instant, awaiting your reply
(BH 152; TM 25)

Rimbaud's telegram occurs in a 'blank instant' partly because the 'Good governors and captains' (BH 151; TM 25) are deaf to the strain

---

[3] *The Poetical Works of Gerard Manley Hopkins*, ed. Norman H. MacKenzie (Oxford: Clarendon Press, 1990), pp. 124, 128, quoted CCW 160.

articulated in and by poetry's subject. Hill, as we have seen, explicitly sets limits to the arena of effectivity available to poets; he writes that 'poets are not legislators, unless they happen to be so employed, in government or law' (CCW 169) (though he recants on this position in the recent lecture 'Milton as Muse').[4] But it is also a 'blank instant' because Rimbaud's phrase disturbs the synoptic intelligence keen to legislate the contexts within which utterances are to be made. The 'I' is estranged, becomes an object perceived by the speaker, an other. '*Je* est un autre' establishes a bond between the self and its social context, or rather loosens confidence in the self as the claims of the world establish their objectivity: it is, rather literally, a 'self / going spare'.

Hill returns to the metaphor of blindness in a late poem that honours another philosopher, Gillian Rose. 'In Memoriam: Gillian Rose' begins with 'a question … for the form's sake'. 'You do not need to answer the question,' Hill writes: 'Whatever the protocol I should still construe' (BH 588; TCP 35). We can perhaps read in this sentence a recantation to accompany that given in Hill's 'Milton as Muse' lecture. 'I should still construe' can be read as accepting the responsibility for the poet to construct his own private history (addressed in the first five lines) or, alternatively, as an imperative to investigate and interpret the terms (the 'protocol') according to which he can do so. It perhaps ruefully notes, too, that even if Rose could answer back, Hill would ignore her and construct his own version of events. But the phrase admits another reading, providing we take (as with Rimbaud's '*Je* est un autre') the subject pronoun as an object pronoun: '"I" should still construe'. The first person singular should still possess grammatical integrity in its relation to other elements in the sentence. This provides a sense that insists on the ethical imperative to seek a way of maintaining the borders of individual subjectivity in the midst of the prevailing powers of public authority.

But despite this possible modification of his position vis-à-vis the responsibilities of poetry, Hill stays close to the formalism articulated in 'Our Word Is Our Bond'. Poetry, like Rose's philosophy, represents a particular kind of achievement:

> There are achievements
> that carry failure on their back, blindness

---

[4] See 'Milton as Muse', lecture delivered at Christ's College, Cambridge (29 October 2008), available as podcast <https://www.christs.cam.ac.uk/milton-muse> [accessed 2 April 2019].

>     not as in Brueghel, but unfathomably
>     far-seeing.
>     (BH 588; TCP 35)

Hill refers to the blindness depicted in Brueghel's painting *The Blind Leading the Blind* (1568), which shows six blind men stumbling towards a ditch; by contrast, Rose's is a 'far-seeing' blindness, one which works not according to a pre-established system, but, equally, not arbitrarily. These lines amount to a formal, aesthetic reworking of Rose's tentative but incremental definition of aporetic ethics:

> If metaphysics is the *aporia*, the perception of the difficulty of the law, the difficult way, then ethics is the development of it, the *diaporia*, being at a loss yet exploring various routes, different ways towards the good enough justice, which recognises the intrinsic and the contingent limitations in its exercise.[5]

Imagined as a conversation, or 'agon', between Hill and Rose, 'In Memoriam' extends this notion in an aesthetic reformulation of, or dialogue with, Rose's philosophy. This is why Hill's initial question is 'for the form's sake': it establishes a provisional arena within which questions of aesthetic and philosophical judgement can be addressed. If form, syntax, and metre are inconvenient checks on a writer's line of sight, they nevertheless provide the necessary constructive edifice within which thought can begin.

What, then, is objectivity for Hill? Austin's empiricism depends on a notion of the world as data given fully formed for study, ignoring the relationship of the subject to that world. For Hill, though, objectivity has something to do with being 'within the process' (CCW 162, quoting T. H. Green), with blindness, with 'a blank in one's ... thinking' (CCW 161), and with a self going spare. It is a formal matter, something to do with 'technical perfect[ion]'. Immersion and literariness are the coordinates for Hill's sense of objectivity, but they also point to a region beyond the world where things get done. In this respect Hill's thought owes something to the philosopher and mystic Simone Weil (1909-1943), and in particular to *Gravity and Grace*, a posthumously published collocation of Weil's notes and fragments. Something of this

---
[5] Gillian Rose, *Love's Work* (London: Chatto and Windus, 1995), p. 116.

mix of immersion, formal composition, and transcendence is legible in the axioms and speculations contained in that volume, as well as in Weil's *The Need for Roots*.[6]

As a collection of fragments rather than a conceptually unified system, *Gravity and Grace* might aptly be defined as 'blind' in the sense Hill gives the word in his elegy for Gillian Rose. Nevertheless, it displays an unnerving quality of single-minded attention, revealing a thinker gripped by the spectacle of the abject, and yet confident that the abject is the necessary though not sufficient condition for the attainment of grace. Gravity, Weil writes, is the moral force that governs our reactions to the contingent aspects of the world, but grace counterposes a barely distinguishable 'law of ... descending movement'.[7] To 'possess the truth of the world' we must willingly submit ourselves to contingency:

> 'He emptied himself of his divinity.' To empty ourselves of the world. To take the form of a slave. To reduce ourselves to the point we occupy in space and time—that is to say, to nothing.[8]

Our one possession, the 'I', must be voluntarily given up, not reduced to a bare, forked thing by tragic forces. The distinction can be hard to make out. On the one hand, matter is that which blinds us to the possibility of justice. On the other, matter is a means of communication with God: 'The essence of created things is to be intermediaries. ... They are intermediaries leading to God'; 'Every separation is a link'.[9] Divine love, as a result, is in the first instance approached by the immersion of the self in the most compromising and degrading conditions, with the attendant risk that we are so degraded by these conditions that grace becomes inaccessible. This *kenosis*, associated with what Weil calls 'decreation', is central to her philosophy, and while it also became important to Hill's late work, its implications are present throughout his career.[10]

---

[6] Hill cited in particular *The Need for Roots* and *Waiting for God* as touchstones. 'A reading and discussion of my own writings in the context of contemporary British philosophy and poetry', lecture at *Collège de France*, 18 March 2008.

[7] Simone Weil, *Gravity and Grace*, trans. by Emma Crawford and Mario von der Ruhr (London: Routledge, 2002), p. 4.

[8] Weil, *Gravity and Grace*, p. 12.

[9] Weil, *Gravity and Grace*, pp. 145-46.

[10] The concept of *kenosis* in Hill's work is usefully covered in Adrian Grafe, 'Geoffrey

I would like to read a poem that has not before been associated with Weil, despite what appear to me to be clear associations with her notes on divine love. 'Ovid in the Third Reich' is the first poem in Hill's 1968 volume *King Log*:

> I love my work and my children. God
> Is distant, difficult. Things happen.
> Too near the ancient troughs of blood
> Innocence is no earthly weapon.
>
> I have learned one thing: not to look down
> So much upon the damned. They, in their sphere,
> Harmonize strangely with the divine
> Love. I, in mine, celebrate the love-choir.
> (BH 39; KL 13)

Hill's title points towards a richly suggestive situation: the residence of Ovid, the poet of love, in a society that has become a byword for atrocity (Weil explicitly compared the Third Reich to Imperial Rome).[11] Love here is felt only as the rehearsed piety of the salaried family man ('I love my work and my children'), who shrugs his shoulders in the face of atrocities: 'Things happen'. These two terse words ascribe an ominous autonomy to impersonal events, suggesting a society where the self has less agency than matter – to whom do these things happen? A sense of resignation pervades the poem ('God / Is distant, difficult'), accompanied by a comfortable self-congratulation in the speaker's confession of spiritual progress: 'I have learned one thing: not to look down / So much upon the damned'. He is quite confident in his distinction from these souls, a confidence only reinforced by the magnanimous recognition of his earlier error.

Weil's conception of divine love, however, makes the poem's erotic language appear less elegiacally ironic. For Weil, divine love is predicated

---

Hill as Lord of Limit: the Kenosis as a Theological Context of his Poetry and Thought', and Jennifer Kilgore-Caradec, 'Kinesis, Kenosis, and the Weakness of Poetry', both in *Revue LISA* 7.3 (2009).

[11] 'The analogy between the systems of Hitler and of ancient Rome is so striking that one might believe that Hitler alone, after two thousand years, has understood correctly how to copy the Romans'. Weil, *Selected Essays 1934-1943*, trans. by Richard Rees (Eugene: Wipf & Stock, 2015), p. 101.

on the atrocities for which the Third Reich is notorious: 'Relentless necessity, wretchedness, distress, the crushing burden of poverty and of labour which wears us out, cruelty, torture, violent death, constraint, disease—all these constitute divine love'. Why? Because, Weil says, without this 'screen' of brute necessity, our selves would be 'evaporated' by the 'direct radiance of his love', and there would then be no self to surrender for the sake of love: 'It is God who in love withdraws from us so that we can love him'.[12] What Hill dramatises in 'Ovid in the Third Reich' is the risk that, in such a world, love does not accept this gamble, or rather accepts God's withdrawal at face value, and becomes reduced to the mechanical piety articulated in the first line. In this, his text realises the sharp tipping point Weil adumbrates when she writes that while 'There is every degree of distance between the creature [inanimate matter, plants and animals] and God', by contrast 'We are at the point where love is just possible. … God has created a world which is not the best possible, but which contains the whole range of good and evil. We are at the point where it is as bad as possible'.[13]

Bearing in mind Hill's claim that he was 'completely moved' by Weil's philosophy, it is interesting to consider how this affects his understanding of her thought. I would argue that one result of this emotional investment is a projection onto her philosophy of a rather private preoccupation. I am thinking of the well-known reference, in 'Poetry as "Menace" and "Atonement"', to Weil's proposal of

> a system whereby 'anybody, no matter who, discovering an avoidable error in a printed text or radio broadcast, would be entitled to bring an action before [special] courts' empowered to condemn a convicted offender to prison or hard labour. (CCW 10)

Anxious that this proposal might provide 'unassailable evidence that the woman was merely an obsessional neurotic', Hill goes on to suggest that a more acceptable assertion is 'that grammar is a "social and public institution"' (CCW 10, quoting Donald Davie). Critics often cite this passage in the context of Hill's interest in grammatical blunders; in this context Weil's proposal seems to imply that language that does not

---

[12] Weil, *Gravity and Grace*, p. 32.

[13] Weil, *Gravity and Grace*, p. 79.

effectively manage its connotative range (what Hill calls 'atonement') is as culpable as theft or murder. Weil, in fact, says nothing of the sort. In *The Need for Roots*, Weil's comment arises in the context of factual errors and false assertions in textbooks and newspapers (her examples include the philosopher Jacques Maritain and the reactionary journal *Gringoire*).[14] It takes place in the context of a polemic in favour of the eradication of misleading or erroneous information from those texts, particularly newspapers, responsible for delivering knowledge to the public. Not one word is devoted to the syntax or grammar in which this information is couched.

But this is perhaps to labour the point, since Hill's main concern – the enmeshing of the writer in an objective world, and the conflicting accounts of truth that result – is clearly at the heart of Weil's proposal. Indeed, Weil offers a particularly important definition of objectivity for Hill. In an early essay '"The Conscious Mind's Intelligible Structure": A Debate', Hill cites another passage from *The Need for Roots*: 'Simultaneous composition on several planes at once is the law of artistic creation, and wherein, in fact, lies its difficulty'. Weil goes on to assert that

> A poet, in the arrangement of words and the choice of each word, must simultaneously bear in mind matters on at least five or six different planes of composition ... Politics, in their turn, form an art governed by composition on a multiple plane.[15]

'The value of her statement', Hill writes, 'is in her recognition that one does not attain objectivity simply by surrendering to the primary objective world'. Rather than mastering the world through discourse, as Austin would have us do, objectivity is a matter of immersion in planes of composition, overlapping realms of discourse that interact as upon a stage. Weil's theory entails that 'lyric poetry is necessarily dramatic', and Hill deploys a theatrical metaphor to describe 'what takes place "simultaneously" in the arena of the poem'.[16] This conception of poem-as-discursive-drama is visible in much of Hill's work, from *Mercian Hymns* to *Speech! Speech!* and beyond.

---

[14] Simone Weil, *The Need for Roots*, trans. Arthur Wills (London: Routledge, 2002), pp. 36-7.

[15] Quoted in Geoffrey Hill, '"The Conscious Mind's Intelligible Structure": A Debate', *Agenda* 9.4 – 10.1 (1971-72), 14-23 (pp. 14-15).

[16] Hill, '"The Conscious Mind's Intelligible Structure": A Debate', p. 15.

In *The Triumph of Love*, for example, Hill's diction shifts between elegy, lyric observation, indignant responses to critics, and petitions to the Virgin Mary, whom he 'approach[es] ... in modes / of rhetoric to which I have addressed myself / throughout the course of this discourse' (BH 276; TL 66). To address oneself to rhetoric, to speak to speech, is a peculiarly reflexive way to approach divine love, but one perhaps in keeping with the immersive spirit of Weil's philosophy. 'Estrangement itself / is strange', the passage continues, before rattling through a heady list of philosophers (including Wittgenstein, Augustine, Pascal, Coleridge, and Bradwardine) in an anxious, self-estranging parody of synoptic erudition (BH 276-77; TL 66-67). But if the drama here seems to be a cynical one, there are compensations to be found in the changes rung on the words faith, real and being in an earlier passage of the book:

> The hedged sun
> draws into itself for its self-quenching.
> If one is so minded, these modalities
> stoop to re-enter the subterrane of faith—
> faith, that is, in real Being;
> the real being God or, more comprehensively, Christ—
> (BH 249-50; TL 20)

In the knitting together of 'being' as noun and verb, and 'real' as noun and adjective, Hill less cynically brings together grammar and Weil's objectivity, decreating the self ('self-quenching') in an immersive exploration of language's ambiguities. Both here and in the addresses to *vergine bella*, Hill plays with various levels of literacy in a mimesis of our contorted negotiations of the intersecting planes of experience that constitute (as Weil suggests) not just our creative but our political lives. As Hill writes early on in *The Triumph of Love*: 'how could there not be a difficult / confronting of systematics ...?' (BH 240; TL 3).

It's hard to imagine a self less likely to seek its decreation than the self of Samuel Taylor Coleridge (1772-1834): his notorious predilection for monologue is the stuff of legend. Perhaps a kinder way of putting it is that his prolixity is a byproduct of the self-correcting nature of his thought. As Hill writes, 'Coleridge's concern is not so much with thought as with "the mind's self-experience in the act of thinking"' (CCW 6-7). What this means is that, as with Weil, Hill is attracted to the theatrical element of Coleridge's thought, particularly with his notion of the 'drama of reason': the putatively dialogic processes by which we establish objectivity. Coleridge is also important to Hill because of Coleridge's intellectual debt to German Idealism, a tradition that would come to exert a considerable hold over the nineteenth-century British imagination, and over Hill's thereafter. In this section I will examine two key concepts in Coleridge's writings, both of which have a significant place in 'the mind's self-experience in the act of thinking': the imagination, and common sense.

Coleridge's famous pronouncement on the imagination occurs at the end of the first volume of *Biographia Literaria*, just after a long passage composed of texts that bear a controversial similarity to the philosophy of F. W. J. Schelling:

> The IMAGINATION then I consider either as primary, or secondary. The primary IMAGINATION I hold to be the living Power and prime Agent of all human Perception, and as a repetition in the finite mind of the eternal act of creation in the infinite I AM. The secondary I consider as an echo of the former, co-existing with the conscious will, yet still as identical with the primary in the *kind* of its agency, and differing only in *degree*, and in the *mode* of its operation. It dissolves, diffuses, dissipates, in order to re-create; or where this process is rendered impossible, yet still at all events it struggles to idealize and to unify.[17]

By contrast with the fancy, which deals only with 'fixities and definites', the imagination goes beyond the arrangement of what merely exists; it reorders relationships in order to *unify*, to make objective. The imagination is the quintessential faculty of the romantic defence of art's diagnostic and constitutive possibilities.

Hill's essay 'Redeeming the Time' is an extended meditation on these possibilities. It focuses on the notion of diagnosis, and on the creation of a community sense, by taking as its theme the impact of social change upon the nineteenth-century imagination (CCW 88-108).[18] Hill asserts

---

[17] Samuel Taylor Coleridge, *Biographia Literaria, or Biographical Sketches of My Literary Life and Opinions*, ed. James Engell and W. Jackson Bate, Vol I (London: Routledge and Kegan Paul, 1983), p. 175.

[18] 'Redeeming the Time' was originally published in *Agenda* 10.4 – 11.1 (1972-1973),

that the early to mid-nineteenth century saw 'a drastic breaking of tempo and ... an equally severe disturbance of the supposedly normative patterns of speech' (CCW 88). The industrial revolution created social changes that effected 'a diremption between perception and utterance, energy and effect' (CCW 100). However, Hill claims that Wordsworth's 'Ode: Intimations of Immortality' 'transfigures a fractured world': art has the power to recognise and, more significantly, to reconfigure suffering (CCW 92). The precise nature of this transfiguration – how and upon whom it operates – is left undefined. Questions accrue, too, as to what Hill's 'diagnosis' entails: how does it relate to historiographical investigations of crisis? How can an art excluded from society's domain of legislation presume to judge it?

The Coleridgean argument for the imagination's diagnostic and constitutive capacities is echoed when Hill recasts Coleridge's passage on the imagination:

> the significance of Coleridge's distinction between primary and secondary imagination, particularly when read in the light of later pronouncements in *Table Talk*, is that the first represents an ideal democratic birthright, a light that ought to light every person coming into the world. In the event, the majority is deprived of this birthright in exchange for a mess of euphoric trivia and, if half-aware of its loss, is instructed to look for freedom in an isolated and competitive search for possessions and opportunity. Therefore the secondary imagination, the formal creative faculty, must awaken the minds of men to their lost heritage, not of possession but of perception. (CCW 101)

Hill's poetics here are quintessentially Romantic and Kantian – art reacting to its exclusion from society by embracing a critical stance.[19] The imagination is counterweight to a commodified society, whose distractions are 'euphoric' but deadening, replacing perception with an appetite for material possessions.

The 'later pronouncements in *Table Talk*' in the light of which Hill reinterprets Coleridge's distinction in all likelihood include a passage which Hill had quoted earlier in the essay. In it, Coleridge deprecates

---

pp. 87-111.

[19] See Isobel Armstrong, *Victorian Poetry: Poetry, Poetics and Politics* (London and New York: Routledge, 1993), pp. 3-4.

the abstruse metaphysics of the *Biographia*'s Schellingian passages, in favour of 'the common sense':

> All that metaphysical disquisition at the end of the first volume of the Biographia Literaria is unformed and immature; it contains the fragments of the truth, but it is not full, nor thought out. It is wonderful to myself to think, how infinitely more profound my views now are, and yet how much clearer they are. The circle is completing; the idea is coming round to, and to be, the common sense. [20]

With 'common sense', Coleridge invokes a long history of reflection upon the notion of a community sense, the *sensus communis* which features centrally in Kant's *Critique of Judgement*, where it is conceived of not as the means by which the majority of people understand the world, but as a sensuous understanding: 'a subjective principle, which determines only by feeling rather than by concepts'.[21] In the *Biographia*, Coleridge had written that 'it is the two-fold function of philosophy to reconcile reason with common sense, and to elevate common sense into reason'.[22] In theory, then, this reconciliation would produce a mode of cognition through which sensuous apprehension would contribute to the diagnosis and creation of existing and future forms of community.

Difficulties arise, however, when the blueprint of a *sensus communis* remains immured in a mind entranced by its own dexterity. In response to the passage quoted above, Hill writes: '[Coleridge] surely foresaw the obligation to enact the drama of reason within the texture of one's own work, since nothing else would serve. His parentheses are antiphons of vital challenge' (CCW 97). But digression can be pretence or diversion as well as self-criticism, and the passage of Coleridge's which inspires Hill's praise is in fact serenely sure of its position ('It is wonderful to myself to think how infinitely more profound my views now are').[23] Not only that, it erases the debt owed by Coleridge to Schelling, in

---

[20] Coleridge, *Table Talk*, quoted CCW 97.

[21] Immanuel Kant, *Critique of Judgment*, trans. by Werner S. Pluhar (Indianapolis: Hackett, 1987), p. 87.

[22] Coleridge, *Biographia Literaria*, I, p. 270.

[23] For a critique of the 'drama of reason', see Peter Robinson, 'Reading Geoffrey Hill', in *Geoffrey Hill: Essays on his Work*, ed. Peter Robinson (Milton Keynes: Open University Press, 1985), pp. 196-218 (pp. 216-17).

its disavowal of those passages derived from the German's philosophy. Coleridge's complacency is indicative of the risks inherent to the notions he bequeaths to post-Romantic thought. Just as historical particulars can be swallowed in philosophy's egotistical sublime (as Hill suggests in 'Discourse: For Stanley Rosen'), so ethical thought can abruptly stop when faced with euphoric notions of community.

Euphoria's deadening effects resound in Hill's poem 'An Apology For the Revival of Christian Architecture in England', a poem which is both a Coleridgean diagnosis, and an exploration of Coleridge's intellectual legacy (Hill said in interview that in this poem, 'to the best of my ability, I'm offering a diagnosis' of English nostalgia).[24] One of its epigraphs is taken from Coleridge's *Anima Poetae*: 'the spiritual, Platonic old England...' (BH 125; T 22). In 'An Apology', this is a nation that hums with audible detail yet remains shadowy and indistinct:

> Pitched high above the shallows of the sea
> lone bells in gritty belfries do not ring
> but coil a far and inward echoing
> out of the air that thrums. Enduringly,
>
> fuschia-hedges fend between cliff and sky;
> brown stumps of headstones tamp into the ling
> the ruined and the ruinously strong.
> Platonic England grasps its tenantry
> (BH 128; T 28)

Common sense in this poem is something 'far and inward', a thrumming air occupying derelict steeples. England's 'tenantry' are partly the Anglo-Catholic movement who struggled to recreate a community through literature and architecture. Section 7's title, for example, echoes the title of John Henry Newman's novel *Loss and Gain: The Story of a Convert* (1848), a fictionalised account of Newman's conversion to Roman Catholicism. And the sequence's title echoes Augustus Pugin's pamphlet *An Apology for the Revival of Christian Architecture in England*, an argument for a national Anglo-Catholic architecture. The frontispiece of Pugin's tract displays an elevated view of the twenty-four Roman Catholic cathedrals, churches and chapels Pugin had

---

[24] Interview with John Haffenden, 'Geoffrey Hill', in *Viewpoints: Poets in Conversation with John Haffenden* (London: Faber and Faber, 1981), pp. 76-99 (p. 93).

been commissioned to design, huddled shoulder to shoulder against a faintly-sketched pastoral landscape: a New Jerusalem populated only with 'lone bells'.[25]

One candidate for 'Platonic England's tenantry', then, is the group of Victorian artists, writers and other cultural figures who were in receipt of Coleridge's intellectual patrimony, and who employed various strategies in an attempt to create or preserve a particular community sense (the other tenantry, of course, are the 'English labourers' and 'Indian peasants' whose labour contributed to the wealth of imperial England).[26] But the tenants have, for the most part, departed from the scene, leaving behind them echoes, heralded in the first sonnet with a series of end-rhymes in '-sts' ('hosts', 'ghosts', 'pentecosts', 'quests', BH 125; T 22). These rhymes recur throughout the sequence and later collide in 'The Laurel Axe': 'tremulous boudoirs where the crystals kissed / in cabinets of amethyst and frost' (BH 129; T 30). They resonate with echoes from 'distant', 'lost' communities whose projected environments acquire a dubious durability in 'inward' spaces. 'An Apology' deploys these sensuous variations on a theme as a more searching analysis of Coleridgean common sense than 'Redeeming the Time' supplies. Yet it is also a resigned, late-Coleridgean sense of community, in which the imagination becomes consolation rather than critical faculty. In a world in which freedom is predicated upon 'an isolated and competitive search for possessions and opportunity', *sensus communis* becomes, as Hill puts it in *Scenes from Comus*, a 'decaying sense' (BH 423; SC 5).

Although Coleridge played a key role in the importation of German Idealism into nineteenth-century Britain, it was the Victorian philosophers known as the British Idealists or British Hegelians who institutionalised this tradition, albeit briefly, in the universities. An examination of Hill's essays and endnotes reveals a particular interest in their thought, yet despite this their presence in Hill's texts has yet to receive attention.[27] This is unfortunate, since their work resonates productively with his meditation on poetry, philosophy, and objectivity.

---

[25] Augustus Pugin, *An Apology for the Revival of Christian Architecture in England* (London: St Barnabas Press, 1969), frontispiece.

[26] *Viewpoints*, p. 93.

[27] For a study of Hill's relationship to Coleridge, the British Idealists, and Rose, see Alex Pestell, *Geoffrey Hill: The Drama of Reason* (Oxford: Peter Lang, 2016), from which some of this material has been taken.

For the sake of brevity, I will concentrate in this section on the two most prominent philosophers from this group: T. H. Green (1836-1882) and F. H. Bradley (1846-1924). As with Hill's fretful address to Stanley Rosen, his essays on these thinkers are concerned with exploitation, arbitration, uncontrollable emotion, and how these factors impact upon poetry's, and philosophy's, wrestle with truth.

The cliché is an apt one, since Hill's writings are particularly adept at embodying the difficulty of pinning down the truth, and the agonising thrill of being pinned down by it. A true thing is difficult to express, since, as the Idealist philosopher R. L. Nettleship says in a passage quoted approvingly in Hill's essay '"Perplexed Persistence": The Exemplary Failure of T. H. Green',

> the consciousness which we express when we have found the 'right word' is not the same as our consciousness before we found it; so that it is not strictly correct to call the word the expression of what we meant before we found it.
> (CCW 123)

As a rejoinder to Pope's 'What oft was *Thought*, but ne'er so well *Exprest*', Hill's approval of this analysis brings him well within the confines of post-linguistic-turn theory: it transfers the weight of expressive responsibility away from the speaker onto the words themselves, and conceives of them as exerting a constitutive effect upon the subject.[28] In the transition from the empty concept to concrete experience, word order, the distribution of clauses, the usage of pronouns, subjunctives, copulas, and prepositions, have the force of arbitration. The speaking subject is at the mercy of words as much as words are in the possession of the subject.

This emphasis on the contingent, accidental, or otherwise unruly components of the media through which human agents define themselves is recalled in the dictum of Green's with which Hill begins his essay: 'Abstract the many relations from the one thing, and there is nothing' (CCW 109). This, for Hill, embodies Green's value as a thinker: his insistence that definition or objectivity is only conceivable if the thing to be defined is considered in its 'many relations' with the world. Again, the 'Archimedean ec-stasis' rears its head. An important outcome of

---

[28] Alexander Pope, *An Essay on Criticism*, in *The Poems of Alexander Pope, Volume 1: Pastoral Poetry and An Essay on Criticism*, ed. E. Audra and Aubrey Williams (London: Methuen and New Haven: Yale University Press, 1961), p. 273.

this, for Hill, is that philosophy's language becomes inseparable from its concepts. Since thought cannot but be modified by its expression, philosophical ideas cannot be extricated from the language they're expressed in without damage. And if this is true for philosophy, it is even more so for poetry. Hence Hill's indictment of Green's 'failure'. This failure is the misrecognition of poetry's unassimilable force, a complex interaction of sensuous and conceptual elements that resist absorption within other discourses. While Green recognises, in his essay 'Popular Philosophy in its Relation to Life', the contribution Wordsworth makes to ethical thought, and deploys chunks of poetry throughout his texts to supplement their argument, Hill argues that poetry cannot be co-opted 'as simple emotional referents' without distorting both the poetry and the philosophy (CCW 122).[29]

In the same vein, Hill disparages those moments in the writings of the British Idealists when they let their emotions run away with them: Sidgwick, for example, in a moment of euphoria writes 'Oh, how I sympathise with Kant!' (CCW 113). Like Austin, their language strives for technical precision, but cannot escape being infected by the diction of their social environment. On the one hand, Hill cites the testimony of Green's students, who refer to his 'perplexing tangle of phrases' and his 'great difficulty in expressing himself' (CCW 116, 119). On the other, as a public speaker, Green was faced with the demand for rhetorical fluency: 'Green,' Hill writes, 'was writing to be received, and, at the same time, was conducting a running battle with the premises of current receptivity' (CCW 120). Two kinds of objectivity are at stake, then: first, the already existing 'premises of current receptivity', and second, the thought that is struggling to come into existence, to make itself objective, but which in its articulation in language undergoes a transformation according to the pressures exerted by the grammar and syntax of the day.

'[C]urrent receptivity' looms large in much of Hill's recent poetic work, perhaps nowhere more so than in *Speech! Speech!*:

> Erudition. Pain. Light. Imagine it great
> unavoidable work; although: heroic
> verse a non-starter, says PEOPLE.
> (BH 289; SS 1)

---

[29] See T. H. Green, *The Works of Thomas Hill Green*, ed. R. L. Nettleship, 3 vols (London: Longmans, Green & Co, 1906), III, pp. 92-125.

The pained euphoria of these initial lines is dampened by the cynicism of the 'PEOPLE', they whose attitudes, feelings and behaviour are determined by what Green called 'popular philosophy', the reigning conceptuality of the day. In his two essays on Bradley and Eliot, 'Word Value in F. H. Bradley and T. S. Eliot' and 'Eros in F. H. Bradley and T. S. Eliot', Hill considers the way these contrary forces affect Eliot's writing, focusing on the expectations deriving from Eliot's public role, and the syntax of Bradley's philosophy.

Eliot's 'exemplary failure', like Green's, is cynically to succumb too easily to the sway of popular diction, and to the thought embedded therein. For Eliot, Hill writes, the material to which the poet must be faithful is

> no longer primarily language; it is Christian Thought; or the People as he understands them. And how he understands people is still very much how he understood them in the pub scene of *The Waste Land*, only now, instead of saying 'Well, if Albert won't leave you alone, there it is, I said', they say 'that is how I should talk if I could talk poetry'. This is not enhancement but impoverishment, and the language of *Four Quartets* also is language that has suffered impoverishment.
> (CCW 547)

The 'People' is no concrete collection of living human beings, but the expectation of a particular kind of language, an objectivity drawing the writer fatally to its centre of gravity. Where philosophy can be of use to the poet is in the conception of new kinds of objectivity, in the idea of truth as something struggling to come into being, rather than being handed to the writer fully-formed. And, as Hill argues in these two lectures, Bradley's philosophy focuses on this very question.

Bradley postulated, as the sole condition for the intelligibility of existence (that without which we could have no meaningful experience whatsoever), a totality or an Absolute the scope of which renders it unknowable, but of which we are constituent elements. As far as we are aware of this totality, we are able to make judgements, or to form binding experiences with objects. However, these judgements are never completely successful – there always remains something unknown. Again and again in Bradley's philosophy the reader encounters partial truths, objects only incompletely identified. Bradley writes: 'When I think of contraries I first take them as being somehow separated and yet conjoined. The special nature of this "somehow", this known or unknown condition, will vary in different cases'.[30]

As with Weil, it can appear that Hill's having been 'completely moved' by Bradley's philosophy sometimes leads to unwarranted assertions. A case in point is Hill's often repeated assertion that 'the crucial step' in writing a poem 'requires' the Bradleian vision of 'getting within the judgement the condition of the judgement' (CCW 566). Yet Bradley specifically denies the credibility of this notion; he asks: 'But can the conditions of the judgement ever be made complete and comprised within the judgement? In my opinion this is impossible. And hence with every truth there still remains some truth, however little, in its opposite'.[31] Hill's enthusiasm led him to the very conclusion which he refuted in 'Our Word Is Our Bond': that the observer, whether philosopher or poet, is capable of establishing the entirety of the field of vision, including his own position in that field.

But if Hill is guilty of drawing groundless conclusions from Bradley's philosophy, he is more acute on Bradley's influence over Eliot's poetry. Central to this influence is Bradley's *'somehow* of realization' (CCW 534): the necessarily nondeterminative process through which truths might be realised (there are parallels with Rose's *diaporia* here). What might it mean to inhabit this 'somehow' in a poetic text? For Hill, one answer is to be found in Eliot's poem *Marina*, which Hill described as 'the most Bradleian of all Eliot's poems' (CCW 552):

> What seas what shores what grey rocks and what islands
> What water lapping the bow
> And scent of pine and the woodthrush singing through the fog
> What images return
> O my daughter.[32]

Hill begs the question of what exactly constitutes the Bradleian quality of the poem, but some provisional suggestions might be made. *Marina*'s syntax is particularly nondeterminative: the poem's object world is never clearly defined, since the lack of punctuation means that the only

---

[30] F.H. Bradley, *Essays on Truth and Reality* (Oxford: Clarendon Press, 1914), p. 271.

[31] Bradley, p. 253.

[32] T.S. Eliot, 'Marina', in *Collected Poems 1909-1962* (London: Faber and Faber, 1974), pp. 115-16 (p.115).

connective between most of the nouns is the simple question 'what'. No particular sea, rock, or island is pointed to, no deictic 'this' conjures an object in front of the speaker, while the deferral of the verb 'return' to the fourth line effectively presents us with a continuum of objects whose relationship to the observer is only belatedly suggested. The vague presentation of objects, slowly perceived through the fog, whose relationships to one another and to the speaker are attenuated by the repeated 'what' and the deferred 'return', occupies a similar sensuous and cognitive realm to the tentative approach with which Bradley deals with partial or incomplete identifications.

As for Hill, he is perhaps most Bradleian in *Canaan*. Several poems from this collection are characterised by a prosodic hesitancy and diffidence in the face of gradually appearing objects that recalls *Marina*. Here is the first stanza of the poem 'Cycle', dedicated to the translator William Arrowsmith:

> Natural strange beatitudes
>      the leafless tints
> of spring touch red through brimstone
> what do you mean  praise and lament
> it is the willow
>     first then
> larch or alder
> (BH 206; C 38)

Like *Marina*, the prosody of 'Cycle' is notable for its lack of punctuation, and its deployment of indentation (both at the beginning and within lines) as a gesture of semantic hesitation.[33] 'Cycle' also shares with *Marina* a syntax of apprehension which allows objects to emerge into the poem's arena, without clearly defining their relationships. Hill's prosody permits a tentative temporality of emergence: see, for example, how 'spring touch red' first reads as a collection of nouns, before 'touch' is quickly restored as a verb, restoring movement to the passage (the red appearing through the yellow 'brimstone', much as the objects in Eliot's poem appear through the fog). We are told that something 'is' the willow, but what the subject of this predication is is left unspoken; a similar uncertainty refuses to decide between the larch and the alder at the end of the stanza.

---

[33] For an analysis of this practice, see Peter McDonald, *Serious Poetry: Form and Authority from Yeats to Hill* (Oxford: Oxford University Press, 2002), p. 192.

If the slightly impatient 'what do you mean    praise and lament' is less pacific than the repeated 'what's of *Marina*, it still establishes a set of priorities by which the object world, in all its gradations of knowability, takes precedence over the taxonomies of poetic comprehension (in this case *laus et vituperatio*). Poetic completion, or atonement, is predicated at moments like this upon a voluntary abdication of perceptive completion. Euphoria is exchanged for hesitation, and being 'completely moved' becomes a cautious uncertainty.

This chapter has only been able to scratch the surface of Hill's involvement with philosophy. His *Collected Critical Writings*, not to mention scattered poems, contain scores of references to philosophers beyond those mentioned above. In particular, much more might be said about the interconnections between Hill's writings and a broad swath of theological thought, including that of the Cambridge Platonists, Bishop Butler, Dietrich Bonhoeffer, and D. M. MacKinnon. His relationship to politics, both secular and ecclesiastical, is informed by such writers as Jeremy Hooker, Thomas Hobbes, John Locke, and Edmund Burke. And figures like Ralph Waldo Emerson, William James, Henri Bergson, and Ludwig Wittgenstein play important roles at various points in Hill's career. More distant in their concerns, perhaps, Walter Benjamin, Hannah Arendt, and Theodor Adorno nevertheless offer fruitful affinities and discordances with Hill's approach to the ethics of aesthetics.

Closer study of Hill's relationship to these thinkers would go some way to disclosing what Dorothea Krook describes as 'the significant common ground that may be seen to exist between poetry and philosophy when both are viewed as products of the creative imagination' (quoted CCW 124). Hill quotes these words in his essay on Green, and it's perhaps the closest he comes to admitting a sense of shared activity between poetry and philosophy. Characteristically, he follows it up with a gloomy caveat: 'It is in this domain that Green, who had so much to say, has so little to give'. If there is 'common ground' shared by poetry and philosophy, it bears the scars of each discipline's pathos-laden debates, of a host of 'sel[ves] / going spare'. On occasion, Hill begs out of this arena, imagining an 'atonement' in which the conditions of making are at one with the made object. But a restless refusal to be satisfied with factitious transcendence draws him back to trace the scars of the ground of judgement, which are visible even when his poems fantasise their healing:

> still to conceive no otherwise: an
> aphasia of staring wisdom
> the soul's images glassily exposed
>                         fading to silverpoint
> still to be at the last
> ourselves and masters of all
>                                  humility—
> (BH 175; C 5)

CHAPTER EIGHT

# Geoffrey Hill's Difficulties

## Martin Dodsworth

Readers do not find Geoffrey Hill an easy poet, nor does he seek to be easily understood. He attaches importance to difficulty: 'I think art has a right – no, an obligation – to be difficult if it wishes. And since people generally go on from this to talk about elitism versus democracy, I would add that genuinely difficult art is truly democratic'.[1] He has in mind the simplifications of totalitarian art; in this respect his argument has something to be said for it. The notion that 'art' has a 'right' to anything is, however, deeply suspect; and the invocation of 'democracy' seems beside the point. As a system of government, despite its manifest defects, it is preferable to anarchy, oligarchy or dictatorship, but outside the sphere of government democracy is a word with little force. Hill's 'difficulty' is more open to question than his forthrightness suggests. In this essay I first consider the kind of difficulty with which his reader is presented by three characteristic features of the poems – allusiveness, indefiniteness of relation, and ambiguity (there are others). I then go on to look at some of the difficulties which, according to his own account, face this poet in the act of writing, hoping that they may cast light on those faced by his reader. Finally, I attempt an interim judgement on the challenge thrown at the reader by the difficulties of Hill's poetry. What is their justification?

Allusiveness marks Hill's poetry throughout; in his first book, *For the Unfallen,* titles such as 'The Troublesome Reign', 'Solomon's Mines', 'Elegiac Stanzas', or 'Doctor Faustus' trail references to literature which the reader must recognize in order to judge their relevance. The poet has to some extent offered help in the form of notes and commentary at the back of *King Log, Mercian Hymns* and *The Mystery of the Charity of Charles Péguy.* But the help is distinctly limited; the notes to the latter

---

[1] 'The Art of Poetry LXXX', an interview with Geoffrey Hill, *Paris Review,* No. 154, Spring 2000, p. 277. This implicitly revises his account of the matter in an earlier interview ('David Sexton talks to Geoffrey Hill', *Literary Review* (February 1986), 27-29 (p.28)), where he suggests that all that is needed to understand his poems is 'the kind of attention which one ought to be able to take for granted'.

volume, for example, do not gloss 'Chateau de Trie', 'St Cyr', or 'Mars-la-Tour, Sedan', all of which require a greater knowledge of France than the poet's own brief account of Péguy would seem to imply. He gives Rimbaud's letter to Georges Izambard as the context for '*Je* est un autre' (BH 152; TM 29), but the force of this reference depends on the place the letter occupies in modern French culture, of which the reader is given no indication. This suggests that the poet finds it as difficult as his readers to know how allusion is to be defined, or where it ends. There are no notes to volumes later than *The Mystery* and the reason may be that, after that, Hill felt that notes could raise as many problems as they solved – or more. Some clues may be picked up from the acknowledgements to *Canaan* and its successors, but, on the whole, readers since 1983 have had to work things out on their own. The reader of 'Improvisation on "Warum ist uns das Licht gegeben?"' (BH 519; WT 82) needs not only to understand the German, but to know that it refers to Brahms's Op. 74 motet. The texts used in that piece are all relevant, and so is the music. Brahms's repeated cry of 'Warum?' ('Why?', that is, 'Wherefore is light given to him that is in misery?' (Job 3:20)) can be heard as a kind of counterpoint to Hill's poem – but only, of course, if the reader knows and understands the music. Earlier in the volume, the same reader, in order to understand 'From the Annals' (WT 75-77) – the annals perhaps those of Hill's early visits to the cinema with his parents – is required to have some knowledge of Michael Powell's *The Man in Black,* a fairly recondite film.

It will be said that such allusions are no problem in the age of the internet (where, for example, without difficulty, you can hear a performance of the Brahms motet). Some allusions are more difficult than others, however. 'On the Reality of the Symbol' (BH 488-90; WT 9-14) identifies Karl Rahner as a 'Fine theologian', which is a clue, but it is probably his particular views on symbolism and on the Psalms that give the poem meaning. The essay to which the poem appears to refer can be found in the fourth of twenty-one volumes of Rahner's *Theological Investigations,* which for many readers will be inaccessible; Hill's own account of it will not (CCW 567), but is an insufficient base for understanding the poem.

Allusion is an established device in poetry, particularly so since the start of the twentieth century. Eliot, Pound and David Jones use it in a distinctive fashion, which Hill adopts and adapts.[2] Pope's use of Horace or Tennyson's use of Vergil (or Lucretius), depends on the common

---

[2] Christopher Ricks, *Allusion to the Poets,* (Oxford: Oxford University Press, 2002).

stock of knowledge of most educated readers of the day.[3] However much Eliot, Pound and Jones vary in other uses of allusion, they all use the device to *recommend* knowledge of some books rather than others. Pound is the most explicit about the pedagogic aspect of his poetry, Eliot the least. Hill's explicit moralism gives to the reading-list constituted by his allusions a Poundian quality; as Pound urges deeper acquaintance with Confucius, so Hill would have us study Bradwardine and Bonhoeffer. It is with them as with the Brahms motet – a more than superficial knowledge is demanded. The difficulty is not only that this puts the reader to a degree of trouble which may, or may not, be rewarding, but also that the poems do not extend much invitation to the reader to do so. Many, evidently, do not find them as inviting as is required. Hill spoke of a refusal to ingratiate himself with the reader, and demanded 'why does poetry have to address us in simplified terms, when if such simplification were applied to a description of our own inner selves, we would find it demeaning?'[4] An invitation does not have to ingratiate, nor does it necessarily entail simplification. It is as though Hill never considered this matter.

The problems associated with Hill's allusiveness do not end here. By allusion, a poet associates a poem with other works of literature; an initial difficulty is to determine how much of what is alluded to is to be brought from its old context into relation with its new context. Such difficulty is generally exacerbated by the way in which Hill uses the English language; he blurs precise relationships among many of the words that make up his poetry. This is largely, though not exclusively, a matter of syntax. For example, 'Ezekiel's Wheel', a poem (or sequence) in memory of Christopher Okigbo, begins:

> Consider now the valley
> of Hinnom—the trucks
> from the abattoir
> skidding their loads,
> the shameless body parts.

---

[3] Michael Edwards writes of Hill's 'imitations', so linking his work, quite legitimately, with that of past centuries (*Poetry and Possibility*, (London: Macmillan, 1988), p. 169 ff.); I use the term 'allusion' to emphasize the gap in context between Hill and the authors of whom he avails himself.

[4] Blake Morrison, 'Under Judgment', *The New Statesman* 99.2551 (8 February 1980), 212-14 (p.214); 'The Art of Poetry', pp. 276-77.

> Ezekiel's wheel
> shall encompass all:
> each flame-warped spirit
> dancing unshriven,
> the righteous no less
> than the jettisoned
> gobbets in limbo.
> (BH 221; C 56)

The poem / sequence is characteristically allusive, requiring some knowledge of Okigbo as well as of Ezekiel and Hinnom. But even with that knowledge it is difficult to make out what holds these lines together. The Biblical Hinnom is traversed by skidding trucks loaded with body parts; this presumably describes the horrors of civil war in Nigeria as experienced by Okigbo. The status of Hinnom is unclear, since the allusion might as well be Miltonic as Biblical. Moloch 'made his grove / The pleasant valley of Hinnom, Tophet thence / And black Gehenna called, the type of hell'.[5] Referred to its context in one of Hill's favourite authors, the allusion evokes the contrast of 'the pleasant valley' and the butchery of Moloch's sacrifices which took place there, and so stresses the enormity of Nigeria's fall into civil war. The Old Testament references to Hinnom are largely topographical, but those in Jeremiah could be relevant, particularly 19:5-6: 'They have built also the high places of Baal, which I commanded not, nor spake it, neither came it into my mind: Therefore, behold, the days come, saith the LORD, that this place shall no more be called Tophet, nor The valley of the son of Hinnom, but The valley of slaughter.' Allusion to Jeremiah would raise the issue of divine responsibility for the slaughter, without, of course, answering it. It would also raise that of human responsibility for the same thing, with a suggestion of 'abominations' (7:30) which could refer to post-colonial misrule or, more unfortunately, to colonial stereotypes of black Africa. Given the scholarly nature of Hill's poetic imagination, we cannot rule out, either, the possibility that St. Jerome's description of the Valley of Hinnom as a type of the 'everlasting punishments with which sinners were afflicted' is meant to be recalled by the reader, too.[6]

---

[5] *Paradise Lost* (i.403-5), *The Poems of John Milton*, ed. John Carey and Alastair Fowler, (London: Longman 1968), p. 486.

[6] St. Jerome, *Comm. In Matt.*; Migne xxvi 68, quoted by Alastair Fowler, *The Poems of John Milton*, ed. John Carey and Alastair Fowler, (London: Longman 1968), p.486.

This would generalize the specific human responsibility for atrocity in Nigeria as an aspect of original sin.

Is 'the valley / of Hinnom' used metaphorically (to signify a paradise horrifically transformed into a hell) or, under the aegis of Ezekiel, are two historical moments being violently juxtaposed (in which case, how much does it matter that Hinnom is associated with Jeremiah rather than Ezekiel?)? The question comes to a head if we ask ourselves exactly where we are to place 'each flame-warped spirit / dancing unshriven'? Are they at once in Nigeria and in Hinnom? Does the flame come from flame-throwers (in which case the spirits might belong to those in control of the weapons as well as their victims) or does it come from God, as the 'flaming flame' of Ezekiel 20:45-49, or as the product of the 'coals of fire' of Ezekiel 10:2? Perhaps these spirits are those of Yeats's 'Byzantium' (or a parody of them): 'flames begotten of flame, Where blood-begotten spirits come / And all complexities of fury leave, / Dying into a dance'.[7] Are all these possibilities comprised in Hill's meaning, and if so what are we to make of that? The allusion to Yeats would seem to explain how it can be spirits, rather than bodies, that are 'flame-warped'. But Yeats's unorthodox beliefs make it difficult to see the relationship this idea bears to Ezekiel, and especially so if the reader is already uncertain about the connection between the Old Testament prophet and twentieth-century Nigeria. Sentence-shape and grammar fail to contain and direct the superabundance of allusion. This is especially true of the lines that conclude this passage:

> each flame-warped spirit
> dancing unshriven,
> the righteous no less
> than the jettisoned
> gobbets in limbo.

There seems to be an antithesis of the righteous (that is, the self-righteous in command of the putative flame-throwers and other weapons) and the 'jettisoned / gobbets' ('shameless body parts') of their victims. Those who wield the weapons and those who have suffered at their hands are equally 'flame-warped spirits', and equally 'encompassed' by Ezekiel's wheel – that seems to be the gist of it. But can 'gobbets' of flesh be

---

[7] *Yeats's Poems*, ed. A. Norman Jeffares (London and Basingstoke: Macmillan, 1989), p. 364.

spirits at all? And why are the weapon-wielders dancing? Are both the righteous and the gobbets in limbo? And if so, where does limbo stand in relation to Hinnom?

It may be possible to resolve all the doubts and hesitations to which these questions give rise, but there can be no doubt of the difficulty with which they present the reader. The overt challenge is from the tendency of allusion to suggest rather than define. The underlying challenge is from the sentence-structure which allows 'each flame-warped spirit' to emerge from somewhere that is neither the 'fire infolding itself' (Ezekiel 1:4) of the vision of the wheel, nor the flames of the Nigerian slaughterhouse, but uncomfortably between the two.

Hill lays great stress on grammar in his writing; he does not mention syntax so often. In fact he is fond of apposition, a device that diminishes the force of syntax. Gabriel Pearson, in his brilliant account of *King Log*, remarked on this some years ago, finding in 'Funeral Music' a remarkable hospitality to 'appositional figurations which turn upon unsettling discordances, oppositions that they complicate rather than clarify or amplify'.[8] Pearson's observation holds for the entire corpus of Hill's poetry. A couple of examples from *Tenebrae* show what is at stake: in 'Lachrimae Antiquae Novae', from the title sequence, 'scentings of love across a wilderness / of retrospection, wild and objectless / longings incarnate in the carnal child' (BH 124; T 20), and, in 'Fidelities', part of 'An Apology for the Revival of Christian Architecture in England', 'Some / who are lost covet scholastic proof, /subsistence of probation, modest balm' (BH 130; T 31). The use of apposition in both these cases leaves it unclear whether the reader is faced with rephrasing of the original entity ('scentings' rephrased as 'longings') or addition to it ('longings' as well as 'scentings'). The lost might covet scholastic proof rather than any balm, however modest; on the other hand such proof might in itself be regarded as 'modest' balm because incapable of the conclusiveness to which it aspires. The intermediate phrase in the second example, 'subsistence of probation', is consistent with either interpretation. Pearson writes of this device in terms of 'a kind of tension between disruption and unity' (p. 33), and that is the effect in both the cases here. Whether any point is served by this tension is another matter.

What one might call appositional play remains a feature throughout Hill's poetry. *The Orchards of Syon*, for example, uses it often:

---

[8] '*King Log* Revisited', in *Geoffrey Hill: Essays on his Work*, ed. Peter Robinson, (Milton Keynes: Open University Press, 1985), p.32.

> My mind, as I know it, I still discover
> in this one-off temerity, arachnidous,
> abseiling into a pit, the pit a void,
> a black hole, a galaxy in denial.
> (BH 408; OS 58)

The pit, the void, the black hole and the galaxy in denial are the same and yet different, and the order of the words emphasizes the difference without overt challenge to their grammatical equality. There is a dramatic form of meaning here; the pit turns out to be a void, the void a black hole, and so on, as the spider abseils down. But the grammar is unclear whether 'the pit' is 'my mind' or not, because 'arachnidous' and 'abseiling' can be applied either to 'my mind' or to myself ('I'). The grammatical ambiguity of the appositions is certainly vertiginous, but difficult to justify. A second example is even more challenging:

> This well-clued business not ways beyond us—
> business meaning here survival, strange lures
> of duress, longevities
> (BH 385; OS 35)

'Survival' might entail 'longevities', but, one has to say, it might not. The relation between the two words is uneasy, and this is more emphatically the case with the 'strange lures' which might be another aspect of the business of survival (you will be subject to such lures in the course of surviving) but cannot be in apposition to 'survival' since there is no identity – no *obvious* identity, that is. This lack of obvious identity queers the pitch for the simple apposition of 'longevities' to 'survival', and makes the relation between the two more uneasy than first suggested. Hill's habitual but, we may be sure, not unconsidered use of apposition is consistent with his reluctance to endorse a poetry of simplicity. For Hill, as for Henry James, 'Really, universally, relations stop nowhere'.[9] His appositions are an expression of this. The reader is not bound to sympathize, nor to consider them enlightening.

In the later poetry (after *Canaan*), this infinity of relations finds expression in the poems' frequently opening in mid-stream.

---

[9] Preface to *Roderick Hudson*, in Henry James, *Literary Criticism: French Writers, Other European Writers, The Prefaces to the New York Edition*, ed. Leon Edel (New York: Library of America, 1984), p. 1041.

'Improvisation on "O Welt ich muss dich lassen"' is an instance:

> *Traurig* as one is between bearers, dancers,
> old comrades from the Crem or at the Palais,
> that's not the issue.
> (BH 483; WT 3)

The situation in which 'one' is *'traurig'* ('unhappy') is ill-defined by 'between bearers, dancers', and it is not clear whether 'one' is to generalize or is specific to the speaker. The effect is disorientating, and presumably meant to be so. Its dramatic force is, however, reduced by the frequency with which Hill uses it; the result can be that the reader resentfully feels subject to unnecessary mystery.[10] The collocation of 'bearers, dancers' may explain itself in the opposites of the next line – [coffin]-'bearers' belong at the Crem, 'dancers' at the Palais (or they did) – but the uncertainty, even if passing, reinforces the haze in which 'the issue' is felt or perceived. Matters are not made easier by the sentence that follows: 'Can't decide among / the cheap comedians' since there is no obvious link from the first sentence to the second, unless the comedians are the bearers and dancers, in which case what makes them 'cheap'? The reader's impression is that of being plunged into a discourse which began with quite other words than those on the page.

The lack of definition in the relations between elements in his poems (though not the use of apposition) is, like Hill's allusive practice, modernist. The apparent beginning in the middle of things, for example, can be paralleled in both Eliot and Pound. 'Modernist', however, has the wrong connotation, if one bears in mind the comfortable place 'modernism' occupies in current ideas of English and American literature. 'Modern' would be a better word, as making plain the conscious link between style and historical moment. Hill's increasingly difficult beginnings embody the difficulty, as he sees it, of beginning in the modern world at all – beginning, that is, on one's own account rather than in response to that world's suspect urgencies, which imply the pressure of 'canting commodity speech' and 'the acoustical din that surrounds us all' and the 'very great difficulty' with which 'the personal note' is realized in the best poetry of our time.[11] It is perhaps

---

[10] 'Ars' (BH 507; WT 62) begins 'Hazardous but press on'; see also *The Triumph of Love* XLVI, LIV and LVI, for example.

[11] *Viewpoints: Poets in Conversation with John Haffenden* (London: Faber and Faber,

a mark of the 'intelligence' to which Hill appeals in his poetry that it should be aware of the threat that the 'acoustical din' represents and of the difficulty of establishing any true relationship in the face of such a threat. On the other hand, Hill's own allusive and appositional practice, when unsuccessful, is itself vulnerable to description as 'acoustical din'.

That difficulty is increased by the omnipresence of the ambiguous in the world as Hill sees it, something which is necessarily reflected in representations of that world and the language in which they are conveyed. As far as poetry is concerned, 'any complexity of language, any ambiguity, any ambivalence implies intelligence. Maybe an intelligence under threat, maybe an intelligence that is afraid of consequences, but nonetheless an intelligence working in qualifications and revelations … resisting, therefore, tyrannical simplification'.[12] Hill's ambiguities are formulated by such an intelligence. They are found throughout his work. 'Knowing the dead, and how some are disposed' (BH16; FTU 30) – disposed physically or in frame of mind? From the same poem: 'We grasp, roughly, the song' – 'approximately' or 'in a way likely to damage'?[13] From the next volume: 'Stung by the innocent venoms of the earth' (BH41; KL 16) – innocent because insentient, though intrinsically harmful, or innocent because the venom of the things of the earth lies in the nature of our desire for them? Two volumes on we find: 'Dominion is swallowed with your blood' (BH 124; T 20) – does that mean that Christ by his sacrifice assumes lordship over mankind, or that those who take the Eucharist acquire thereby a taste for lordship over others?

The questions to which such ambiguous expression gives rise do not necessarily have a single answer. They are not sought out in order to perplex the reader, however. Ambiguity *arises* for Hill in the process of writing, and is not, as far as he is concerned, to be identified with the *manner* in which he chooses to handle his material:

> I query the idea that I 'address myself to subjects', which seems to imply some kind of settled policy. It may be that the subjects present themselves to me as being full of ambiguous implications, but this is surely a different matter. The ambiguities and scruples

---

1981), p.86; 'The Art of Poetry', p. 279.

[12] 'The Art of Poetry', p. 277.

[13] These two examples are discussed more fully, and finely, by Christopher Ricks, *The Force of Poetry*, (Oxford: Oxford University Press, 1984), p. 291.

seem to reside in the object that is meditated upon.[14]

Ambiguity inheres in Hill's subject-matter; but his attitude to it is very different from that of the poet and critic with whom the term is most readily associated, William Empson. Hill's early essay on Empson is revealing in this respect. First of all, he recognizes kinship; in opposition to Bernard Bergonzi's sense that in Empson 'so often nothing leads behind or beyond the words', Hill suggests that there is something there after all, something that Hill's own readers will readily recognize: 'some presence as vaguely numinous as "suffering"'.[15] The poems by Empson that he admires are those, like 'Let It Go', that embody such suffering. Empson's ethical sense, however, is very different from Hill's. Although desperation is certainly the note of 'Let It Go', its presence in Empson's criticism is subdued in favour of an emphasis on 'balance': 'The object of life … is not to understand things, but to maintain one's defences and equilibrium and live as well as one can'.[16]

Hill would like to *understand* things, but lays down conditions on which understanding is to be achieved, such as the existence of 'intrinsic value', which proves illusory; balance does not appeal to him.[17] He dislikes Empson's 'Arachne', a poem about 'balance', for the 'banal obviousness' with which its theme is developed, but it is at least plausible that what he really dislikes is the theme itself.[18] He takes the view of Johnson, who 'could see no bicycle would go; / "You bear yourself, and the machine as well"'.[19] Similarly, he rejects the idea of John Crowe

---

[14] *Viewpoints*, p. 90.

[15] 'The Dream of Reason' (review of *The Review, Special Number: William Empson*), *Essays in Criticism*, 14.1 (January 1964), pp. 91-101 (p. 95).

[16] William Empson, *Seven Types of Ambiguity* (Harmondsworth: Penguin, 1995), p.285. On 'balance' in Empson, see my 'Among Contradictions' (review of John Haffenden, *William Empson: Among the Mandarins*), *Essays in Criticism*, 56.2 (April 2006) 199-209 (pp. 208-9).

[17] See Marcus Waithe, 'Hill, Ruskin, and Intrinsic Value', in *Geoffrey Hill and his Contexts*, ed. Piers Pennington and Matthew Sperling, (Peter Lang: Oxford), pp. 133-49 and Lee Spinks, 'Geoffrey Hill and Intrinsic Value', *Essays in Criticism*, 68.3 (July 2018) pp. 369-89.

[18] 'The Dream of Reason', p. 99. Hill's impatience with Empson's early poems 'where the strength occasionally seems more assured than real' (p. 96) connects with a reluctance to endorse the balancing act they perform.

[19] 'Invitation to Juno', *The Complete Poems of William Empson*, ed. John Haffenden (London: Allen Lane, 2000), p. 12.

Ransom as 'the supreme equilibrist': 'despite the consensus we may better appreciate Ransom's final achievement by not shirking the occasions when he is thrown off balance' (CCW 129). It is basic to Hill's poetry that truthfulness (to *his* own need to understand and to the moral-aesthetic requirement of the poem as *he* conceives it) takes priority over the pragmatism represented by Empson's 'balance'.[20] It is not fascist to question this point of view.

Hill attaches great importance to an observation by Simone Weil in *The Need for Roots*:

> Simultaneous composition on several planes at once is the law of artistic creation, and wherein, in fact, lies its difficulty.
>
> A poet in the arrangement of words and the choice of each word must simultaneously bear in mind matters on at least five or six different planes of composition. (CCW 573)[21]

The poet uses language in order accurately to represent the world as he perceives it. Since the world is intrinsically ambiguous, it is a requirement of its representation that there should be 'five or six different planes of composition'. But it is in any case intrinsic to the language which embodies his subject-matter that it functions on multiple levels. The result can be a kind of poetic stalemate: 'though the grading and measuring of words presupposes the ability to recognize ambiguities, there are some ambiguities so deeply impacted with habit, custom, procedure, that the "recognition" is in effect the acknowledgement of irreducible bafflement' (CWW 228).

Readers of Hill have to be prepared for poems that present such bafflement without any advocacy of the sort of 'balance' which Empson aimed at. The unresolved paradoxes of 'The Pentecost Castle' evoke this bafflement: 'And you my spent heart's treasure / my yet unspent desire / measurer past all measure / cold paradox of fire' (BH 117; T 11). Even though such poetry lacks 'balance', and because it resists 'tyrannical simplification', Hill regards the writing of it as a positive act, and he

---

[20] Ricks cites Hill as writing in 1954 of the need 'to walk the tight-rope over the jaw-hole' (*The Force of Poetry*, p. 355). In the passage quoted above from *The Orchards of Syon*, 'abseiling into a pit' seems to be preferred to walking a tight-rope.

[21] Also quoted by Hill in '"The Conscious Mind's Intelligible Structure": A Debate', *Agenda*, 9.4/10.1 (Autumn/Winter 1971-2) 14-23 (p. 15); see Michael Molan, 'Milton and Eliot in the Work of Geoffrey Hill', in *Geoffrey Hill and his Contexts*, pp. 100-01.

wants the baffled reader to regard it in a similar light. It is truthful to the way he sees the world, whether he or his reader likes it or not. In so far as his poetry deals, as it generally does, with ambiguities 'deeply impacted with habit, custom, procedure', it cannot be other than baffled. In so far as it extends an invitation to the reader, it is to share in the poet's own frustration. The reader follows the poet in searching for meaning within the language of the poem and within the world to which language is the mode of access. In this search, bafflement signifies failure, but also a kind of success, that of a sustained attempt at truthful utterance. Some readers, however, may with reason find this success difficult to accept.

It is at this point that the argument must turn from a consideration of the demands made on Hill's readers to the demands made on himself. Indeed, in the opposition of Hill's 'bafflement' to Empson's 'balance', that turn has already been made. I have suggested that Hill is able to justify his baffled poetry by the claim that it is truthful. This accords with the high moral demands he makes on poetry and articulates in his criticism. On the other hand, the opposition of truthful Hill to pragmatic Empson feels like one based on temperament rather than reason alone. To consider Hill's difficulties in the writing of poetry may help us to determine how far the difficulties of the poetry are required by the internal logic of what is said and how far by an ungeneralisable personal bias.

As far as the poetry before 1998 is concerned, the question might seem irrelevant. That poetry is often described as 'impersonal'.[22] Hill at this time conceives of the poem as an object distinct from its maker, associated with Yeats's remark that 'a poem comes right with a click like a closing box' (CCW 4 – also alluded to in the interviews with John Haffenden and Blake Morrison).[23] The poem-as-box is consonant with the poet-as-technician: 'I would claim the utmost significance for matters of technique' (CCW 4).

After 1998, the poetry takes on a self-consciously unfinished air. 'I don't much have / the patience, now, of the artificer' (BH 601; TCP 51). Whereas the first person is uncommon in the pre-1996 poems, and rarely to be identified with the author, the reverse is the case in later books: '– Urge to unmake / all wrought finalities, become a babbler / in

---

[22] For example, Martin Dodsworth, 'Ted Hughes and Geoffrey Hill: An Antithesis', in *The New Pelican Guide to English Literature*, ed. Boris Ford, 9 vols. (Penguin: Harmondsworth, 1982-88), VIII: *The Present* (1983), pp. 281-93 (p.291).

[23] *Viewpoints*, p.83; 'Under Judgment', p.212.

the crowd's face –' (BH 601; TCP 51).²⁴ 'Forty or fifty years ago I would have said the poem is achieved by the fullest possible objectification of individual subjectivity. Obviously I no longer think so'.²⁵

It might seem that the explanation for this contrast between early and late styles lies in what the poet has told us of himself. 'From late childhood I suffered from chronic depression, which was accompanied by various exhausting obsessive-compulsive phobias'; after he went to America in 1988, he was prescribed the drug serotonin as an antidote for this depression, with startling results.²⁶ Such an explanation, however, explains nothing, since it assumes a passivity of will on the poet's part for which there is absolutely no evidence. Furthermore, it can, and, I think, should be argued that the change in attitude and procedure is more apparent than real. Language is so deeply implicated in human affairs that 'impersonality' in a poet can only be a relative matter.²⁷ The element of 'feeling' in a poem looks two ways, toward the writer who feels, and toward what is felt about; feeling in the poem may be thought to cohere around its subject-matter without overt reference to the poet who feels – this does not mean there is no reference at all. 'Funeral Music' might serve as an example. It demonstrates perfectly Hill's concern with 'those processes of the past which were the original betrayals ... in the governance of England', registered in a language and with an intensity that are also typical of Hill's 'objective' style.²⁸ He has said of this style that 'the kind of perfectionism at which I was aiming in the earlier books was, so to speak, the acceptable fact [*for* face?] of [my] obsessive-compulsive disorder'.²⁹ It is hard not to feel that in lines from 'Funeral Music' like 'I believe in my / Abandonment, since it is what I have' (BH 52; KL 30) – the first-person is that of an actor in the Wars of the Roses – the deliberation of the line-ending should be felt as the sign of the poet's

---

²⁴ BH omits the concluding dash

²⁵ 'The Art of Poetry', p. 282.

²⁶ 'The Art of Poetry', p. 288. The experience of medication is alluded to in section CIX of *The Triumph of Love* (BH270; TL 56).

²⁷ '[A] poetry of true diffidence would seem to be a contradiction in terms': John Bayley, 'The Tongue's Satisfactions', *Agenda*, 30.1-2 (Spring-Summer 1992), p.9. Hill approves Eliot's account of Valéry as putting himself into 'Le Cimetière marin' 'to the point at which the surrendering of the maximum of [his] being to the poem ends by arriving at the maximum of impersonality' (quoted CCW 543).

²⁸ 'Under Judgment', p. 213.

²⁹ 'The Art of Poetry', p.288.

own sympathetic, and possibly obsessive, participation alongside the speaker in the drama of the poem. There can be no doubt of the personal investment in poems like 'September Song', or in the sequence *Mercian Hymns*, or in 'The Stone Man' ('Soliloquies' in *King Log*). It may be less overt in 'The Songbook of Sebastian Arrurruz' or 'Lachrimae', but it is there too. Hill's 'impersonal' poetry has much of the personal about it.

This is perhaps why he has had so much to say about the evil of the confessional impulse in poetry, especially contemporary poetry. He comes back again and again to the matter of 'self-expression' because he himself finds it difficult and because his attitude to it is not determined. 'Poetry is not self-expressiveness of a vulgarly spontaneous kind' because 'expression' of self gets in the way of the attempt at truthfulness proper to Hill's idea of poetry.[30] On the other hand, as we have seen, the self *is* involved in it somehow.[31] Hill has touched upon this a number of times. In 1980, for example, he argued, surely with himself in mind, that 'self-affirmation may be very different from self-expression, and can take anonymity [of 'The Pentecost Castle' kind?] as one of its forms' (CCW 134).[32] In the *Paris Review* interview of 2000 he was still worrying at 'self-expression' and what is wrong with it: 'One's idea of the authentic self may be quite different from the authentic self as it really is. The dividing line between innocent stupidity and fakery is very unclear; and I think that innocent stupidity and deliberate fakery can coexist in the same writer'.[33]

'Self-expression' was still of concern in 2005. When a poem is good, he says, in 'A Postscript on Modernist Poetics',

> the anecdote is no longer the agency of our self-promotion; something recalcitrant has come between us and our expectant and expected satisfaction ... 'A being,' says Rahner, 'comes to itself by means of "expression", in so far as it comes to itself at all' (CCW 566-67).[34]

---

[30] *Viewpoints*, p. 87.

[31] A Bradleian 'somehow' (CCW 549), rather than 'the *somehow* of abdication' (CCW 534).

[32] This antithesis of self-affirmation and self-expression anticipates the distinction between self and personality which Hill later picks up from Rosenzweig (CCW 496).

[33] 'The Art of Poetry', pp. 383-84.

[34] 'There's a fine phrase of Nietzsche's about "this delight in giving a form to oneself as a piece of difficult, refractory, and suffering material". In such a phrase the difficulties, refractoriness and suffering of the personality and the difficult and refractory nature of

Hill's prolonged meditation on the issue of 'self-expression' and the 'recalcitrant' is indicative of the extent to which he is personally involved in his own poetry.[35] If, nevertheless, we learn a great deal more about him as a fallible human being in his later poems, it is because he is now willingly present in his poems as suffering equally with his readers the effects of that 'terrible aboriginal calamity' (CCW 475) in which, like Newman, he believes.[36]

Hill's self-implication in the poetry tells in the way his stylistic preferences can so easily – perhaps too easily – be related to his own beginnings. He was the child of a village policeman; his father was at once an important member of the community and yet, by virtue of his job, apart from it. The impact of this on an only child, gifted beyond the expectations of those around him, cannot be underestimated. The gifts were intellectual and imaginative, setting him also, we may assume, perilously, bafflingly, apart. The poet's allusiveness suggests a second home in literature, but, in its indefiniteness, not a certain one. His instinct for apposition embodies such uncertainty in the poetry, matched by a contrary need to assert himself as prophet and, in the criticism, man of slaughterous judgement, as in the case of T. S. Eliot. This form of presence in his own poems is not always problematic. *Mercian Hymns* is in part concerned with Hill's own childhood but it is neither confessional in the senses to which Hill objects nor problematic in its procedures, St.-John Perse and David Jones providing a frame of reference for the reader. Even in this relatively benign work, however, anxieties about language and about power, including the poet's own power, are visible.

Hill rarely expressed joy in his gift of language. One reason may be that the extraordinary sensitivity to word-usage displayed in the criticism has only led to the terrible 'bafflement' we have already discussed. What is certain is that he felt being a poet as, among other things, a burden and a pain. When, in *Mercian Hymns,* Hill declares 'I am your staggeringly gifted child' (BH 111; MH XXIX), Andrew Roberts rightly finds the words expressive of 'gratitude and humorous hubris'; but, clearly, the

---

language itself are seen to cohere'. *Viewpoints*, p. 87.

[35] See Kenneth Haynes, '"Perplexed Persistence": The Criticism of Geoffrey Hill' in *Geoffrey Hill and his Contexts*, pp. 213-25.

[36] John Lyon writes of 'the Hill of self-conscious imperfection' ('Geoffrey Hill's Eye Troubles', in *Geoffrey Hill: Essays on his Later Work*, (Oxford: Oxford University Press, 2012), p.115). It seems plausible that Hill should associate his eye trouble with the post-lapsarian 'film' removed from Adam's eye by Michael (*Paradise Lost*, 11.412-130).

phrase also implies a poet staggered, that is, taken aback by, his gift.[37] Hill not infrequently writes as though unhappily coerced by his own supreme ability. In *Scenes from Comus*, for example, we find the lines: 'Say that I ám gifted – and I'll touch you / for ordinary uncommon happiness' (BH 445; SC 29).[38] In *The Triumph of Love* there is, interestingly, a possible note of self-blame: 'Why do I / take as my gift a wounded and wounding / introspection?' (BH 258; TL 35).

The bafflement to which his deep intimacy with language has led him is not the sole or even principal cause of the pain with which he associates the writing of poetry. More than once, Hill quotes this passage from Coleridge: 'For if words are not THINGS, they are LIVING POWERS, by which the things of most importance to mankind are actuated, combined, and humanized' (CCW 95).[39] These living powers sound benign, but if you reflect on Hill's ideas about fallen humanity they may take on a sinister quality. Coleridge also described words, in a passage of which Hill is surely aware, as 'Spirits and Living Agents that are seldom misused without avenging themselves'.[40] Their vengeful power is frequently remarked by Hill in his criticism; and consciousness of that power also plays a large part in his account of the creative process: 'In a poet's involvement with language, above all, there is, one would darkly and impetuously claim, an element of helplessness, of being at the mercy of accidents, the prey of one's own presumptuous energy' (CCW 155).

For a writer so highly alert, to himself and others, this helplessness must have been deeply disturbing. When John Haffenden asked him 'whether any particular poems were predetermined or preconceived, or is it the case that your insights and concerns always realize themselves in the process of composition', Hill replied 'It's a mixture of the two.'[41] He then elaborated on the pains of waiting for a poem to shape itself in him, before going on to describe the process of 'slow, common

---

[37] Andrew Michael Roberts, *Geoffrey Hill*, (Horndon: Northcote House, 2004), p. 25. Compare 'The cross staggered him', 'Canticle for Good Friday' (FTU 39).

[38] BH omits the stress mark in these lines.

[39] See Matthew Sperling, 'Hill and Nineteenth-Century Linguistic Thought' in *Geoffrey Hill and his Contexts*, pp. 107-31.

[40] Letter of 28 May 1822, quoted in S.T. Coleridge, *Aids to Reflection*, ed. John Beer (*Collected Works of Samuel Taylor Coleridge*, vol. 9, Princeton, NJ: Princeton University Press, 1993), p. 10 n.11.

[41] *Viewpoints*, p. 82.

craftsmanship' of 'when I'm able to write'.[42] In the first case, he depicts himself as all together at the mercy of the unwritten poem – helpless:

> I've gone sometimes for ten years knowing ... that something is waiting to be written; the only obstacle is a total inability to write it ... Then, if I'm lucky, various germinal phrases or a hint of rhythm or something ... will begin to stir, and for a time I have to be content to let the work grow by a process of accretion ... if I'm lucky there will come a point when things begin to click into shape ... I know the subject but I don't know the argument. I don't think I've ever conceived a poetic argument as a thing in itself which merely required words to embody it. I only discover my argument in discovering the words for it.[43]

Once he is writing the poem, the emphasis is on the *labour* of composition and the poet's control of what is going on. There is no longer talk of being 'lucky':

> With my own poetry, when I'm able to write it, the process seems a slow, common craftsmanship, an ordinary *occurrence*. There comes a moment, after all the anxiety and doubt, when one is working to a conclusion and feels fully in command of the material and the situation. Obstacles will occur, but you do not at a deep level lose confidence.[44]

What is interesting is that the poet does not attempt to harmonize the two accounts for Haffenden's benefit. On the one hand there is helplessness, on the other there is the poet feeling 'fully in command'. The process of writing as he describes it could suggest a struggle for control between the writer and the words that have him at their mercy; Hill encourages such an interpretation by saying of Blake's phrase 'struggles of entanglement' (from *Jerusalem*) that 'in moments of either elation or depression I feel that [it] could stand as an epigraph to my whole writing life'. Unsurprisingly, he speaks of an 'exhaustion' which is necessary for the 'breakthrough' that brings the labour of writing to an end.[45]

---

[42] *Viewpoints*, pp. 82-4.

[43] *Viewpoints*, p. 82.

[44] *Viewpoints*, p. 84.

[45] *Viewpoints*, pp. 82-3.

Given the sensation of helplessness before language which this poet endured, it is not surprising that he should be greatly concerned with issues of power. It is scarcely necessary to invoke the power of the policeman-father. 'Being in command', as he describes himself in the second stage of the writing process, is the antithesis of 'being at the mercy of accidents', and must bring with it a sense of relief, or even relish, in the power that is exercised over the words that previously kept him waiting, in the dark about what would emerge, helpless. The poetry that results is characterized by the power it exerts over the reader, most obviously in the way enjambment drives the reader on, as in 'Terribilis est locus iste':

> Briefly they are amazed. The marigold-fields
> mell and shudder and the travellers,
> in sudden exile burdened with remote
> hieratic gestures, journey to no end
>
> beyond the vivid severance of each day,
> (BH 134; T 38)

Anyone who heard Hill read his own poems will have recognized, too, the intelligence with which he modulated a powerful voice in command of his audience. As Professor of Poetry at Oxford, he spoke of 'policing his patch'.[46] Power, specifically the poet's power, but not only that, is an issue from beginning to end in the poems; *Mercian Hymns* should be the *locus classicus*. It associates Offa, 'a tyrannical creator of order and beauty' (and potential totalitarian?), with 'the tyrannical streak in oneself as a child'; the child is a poet.[47] But it is too easy to name poems which take power for their subject-matter: 'Of Commerce and Society', 'Funeral Music', 'De Jure Belli ac Pacis', *Scenes from Comus*, *A Treatise of Civil Power*. The matter of power is associated by the poet himself with the power to which his own working-class family was subjected. *Mercian Hymns* XXV commemorates his grandmother, who made nails by hand (BH 107). 'Coda' (BH 599-600; TCP 49-50) places that subjection as the antithesis of the power the poet has over words: 'how much is gift-entailed / great grandson, and son, of defeated men' (BH 600; TCP 50). A further aspect of the poet's power is the reading-list aspect of his allusions.

---

[46] Lecture of 10 May 2011; may be accessed in an audio version at http://www.english.ox.ac.uk/news-events/regular-events/professor-poetry .

[47] *Viewpoints*, p.94.

Power is present in the poems in a particularly Hillian way. The poet exerts his power through language, but language exerts its power through him. He is both outside the poem, forcing it on, and inside it, painfully registering the force which is exerted, present alongside the reader, sharing the reader's frustration which is his own (and, if 'sharing' involves a kind of unloading, not his own). A section from *Scenes from Comus* illustrates the distinctive play of power that emerges:

> That we are inordinate creatures
> not so ordained by God; that we are
> at once rational, irrational – and there is reason.
>
> That this is no reason for us to despair.
> The tragedy of things is not conclusive;
> rather, one way by which the spirit moves.
>
> That it moves in circles need not detain us.
> Marvel at our contrary orbits. Mine
> salutes yours, whenever we pass or cross,
>
> which may be now, might very well be now.
> (BH 421; SC 3)

The poem, the second in the section 'The Argument of the Masque', proposes a series of topics which may or may not be addressed in Milton's masque or Hill's book. There is something impassive in the way they are voiced – it is not clear to what extent the poet endorses these propositions, or what is expected of the reader in relation to them, except assent. 'That we are inordinate creatures / not so ordained by God' implies the possibility it denies, that God decreed that human beings should be 'inordinate', that is, without rule. No feeling about this possibility appears. The same is true of 'that we are / at once rational, irrational – and there is reason.' Is there reason in us for our being at once rational and irrational? Or is it simply that reason exists, perhaps as some kind of rule, even though, gifted with reason, we do not recognize it? The propositions have the ability to unsettle, by the very fact of their unyieldingness. There is an implicit challenge to the reader, and to the poet within the poem, and yet there is also a sense in which the challenge is *issued* by the poet who commands and endorses the poem.[48]

The language is formal, and what is said observes form, in that the line-endings give emphasis to what is being said. And yet the lines exert power which exceeds a matter of form. They *insist:* 'inordinate ... not so ordained', 'rational, irrational ... there is reason ... this is no reason'. The poet's own comment, 'this is no reason to despair', leaves the reader to intuit the reason he should think despair a possibility; as a sentence of comfort it is, then, self-defeating. There is something obdurate about the poem's brooding on reason and order by which the poet himself seems to be oppressed. He speaks of tragedy, the spirit, movement in contrary orbits, passing or crossing, but in such a way that it is difficult for the reader to get purchase on what is said. One cannot be sure, even, that the poet himself has such purchase (the phrases he produces may be only gestures of his own helplessness), or that he knows to what extent he wants the reader to achieve it. The poet addresses Hugh Wood, the dedicatee of the volume, but it is hard to tell whether he does so consistently through the section, or whether he has any other reader in mind. If the propositions made in the poem are unyielding, so is the poet in his self-presentation. The reader is helpless before both, is subject to poetic power.

Nevertheless, the poem is obstinately present to both reader and poet – 'obstinately', because its procedures imply meanings that are not made explicit, and so cannot be dismissed until explicitness has been achieved. The poet, like the poem, brings nothing to resolution. Is the poet passing or crossing his friend's orbit or not? Is he saluting him or not? The diminuendo of 'may' into 'might' in the last line suggests not, but a lot depends on the kind of circles 'we' are supposed to be moving in. It may be that sufficient salute has been made just by introducing the idea of saluting into the poem. The effect is puzzling, and all the more so for the poem's not appearing to admit that it might be so regarded. It rests heavily on us, partakes of this poet's peculiar sense, one that resists generalization, 'That weight of the world, weight of the word, is' (BH 430; SC 12). Commentators' willingness to take this statement as generally applicable is unwarranted and wrong-headed. There is no doubt, however, that the word was a burden for Hill. His poetry can

---

[48] In *Broken Hierarchies*, 'and there is reason' is revised to 'possessed by reason', while 'by God' is replaced by 'of God'. The effect of the former change is to render the lines more subdued, though the evocation of demonic possession in relation to reason is still challenging in the former way.

be oppressive, and it can be painful. Hill writes a poetry of witness ('the only way I can effectively witness is by writing and trying to write as well as I can. There are things one has to witness to'); he is aware that etymologically 'martyrdom' is 'witness'.[49] He has borne witness to the atrocity of the death-camps, to the heroism of von Haeften and his comrades, and others, to the corruption of modern parliamentary politics, as the martyr Robert Southwell bore witness to his faith. These are matters painful to contemplate; the writer has to determine his own relation to them as a fallible human being, and also to fight the vengeful living powers of language in doing so. In his 1983 sermon preached at Cambridge he attempts a positive view, seizing on Yeats's reproach to Margot Ruddock for her sloppy poetic technique ('there is no difficulty to force you down under the surface – difficulty is our plough') in order depict the act of writing:

> One is ploughing down into one's own selfhood and into the deep strata of language at one and the same time. This takes effort and may be painful. Selfhood is more vital, recalcitrant, abiding, than self-expression ... The pains to which I refer are those examples of self-discovery and self-rebuke which seem inseparable from the technical process itself, when the most accomplished maker turns upon his mastery.[50]

Hill's best poems witness as much to the pains of his difficult search for truth as to the pain in the world that is also his concern. The balance, achieved or declined, between the poet's pains and the world's is often difficult for the reader as well as the poet.

Hill quotes Crowe Ransom's 'celebrated definition of the poem as "nothing short of a desperate ontological or metaphysical manoeuvre"' and says that it seems 'a formula at once all-embracing and exclusive' (CCW 128). The description may be reasonably applied to Hill's own poems; Hill sees Ransom as a version of his poetic self, someone writing, as he does, under a sense of constraint, and enduring the 'agony' to which this 'constraint' gives rise ('constraint' CCW 128, 'agony' CCW 128, 131, 138).

---

[49] 'The Art of Poetry', p. 292.

[50] 'Thus my noblest capacity becomes my deepest perplexity', *A Sermon preached at Great St Mary's, the University Church, Cambridge*, 8 May 1983, duplicated sheets, p.2.

The 'agony' of writing and the burden of being a poet are accompanied by a tendency to adopt or endorse extreme points of view. His description of existence as something to be endured springs to mind. [51] So does his endorsement of Simone Weil's 'greatness as an ethical writer' on the basis of her proposal that '"anybody, no matter who, discovering an avoidable error in a printed text or radio broadcast, would be entitled to bring an action before [special] courts", empowered to condemn a convicted offender to prison or hard labour' (CWW 9-10). Weil seems not to have heard of lesser penalties, nor to have considered them; thankfully she does not think capital punishment appropriate. Hill goes along with her defiantly, allowing that the remark might strike others 'as unassailable evidence that the woman was merely an obsessional neurotic'. 'Merely' here is gratuitous, but otherwise he makes a good point. Hill brings in Weil in order to buttress his own sense of 'empirical guilt', one extremity to hold up another. It is a high-risk strategy, an illegitimate use of professorial power.

Hill's rhetoric is not infrequently all there is to carry off quite unacceptable judgements. In 'A Postscript on Modernist Poetics', he discusses two lines by Keats:

> Instead of sweets, his ample palate took
> Savour of poisonous brass and metal sick.

His argument hinges on the phrase 'took savour' and the enjambment which separates the two words; 'savour', he says, is a normal word to use of eating and drinking, but 'took / Savour ' suggests 'a degree of petulance' within Hyperion's suffering, whilst the enjambment dramatizes the moment when 'presumably, he might have come up with some alternative less satisfyingly wounded.' Hill goes on to characterise the lines' effect via a slighting comment on Eliot:

> Eliot's recurring commonplace phrase – 'the enjoyment of poetry' – seems not to apply to anything that really matters here; the phrase savours more of the question whether or

---

[51] 'L'existence est ce que nous sommes, par nécessité, tenues d'endurer. La spiritualité constitue, pour quelques individus seulement, une dimension supplémentaire.' Interview with Anne Mounic (who also appears to be responsible for the translation, seen and approved by Hill), in *Temporel: Revue Littéraire & Artistique*, 28 September 2008: http://temporel.fr/Le-poeme- moulin-mystique-Entretien. [accessed 12 January 2013].

not one should, in lifting the teacup, crook the little finger. Whatever strange relationship we have with the poem, it is not one of enjoyment. It is more like being brushed past, or aside, by an alien being. (CCW 566)

The denigration in that crook of the little finger coerces agreement that Hill knows what 'really matters here'.[52] In fact, it is not clear what 'really matters', or even where 'here' is (the quoted lines? The first *Hyperion*? 'the' poem?). The absoluteness of Hill's position takes the breath away and his tone discourages a reasoned response. In earlier days he himself found 'pleasure' to be experienced in the 'conflicting yet colluding' force-fields of 'sin' and 'anxiety' in poetry (CCW 11). In the light of this, we might allow ourselves to find 'enjoyment' in the lines from Keats, whether or not we assent to the analogy with an 'alien being'. Not many of us will have met with one of those, or thought 'being brushed past, or aside,' by one an appropriate analogy for, say, the experience of reading or hearing poetry which is essentially human, like the two songs that end *Love's Labours Lost*.

These examples of unguarded extravagance find their counterpart in the way Hill's poems push the reader to extremity, challenged by the authority the poet claims for himself and yet which he also undermines: 'This is quite dreadful – he's become obsessed. / There you go, there you go – narrow it down to *obsession*!' (BH 250; TL 21). Hill habitually puts the reader on the spot, and not just by his aggressively self-deprecating humour ('It's good of you to mention the humour').[53] The 'ragged-edged', unfinished quality of the later work looks for completion in defiance of the perfection its author once strove for, and, in its claim to be 'art', calls art into question.[54] Is it or is it not the realm of alien beings? Is Hill such an alien being himself? At times, perhaps, he would find these questions difficult, at others he might assent to the extreme position they imply.

---

[52] Hill is depending on previous discussion of Eliot's unsatisfactory uses of 'enjoyment" (CCW 535-37, 557, 560). He makes his point as far as 'amusement' is concerned (CCW 555-56), but I see no reason why he should be unwilling to incorporate Eliot's admirable description of 'the full surprise and elevation of a new experience of poetry' (praised at CCW 559) into the sense of 'enjoyment' as he uses it elsewhere.

[53] *Viewpoints*, p.95.

[54] 'The Art of Poetry', p. 290.

Hill's poetry is intrinsically difficult. It challenges understanding, it challenges the reader's sense of poetry as an art, and it challenges that same reader to submit to the power of the poet. As far as understanding is concerned, the challenge is not just the one that ambiguous expression, indefinite relationships between words, and allusions normally present a reader. The poet's existential difficulty infects these elements of the poetry. The imponderable nature of Hill's ambiguity and the uncertainty of the relationship between elements of the poem are implicit within his account of the poem as the outcome of a baffled attempt at truthfulness. His allusiveness represents the 'habit, custom, procedure' (CWW 228) in which the ambiguities which concern him are so 'deeply impacted'. In some cases it stands for the power that language has over him; in others, for a power which is asserted over the reader.

Those of Hill's admirers who insist on how entirely comprehensible are his poems are quite beside the point, then, and do him a disservice because they radically misrepresent him.

> We think nothing of exerting ourselves to learn a language or master a new software program – why should it be regarded as anachronistic to demand a fraction of such effort to understand a poem? If a poet has something to teach, poetry lovers should be prepared to make the effort to learn.[55]

Poetry is not a code, or written according to a program, nor are Hill's poems designed to 'teach'. We need to take seriously the poet's own views on his work, so copiously offered, presumably in the hope that he should not be misunderstood as a 'simple' poet. There is a passage in the *Paris Review* interview, which many of his admirers need to take to heart; he speaks of himself in the third person, as though to underline his own objectivity: 'they say that Hill claims for himself the status of a prophet ... And all I can say is that no such claim is made by the author'.[56] The very real difficulties of allusion, syntax and ambiguity in the poetry bear this out, and challenge the reader to ask what the poems are trying to do.

Hill said of 'Funeral Music' that he 'was attempting a florid grim music broken by grunts and shrieks' (KL 67). This is consistent with the refusal to be a prophet, or (often repeated) to allow poems to be reduced

---

[55] Peter Popham, 'Think of England', *New Statesman*, 7-13 December 2012, p. 52.
[56] 'The Art of Poetry', p. 284-85.

to statement. His poems offer a particular kind of experience, as music does in a different kind. They should be received in something of the same spirit as music, though this does not mean that they should be reduced to exercises in acoustic. They each have a specific subject-matter which gives rise to a particularity of experience which is unmistakably Hillian. This particularity must be what he had in mind in writing of the effect of poetry as 'being brushed past, or aside, by an alien being'. Being brushed aside is an experience most readers of Hill will recognize; they should also recognize that many poems bring them close to the poet's own 'irreducible bafflement' before 'deeply impacted' ambiguity, a feeling which might well be represented in terms of 'florid grim music', though in fact the varieties of music in his work are many and diverse.

Hill is very uncomplimentary to Eliot's attempts to associate music and poetry (CCW 11, 546, 547, 557). This is partly because he likes to distance himself from Eliot from whom he has learned so much, partly because his notion of poetic music is much closer to Pound's, to which he devotes part of the last of his Clark lectures. Two of the passages he quotes there from Pound are relevant to his own work. The spirit of Hill's earlier poetry is implicit in Pound's account of 'the old music' revived by Arnold Dolmetsch: 'You played it yourself as you read a book of precision ... It was not an interruption but a concentration' (CCW 250). Later, Hill discusses Pound's idea of 'tempo'; this applies to himself also, but even more important is the idea of the 'great bass', particularly to an understanding of Hill's later poems:

> Pound's theory of the 'great bass' in music is that 'down below the lowest note synthesized by the ear and "heard" there are slower vibrations ... The whole question of tempo, and of a main base in all musical structures resides in use of these frequencies'. (CCW 254).

Hill's judgement that in 'Envoi (1919)', 'Pound's melopoeia is itself drawn into a "dance of the intellect among words and ideas, and modification of ideas and characters' (CCW 258) is also pertinent to the musical nature of his own poetry. And it is difficult to grasp. One should probably associate with the idea of the 'great bass' as a principle in Hill's poetry his sense of something hovering about the poems of the metaphysicals: 'There is a kind of poetry [e.g. 'Donne, Herbert, Vaughan'] ... in which the language seems able to hover above itself in a kind of brooding, contemplative, self-rectifying way'.[57] The association is natural because he had his own sense of 'hovering' in the course of composition:

> I have a kind of hovering *feeling*. I see, speaking by analogy, an aura, and I can hear certain phrases just beginning to emerge, phrases of considerable latent possibility. And the difficulty for me is to discover where they might be leading or going.[58]

The 'great bass' in *The Orchards of Syon* and *Speech! Speech!* is thematic, and meant to give direction to the 'phrases of ... latent possibility'. In the case of the lines from 'Ezekiel's Wheel', theme fails, in my judgement, to give direction to a series of striking phrases. The risk of failure is always present for a poet who has 'never begun a poem actually knowing, really, where it was going to end'.[59]

Poetry is not, as Hill knows well, music. The 'hovering' presence of the analogy with music does, however, call into question what poetry *is* for him, and, indeed, for the reader. *The Triumph of Love* is particularly challenging in this respect; but, throughout the *oeuvre*, the status of the poem is a cause of concern. 'September Song' illustrates this. Hill's own 'recalcitrance' is built into his poems:

> there is something naturally incoherent in me, just as ... there is probably something, at some level, anarchic, because the kind of obsessive concern I have with order in the early work is one that somebody has who feels all the time how endangered order is, and what a potential threat to order *he* is.[60]

The 'anarchic' side of the poet is out in the open in the later poetry.

The challenge of the poetry is partly to grasp the kind of 'anarchic' music it makes (there is some resemblance to the music of Harrison Birtwistle in the demands made upon the audience, and in the bafflement which the work of both artists embodies). But partly the challenge is to the reader to exert a contrary force. If Hill's commitment to power has a lot to do with finding a counterpoise to the pressure of

---

[57] 'The Art of Poetry', p. 283.
[58] 'The Art of Poetry', pp.289-90.
[59] 'The Art of Poetry', p. 289.
[60] 'The Art of Poetry', p.290.

language upon the poet that leaves him helpless, then a questioning, determining pressure upon the poems from his readers is needed to confirm the reality of their poetic power and, in so far as he is within them, of their creator also. Hill has praised the 'dogged resistance' of Hopkins to the 'inertial drag of speech' (CCW 108, 91). He exemplifies a similar resistance, but we devalue it if we, in turn, are not prepared to resist it if and when it appears wrongly directed. Hill's way of being difficult often flatters current notions of what poetry, especially a modern poetry, ought to be. It is too easy to argue that his 'complexity ... is ... a complexity of our time'.[61] It has an alienated – or even alien – quality after all, that such a judgement denies. The reader is, and should be, hard put to it to know what to make of it. He *is* a difficult poet. It was deeply misleading of him, in reply to a question (in 1986) about his alleged difficulty, that it was his 'fate, within the domain of rumour, to be regarded as "this notoriously difficult poet"', and his recantation ('We are difficult' and so on) was called for.[62]

At one or two points, this essay has suggested a resistant response to one aspect or another of the poems, and sometimes to a poet whose sense of the poetic invitation is often absent, and (implicitly) to a nascent expository tradition that has too much of the inert about it. But it would be wrong to conclude without acknowledging that Geoffrey Hill has a place among the greatest of our poets, and, one might add, the most generous, for what is it but generosity that takes the poetic risks and suffers the poetic pains that he does? I should like to conclude with a list of some of the poems and volumes for which I am most grateful: 'Funeral Music', 'The Songbook of Sebastian Arrurruz', *Mercian Hymns*, most of *Tenebrae*, *The Mystery of the Charity of Charles Péguy*, 'Sorrel' and 'Sobieski's Shield' (at least) from *Canaan*, many poems in *Without Title*, and the bulk of *A Treatise of Civil Power*, not to mention the extremely beautiful 'Sei Madrigali' in *Al Tempo de' Tremuoti* (BH 930-32). These are the justification for Hill's difficulties.

---

[61] Dodsworth, p. 290.

[62] 'David Sexton talks to Geoffrey Hill', *Literary Review*, February 1986, p.28: 'We are difficult. Human beings are difficult. We're difficult to ourselves, we're difficult to each other ... One encounters in any ordinary day far more real difficulty than one confronts in the most "intellectual" piece of work.' ('The Art of Poetry', p. 276).

*Postscript 2017*
This essay may reflect some of my own difficulties in writing about those of the poet in his own lifetime. I found Geoffrey Hill's remarks about difficulty disingenuous and unhelpful, and the adoption of his account by his admirers unhelpful to interested readers. Hill's conflicting feelings about the exercise of poetic power result in an unusually complex poetry of very variable degrees of success, particularly at the level of expression. This made it difficult for me to deal with the later poetry, in which ideas of 'balance' are less evident and achievement more erratic. If my account of difficulty in the second part of the essay has a certain circularity, this is because I was mindful of the later poetry's power to grip the reader intellectually and expressively at the same time as tending to dissipate itself in incoherence and desperate gesture. There is a parallel in this with the late poems of Paul Celan, which one would not be without, but which have a similar quality of often not coming together as the author seems to require. Hill's later poetry, like that of Celan, asks for a way of reading that is both engaged and resistant, which I tried to exemplify without too much insistence on what I found unsatisfactory. In the result, some of the ambivalence ascribed to Hill's difficulties may be felt to be reflected in my response to them. Hill's feelings about power seem deeply involved in his upbringing as the only son of a village policeman, isolated from the community in one sense and deeply implicated in it in another. The essay does not go far into this sensitive matter, partly out of respect for the poet himself, partly because, if you think of the poems as 'brushed past, or aside, by an alien being', Hill is that alien being, and I would not wish the alien quality to be dissipated in speculation about the life.

*Post-postscript 2019*
The passage of time has given me the chance of a few words on Hill's posthumous sequence *The Book of Baruch by Justin the Gnostic*.[63] There is menace in the title but atonement in the text, which is noticeably relaxed and relatively accessible. It is extensively allusive and there is ambiguity, but the allusions are mainly familiar (to readers of Hill) and ambiguity is kept within limits. The publisher describes the sequence as 'written in long lines of variable length, with much off-rhyme and

---

[63] *The Book of Baruch by the Gnostic Justin*, ed. Kenneth Haynes (Oxford: Oxford University Press, 2019).

internal rhyme'.[64] It is, in effect, rhythmic and musical prose. The form is described by the poet as 'a cyclic pindaric ode' (section 260), cyclic in the recurrence of themes and Pindaric in its commemoration of heroes. The poem is also a journal – 'more of a daybook than ever *The Daybooks* were' (section 186) – and the agony of creation is considerably abated: 'Notice how comfortably unsettled I become the more this sequence is revealed as my real home' (section 256). 'Home' is poignant in the light of the glimpses given of the poet's early days: 'that marred childhood of which I am both ashamed and proud' (section 260). The Gnosticism referred to throughout the poem reflects a dualist view of the material world as, at the least, hopelessly flawed and a spiritual world which expresses itself in terms of 'intrinsic value', though there is a good deal more to it than that.

*Baruch* shows a poet whose self-awareness did not exclude some awareness of the problems outlined in the first part of my essay, and its function as a kind of 'home' for the writer obviously connects with my account of some of the poet's personal difficulties. 'My odes are a form of "oppositional defiance disorder"' (section 268), he says, and this re-affirms his insistence that he was not a prophet and encourages (in my opinion) a more modest, human and inspiriting view of what the poems do, as do the many references to music and his own musical gifts.

It is a generous book and reflects the best of his nature (he was a very lovable man); it is also in continuity with his most serious concerns to which a new humanity is added. With *The Book of Baruch*, we are once more emphatically in the poet's debt.

---

[64] https://global.oup.com/academic/product/the-book-of-baruch-by-the-gnostic-justin-9780198829522?q=book%20of%20baruch&lang=en&cc=gb# [accessed 29 March 2019].

Chapter Nine

# Playing (to) the Crowd: Examining Performance in *Speech! Speech!*

## Samira Nadkarni

In an interview in the spring of 2000, Geoffrey Hill discussed his then latest work, a long poem entitled *Speech! Speech!* which dealt extensively with the notion of the self and one's voice in the world. In doing so, he raised several important questions, stating:

> The world is full of noise, the noise of opinion. Are you going to be able to master some small aspect of it, and use it in the making of your own voice? Or is it stronger than you are? Do I mean stronger or just louder? These particular difficulties, and other vaguer apprehensions seem to me to be the force field of making and, in a way, self-making.[1]

Hill's statement suggests that selfhood in the contemporary world is manufactured or created, produced either by a controlled amalgamation of opinion, or by the self being overwhelmed by opinion. While Hill's stance in the poem is far from unique in this regard, it manifests itself uniquely to depict this theorising of the construction of selfhood within the space of the poem's performance; the poem representing not simply the voice of the primary poetic persona, but also the surrounding din that constitutes the 'noise of opinion'. A music-hall-inspired tirade of fragments, allusions, quotes and imperatives does much to depict the discourse of contemporary culture through its frequent references to various historical events, literary works, music, the radio, as well as the media at large. The poem deliberately presents itself as satire or farcical performance, with the poetic persona in the role of paid performer, underlining the manufactured nature of selfhood and the performances that allow for this creation to occur. This essay considers the poem's

---

[1] Carl Phillips, 'The Art of Poetry LXXX: Geoffrey Hill', *The Paris Review*, 154.42 (Spring 2000), 272-99 (p. 290).

performance in detail and its relation to this theorising of selfhood.[2]

The poem enacts the discourse of the contemporary world, what Hill has referred to as the 'noise of opinion', raising questions about the constitution of the self, the language used in its expression, and the loss of self associated with living in contemporary society. The poem is concerned with the self whose struggle for expression is threatened by all things in discourse and communication that are alien to its own being. Through the performance of this poetic persona, the reader is exposed to the notion that a number of aspects of contemporary life have degenerated into farcical performances – from the appearance of mourning the dead to the erotic, the commodifying aspect of modern life appears to pervade it all. It is clear that *Speech! Speech!* is essentially intended to be read as a farcical representation of the contemporary world, which at times appears more or less a farce itself. Yet there exists within the poem the search for an authentic voice among the many inauthentic voices of our time. The authority assumed by the primary poetic persona does not stand in for authenticity, for, as the poem shows, the poetic persona is just as likely to be inauthentic as the din of voices that surrounds his own. Hill's complicated suspension of the poem between authoritative and farcical, and between artistic and consumerist, then suggests that a discussion regarding his use of performance as simultaneously theme and technique is of particular importance.

The use of the term 'performance' is both considered and specific, and requires a certain amount of explication. Any critical undertaking that chooses to deal with Hill's work must simultaneously undertake a concern with the nature of language, with its specificities; the terms themselves must be made explicit as far as language allows. A discussion of performance, therefore, does not merely constitute a summarised notion of the term as per its conventional usage, as a literary, artistic or creative work, but requires that it be used as per the entirety of its contemporary definitions in the *OED*. 'Performance', apart from the definition just given, is also used to refer to the doing of an action or operation; the competence or effectiveness of the person in carrying out the action required of them as measured against the standard; a notable deed or exploit; the accomplishment of the commanded action; a ceremony, rite or ritual; the execution or interpretation of a piece; a public appearance by a performing artist or an occasion on which the

---

[2] Quotations from *Speech! Speech!* are based on BH. The differences from SS are in most cases changes of punctuation, especially the removal of accents and / or caesura marks.

work is presented; a display of anger or exaggerated behaviour; a fuss or a scene; a difficult, time-consuming, or annoying action or procedure, as well as the fulfilment or discharge of a duty, command, purpose or promise. Moreover, the term can be used in specific ways in specific contexts. For example, in business, the term refers to the extent to which an investment is profitable, especially in relation to other commodities, whereas psychology refers to performance as indicating the observable or measurable behaviour of a person or an animal in a particular, usually experimental situation. All of these definitions will play a part in the discussion of performance that follows, differentiating themselves within the poem as per their use as either theme or technique, and occasionally overlapping each other.

It is worth clarifying at the outset that the poem will not be discussed as performance poetry as this concerns the spontaneous creation of poetry during a performance and its later transcription. Nor will there be a discussion regarding Hill's own reading as the stresses and pauses of the performance are already included in the written copy; although the sequence of the poem is structured so as to be considered in the vein of an actual performance, complete with differing voices, interruptions, and the occasional digression, the poem itself is written, conceptualised and edited, each stanza consisting of exactly twelve lines. And though the poem occasionally attempts the pretence of spontaneity, the poetic persona openly admits to editing his copy and to a lack of spontaneity in stanzas 6, 86, 92, and 115 (BH 291, 331, 334, 346; SS 3, 43, 46, 58). It would seem that the poem repeats the manufactured status Hill has accorded to the selves of the contemporary world. The poem is a made thing, is the poet's attempt to control and mould this contemporary discourse, presenting it as performance, in the shape of a creative, literary work. Performance is therefore presented as both theme and technique.

This then plays into the fact that *Speech! Speech!*'s staged performance relies upon the reader's understanding of its satirical aspect, its role as simultaneously authentic, as well as a sham. John M. Lyon has noted that *Speech! Speech!* draws on the theatricality of music-hall comedians and is greatly indebted to the work of veteran performers such as Hylda Baker, Frankie Howerd and Charlie Chaplin. Hill draws upon the sheer physicality of these acts – the need for gestures and facial expressions – and transposes them into language, effecting their sheer ferocity and humour through the use of word play, line division, caesurae and enjambment. The poem is by turns probing, grotesque, satirical, farcical, and melancholy; the sequence moves rapidly between different tones and emotions, using music hall's juxtaposition of serious and humorous issues to provoke a reaction from his audience of readers.[3] Furthermore, the speed of delivery, the inclusion of stage directions and the reactions of the fictional audience, all add to the notably theatrical tone. Much like an actual performance, the sequence takes moments in which to break the tension, usually through misquotes or tongue-in-cheek references to desire or scatology, a fact that is overtly acknowledged within the framework of the poem itself at the close of stanza 74 (BH 325; SS 37). It is worth noting that the sequence's pretence of spontaneity gestures once more towards its basis as a music-hall performance – that these performances are generally rehearsed, timed and scripted for best effect upon the audience is a well-known fact; despite their pretence of spontaneity, all the movements on stage are planned. The poem emulates this aspect as well: that it is meant to be read as a pre-written performance, complete in itself, is clear from the fact that all the performers, from the critics to the audience, from the questioning and dissenting voices to the catcalls and cheers, are contained within the sequence. The execution and interpretation of the piece are written into its body. In this respect, the sequence appears to trap the reader into following the staged performance – both accord and discord have been accounted for within its framework.

It seems that in drawing on the British music-hall tradition, Hill lays notable emphasis on the poetic persona himself, the primary performer within the poem. However, the connection implied between the self and the poetic persona makes this a particularly complex arena, especially with regard to the notion of the personal within Hill's work. The poem makes clear at the outset that it is, in fact, a performance, thus implying a distance between the actuality of performer and his act. However, Hill's inclusion of numerous aspects of the personal within the poem complicates any analysis of this performance.[4] As numerous critics have noted, Hill's previous alignment with T.S. Eliot's famous assertion in 'Tradition and the Individual Talent' that 'Poetry is not a turning loose

---

[3] John M. Lyon, '"What are you incinerating?": Geoffrey Hill and Popular Culture', *English*, 54.209 (Summer 2005), 85-98 (p. 90).

[4] Personal elements from Hill's own life, such as the medication required for his depression and its effects upon his work, his then-recent heart-attack, his early memories of radio programmes such as *Worker's Playtime*, and a reference to the death of his friend David Wright, all make an appearance within *Speech! Speech!*.

of emotion, but an escape from emotion; it is not the expression of personality, but an escape from personality' assured the reader that the personal was evicted from his work whenever possible, resulting in 'the fullest possible objectification of individual subjectivity'.[5] However, over a period of time there appeared to be a softening in Hill's views with regard to his position on the presence of subjectivity in his work, confirmed in interview when he stated that, while he still agreed with Eliot's assertions, he thought his previous views too absolute, and the result of a misinterpretation of Eliot's words.[6]

Arguably, Hill's modified understanding of Eliot's argument has led to a significant shift in the construction of his poetic personae. The critic is led to assume that his current work with its inflection of the personal, now mediated by self-knowledge and self-awareness, or what Hill himself terms 'autobiographical comedy, or even clownishness', will continue to follow the argument set out in Eliot's essay, although now adhering to a new understanding of what this argument entails.[7] Eliot's assertions in 'Tradition and the Individual Talent' suggest that the poet is called upon to achieve a state of impersonality in order to adhere to tradition, by 'surrendering himself wholly to the work to be done' in order to depict, not the singular emotions of the individual as poet, but rather an emotion or set of emotions which would have their life in the poem, and which would for their power call upon the materiality of the poem itself.[8] Eliot even goes so far as to suggest that his position may imply an 'attack' upon 'the metaphysical notion of the substantial unity of the soul'.[9]

Following this trend, Hill's own statements in the *Paris Review* interview would appear to adhere to this rejection of a single individual personality; despite the appearance of the personal, or rather the biographical, within his work, Hill's poetry would still appear to reject any notion of an authentic self implied by the metaphysical notion of the unity of the soul. Rather, he states outright that the creation of a poetic persona that evidences traits of the personal does not necessarily signify its authenticity:

---

[5] *Selected Prose of T. S. Eliot*, ed. Frank Kermode (London: Faber & Faber, 1975), p. 21; 'The Art of Poetry', p. 282.

[6] 'The Art of Poetry', p. 282.

[7] 'The Art of Poetry', p. 284.

[8] *Selected Prose of T. S. Eliot*, p. 22.

[9] *Selected Prose of T. S. Eliot*, p. 19.

as if the self-expression were ectoplasm emanating in a continuous stream from the allegedly authentic self. One's idea of the authentic self may be different from the authentic self as it really is.[10]

In this manner the supposedly authentic self is both presented and disavowed, accord and discord are both accounted for within the poem, and the critic cannot help but be aware that any presumption on their part could pose them as merely another haplessly grinning fool in the crowd, a reference no doubt underlined by the use of Daumier's '*On dit que les Parisiens sont difficiles à satisfaire*' for its cover image. And as Romana Huk states, these methods then:

> present an example of a developing strain of poststructuralist practice that, instead of calling for the total absolution of the subjective principle ... advocated "using the force [or struggle] of the subject to break through the deception of constitutive identity" in order to reveal the structure of contradiction that forges it.[11]

It would appear that in applying Eliot's guidelines, Hill presents the reader with the made thing, the poem itself, rather than with any connection to Hill himself as a single linking persona, although to completely disavow this persona would be a grave error. Moreover, the role of this poetic persona is further complicated by Hill's patterning of the poem as a theatrical performance as this implies that the role of the performer is in fact simply that: a role that could be played by any actor with the appropriate script. The role of the performer thus presents itself as a free-floating 'I' that is non-subjective and cannot be seen as a single self. Thus the effacement one encounters in the reading of this poem is not simply Hill's own, but also the effacement of the poetic persona as poet, who presents himself as publicly playing a role for the masses. As Andrew Roberts has noted of the poem:

---

[10] 'The Art of Poetry', pp. 283-284.

[11] Romana Huk, 'Poetry of the Committed Individual: Jon Silkin, Tony Harrison, Geoffrey Hill, and the Poets of Postwar Leeds', in *Contemporary British Poetry: Essays in Theory and Criticism*, ed. James Acheson and Romana Huk (New York, NY: State University of New York Press, 1996), pp. 175-220 (p. 180).

The voice of Hill's own persona is a persistent linking thread, but is constantly interrupted, undercut, and quarrelled with, from within and without, by other voices and other discourses. These works bring Hill somewhat closer to those forms of postmodernist or avant-garde poetry which displace subjectivity into discursive multiplicity, partly in response to the deconstruction of subjectivity in postmodern literary and cultural theory. Yet, characteristically, Hill's trajectory remains unique.[12]

Roberts' description of Hill's having displaced subjectivity into discursive multiplicity would then hold true not only for the subjective voice of the figure of the poet being displaced into the added multiplicity of his critics and audience, but the further displacement evidenced by the poetic persona himself as performer merely playing the role required of him. In Hill's revised adoption of Eliot's stance, the 'I' figured is one that balances itself between Hill's own 'I' inflected and mediated by 'autobiographical clownishness' and the 'I' of the performer playing a role. The coalescing of these two 'I's then produces nothing so much as the poet's own continual surrender to that which is considered most valuable – the work. Hill's displacement of subjectivity into discursive multiplicity and its pretence of fragmentation, moments of recitation or repetition underlining his depiction of modern slavish not-selves, displays not the voice of an authentic self existing and being overwhelmed, but rather a questioning of any self at all, authentic or otherwise. The 'I' presents itself as merely part of the work, the element of the personal both present and evicted, and displaying at its close nothing more than the medium, the 'I' of the poet in which impressions and experiences combine and are described in his speech.[13] The poetic

---

[12] Andrew Michael Roberts, *Geoffrey Hill* (Devon: Northcote House Publishers Ltd, 2004), p. 30.

[13] The term 'medium' here would be intended in both its senses, as an intervening state or substance in which something is achieved, but also as a spiritual medium. The figure of the poet is depicted as a prophet who speaks for the past and the present, yet evicts himself before he speaks for the future; as Bromwich notes, 'He speaks perhaps as a lesser prophet in the hope of a greater to come' (David Bromwich, 'Geoffrey Hill and the Conscience of Words', in *Skeptical Music* (Chicago, IL and London: University of Chicago Press, 2001), p. 160). The prophetic performance is undermined by the unwieldy nature of language itself and the poet's knowledge that his words will probably be either misunderstood or silenced as evidenced by the final stanza of the poem. He

persona that speaks in the field of the poem is constructed in a twofold manner, as part of the literary work, and as being constituted through his representation of self, a representation that appears strongly influenced by the media.

The poet offers a possible respite from this bleak presentation by urging the reader once more towards memory and the need to honour the dead, underlining the significance of the individual's own relation to historicity. The performer's mixture of formal and colloquial speech, his use of canonical literature, art, and popular culture, continue to underline Hill's adherence to the prescriptions set out in 'Tradition and the Individual Talent', this time with regard to a poet's association with the past, and the need for historicity in his work. As Eliot states:

> the historical sense involves a perception, not only of the pastness of the past, but of its presence; the historical sense compels a man to write not merely with his own generation in his bones, but with a feeling that the whole of the literature of Europe from Homer and within it the whole of the literature of his own country has a simultaneous order. This historical sense, which is a sense of the timeless as well as of the temporal and of the timeless and of the temporal together, is what makes a writer traditional. And it is at the same time what makes a writer most acutely conscious of his place in time, of his own contemporaneity.[14]

Hill's use of numerous historical, literary and media-related allusions, when seen in this light, suggests the creation of a historical sense ('timeless' in Eliot's sense), and of memory; a moment in which the poet is commenting not just on the present, but also on the past. Thus the poem, although based in contemporary culture, is viewed through the medium of the past; much like Adorno's elaboration on Sartre's view of the committed writer, he writes not only from within history but also from within the framework of its complicitous medium,

---

speaks in hope of a future prophet who will reconstitute the meaning behind these words into precise and more meaningful terms; one who will recognise the value of the past and the knowledge provided within the poet's speech, and enact his own future performance to a better and more discerning crowd.

[14] *Selected Prose of T.S. Eliot*, p. 14.

language.¹⁵ *Speech! Speech!* displays Hill's concern with the need for the poet to awaken the masses, to attend to language in its fallen state, and to honour and remember the dead; the poem performs Hill's discharge of this undertaken duty.

However, despite the poetic persona having urged the reader towards the relative safety of memory and historicity, these notions are not excluded from the field of the poem's satire, forcing us to view them with a certain degree of scepticism. It is possible that these values could be misconstrued within memory, thereby constituting a false myth, an example of which could be the wondrous fictionalised version of England, the 'Good Old England' that is then mocked in stanza 35 (BH 306; SS 18) of the poem. It is this world that the poet inhabits, a world in which 'the PEOPLE' have been reduced to merely corporate buzzwords and performance has taken over all aspects of life. The sequence suggests the manipulation of the emotions of the masses with regard to the fields of faith, patriotism, the erotic, to even the acts of mourning the dead. Even the poetic persona is not spared as his performance is intended for the consumption of 'the PEOPLE', a layered reference that manages to simultaneously indicate not only the masses of the contemporary world, but also the popular magazine of the same name. The poet-performer himself is not excluded from participation in this commercialisation; despite his clearly satirical jabs at the commercialist nature of post-modern society, he relies upon the sale of his work in order to actually promote his own philosophy. It is in this manner that the poem balances itself between the extremes of the capitalistic media and its satire; the speaker speaks directly from within the system he seeks to circumvent.

However, despite the fact that the poetic persona is active in the consumerist culture in which his orations are marketed and sold, he still exerts what control he can over his work; he refuses to simplify the complexities of language within which he attempts to constitute self-expression. The performer displays anger at the calls to oversimplify and further commercialise his work, stating:

> Consensual
> the gifts of sex, of oratory, in both

---

[15] Romana Huk discusses the ways in which Adorno, in his essays 'Commitment' and 'Lyric Poetry and Society' 'critiques (and historicizes) Sartre's model of transcendent intersubjective praxis based on a writer's freedom to choose' (Huk, pp. 179-181).

> unequalled. Ogled by reborn commerce,
> nó, I will nót speak straightly but abide
> my chainhood on the block.
> (BH 327; SS 39)

This echoes Hill's own stance:

> one of the things the tyrant most cunningly engineers is the gross oversimplification of language, because propaganda requires that the minds of the collective respond primitively to slogans of incitement. And any complexity of language, any ambiguity, any ambivalence implies intelligence. Maybe an intelligence under threat, maybe an intelligence that is afraid of consequences, but nonetheless an intelligence working in qualifications and revelations ... resisting, therefore, tyrannical simplification.[16]

In refusing to restrain the poem's difficulty, to convert his methods of expression into an easier format, the performer acts against the current commodifying culture, one that appears to be equated with the current totalitarian doctrine of the media. The poem displays its simultaneous theme and technique of performance once more, its enactment being time-consuming and difficult to approach on the part of the reader, and this difficulty openly declaimed by the performer. The poetic persona's resistance to simplifying his words largely mirrors Hill's own critical reception; it appears that on this topic both Hill and his persona speak with the same voice. If one accepts that the self is negotiated through a mediation of the personal in language, then the need to simplify the work implies a corresponding simplification of the self, a demotion to another simple and easily defined catch-phrase, a not-self:

> You áre
> wantonly obscure, *man sagt*. ACCESSIBLE
> traded as DEMOCRATIC, he answers
> (BH 347; SS 59)

This echoes Hill's stance with regard to the nature of communication in the contemporary world, as he has stated:

---

[16] 'The Art of Poetry', p. 277.

> I think that the field of modern communications would like to think that it is neo-Lockean, but in fact, at its worst it has none of the limited but definite virtues that Locke had. It is reductive, and yet chaotic. Or, let us say, reductive, oversimplified, and yet violently confrontational. Such simplification of language – what one might call a kind of mass-demotic – is gripped by its own oxymoron; purporting to be accessible, it is in fact haughty and condescending, because it will not respect the intelligence of those from whom it demands a response.[17]

The poet's refusal to entertain the simplification of language in his work exemplifies what Andrew Roberts has noted – that Hill appears to fear the trivialising influence of the public sphere on poetry.[18] But it appears that Hill's fears extend beyond the bounds of poetry, to all the multiplicities of contemporary life that are now governed by performance and production. If various aspects of life are to become performances, then it raises the question of an audience and the need to market it to the masses. That the dead, the erotic, language (and its use in poetry in particular), the personal, faith and patriotism all appear to be performances in the contemporary world raises the notion that it is simply a matter of time before these too are marketed out to the public sphere; that is, if it has not already begun.

The media circus surrounding the death of Diana, Princess of Wales, extensively referenced in *Speech! Speech!* (BH 299, 306, 319, 324, 335; SS 11, 18, 31, 36, 47), shows that these fears are not unfounded. The poem satirises the apparent mythical stature awarded to Diana upon her death by the people of England and the world at large, the near reverence accorded to her memory. The sequence suggests that the media played a large role in the idealisation of the consequent mourning that took place, a fact that the performer mocks overtly:

> Age of mass consent: go global with her.
> ...
> Pledge to immoderacy the outraged
> hardly forgiven mourning of the PEOPLE,
> inexorable, though in compliance,

---

[17] 'The Art of Poetry', p. 280.
[18] Roberts, p. 34.

>     media-conjured. Inscrutable Í call
>     her spirit now on this island: memory
>     subsiding into darkness, nowhere
>     coming to rest.
>     (BH 299; SS 11)

The poet-performer believes that this media-conjured relentless mourning for the death of Diana robs it of much of its authenticity. The result of this manipulation is that it fails to hold true, fails to be converted into lasting memory. Instead, it is created and marketed as commodified suffering that is then sold to and consumed by the masses. The manipulation that occurs does not restrict itself simply to the exploitation of the memory of Diana, as there is also the manipulation of the people of England, the media-encompassed PEOPLE, whom the poet-performer exhorts to awaken to their reality:

>     It is not Ceres' living child I see
>     broken asprawl inside the wind-tunnel,
>     from limo to limbo in a soundbite,
>     fuck-up as obligation. ENGLAND AWAKE.
>     You fell for Aladdin's Uncle—one of those.
>     (BH 319; SS 31)

The sequence labels the media 'Aladdin's Uncle', the villain of the piece who attempts to manipulate the characters of the story in search of constant and greater power; the two are equated within the bounds of the poem. The poetic persona is attempting to awaken the people of England to the fact that they are being misled, manipulated into performing the memory of Diana as idealised myth rather than conventional mortality. It is in this manner that memory and history are misread and misconstrued, turned into 'a botched business, / out of our hands, *reduced* to the Sublime' (BH 324; SS 36).[19] Despite the fact that there is an acknowledgement of the dead, a ritual of mourning that is enacted, it is corrupted by this overt and false idealisation that elevates them beyond reality; the memorial and remembrance are converted into a sham, a performance, one that the poem echoes within its satire.

Unable to trust the media and the now commercialised acts of mourning, the sequence's satire is enacted from a position of doubt.

---

[19] My italics.

It is from this same position that the question of religion is discussed. The performer questions the system of belief within his performance, presenting the possibility that the performance of religion may have always been an idealised myth constituted by the promotion of 'magistrates, prophets, / and visionary infants', and likened to 'fanatical / expressionless self-creation on a stuck-track' (BH 290; SS 2). After all, as the poetic persona questions, 'who on earth will protest?' (BH 290; SS 2) as spirituality requires the assumption of faith. However, the poet figure is less interested in the question of belief than the need to believe in a *real* and *true* spirituality. The sequence is notably concerned with the possibility that religion and spirituality have also been manipulated and media-conjured, similar to the death of Diana; the poet-performer is involved in the seemingly notable deed of attempting to awaken his audience to this possibility. It is in this manner that the poetic persona appears to equate religion with the blind followers of a cult, likening the gestures that emphasise spirituality to a sort of ritualistic lip service, an enactment of that which is expected. The use of images such as that of a welcoming show-host, the terms 'communications breakdown' and 'stuck-track' (BH 290; SS 2) all imply that religion has been appropriated by consumer-based popular culture, associated and run under the unnamed god, the media. And it is important to note that the poetic persona does not merely imply that the performance associated with religion is a contemporary phenomenon; rather he equates it with the performances of Reformation woodcuts, a popular means by which to enact morals and religious principles of the Lutheran faith in the sixteenth century. It is made clear by this conjunction that the performance of religion has been a component from the moment of its conception; it is not simply another aspect of the modern phenomenon. However, as the performer notes, religion's relation to spirituality makes it particularly hard to pin down to a single position, his own work shifting to reflect this melding:

> It was not so much
> cultic pathology I had in mind
> as ethical satire; but you wriggle so,
> old shape-shifter.
> (BH 298; SS 10)

The poetic persona both fears and questions the fact that the masses may be led by the media to settle for this myth rather than any actuality of the divine, manipulated by their following of the 'unnamed god'. The dominion of the media over 'the PEOPLE' thus appears insurmountable as questioning would go against the need for unassailable faith. The poem's ethical satire is therefore concerned with a need to question the contemporary state's establishment of the notion of selfhood as defined by these various facets of culture – the enacting of the act.

Upon consideration, it appears possible that the not-selves of the contemporary world, which, mired in directive-ridden culture, currently evade authenticity, come to reflect (albeit in a skewed manner) Hill's own past need to evade the self within language. His previous burial of the self in the not-self of language in order to objectify to the fullest possible means any expression of individual subjectivity, seems to mirror the state of 'the PEOPLE' of the modern world who have buried themselves in the meaningless phrases and prescriptive normalities of contemporary culture. This is underlined by the sequence's stressing of the undeniable influence of the media through television, radio, and popular magazines such as *The People*, *Time*, *Life* and *Variety*. It appears that the poetic persona fears the lack of individuality caused and expressed through mass culture, or pseudo-culture, created not by the masses but by the media governing them, and mediated by capitalism:

> COMPETITIVE DEVALUATION—a great find
> wasted on pleasantries of intermission.
> Say it: licence to silence; say it: me
> Tarzan, you ǀ diva of multiple choice,
> rode proud on our arousal-cárrousel.
> (BH 315; SS 27)

>         Say this was my idea. THIS
> WAS MY IDEA.
> (BH 323; SS 35)

Mass culture appears to be largely governed by commercial directives, the repetitive 'say it' ingraining it into mass memory, culture itself becoming a mass act presided over by the body of the media. The performer underlines this directive-driven aspect of language by peppering his speech and the audience's response with a number of such directives as in stanzas 26, 40, and 94 (BH 301, 308, 335; SS 13, 20, 47). However, the performer is unable to exist outside of the pseudo-culture that encompasses contemporary life, so that all he can do is include this aspect within his performance. His work protesting this commodification is sold, its ability to reach the masses relying on its profitability, especially in relation to other commodities of the same nature; as the performer notes, 'EITHER WAY THEY GET YOU ... Not everything / is as we want it' (BH 320; SS 32).

The poetic persona's orations now appear more terrifying than before: if religion, patriotism, the act of mourning and honouring the dead have all been reduced to mere commodities, if one's self constituted within these acts is merely another performance on the world's stage, then it may in fact be impossible to retain a relation to one's own historicity without it being tainted by media-manipulated performances. Individuality and selfhood appear beyond hope if they are to be confirmed in this manner. The mediation of selfhood that Eliot and Hill recommend then seems redundant, as the self as individual has potentially ceased to exist. Arguably Hill's own mediation of subjectivity, both past and present, is distinct from the loss of individuality implied in mass culture: the two cannot simply be equated as the not-selves of contemporary culture are mired in the prescriptive generalities of language, whereas Hill's own mediation of self takes place within the bounds of an extremely particular and defined use of language. However, it is worth noting that *both* uses of language subdue any hint of subjective individuality. The poetic persona's apparent awareness of this possibility reveals the need for his performance, his need to engender some form of response from the crowd, if only to awaken them to the possibility of their participation in this performance and subsequent loss of individuality and selfhood.

The poem's use of contemporary language evidences a medium that appears to fragment with an eventual lack of eloquence; as David Bromwich notes, the poem is concerned with disintegration.[20] The poetic persona is therefore not simply conscious of himself and his place in terms of the past and present, but also of his place within language, and in its means of expression:

---

[20] David Bromwich, 'Muse of Brimstone', *New York Times*, March 11 2001.<https://archive.nytimes.com/www.nytimes.com/books/01/03/11/reviews/010311.11bromwit.html> [accessed on 14 June 2017], (para. 2).

> Thís lays it ón | a shade: in the arms
> of his claustral love. A pun, then, *arms*? He's that
> sort of a mind. Another one on *lays*:
> lays it | on a sháde—are you still wíth me
> yet wandering, blocked words hung round neck
> on a noose of twine: his own name included.
> (BH 334; SS 46) [21]

The performer is notably conscious of means by which language can be twisted to multiplicities of meaning; the performer questions 'Why and how / in these orations do I twist my text?' (BH 301; SS 13). Language is a primary concern for many performers, and there remains the need to choose words wisely so as to evoke the desired response from the crowd. As Hill has stated on more than one occasion, words are meant to be difficult for a poet; the same is applicable to the entertainer. It appears that one of Hill's themes within *Speech! Speech!* is the apparent opposition of the conventional aesthetic view of poetry with the broader conception of language as performative utterance or propaganda; a concept that appears to be taken from his early essay 'Our Word is Our Bond' and further explored within his poetry. The sequence attempts to escape these confining classifications by constituting what Hill terms 'an atonement of aesthetics with a rectitude of judgement.' (CCW 12) Thus, Hill's use of music hall, his utilisation of contemporary jargon, and the juxtaposition of the same with more traditional forms and styles through the poem's broad use of inter and intra-textuality immediately places the sequence outside of this traditionally aesthetic view. Furthermore, the breaks, diversions and interspersions prevent the poem from achieving the fluidity necessary for what has traditionally been considered to be poetry. This opposition is further complicated by Hill's fear of the trivialising influence of the public sphere and its possible effect on poetry; the speech of the public persona, while couched in and around performative propaganda, is in fact ethical satire that mocks itself while assuming its form. And yet, the poetic persona believes that this satire will fail to hold true; his final words predict a world where he has been silenced, his use of language critiqued and evicted. As Bromwich notes, in his work 'Hill seems to be pointing to a world of speech in which poetic assertions, if rightly

---

[21] In SS the fifth line quoted reads 'Wandering again, blocked words hung around neck'.

framed, will never be liable to persuade – as if poetry might succeed at last in making nothing happen'.[22]

The description of the manipulation of this medium thus provides Hill with the means by which to discuss the potential reception of the performance itself. The poetic persona is constantly concerned by the need to evoke a greater sentiment than that which has been evoked by his numerous critics, the RAPMASTER of the piece, measuring his competence of ability to perform as measured against these critics:[23]

> Hopefully, RAPMASTER, I can take stock
> how best to out-rap you. Like Herod
> raging in the street-pageants, work the crowd.
> (BH 335; SS 47)

And the fact that Hill uses the term RAPMASTER to define his many critics, combining them into a single insurmountable entity defined by a pithy catch-phrase, appears to be doubly layered. The first association is the fact that the *OED* defines 'rap' as a rebuke or an adverse criticism; thus the term 'RAPMASTER' refers to the performer's many critics. Secondly, *Speech! Speech!* is written with a definite rhythm and meter in mind; the associations of a performance of free-verse rapping, a form of popular music, are then simply adding to the aural aspect of the performance implied by the constant allusions to the radio, and music. Hill adds to this by mentioning John Skelton in stanza 95:

>                     Skelton Laureate
> was a right rapper: outdance yoú with your shades
> any day. And is gone.
> (BH 336; SS 48)

---

[22] Bromwich, pp. 157-58.

[23] It is worth noting that the performance of the critiques presented within the poem greatly resemble critiques levelled against Hill himself by contemporary critics. While it is possible to read the poem as a response, I would argue that Hill's loose incorporation of these critiques as well as his collation of these critics into the singular form of the farcical RAPMASTER potentially undercuts any attempts to consider his response as serious engagement with these critical evaluations.

It is worth noting that Skeltonic verse has been likened to rap music with its short lines of rapidly tumbling rhymes.[24] Moreover, the overt association between Skelton, whose work dealt largely with the morals and ethics of his time, and the performance of ethical satire by the poetic persona is evident. By evoking Skelton, Hill appears to reference his own essay 'The Tartar's Bow and the Bow of Ulysses', in which he states, 'Skelton … makes his metrical variations, from rime royal to macaronic hexameter or to the so-called tumbling verse, embody and enact his ethical priorities.' (CCW 197). That Hill should attempt to do the same is merely to employ Eliot's traditional methods – the performance is creating a sense of timelessness that is brought into contemporaneity by its associations with the present. The performer is attempting to out-critique his critics, out-rap the RAPMASTER, by manipulating the medium of language, and alluding to past associations where the same may have taken place.

Thus, the poetic persona is attempting to make himself heard over the multiplicity of voices that constitute his audience; he is attempting to give rise to a voice that aspires to authenticity – one that speaks with a sense of historical timelessness through its evocation of the past as well as its place in the present. However, as previously stated, this historicity is put in question and, although the performer's voice aspires to express a self, it is repeatedly undercut and undermined by the various voices within the poem that represent both the critics and the audience at large, as well as the self-conscious questioning that arises from Hill's own mediation of the personal. The creation of this voice is therefore fragmented, rapidly disintegrating as the performance proceeds, the poetic persona's early satirical eloquence appearing to give way before an exaggerated, almost manic rush to get the words out before the close of the piece. Nevertheless, it is in this ineloquence that the poem actually achieves its greatest moments; its incoherence lends it strength. The break in which the poetic persona is forced to abandon his point then forces the reader or his apparent listeners to evaluate what is left unsaid; it is in the moment of this break that one is led to reflection. Thus, it appears that one of the methods that Hill applies to the performance itself is the need for the listener or the reader to read between its actual lines, the moments depicting the breakdown of ritualised coherency providing the act with a great deal of its impact. As Hill states:

---

[24] David Mikics, *A New Handbook of Literary Terms* (New Haven, CT and London: Yale University, 2007), p. 92.

the uneloquent is a form of eloquence. Incoherence, like spontaneity itself, may very well be effect, rather than cause … The respect in which I remain consistent is that the only answer is the poem itself, the made thing.[25]

Thus, despite the fact that the performer is concerned with giving the masses what they desire, this in no way diminishes his own moral or ethical stance; the performance of the poetic persona appears to follow Hill's reflections on the character of Clokyd Colusyon in Skelton's *Magnyfycence*, a performer in his own right:

Idle people desire to be entertained; Clokyd Colusyon is entertaining them … Clokyd Colusyon is rightly estimating his place in the world's business; that is his *métier*; but Skelton is also considering him rightly, according to the measure of righteousness. The rectitude of such verse is manifested in its capacity to measure up to the demands of active vice and to the authority of active virtue; it is a brooding third force in which the magisterial rime royal and the cynical travesty of the magisterial style are balanced but not equated. (CCW 197)

While the primary poetic persona within the poem appears particularly concerned with the morality of his act, the need to awaken 'the PEOPLE' to the truth of their historicity, he remains bound within his own associations with this world as well; the poetic persona is not completely innocent, as he has admitted. Hill's method in the performance then, in his search for authenticity, is to walk the thin line between the poetic persona's performance within the performance that appears to constitute the contemporary world, to create a mediating point wherein the two are balanced but not equated. And it appears that Hill succeeds most at the close of the sequence where the primary poetic persona finally falls silent, fragmented, ineloquent, and defeated; the possibility of an authentic voice is situated in the final silence of the piece, within the knowledge of its own futility.

The performer's silence at the close of the piece, his coma-induced loss of self then mirrors the loss of self he believes to be present in contemporary culture. In a world where we *might* once have been products of god, of faith, of history, we are now merely products of the

---

[25] 'The Art of Poetry', p. 289.

media. This is the basis of the performer's speech, his call to awaken, his doomed performance, his prophetic understanding that most of these scripted lines will fall on deaf ears in the present. It is clear that the poem's towering mass of allusions, inter- and intra-textuality, its references to the past and to contemporary culture all make it a particularly dense and complex piece, a long poem that will never be a comfortable read. Hill forces the reader to aspire to understanding, much as he aspires to regain his supposedly lost inspiration. Comprehension of the poem comes at the price of acknowledging that one may be no more than another haplessly grinning fool among the crowd. Hill's mocking encompasses us all, and stunningly, himself as well.

CHAPTER TEN

## 'Like a Mason Addressing a Block': Materiality and Design in Geoffrey Hill's Poetry

NATALIE POLLARD

> [W]hat we should have had around us now, if, instead of quarrelling and fighting over their work ... they had guarded the spoils of their victories. Fancy what Europe would be now, if the delicate statues and temples of the Greeks, – if the broad roads and massy walls of the Romans, – the noble and pathetic architecture of the middle ages, had not been ground to dust.
> —John Ruskin, *Political Economy of Art* [1]

From its investigations of the courtly basilica to the war memorial, portraiture to church design, consort music to pattern poetry, the work of Geoffrey Hill offers a compelling example of the way contemporary British poetry has probed – for its own advantage – the intersecting links between ancient and modern European art and architecture, patronage and the politics of design. Taking an interdisciplinary approach to material culture, this chapter explores how contemporary poetic works make strategic use of the built environment – constructed artefacts to be moved through, inhabited and looked up at – in order to negotiate their cultural inheritance and personal artistic legacy. Reinvesting in built structure on the poetical page, Hill's eye for aesthetic detail is historically and politically attuned to the purposes for which stones, tablets and building blocks have been used and re-used across the arts. He is highly alert to their ability to attract new audience gazes, and to both found and bolster reputations. Money, history, economic nous, and the contribution of Italian, French and German design models to social, rhetorical and moral thought interlace, both in the works Hill redeploys, and in his own English lyric appropriations of the politics of structure.

---

[1] John Ruskin, *The Political Economy of Art: Or, 'A Joy Forever' (and Its Price in the Market), Selections from the Writings of John Ruskin* (London: Smith, Elder & Co, 1871), p. 438.

On the front jacket of Hill's 1998 edition of *The Triumph of Love* is his adaptation of a woodcut from the title page of Lord Morley's *The Tryumphes of Fraunces Petrarcke*, the first English translation of Petrarch's *Trionfi*:

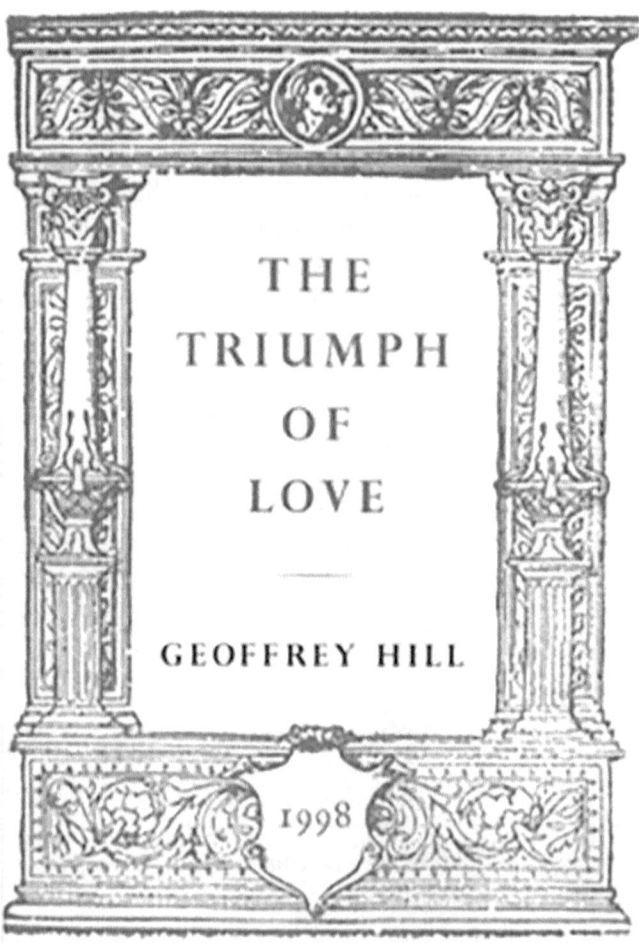

Front jacket illustration of Houghton Mifflin edition of *The Triumph of Love*.[2]

---

[2] Front jacket illustration of Geoffrey Hill, *The Triumph of Love* (Boston, MA and New York, NY: Houghton Mifflin Company, 1998), adapted from the title page of *The Tryumphes of Fraunces Petrarcke*, edited and translated by Henry Parker, Lord Morley, c. 1553.

We gaze on a re-worked copy of a copy, a carrying-over from the already existing translation of Italian to English, and from stone to page. The reader's eye moves from a design reminiscent of an ancient Roman triumphal arch, to its reconceptualisation as the early modern frontispiece of Morley's English translation from Petrarch's Italian, and again to the promotional tactics of Hill's late twentieth-century jacket, designed for his Anglo-American audience.

What do we see? An architectural frame surrounds the contemporary poet's name and title with highly decorated structural motifs, listening back on imperial authority, and its spectacles of might. A row of pilasters spans two levels, and acanthus scroll capitals support the ornate entablature. Elaborate foliate decoration covers the aedicule, and on the stylobate a cartouche announces the date of publication: '1998'. This busy frame draws the eye toward the central uncluttered space of the lettering. The viewer's gaze traverses exterior space as it moves within, crossing a boundary between orders of space as one reads inside the opening, and then again as one turns over into the volume's contents. These boundaries are emphasized by the decision to redeploy a version of a woodcut from the (inner) title page of the first English translation of Petrarch's *Trionfi* as the (outer) jacket of Hill's *Triumph of Love*. Different levels of interiority and exteriority, design style and temporality are traversed as the viewer negotiates both architectural and literary frontispiece: the physical frame that adorns the main entrance to a building is allied with the decorated aperture that appears opposite the title page in many sixteenth-century books, and which itself often employs columns and pediments.

The reader is confronted both by a built structure – which must be passed through in order to enter – and by the physicality of the bookmaker's, printer's, etcher's, publisher's labours with matter and space. The sixteenth-century woodcut blocks that ornamented Petrarch's *Triumphs* emphasized the book as *thing*: an inked and pressed object to be displayed, viewed, handled, and admired as well-made. Anticipating the eyes and the bodies of readers moving through carefully arranged textual and physical space, the frontispiece draws analogies between architecture and text, bookmaking and engraving. In using a reproduction of his predecessor's own reproduction of historico-architectural material for his cover, Hill is freshly alert to the audience-negotiations of early modern bookmaking, and their use-value in the present. Morley's frontispiece not only invited viewers to *enter*, as well as read, his English version of Petrarch's text, it also impressed upon them a sense of restraint and order through its design model: the reader passes through a physical aperture modelled on the stately heroism and formal control of the Greco-Roman triumphal arch.

As such, Hill's pillared frame wields a design authority derived from earlier derivations from the neoclassical organization of space and matter. Hill's *Triumph* lures in readers, and impresses on them the antique authority of its structure. If the printed page invites admiration for its decorative manifestation of the craft of print and textual arrangement, it also marks out for its own ends the historical authority of the built environment. In Hill's use of the sixteenth-century frontispiece as his cover, the orders of classical and early modern architecture – as well as inked material – go in search of public recognition as honed, finished products. They do so through recourse to historical precedent, redeploying the authority of the strictly proportioned materiality of the triumphal arch. Hill's page also draws attention to its borrowing of an already bastardised, copied form; it uses a replication of an already-existing replication; the early modern re-translation, across media, from the Italian. As Pierre de Nolhac observes: 'Petrarch has no credit for the illustrations of his *Trionfi*, which were repeated, again and again in the fifteenth and sixteenth centuries, in paintings, bas-reliefs and tapestries.'[3]

Critics have often noted Hill's lyric focus on labour, materiality and historical reworking; traits that can be seen across his oeuvre, from his early interest in the trade of names and the power of English medieval patronage in *Mercian Hymns* (1971) to his later circumspection about the modern artist's 'genuflections to an audience' and 'benedictions' in *Orchards of Syon* (2002). More rarely has attention focused on Hill's use of the history of argumentation carried in the built environment, and the appropriation of its authority in commissioned work across the arts, as well as in the publishing industry.[4] In order to do so, this chapter will

---

[3] Pierre de Nolhac, *Petrarch & the Ancient World*, Vol 1 (Boston: Merrymount, 1907), p. 31.

[4] For allusions to printing processes see *Clavics*: 'printers' founts' (BH 793; CL 14), 'smudge-typed' (BH 816; CL 34). For the monetary contexts informing production across the arts see the concluding section of *Clavics*: 'cost- / Estimates fall / Short of cost' (BH 832; CL 42), and 'Pindarics' in *Without Title*: 'All-funding eloquence', 'admission charge is the true price of fame' (WT, 41, 43). For architecture see 'An Apology for the Revival of Christian Architecture in England' *passim* (BH 125-31; T 22-34) and *Mercian Hymns* I (BH 83), *Odi Barbare* sections I, XXIX and LI (BH 835, 863, 885; OB 9; 37; 59), Hill's reproduction of an architectural plan in the front matter of *Clavics* (CL 5); and the publicity for Hill's readings at Boston, MA, which make use of Doric

attend in particular to *A Treatise of Civil Power* and two of the *Daybooks*: *Clavics* and *Odi Barbare*. It will also dwell briefly on 'An Apology for the Revival of Christian Architecture in England' and *Mercian Hymns*.[5]

Let's take as example Hill's 2007 poem, 'In Memoriam: Ernst Barlach'. In this text, both poet's and sculptor's tools – inked and built materials – visibly bend in service of the economics of construction and re-construction (BH 597; TCP 45). Hill is looking at an image of the 1921 oak tablet, *Schmerzensmutter* (*Mother of Sorrows*), which had been commissioned in memory of the dead of the Great War.[6] The original structure, which had been displayed at the Nikolai church in Kiel, was destroyed in bombing during the Second World War. Hill's use of the earlier artefact and his consciousness of his contemporary work's modeling on, and recollection of, the missing object prompt – in us and him – awkward questions about the re-appropriation of his twentieth-century German source. Hill's lyric construction of a print memorial circles uneasily around its production of new commemorative matter:

> *My heart bleeds with grief but you give me strength*
> you carved in Low German for an *Ehrenmal*
> or *Mahnmal* on which the Mother of God
> is rayed around by seven swords that have the appearance
> of stabbing her in the back. The vertical one
> we call *crucifix* without too much straining
> of faith or credulity. But the Low German
> snapped at an angle is a right bugger
> *Min Hart* I think I can read, but the squinching
> obscures things. Anyhow, the War did for it: Kiel
> was ill-used.
> (BH 597; TCP 45)

---

columns (Brotherton collection: BC MS 20c Hill 6/Bos – 6/Bur Boston Univ-Burch). See also Rosemary Hill, 'Ruskin and Pugin', in *Ruskin and Architecture*, ed. Rebecca Daniels and Geoff Brandwood (Reading: Spire, 2003), pp. 223-248.

[5] I have in mind especially the forces that shape the production of the twenty-first century phototypeset pages of Hill's small press volumes brought out with Enitharmon and Clutag, and the demands of publishers and editors in the proofing and printing, marketing and disseminating processes of larger houses Hill has collaborated with, such as Penguin.

[6] Ernst Barlach, *Schmerzensmutter* (*Mother of Sorrows*) 1921. Bronze relief. Nikolaikirche, Kiel, destroyed 1944. Copyright Archiv Ernst Barlach Stiftung Güstrow. Viewable at: http://www.wege-zu-barlach.de/index.php?id=79

The lines are attentive to numerous forms of 'ill-use' – artistic, as well as political and national. They allude to the deployment of Kiel's maritime resources for the Nazi agenda (the city became a key naval base and a production site for submarines in the Second World War), and to the destruction that resulted from Allied bombing, which 'did for' over eighty percent of the historic old town.

At the same time, Hill probes a quite different form of ill-use; that of artistic re-appropriation of material, which arises in the attempt to commemorate, revisit, and refashion earlier artefacts. The lines do not discourage such use, but they do imply that even the most apparently honourable of commemorative agendas across time and culture risks betrayal and sabotage. That can be seen in Barlach's recollection of the *mater dolorosa* (though Hill does not suggest naïvety on Barlach's part). The engraver's arrangement of the swords that are luminously 'rayed around', and which imply devotion and longing for heavenly ascent, simultaneously gives the appearance of 'stabbing her in the back'. Barlach is reworking the traditional figure of the mother of sorrows in terms of anti-war intent, pleading for an end to bloodshed, yet the language he uses to emblematise pitiably fallen, pained and penetrable human flesh makes recourse to the violent iconography of rayed swords. It is not entirely clear whether such redeployment of the mother of sorrows to fit a pacifist post-First World War agenda, strains 'faith and credulity' in quite a different respect by twisting the religious iconography into the service of peaceable ends.

A more profound sense of ill-ease, however, hangs about Hill's appropriation of Barlach's memorial. Below the carved image, in the region's Low German dialect, the oak panel bears an inscription: 'Min Hart blött vör Gram awers Du giest mi Kraft 1914 – 1918'. As Hill keeps reminding us, he can't read Low German, which may be why only snatched fragments of this phrase make their way into the poem. Hill is willing to translate for us, or to reiterate a previous translation: 'My heart bleeds with grief. But you give me strength'. Yet even with the English gloss, Hill's lines emphasize distance, and the perils of his own and others' misreading. The oak tablet is estranged from poet and readers at least thrice over. First, Barlach's artefact is lost. Second, the poet is abashed that he doesn't have Low German, and he worries over the limits this imposes on his wider knowledge of, and reading of, Barlach: 'I should have known Low German' (BH 597; TCP 45). Third, there are physical difficulties in looking at the reproduced image rather than the physically present *Ehrenmal*: the poet can scarcely see the detail: 'I *think* I can read…'.

One shares his visual difficulty in regarding an image of the object: '[T]he Low German / snapped at an angle is a right bugger', writes Hill: '*Min Hart* I think I can read, but the squinching / obscures things' (BH 597; TCP 45). The reproduction of Barlach's piece draws the poet into an unhappy physical relationship with the memorial's absent materiality. 'Snapped', 'straining' and 'squinching' gestures characterize Hill's attempts to view it. Though he has at his disposal images of the sculptor's work, and translations of the text, Hill cannot come face to face with the original. This lost object puts the poet in an uncomfortable predicament. It prompts and structures Hill's new act of lyric composition, and disorients his creative-conceptual responses. Both in viewing Barlach's literary memorial, and in attending to his literary interpretation of the original, the audience becomes conscious of obscurities, errors, misreadings, and potential misuses.

Part of what Hill's ink memorial worries over, perhaps disproportionately, is that lost or destroyed commemorative objects will generate distortingly nostalgic forms of recollection. Refusing to move in service of the Yeatsian apothegm, 'Man is in love and loves what vanishes', Hill's poem looks leanly at the way legacy is established over time.[7] The poem focuses on the uneasiness of the relationships between literary memory, commissioned artefacts and historical interpretation, and attends to the way particular socio-economic conditions of commemorative production result in preservations and perversions of legacy. Amongst Hill's targets are those who have recalled Barlach's pieces in a misleading language:

> And independent peasantry
> is a myth, and *Artist Against the Third Reich*
> something of a misnomer. You tried to buy time
> and to stave off calamity as I would have done
> you were not Haeften nor could I have been.

Hill's lines keep in mind the artist's determined resistance to a dictatorship's silencing of expression. At the same time, his own poetic tribute is conducted in the rhetoric of struggle, compromise and barter:

---

[7] W.B. Yeats, 'Nineteen Hundred and Nineteen', *Collected Poems of W.B. Yeats*, ed. Richard J. Finneran (New York, NY: Macmillan, 1989), p. 207.

'You tried to buy time', Hill writes, 'and to stave off calamity'.[8] Far from triumphant, the negotiative phrasal verb forms end in collapse and non-fulfilment: 'You tried', 'you were not'. If Hill's lines are offered in tribute to the deceased artist, their disappointed verbal constructions work against the temptation to gloss Barlach's continued legacy as a victory over, or freedom from, brute political and economic forces. Reiterating that art cannot be 'independent' from worldly power, Hill also wants to apply this recognition to his own situation: 'as I would have done', 'you were not … nor could I have been'. This recognition informs Hill's objection to Peter Paret's book, *An Artist Against the Third Reich*, as 'something of a misnomer': its wording implies a romanticised form of recollection. Art is not to be pressed into service as '*against*' the Third Reich ('you were not Haeften'), but to be recognized as a humbler form of defiance, which is compromised and non-self-reliant. Rather than depicting Barlach as a victor over repressive forces, Hill casts him as an ordinary all-too-human 'you' to be spoken to, doing merely what 'I would have done' under oppressive economic and political conditions – both an admirable and circumscribed achievement.

It is a contemporary poem in which absent matter tells of modern art's compromises in the face of historical calamity and economic necessity. One wonders what is at stake for Hill in the comparison. The poet's first-personal 'I' suggests identification with his German forebear's personal and politico-aesthetic struggles. Even as Hill's memorial makes Barlach's lost material sing of the survival and circulation of artworks and origins, its acoustic transmits the noise of patronage, reputation, linguistic affiliation, and social ideals about art and objecthood. In the act of writing about artistic humility and economic circumscription, the contemporary 'I' also takes on a contradictory kind of grandeur. Hill not only draws himself into direct relations with the imperilled artist ('you'), he aligns with the sculpted *Ehrenmal* the wartime dead and his own textual monument for the sculptor. A presumptuous aura hangs over Hill's intimate alignment of 'I' and 'you', and his enactment of a 'dialogue' between very different kinds of work and culture. Both objects raise questions about political struggle, aesthetic modesty and appropriate

---

[8] Barlach's memorials were banned under National Socialism as 'degenerate art', removed from public sites and threatened with destruction. Many of these pieces were acquired by Hermann F. Reemtsma, who restored them after the war. He also commissioned new work, enabling Barlach to continue producing in his idiosyncratically spare, introspective style.

public recollection. But engraving and poem act in materially different economic situations and under different ethical conditions. What the perceived parity affords is an opportunity for Hill to exhibit himself in fluent conversation with an imagined artistic ally across time and nation.

At once negotiating particular artistic legacies, and invested in its own literary self-fashioning, Hill's work focuses on the relationship between the politics of design style and the materiality of making, in wood, stone and poetic print. It is a concern for artistic labour and matter that takes shape through the contemporary poet's painstaking care with his own handwritten, ink-and-paper manuscript drafts, and their manifestation in printed, published form. Across his career, Hill has insisted on precise typographical effects. Complex systems of lineation, hyphenation, pagination, typographical marks, and the use of upper and lower cases and small caps are in evidence in *Speech! Speech!*, *The Triumph of Love*, *A Treatise of Civil Power*, and *Clavics*. These are adjustments that are difficult for the typesetter to get right, or rather, they require that highly specific instructions are communicated by the poet to the publisher – from the correspondence between point size and leading (the size of space between lines) to the alignment of individual letters within words and between lines; from the carefully calculated distance of the text from gutter, to the spaces of indented half-lines.[9] Letters in Hill's archive at the Brotherton show a history of intense collaboration over textual variants at proof stage through his career.[10] Even in the more regular-

---

[9] 'The typography of the whole is his', says Andrew McNeillie, of his correspondence with Hill over the Clutag Press *Treatise of Civil Power*, 'except for the blue rules above and below his name'; 'We followed Geoffrey's wishes pretty much to the letter and were of course happy to. The mix of fonts on the cover / title meant we had to acquire a font we didn't have'. McNeillie also notes the invaluable involvement of Kenneth Haynes, who produced a clear typescript of *Clavics*, including specific details as to layout and type design. Personal correspondence with Andrew McNeillie, 29 Nov. 2012.

[10] See letters between André Deutsch and Hill, 1981-83. Here, a discussion of the kerning – the typesetter's adjustment of the spacing between the letters – of the 'M' and the 'y' of the 'Mystery' of *The Mystery of the Charity of Charles Péguy*, so as to achieve the impression of an equal distance between all the letters, takes place. See also the correspondence between Hill and William Cookson in 1972, where Hill worries over how to keep costs down whilst making late changes to proofs, and articulates his anxieties over errors and infelicities in the 'irrevocable' medium of print. See also correspondence with Cookson in 1993, over the proofs of 'Psalms of Assize', where concerns about the alignment of the final words of lines, and stipulations about the alignment of single letters (the letter 'd') between words on different lines, are made. Page breaks, line breaks, indentation and the space between the title and epigraph are all considered and amended. See BC MS 20c Hill/6/AGE/William Cookson 1/2.

looking typologies of *King Log* and *Mercian Hymns*, there are elements which are the product of editorial discussion and re-alignment, notably the setting of two sections of 'The Songbook of Sebastian Arrurruz' (BH 76, 79; KL 60, 63) and of the *Hymns* (BH 83-112), laid out in justified, rectangular blocks, with regular margins and unobtrusive hyphenation. The mixture of typographic rules in the layout of these poems – reverse indentation in *Mercian Hymns*; an alternation between centred and flush left organisation in 'Songbook' – are subtle modulations of print. They act on the eye very differently from the noisy marks of Hill's later volumes, but their gentler refashionings of the printed page are just as much the result of close editorial collaboration and conversation.[11]

In choosing to publish with Penguin and Yale, Hill's meticulousness about jacket and page design was more restricted than it had been with his smaller press ventures. These houses' imperative to produce pages that regulate design features, so that books fit into a distinctive house style (the consumer's eye should not be distracted by anomalous-looking covers or arrangements of printed matter within) has tended to preclude close authorial collaboration over the fine-tuning of typographical details. In Hill's post-1990 volumes, this has led to a more homogenized design, which is perhaps most evident in the rather grubby production of the 2007 *Treatise* (the paper quality is poor; the cover design weak, particularly in comparison to Hill's later volumes). Another troublesome issue arose with that book: Penguin failed to print the '*power*' of Hill's title entirely in lower case, as he had requested, and as it had appeared in the Miltonic original.[12] It is tempting to think this influenced Hill's decision not to issue *Clavics*, *Oraclau | Oracles* and *Odi Barbare* with Penguin, and to bring them out with the smaller presses Enitharmon and Clutag instead. (Hill knows the editors at these houses personally, has been able to collaborate with them closely, and their production methods and economies of scale allow the author much greater freedom over the look of the finished product.) But there is another more practical reason for the three volumes having come out with these presses. Hill's collected poems, *Broken Hierarchies: Poems 1952–2012*, had already

---

[11] See also the typesetting of 'Four Poems Regarding the Endurance of Poets' especially 'A Prayer to the Sun' (BH 56; KL 36). See Hill's earlier adventures in small press publishing: *Preghiere* (University of Leeds: Northern House Pamphlet, 1964) and Hill's Fantasy Press pamphlets (Oxford, 1950s).

[12] And as it appeared in an earlier publication by Hill: *A Treatise of Civil power* (Thame: Clutag Press, 2005).

been signed up at OUP, and the commercial Penguin are reluctant to publish volumes that would be swiftly superseded by a *Collected*. So too, from Hill's, and OUP's, perspective, the issue of acquiring permissions for *Broken Hierarchies* would not arise for the three volumes if they were brought out with Clutag and Enitharmon, as neither Andrew McNeillie nor Stephen Stuart-Smith would lay claim to any.[13]

Hill's late work in particular interlaces these economic and material preoccupations with his sensitivity to the role of trans-continental linguistic trade and artistic imitation, which powerfully structures contemporary English poetic form. In *Odi Barbare*, for instance, Hill carefully balances his Italian inheritance – the title is lifted from the nineteenth-century *Odi Barbare* of Giosuè Carducci (a three-volume work that had transposed the quantitative metrics of Ancient Greek and Latin poets into accentual Italian) – against his redeployment of the English Sapphic stanza that he derives from Philip Sidney's *Arcadia*. The complex cross-cultural shards of this contemporary work keep our gaze trained on the intersections between art, literature and the politics of their (re)production. Through the politics of this borrowing, Hill also trains attention on the thinginess of aesthetic creation. Hill's 2012 collection self-consciously attends to the parity between artistic and literary raw material, as the ink of his poetry is refracted through the glass, wax, paper and leather of the Irish artist, William Orpen's, early twentieth-century self-portraiture:

> But imagine, shall I, the mirror broken,
> Treading slivers. Pray not to be a sophist.
> Nor would you find dramatization fitting
>     Such a persona
>
> So to be whipped up out of wax and stylus,
> …
> Conjured shards dancing on the leather desktop,
> (BH 882; OB 56)

---

[13] He is also highly aware of commercial pressure in public performances. In Hill's 'Lines of Force' lecture as Oxford Professor of Poetry, 27 Nov. 2012, Oxford, he begins by speaking of 'this weird and demanding event', the marketing and events management for which began months in advance: 'there are faculty demands to be met. A time has to be supplied, so that advertising, commissioning may begin. … The presumption is that one has something to *sell*.'

At one moment paper thin, and the next conjurings of light and glass, Orpen's historical apparitions are made to 'danc[e]' on the writerly desktop, paraded for Hill's readership. The poet's verbal conjuring with slivers of light and enigmatic fracturing, reflects and refracts the prominent use of mirrors in Orpen's paintings throughout his career:

> Orpen's self portrait in the French hotel room
> > Quizzing his helmet
>
> (He was no combatant), the brandy bottle
> Concentrated sluttish within reflection;
> Peril implicate but not here intrusive.
> > There will be shadows.
> (BH 882; OB 56) [14]

Hill's lines have within their purview Orpen's self-scrutiny in his *Self Portrait* of 1924, in which the artist's reflected face infinitely recedes through interior space and out into the Parisian skyline. Hill also recalls the mirrors that appear, publicly, in Orpen's large-scale commissioned work: *The Signing of Peace in the Hall of Mirrors, Versailles, 28 June 1919*. Although that canvas depicts a moment of apparent historical resolution, when Allied politicians demonstrate unity through signing, the scene is distorted and broken by the enormous reflections behind and above their heads, which throw the light and the clean classical dimensions of the hall out of proportion. Orpen's brush makes the architectural structure teeter, challenging the harmony of staged political intent. Critics have read the piece as typical of the commissions Orpen fulfilled at this period in his career: in this 'remarkable series of canvases he quietly belittled the "frocks", as he called them, by devoting the major part of his compositions to the splendour of the conference venues whilst relegating the participants to the bottom quarter of his canvases.'[15] Once more, Hill's verbal textures are closely attentive to

---

[14] This is the OB version; in BH the third line quoted has been revised to '(He was no war man) and the brandy bottle'. See *Standpoint* (July/Aug 2010) for a version of the poem punctuated very differently. Online version also at: https://standpointmag.co.uk/issues/july-august-2010/text-july-10-geoffrey-hill-new-poems/ [accessed 29 Nov. 2012]. See also Clutag archive at the Bodleian Library, Oxford, which contains the earlier drafts of *OB* punctuated with em-dashes and colons rather than commas and stops. '[S]luttish' has also been changed from the earlier 'uppish'.

[15] Elizabeth Cayzer, 'Sir William Orpen', *Changing Perceptions: Milestones in Twentieth-*

the politics of the war commission, and the circumstances in which commemorative artefacts are crafted. 'He was no combatant', we are informed of Orpen, the simple past tense of this negative clause reflecting the brevity of Hill's earlier reminder: 'you were not Haeften'. It is as if Hill imagines some sentimentalising, aesthetically idealising listener must keep being prompted to recall that the 'peril[s] implicate' in soldiery and artistry involve very different recoils and hazards.

One also keeps in mind the grandeur of the artist's own commissions. Orpen was the highest paid portraitist of his day. The *Hall of Mirrors* secured him the (then) princely sum of £3000. But money also kept him, as Elizabeth Cayzer sees it, 'chained to the treadmill of commissioned portraiture'.[16] His earlier paintings of labourers and intimate models are frequently lauded as his best work; and his later formal portraiture have often been dismissed as routinized 'mechanical marvels'.[17] Yet Hill's vocabulary directs attention to the insistent workmanship of making, imagining the din and mess of equipment reverberating around printer's and artist's studios: 'slate', 'wax', 'stylus', 'paper ... paper', 'shards'. It is a refraction of Orpen's attention to the materiality of creation. Integral to the historicity Hill recalls – and the new work he makes – is its crafted objecthood. Seeking the company of a painter who attended to the pragmatics of making in the early to mid-twentieth century, Hill self-consciously attends to their shared fashionings from glass, wax, paper, leather, ink. For the 'conjuring' acts, even those at the leather desktop, are Orpen's as much as Hill's. A keen letter-writer, the painter frequently dispatched pen-and-ink drawings of his portraits to correspondents. In *Leading Life in the West*, sheets of paper, painting and writing material, as well as a liquor bottle, are clustered beneath the frame of the mirror in which Orpen studies his reflection in the self-portrait. Such materials seem to compel both artists to place them in the foreground. Hence the succession of self-portraits, in which the canvases capture Orpen in the act of painting himself in, eyeing the scene (i.e. himself) warily. The effect is one of live performance of personae. His succession of self-portraits make him seem to appear – before our eyes and his own – in camouflage. Posing stagily before his own brush, the artist evades direct identification with the selves he paints. At once handling his face as a prop, to be looked

---

*Century British Portraiture* (Alpha Press, 1998), pp. 21-25 (p. 22).

[16] Cayzer, p. 24.

[17] Sir John Rothenstein, *Modern English Painters* 1 (London: Macdonald and James, 1976), p. 226.

at through the many the mirrors he uses to capture his visage, and as intangible, posed reflection, the painter comes to seem a succession of refractions of the mirrored images of a disguised 'William Orpen', which has slid out of contact with any single, identifiable source. Both Orpen and Hill place themselves face to face with the materials of art – and with themselves – as their subjects. A self-consciousness about compromised originals structures these men's relations with audiences; the body of commissioning viewers who made Orpen among the richest, most famous artists of his day, or the readership courted by the contemporary poet, who may be ambitious for canonicity, but can be under no illusions about eking financial reward, or even a living from his work.

However, if the contemporary poet's eye is on legacy and not economic reward, it remains unclear why he redeploys the lexicon of artistic trade and exchange, recalling works produced as part of luxurious courtly display and for lucrative commission. What do Hill's collaborations over correctly phototypeset pages have to do with the political realities he recalls Orpen being paid to depict at Versailles, or with those literary figures, performers and designers Hill keeps returning to at the early modern court? I want to explore more closely, first, the link Hill perceives between the politics and economics of patronage systems and his audience-publisher relations in the twenty-first century; and second, the relationship between Hill's use of earlier, historically allusive styles of artistic structure that have been judged appropriate to commission for public or personal consumption, and his exploration of the negotiations and labour of styling the published pages of his own poetry books for contemporary audiences (negotiations that manifest differently with large and small presses).[18]

For Hill, the 'thrusting / Forward of rhyme', and the sense that, at a patron's hands, 'aesthetics are an inclined plane', draw commissioned performance and the production and re-interpretation of certain forms of *aesthetic* matter into relation (BH 832; CL 42). When, in *Clavics*, Charles I is cast as 'that king-martyr. / He was a double-dealer, betrayed friends

---

[18] See 'Why Publish Poetry?', Discussion between Rupert Hart-Davis, Charles Monteith, Diana Athill, Colin Franklin and Erica Marx, *Poetry Review* 53:2 (1962), in *A Century of Poetry Review*, ed. Fiona Sampson (Carcanet, 2009), pp. 84-99. See review of the event 'Making Books for Love and Money: On the Value of Small Presses', Discussion between Charles Boyle, David Lea, Nicholas Lezard, and Nicholas Murray at *The London Review of Books*, Thursday 15 Nov. 2012 at: http://fiveleavespublications.blogspot.co.uk/2012/11/mammals-versus-dinosaurs.html, by Ross Bradshaw [accessed 28 November 2012].

/ Without quarter', Hill performs his own double-dealing with the term 'without quarter' (BH 793; CL 14). If the poet has in mind the politics of suspicion and dissent at the Caroline court, his lines also refer to Charles's manipulation of physical quarters, in line with Classical stipulations about the correct ways for approaching and moving through built space. In earshot are the king's hierarchical demarcations of roles, persons, movements, and positions at Whitehall, as well as his enthusiasm for the rule-bound proportions of neoclassical buildings, such as the Banqueting House, that accommodated commissioned entertainments to indulge Charles's fine taste: masques, music, and dances were performed for assembled dignitaries and audiences. Also relevant is the construction of Henrietta Maria's Catholic 'quarters', which caused widespread public unease. In such lyric work, the built environment of the early modern court – and the economic, theological and aesthetic negotiations staged there – are a means of scrutinising the politics of design authority and of economic power, as well as the manipulation of numerous audience bodies, patronised artists, political figures, theologians and the people. *Clavics* is a volume in which the power play of contemporary inclination and its aesthetic dealings are mapped onto the claustrophobic atmosphere of the Caroline court – where both illustrate investments in the power of form – but, as we will see, the analogy involves Hill's own not entirely unproblematic appropriation of historical sources.

*Clavics* is a tribute to William Lawes, the court musician to Charles I. On display are the broken bodies of the English Civil War, the violence of commissioned pens and strings, the memorialized musician – 'Will Lawes is slain / Permit me, sire, is slain by such whose wills / Be laws' (BH 792; CL 13) – and the politics of Hill's own awkwardly re-vamped style: 'grinding the textures / of harmony' (BH 805; CL 23). Hill's punning on Lawes's name captures both the spirit of his notes' licensed play, and the constraints of the King's rule-bound commission, emphasizing the negotiations between aesthetic 'will' and royal 'laws'. We watch the composer's '[s]wift and neat hand':

> Notate the viols
> Flexures of styles
> Extravagant command
> Purposeful frills
> What comes of the upthrust and downthrust pen

(BH 792; CL 13)

Like Pound's Canto 81, which also angularly alludes to Lawes, Hill's poem flexes a self-conscious, grim artfulness of jolts, skirmishes and typographical disruption that contrasts with the intimate lyricism of his subject; the well-modulated consort and chamber music written for the king and his close circle.

> These fantasies constrained by their own strings
> ...
> Jolt into the epilogue by your leave
> As into a mixed skirmish, a rout,
>         Punched semibreve
> Like fatal bullet through the fine slashed coat.
> (BH 792; CL 13)

The sense of gravity that one might expect from Hill's tribute is further punctured by ungracious punning and metapoetical interjection: 'Permit me, sire', 'by your leave', 'Lawes ... laws'. It is an effect that echoes Pound's own askance rhetorical approach to musical-lyric harmony: 'Pull down thy vanity. ... what can be thy place / In scaled invention or true artistry';[19]

> Has he tempered the viol's wood
> To enforce    both the grave    and the acute?[20]

The 'Libretto' section of Canto 81 ends with an irked pronouncement, and a lone line: 'And for 180 years almost nothing'.[21] Pound's ruptured typographies go out of their way to draw attention to lyric artifice. Ellipses emphasise the artist's imprecisions of memory and the gaps that appear in trans-historical recollections. Hill's formal textures are quite different: his short lines bend the page into an over-produced cadence. Yet they too use the formal architecture of interruption to draw the eye, distancingly, away from lyrical smoothness, and toward a jumpy, fractious reading experience that is further punctured by meta-commentary on the creative process and strained full rhyme: 'Notate the viols / Flex-

---

[19] Ezra Pound, Canto 81, *The Cantos of Ezra Pound* (London: Faber, 1987), p. 521

[20] Pound, Canto 81, p. 520.

[21] Pound, Canto 81, p. 520.

ures of styles'. Both poets use typography to 'temper' their instruments, and to show how such grace is 'enforce[d]'. Both employ the clipped critical registers of disappointed connoisseurs and fractious commands: 'Pull down thy vanity', consider 'thy place'. These are techniques that prevent close identification with recalled or memorialised composer.

What Hill's page makes clear is that the strings that set down music and lyric are highly dependent on command and reputation. Both the formal properties of *Clavics* and its invocations show Lawes's '[s]wift and neat hand' (BH 792; CL 13) bound up with negotiations of the acoustic and artistic commands of court, and with Charles's investments in music, poetry, masquing, art and architecture. 'Permit me, sire' (BH 792; CL 13) artfully speaks the language of obedience, even as it stirs up 'a rout'. The address is at once that of Lawes, respectfully, to his patron ('sire'), and Hill's, disrespectfully, to a cod-critical reader in a tone of faux-obsequy. 'Permit me' echoes the addresses of earlier volumes' genuflections before a vast public body, the poet ostensibly as commissioned singer, to please and antagonise gentle listeners and critic-reviewers.[22] Such language emphasises the links between composition, reception, and the artist's economic situation. '[T]he swift and neat hand' is that of the writing musician whose fingers move fast across the page, composing the score, and the textures of handwriting, the black marks of Lawes's pen on the parchment. It is a strangely textual way to speak of sound.

What arrives on the contemporary poetic page is a 'mixed skirmish' between the 'frills' of the musician, his sticky end from the 'fatal bullet', and the embattled 'upthrust and downthrust pen' that belongs simultaneously to musician, poet, swordsman and recording literary historian. Hill's fingering of the legacy of sounds is mindful of the scholarly interest Lawes has generated: Lawes' work has been read not only in terms of English music theory and the historical context of courtly production, but has also – especially around the time of Hill's own longhand drafting of his poem – prompted critical debate about the instabilities of the music's manuscript history.[23] Hill's lines likewise

---

[22] See SS and OS.

[23] Published the same year as *Clavics* is John Cunningham's book on Lawes's consort music; a detailed study of the composer's handwriting, advancing new interpretations of chronology and of patronage systems at Charles's Whitehall. Cunningham has a subchapter on 'Lawes's Hand' that attends to its consistency, to dates of composition, and the main problems with attempting to work out chronological changes. From this, he attempts to construct a modern understanding of the mechanisms of court patronage, the social practices around musical composition, dissemination and performance. See

gesture toward the authority of that royal hand. The king's agency may only appear at the margin, sonically speaking, but in another sense it is his command (and commission) that set to work all these pens and strings and hands. Accompanying the monarchical tune, Lawes's musical constraint arrives materially, through the strings of the instrument to be played, and the lines of the stave on which the notes are being written in, as well as in the strictures and purse-strings of seventeenth-century patronage. Purposeful frills are part of the king's design, which requires an elite group of lutenists, violists and singers to play privately to him, as well as to perform music in public, at masques, and for privileged guests, when the occasion demands. (Lawes's crafted sounds are not just an entertaining exhibition of his ingenuity and will as composer.) What arrives on the page interweaves musical, poetical and political lexicon – a synaesthesia of artistic practices and agencies.

Drawn into, and re-focusing, this entanglement of forms, agendas, monies, and conjoined artistic hands is Hill's epigraph to *Clavics*: an image of an architectural structure. We look on a plan for a new palace at Whitehall. Before the first word, the stage is set by a drawing derived from a classical design by the Renaissance court architect and designer, Inigo Jones. The Banqueting House (toward the top right), which housed and shaped the reception of music penned by Lawes, as well as masques by Carew and Jonson, dances and banquets, shows the stirrings of a developing English taste for the strictly proportioned structures of classical design. The politics of taste underlying the preference for rule-bound, cool elegance in design – rather than the Tudor / Gothic organicist development of structures visible across the early seventeenth-century skyline – are legible in the plan reproduced in *Clavics*:

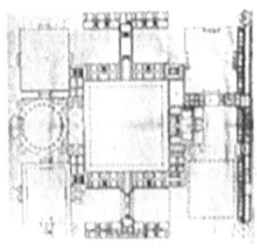

*Drawing by Robert Webb, after a design by Inigo Jones for Whitehall Palace.*[24]

---

*The Consort Music of William Lawes 1602-1645* (Woodbridge: Boydell Press, 2010), pp. 25-27.

[24] Drawing by Robert Webb, after a design by Inigo Jones for Whitehall Palace, reproduced from John Harris, Stephen Orgel and Roy Strong, *The King's Arcadia: Inigo Jones and the Stuart Court* (London: Arts Council, 1973); appears on p.5 (facing title page) of the Enitharmon edition of Geoffrey Hill's *Clavics* (London: Enitharmon, 2011).

The image echoes the classical Palladian lines of Jones's plan for an immense rectangular palace, erected around a series of quadrangles. Unlike the Tudor Whitehall, which had resembled a small village rather than a unified building, Jones's envisaged structure was modelled on strict proportions of Roman design in accordance with Classical rules about columnar heights and spacing, the use of pediment, cornice and giant order. In showing favour for this continental style, Charles privileged an architecture that took stately uniformity as its chief virtue, over the accepted haphazardness of the existing assorted Tudor buildings, courtyards and thoroughfares. [25] He wanted to refashion court structures in line with the strict emphasis on proportion, rather than to continue in the organicist line of 'English' architectural development.[26] Charles did not raise the necessary funds, and the structure was not built. By the time of his execution, the only part of the planned Whitehall that had been brought to fruition was Jones's Banqueting House, which had been commissioned and constructed by James I, and which already stood as a forerunner of classical design (then unpopular) in early seventeenth-century England.

Criticism of Hill has focused extensively on relationships between identity, place, and history. What can account for its reluctance to attend to the authority inscribed architecturally? When Charles Bennett writes that 'interlineation of Latin and Anglo-Saxon suggests for Hill the rhetorical division from which the community of English language, literature and culture will arise' he aligns Hill's historical sensibility with verbal roots, the soil, and archaeology, but not the built environment.[27] David Gervais, Vincent B. Sherry and Jeffrey Wainwright have all dwelt

---

[25] See Susan Foreman, *From Palace to Power: An Illustrated History of Whitehall* (Brighton: Alpha Press / Sussex Academic Press, 1995), p. 11; Colin Brown, *Whitehall: The Street that Shaped a Nation* (London: Simon & Schuster, 2009), pp. 100-01.

[26] Foreman writes: 'Evident in many sixteenth- and seventeenth-century commentaries are anxieties about new tastes for buildings that are '*all antica*'. These accounts inveigle against exotic, foreign-led corruption. Classical buildings are 'idle foreign toyes'; a danger to the traditional social order and its Tudor and Gothic codes of visualization. Not all English writers of the period held this opinion. Britain had its own Roman past, its own classical age, and British classicism was, for them [and Charles I] an attempt to revive the national past. But the archaeological work on Roman Britain had not yet provided substance to these declarations. Early seventeenth-century British classicism, positioned at the nexus of the indigenous and the foreign, was tied with the contestatory discourse of national identity' (Foreman, p. 102).

[27] Charles Bennett, 'The Use of Memory', *Politics and the Rhetoric of Poetry*, ed. C.C. Barfoot Tjebbe, Jane Mallinson (Amsterdam/Atlanta, GA, 1995), pp. 95-106 (p. 101).

at length upon the significance of *Mercian Hymns*'s 'crypt of roots' (BH 86; MH IV), and its fecund natural imagery, but not on its use of bridges, a citadel, a motorway, modern estates, a mansion-house, as well as its 'tympanum and chancel- / arch', 'master-mason' (BH 106; MH XXIV), or 'West Midlands sculpture of the twelfth century'.[28] Nor have any extended studies been penned on the many built structures of the first Hymn, or on Offa's status as architect and commissioner of 'the M5', 'the citadel at Tamworth', 'the Welsh Bridge and the Iron Bridge' and 'the desirable new estates' (BH 83; MH I).

It seems that the critical eye has been drawn more toward *subterranean* structures, and to verbal ruins and remains in the poems, than to standing buildings and monuments. It is a habit of looking that has, I think, contributed to the sense that Hill's historicity is motivated chiefly by representations of lost or degenerating English heritage, and nostalgic recollections of landscape and the soil.[29] There are other structures in place. Such accounts render invisible Hill's long-running investment in architecture, and his fraught attention to the politics of re-deploying existing built forms, both literally, as erected structures take on successive inhabitants, viewers and functions, and are added to and reformed, and in the work enacted though literary and historical re-descriptions and reinvestments in their forms. When Seamus Heaney, in 'Englands of the Mind', describes Hill's work as implementing 'a kind of verbal architecture, a grace and sturdy English Romanesque', he draws us closer to an appreciation of Hill's investment in the complex politico-cultural inheritance of built structure.[30] Heaney's remarks were

---

[28] Author's note to *Mercian Hymns* XXIV, MH, n.p.

[29] Jeffrey Wainwright writes that *MH* nostalgically recalls an 'endlessly fecund', 'nose-level sense of vegetation', where '"great creating Nature"' is linked with lost childhood and 'fancied martyrdoms' (*Acceptable Words: Essays on the Poetry of Geoffrey Hill* (Manchester: Manchester University Press), pp. 35-36). Henry Hart thinks Hill's 'enchanting polysemous patterns of entwined Latin and Anglo-Saxon roots' and his 'English Romanesque' interlace with 'vegetative undergrowth' (*Seamus Heaney: Poetry of Contrary Progressions* (Syracuse University Press, 1993), p. 104). E.M. Knottenbelt writes that 'the literary (poetic) legacy of Mercia is small and must be reconstructed from fragmentary remains ... unearthing the fragmentary remains of memory and history which are effective in language' (*Passionate Intelligence: The Poetry of Geoffrey Hill* (Amsterdam and Atlanta, GA: Rodopi, 1990), pp. 171-72).

[30] Seamus Heaney, *Finders Keepers: Selected Prose 1971-2001* (London: Faber, 2002), p. 86. The architectural terminology used to describe the Romanesque is comparable to those that describe lyric structure. See Michael W. Fazio, Marian Moffett and Lawrence Wodehouse, *Buildings Across Time: An Introduction to World Architecture* (London:

at once specific about the history inscribed in 'English Romanesque', and alert to the particular political ramifications of styling space and stone. (One might read the architecture of *Mercian Hymns*, as Heaney's account underlines, as an argument against barbarised Roman design, or against an 'English' cultural renaissance brought about by Christian structures: the built forms are argumentative, not innocently laying bare their raw materials, or their local characteristics.)[31] In writing that 'Hill addresses the language … like a mason addressing a block', Heaney is attentive to the politics of the Puginesque workmanship and labour of such construction, as well as its site – and type – specificity.[32]

Heaney's discussion of the built environment, however, treats its power figuratively. In his account, the 'sturdy English Romanesque' is an analogy for linguistic concerns; a metaphorical device that helps him probe the struggles between 'Anglo-Saxon' and 'Latinate' *tongues*. Hill's focus on citadels, bridges and palace plans, by contrast, takes design authority *literally*. For him, architecture is an operative political and epistemological force; its forms have reached into and been shaped by historical, theological and national account-making, as well as providing sites on which aesthetic relations are negotiated.[33] Palaces and churches,

---

McGraw-Hill Higher Education, 2009), p. 190: 'the supporting nave arcade has a subtle A-B-B-A rhythm established by piers alternating with two columns'. See also Allison Lee Palmer, *The A to Z of Architecture* (Plymouth: Scarecrow Press, 2009): the Norman Romanesque cathedral at Durham has an 'A-B-A-B rhythm down the nave' (p. 95).

[31] Hill takes the title of his 1978 sequence from Pugin's 1843 *An Apology for the Revival of Christian Architecture*, in which the architect altered his earlier advocacy of obedience to the authority of English Gothic, insisting that tradition should be 'modified to suit actual necessities' (*The True Principles of Pointed or Christian Architecture and An Apology for The Revival Of Christian Architecture* (London: Gracewing, 2003), p. 38). Hill is drawing on a text that urged architects to look not on grand structures but on barns, gates and the 'essentials of good masonry' as design models (p. 15). Ruskin recommends the virtues of masonry which is given 'a certain nobility by building it of massy stones', and modelled on organic structures 'governed always by a certain rude symmetry' (*The Seven Lamps of Architecture* (New York: John Wiley, 1866), pp. 67, 115). Both men were scornful of the 'pointless' elaborations of neoclassical structures, and 'the burnt sugar ornaments of elaborate confectionary' (*The Seven Lamps*, p. 32).

[32] Heaney, pp. 85-6.

[33] 'The discourse of national identity clearly underpins Jones's critical position as the "British Vitruvius". He was Britain's response to the heroic individualities of Vasarian narratives, a faithful imitator of the ancients (even superseding them) and as a master challenging the supremacy of the French and the Italians in architecture.' (Barbara Arciszewska, *Articulating British Classicism: New Approaches to Eighteenth-Century Architecture* (Aldershot: Ashgate, 2004), pp. 14-16).

memorials and banqueting houses – as well as bridges, houses, vaults and crypts – are not analogies for what is 'really' an etymological battle between English and continental tongues. They *are* the sites of socio-cultural struggle, and actively construct, preserve and restructure shared understandings. They have been as fiercely contested as language.[34] Like Hill, when Heaney reads 'that barbaric scrollwork of fern and ivy, .... set against the tympanum and chancel-arch, against the weighty elegance of imperial Latin', he wields specific architectural idiom. But unlike Hill, he employs that architectural specificity weakly.[35] The 'tympanum and chancel-arch' are stony illustrations of what Heaney views as Hill's handling of a *linguistic* power struggle between the organic 'English' historicity of Anglo-Saxon, and the imperial power of Latin.

'Nothing connects us affectively to the dead more than language ... there is a special kind of contemporaneous community which language alone suggests – above all in the form of poetry and songs' Benedict Anderson has written.[36] Both Anderson's and Heaney's remarks have been highly influential in subsequent critical accounts of Englishness, inheritance, art and landscape in Hill – especially with regard to *Mercian Hymns* and 'An Apology for the Revival of Christian Architecture in England'.[37] Yet in Hill, what 'connects us affectively to the dead' at least as eloquently as language is built form. Repeatedly, the historicity of configuring architecture, the complimentary and conflicting traditions of organising habitable structures, inform his theological, national and local understandings of a 'contemporaneous community' – in the Caroline era,

---

[34] 'It is difficult to appreciate through modern eyes the shock – and to many Londoners, the outrage – that the Italianate Banqueting House had on the London public, which loved and revered the traditional Tudor buildings ... warm red brick, or black-and-white checks, haphazard and homely' writes Colin Brown. In contrast: 'the Banqueting House was cold stone and appeared wholly alien to English cultural heritage' (*Whitehall*, p. 100).

[35] Heaney, p. 86.

[36] Benedict Anderson, *Imagined Communities: Reflections on the Origin and Spread of Nationalism* 2nd edn (London: Verso, 1983), p. 145.

[37] Many have focused on the extent to which 'An Apology' should be considered 'apologetic'; few have made more than passing reference to the architecture and to Pugin's arguments about built form. See Calvin Bedient, 'The Pastures of the Wilderness: Geoffrey Hill's "An Apology for the revival of Christian Architecture in England', *The Yearbook of English Studies* 17 (1987) pp. 143-165 (p. 143). See also Tom Paulin's infamous attack in 'The Case for Geoffrey Hill', Review of *Geoffrey Hill: Essays on his Work*, edited by Peter Robinson, in *London Review of Books* 7:6 (April 1985), 13-14.

the age of Offa Rex, and in the twenty-first century.[38] Architecture is not a version of language, or a reflection of linguistic battles translated into masonry. For Hill, constructions are contested matter, and are political. One might apply that recognition to the site of a commemorative work, the palatial rooms at Versailles and the events taking place within, the architectural politics of design, access, performance and patronage at the early modern court, and many other things besides.

The vulnerable majesty of the built environment, specifically the Whitehall of Charles I, and his arrangements of movement through the Palace's physical space, is much on Hill's mind in *Clavics*. In section 10 he writes:

> You who have edited Ben Jonson's masques —
>   All credit to your endeavours.
>    (*Coelum Britannicum*
>      Is not Jonson's)
>       That said
>        He had
>       Many mansions
>     Each with many a room;
>    Majesty's divine cadavers
>  Poised as presiding deities sans tusks.
>                    (CL 20)[39]

Lines 6-8 direct us to *John* 14:2: 'In my father's house there are many mansions. If it were not so, would I have told you that I go to prepare a place for you'. The words are Jesus's reassurance, upon parting from his disciples, that a space will be ready for them with God, in one of his many 'heavenly mansions'. They have been interpreted as an extension of God's hospitality to all virtuous peoples, no matter what their denomination. When refracted through the Caroline court, *John* 14:2 does not illustrate the Christ-like tolerance of Charles's accommodation. The lines are an injunction for an active relationship with the monarch, obliging his

---

[38] For modern architecture in Hill: 'Four days on floor six of the Radisson / Saga ¦ and this had to happen: high density / high intensity spaces' (SC 51); in BH this reads 'Four days on floor six of the Radisson / Saga. I am translated: high density / high intensity spaces' (BH 467); 'Find poetics' entrails exposed as at the / Pompidou Centre' (BH 863; OB 37).

[39] In BH, the last two lines read: 'Mail this *Jonson Redivivus* / Eunomy leading on regal grotesques.' (BH 798).

subjects to sign up to the doctrines of His church, and to sing by his hymn-book. Within earshot are Catholic interpretations of the passage, where 'many mansions' are churches one is compelled regularly to attend, and each churchgoer is a room in which the Host dwells in the taking of the Holy Eucharist. The lines 'He had / Many mansions / Each with many a room;' play out the authority of theological hospitality at Whitehall, which hosted the magisterial Christ-like presiding of the king.[40] However fervently or faithfully practised, it was a paradoxically unstable poise. As the teetering architecture of *Clavics* hints, Charles's mansion houses many traitorously dissatisfied subjects; and its many rooms accommodate the treasonously heterogeneous minds of a kingdom on the brink of civil war. Hill's lines satirise the idea of dwelling safely within any court building, no matter how perfectly proportioned or grandiose its structure.

Building its own disproportionate sense of worldly and divine authority is *Clavics*'s contorted structural aesthetic. The sense of broken, historical bodies is brought into contact with forms pulled apart or stretched out on the rack. Hill puts before us the very different politics and aesthetics of Metaphysical lyric shapes, specifically the obedience of George Herbert's emblem poems, or *technopaegnia* – 'Easter Wings' and 'The Altar' – and Henry Vaughan's 'The Morning Watch'.[41] Hill's extraordinary, wincingly mannered structure struggles to pull itself into line with the literary form of its forebears. Each of its thirty-two sections bends and strains to perform in a manner complimentary to emblem poetry. Is this a failed attempt to shuffle into the key of tradition? Or a flamboyant restyling of the form? On the one hand, Hill's structure ungracefully restructures both things in the world – wings – and their published lyric shapes. On the other, it is an innovative, formally irreverent opening up of spaces between letters, which not only stretches pagination and typography to fit the conceit, but also runs together quite different early modern precedents in thinking through the politics and economics of worldly and divine obedience. It not only emulates Herbert, but Vaughan's own refashioning of Herbertian *technopaegnia*.

---

[40] The identification of Charles with Christ was a lived reality at court. When the king dined with senior members of the Privy Council and Church, they would bow to him to say grace, uttering to Charles the sacred words: 'Give us thy daily bread'.

[41] Herbert, *The Temple: Sacred Poems and Private Ejaculations*, ed. Christopher Harvey, 2nd edn. (London: Pickering 1838), pp. 35, 17. Vaughan, *The Poetical Works of Henry Vaughan: with a memoir*, ed. Henry Francis Lyte (Boston, MA: James R. Osgood, 1871), pp. 93-94.

*Clavics* enacts a peculiar combination of ill temper, temperance and humility. Chafing against the bit, it offers supplication to the existing structure, stretching its phrases to fit the Metaphysical schema, even as it realigns Herbert's winged blocks. Like Herbert's, Hill's lines tug wilfully against their earthliness: they are desirous of ascent, even as their very longing to conform shows earth-bound pride. Hill makes spirited structural sport with Herbert's wings, showing how even the familiar emblem form can be creatively realigned. The shape of 'Easter Wings' also indicated earthly ambition to overcome sin and rise closer to heavenly virtue. Frustrating that aspiration are both men's stony natures, which check ascent, pulling them back to mortar and ground.

If Hill's work has been accused of passive acquiescence, of nostalgic conformity to timeworn poetic contours, it has also been seen as faddish reinvention; an embarrassing display of technical skill.[42] Yet investments in the authority of form and their redeployment are hardly original to Hill. Herbert himself was borrowing from ancient Greek *technopaegnia*.[43] Vaughan's later reworkings of pattern poetry drew on both Metaphysical and Hellenistic sources. He also took Herbertian social and theological critique as a model.[44] For in organising its ecclesiastical architecture in antithesis to the theological structuring of the Caroline court, Herbert's *The Temple* critically considers the hierarchies of Caroline worldly and divine organisation (the emulative literary culture of praise and reward, the complex hierarchies of Charles's systems of monarchical and divine access, and the finery of religious display). The poet's temple takes shape against 'all this glory, all this pomp and state'. Herbert laments that 'now thy Architecture meets

---

[42] See Paulin, 'The Case for Geoffrey Hill', 13-14; Vincent B. Sherry, *The Uncommon Tongue: The Poetry and Criticism of Geoffrey Hill* (Ann Arbor, MI: University of Michigan Press): *Tenebrae* is 'mannered and overworked; it resorts too often to a mastery of techniques merely conventional' (p. 157).

[43] See Simias of Rhodes, 'The Wings' (300 B.C.), a poem that appears to have been inscribed on the wings of a statue of Eros, and whose shape is a pair of wings, in *The Greek Bucolic Poets*, trans. Edmonds, J M. (Cambridge, MA: Harvard University Press, 1912), p. 488. See also Margaret Church, 'The First English Pattern Poems', *PMLA* 61:3 (Sep 1946), pp. 636-50 (p. 636).

[44] See Herbert, 'Jordan II', which distinguishes aspirational self-fashioning rhetoric 'copied' at court from the obedient language of personal devotion: 'As flames do work and winde, when they ascend, | So did I weave my self into the sense. | But while I bustled, I might heare a friend | Whisper, *How wide is all this long pretence!* | *There is in love a sweetness readie penn'd:* | *Copie out onely that, and save expense.*'

with sin;' and that the authority of classical structure has been debased: 'LORD, with what glory wast thou served of old / When Solomon's temple stood and flourished! / ... / Wherefore thou quitt'st thy ancient claim:'.[45] The architecture of Herbert's volume establishes a space in which intimate personal relations with God might be re-established: here, one enters directly and moves unfettered through sacred space. Passing in via 'The Church-Porch', the individual is conducted swiftly to 'The Altar'. It is a quite different object from that fraught site of public offering and sacrament, the early seventeenth-century altar.[46]

One the one hand, the divine architecture of *The Temple* aligns itself with simplicity and humility. On the other hand, Herbert's poems stretch themselves with greater ambition. Actively refashioning their models, they pull wings and altars into new shape. In the act of observing ancient precedents and material phenomena, Herbert reworks them. In this sense, Hill's further redeployments enact neither blind obedience to legacy nor an exhibitionist intervention, but rather an unwillingly surrendered protest against the weighted and imperfect nature of human tribute and recollection, which draws the soaring forms back, often through pride and egotism, toward fallen foundations.[47]

Stones, cement and building work were, of course, explicitly linked with the pride of human ambition in 'The Altar', where the poet's 'heart ... / Is ... a stone' that checks his built offering to God: 'each part / Of my hard heart / Meets in this frame, / To praise thy Name'.[48] Yet broken forms move *especially* well in service of the divine, shaping their tribute from earthly, fractured language. Herbert's longing for ascent

---

[45] Herbert, 'Sion', *Temple* 106.

[46] The altar was a contested site under Charles I. The Laudian relocation of communion-tables altar-wise to the east end of chancels was perceived as popish subversion of Calvinist doctrine, through its visual emphasis on the sacrament. Altar-rails, ostensibly used to prevent animals entering the sacred space, barred access to the congregation: only priests and acolytes could enter. The latter prompted public anger and debate through its association with Catholic demarcation of the space in which Christ becomes incarnate.

[47] See Augustus Welby Northmore Pugin, *The Present State of Ecclesiastical Architecture in England* (London, 1843), which argues for the modern redeployment of the soaring vertical forms of antique Gothic design; for design 'obedience' and 'authority over originality' (p. 113). His structures link ascent with godliness and social goodliness; the authority of formal acclivity with good political-ecclesiastical order. These ascending structures – like lyric wings – are designed in accord with antique sources, and use them to critique contemporary models of political and social order.

[48] Herbert, *The Temple*, p. 17.

produces a structure of quite different quality from those produced in the aspirational acclivity at court. His praise is built for different ends and means. It does not hold as its highest principle those structures that will showcase rule-bound proportion, or please invested audience ears, but rather those which accommodate imperfection and attest to the workmanlike humilities of labour:

> A broken ALTAR, Lord thy servant rears,
> Made of a heart, and cemented with teares:
> Whose parts are as thy hand did frame;
> No workmans tool hath touch'd the same

Like Herbert's, Hill's emblem poems cast persons as kinds of building work, tools and material construction. The 'heart, … cemented with teares' and 'workman's tool' are echoed in *Clavics*'s struggle to 'From 'blood-clay build what ennobles', and its references to 'Inessential repairs' or 'Cracked squires' (CL 40; 12; 12). [49] But unlike Herbert, Hill is shaping monuments for public consumption. The contemporary poet's work moves in service of the audience it will go out to meet: a book-buying readership in the present, the eyes of literary posterity, and (chastisingly) critical and editorial bodies: 'Long harbouring with grin / My enemy' (CL 41), 'Those so barely moved by such recital' (BH 832; CL 42), 'Poor recompense' (BH 816; CL 34). [50] Hill writes as though published words had resiliently to bear the scrutiny of flesh-and-blood others, who brought to the page, the temple and the mansion, their tastes, foibles, aesthetic expectations, and the particular design preferences and prejudices of their era.[51]

'[I]s the work ever in itself accessible?', writes Heidegger: 'the Aegina sculptures in the Munich collection, Sophocles' *Antigone* in the best critics' edition, are, as the works they are, torn out of their own native sphere'.[52] Hill's attention to the material form of the artwork is, like Heidegger's, mindful of its coming-to-being through acts

---

[49] The first quotation is not in BH; the second appears at BH 823; the third, also at BH 823, as 'Cracked fliers'.

[50] The first quotation appear as: 'Long harbouring with grin / Blithe enemy' at BH 820.

[51] See Jonathan F.S. Post, *English Lyric Poetry: The Early Seventeenth Century* (London and New York, NY: Routledge, 1999), p. 136.

[52] Heidegger, *Poetry, Language, Thought*, trans. Albert Hofstadter (New York, NY: Harper & Row, 1971): 40.

of connoisseurship, criticism, classification. Yet Hill does not draw Heidegger's conclusion. For Hill, the work is incapable of existing 'in itself'. From its inception the artefact is shaped by its considerations of supply and demand; in its use of begged, borrowed or reappropriated aesthetic materials, and in its anticipation of reception. That is as much the case for the destroyed memorial sculpture, the painting of dignitaries at the Palace of Versailles, or the consort music played to Charles I; so too for a neoclassical frontispiece, an emblem poem stretched into the shape of wings, or the fine geometric proportionality of a seventeenth-century architectural plan. These artefacts come to being *through* the involvement of commissioners and audiences, labourers and curators, past masters and present agendas: they do not possess an originally inviolate integrity that is secondarily distorted by their removal from a 'native sphere'. What becomes visceral in Hill's literary redeployment of classical and early modern, nineteenth-century and modernist architectural, literary and visual works is that the mechanisms of trade and judgement have been integral to cultural production across continental artforms – just as they are essential, as we keep discovering, to the English lyric imagination.

Hill might have depicted a stand-off between contemporary poetry and redeployed 'originals', in which earlier artefacts are 'torn out of their own native sphere' by usurping literary pieces. But his *Treatise*, *Odi Barbare,* and *Clavics* derive their compromised verbal-visual form in dialogue with the hybridity of the earlier commissions, which themselves appropriated trans-cultural material across the literary, visual and plastic arts. Hill's verbal structures return us to the tastes that shaped the design models that they themselves negotiated. He scrutinises the politics and economics that shaped their earlier works' creative production. In so doing, his poetry also directs attention to the materiality of its own creation and reception. Hill attends not just to stone and canvas but to *print*, and what it is like: we observe the look and feel of inked and bound pages. If his eye for masonry, engraved and printed work is fascinated by the hybrid physicality of matter – books' codices, printed pages, 'printers' founts' (BH 793; CL14), 'smudge-typed … communiqué' (BH 816; CL 34), 'Conjured shards dancing' for attention (BH 882; OB 56) – their imperfections and compromised borrowings remind us of thingly workmanship, competition, and struggles for recognition, demonstrating the range of inky human intervention and counterpoint. The diligent historicity of Hill's work – as well as his fascination with the processes by which it is brought into, and released for, a contemporary audience – demands new modes of interdisciplinary critical attention to the historico-political forces that have structured the production, display and canonicity of aesthetic form across the ages, and across nations, cultures, and genres. Drawing together modes of crafting, displaying and viewing, the marks on Hill's inked pages – from *technopaegnia* to frontispiece; memorial to architectural plan – scrutinise the roles of those who have wielded particular, invested tastes in the processes of commissioning, supporting, or receiving and judging the value of text, image, music and built structure.

CHAPTER ELEVEN

# Geoffrey Hill and Publishing: 'The Recalcitrance of the World'

## Matthew Sperling

'Publishing is an exercise every author ought to confront', Geoffrey Hill has said, because in doing so, in bringing poetic design up sharp against the designs of the literary marketplace, an author 'confronts the recalcitrance of the world itself'.[1] Hill spoke these words in 2009 in a public dialogue with Andrew McNeillie, the publisher of several of his later works at Clutag Press, when he looked back on his lifetime engagement with publishing as 'sixty years of inescapable error'. There was an instance of inescapable error in Hill's first Clutag Press publication, *A Treatise of Civil Power* (2005). Poetic texture came up against the recalcitrance of print technology when the last sentence in stanza XIII of the pamphlet's title-poem found its final two letters slipping off the baseline:

Let's get in deep$_{er.}$[2]

An unusual sort of 'howler'; yet the misalignment of the comparative suffix could be taken, and probably has been taken by some readers, as a fruitful species of semantic-typographic playfulness.

That Clutag book appeared in a limited edition of 200 copies, and preceded the paperback of the same name published by Penguin Books and Yale University Press in 2007. Hill told McNeillie that he used the Clutag book as the occasion for an experiment: he wanted to write in a 'loosened' style of 'dramatic loquaciousness' in the spirit of John Berryman – 'to sound not always biting back on my words' – but later came to judge the experiment a failure. He rewrote the poems for the Penguin / Yale book, discarding most of the long title poem, with eight of its forty-two stanzas transformed into the components of six separate

---

[1] 'A Literary Manuscript Masterclass: Geoffrey Hill in Conversation with Andrew McNeillie', at St. Anne's College, Oxford, 27 February 2009.

[2] Geoffrey Hill, *A Treatise of Civil power* (Thame: Clutag Press, 2005), n.p.

short lyrics. Trade publication allowed Hill to improve the contents, but in other ways the Penguin paperback fell short. As Sophie Ratcliffe wrote in a review at the time, its cover 'offers a photographic reproduction of the original's embossed paper', with 'something naff' about the 'comically ersatz feel' of the result, 'akin to wood-effect vinyl'.[3] Printing a photograph of luxurious heavy paper onto the cheap card of a trade paperback seems to poke some resentful fun at the distance between poetry's high-grade cultural ambitions and its diminished material circumstances. Another bibliographic difference: Hill gave a lower-case p to the word 'power' on the title page of the Clutag pamphlet, in homage to the typography of John Milton's 1659 pamphlet, from which he took his title, but this was regularized into upper-case 'Power' by Penguin.[4] For Hill, talking to McNeillie, the trade publisher's refusal of his lower-case *p* represented 'a loss of a sense of historical depth'. Likewise, Penguin had been reluctant in 1998 to allow Hill to publish a book with a title as obscure as the one he wanted, *Tempus Aedificandi Tempus Destruendi* – a play on the Vulgate translation of Ecclesiastes 3:3 ('a time to break down, and a time to build up'), and on the title of the 1971 choral work by Luigi Dallapiccola. After dalliance with the potential title *Hercules Buildings*, Hill's book was eventually renamed *The Triumph of Love*, and its original title only returned in 2013 when the text printed in *Broken Hierarchies* gave 'Tempus aedificandi tempus destruendi' as an epigraph to the sequence (BH 237).[5]

'The recalcitrance of the world'; 'inescapable error': these were unrehearsed, unpolished words, on which it would be wrong to place too much weight, but nonetheless they are true to themes from Hill's major work.[6] They testify to the continuity between Hill's thinking in and about poetry and his thinking in and about publishing and book-making. Although some of his works are more bookishly conceived

---

[3] Sophie Ratcliffe, 'Awkward Beauty', *New Statesman*, 11 October 2011, archived online at <http://www.newstatesman.com/poetry/2007/10/civil-power-hill-love-treatise>.

[4] See Charles Lock, 'Beside the Point: A Diligence of Accidentals', in *Geoffrey Hill and His Contexts*, ed. Piers Pennington and Matthew Sperling (Oxford: Peter Lang, 2011), pp. 43–60 (pp. 49-50), on the typography of the two books.

[5] For evidence of TL's various early titles, see Poetry Notebooks 42-47 (BC MS 20c Hill/2/1/42-47) and the drafts in BC MS 20c Hill/1/11/1-4, in the archive collection 'Literary Papers and Correspondence of Geoffrey Hill' at the Brotherton Library, University of Leeds.

[6] On error, see Andrew Michael Roberts, 'Error and Mistakes in Poetry: Geoffrey Hill and Tom Raworth', *English*, 56 (Autumn 2007), 339-61.

and intended than others, Hill has always been a writer who takes the book as a form to compose in; there is no volume of his in which bibliographic form is not doing some part of the work of meaning, and all of his books bear considerable scrutiny for the care and intelligence with which their bibliographic codes have been shaped.

*Broken Hierarchies: Poems 1952-2012* is a good instance. As a poetry book it is remarkable in several ways. Coming from Oxford University Press, it is a poetry book from a publisher which notoriously stopped publishing new poetry a decade and a half earlier, when it gave free transfers to all the poets on the list which had been built up across many years by editors Jon Stallworthy and Jacqueline Simms.[7] So Hill is on a contemporary poetry list of one; the next youngest Oxford poet after him is Isaac Rosenberg, who died in 1918. Although published in Hill's lifetime, it is a book which has a professional scholar, Kenneth Haynes, named as editor on the title-page and cover, in the manner one would expect for a scholarly edition of work by an author no longer present to curate his own texts, and yet, unlike the *Collected Critical Writings* of 2008, also edited by Haynes, it has no apparatus to explain the editor's role in textual decision-making. It is a book of books, presented in their chronological order, each with its own half-title page bearing an array of dedications and epigraphs. Usually today we think of a 'book' as a gathering of pages in bound folio format (most often, for poetry, in the form of the 'slim volume'), but several of the books in *Broken Hierarchies* have a curious status; they are virtual books, books which had no prior appearance between separate covers. This was already the case with 'The Songbook of Sebastian Arrurruz' when it appeared in *King Log* in 1968, but *Broken Hierarchies* goes further in presenting four new 'books' never before printed, and promoting 'Hymns to Our Lady of Chartres', originally a short sequence of three poems (CP 175-9), to *Hymns to Our Lady of Chartres*, a book of 21 sections, 420 lines long (BH 155-168). This new book takes its chronological place between books published in 1983 and 1996 respectively, but its own date is given as '1982-2012', so that it exists in a double time-scheme: a poem of the early 1980s made contemporary with the books which begin almost 500 pages later, *The Daybooks* (2007-2012).

---

[7] See Matthew Sperling, 'Books and the Market: Trade Publishers, State Subsidies, and Small Presses', in *The Oxford Handbook of Contemporary British and Irish Poetry*, ed. Peter Robinson (Oxford: Oxford University Press, 2013), pp. 191-212 (207-8).

This chapter will give an account of Hill's confrontation with 'the recalcitrance of the world' during the first three decades of his engagement with poetry publishing, by considering the evidence supplied by the André Deutsch Collection of archive papers held at Tulsa University in Oklahoma. André Deutsch Ltd was the sole publisher of Hill's first four book-length poetry collections, *For the Unfallen* (1959), *King Log* (1968), *Mercian Hymns* (1971) and *Tenebrae* (1979) and of his first collection of essays, *The Lords of Limit: Essays on Literature and Ideas* (1984). It was also co-publisher of *The Mystery of the Charity of Charles Péguy* (1983) with Agenda Editions, and of *Collected Poems* (1985) with Penguin Books. (Hereafter, 'André Deutsch' refers to the publishing company, 'Deutsch' to the man who founded the company.) Apart from Hill, the chief poets to have been on the André Deutsch list at one time or another were Stevie Smith, Elizabeth Jennings, David Gascoyne and Roy Fuller. The back cover of Hill's *Mercian Hymns* lists sixteen authors with books currently in print in the André Deutsch Poetry Books series, including some of those listed above, along with Kevin Crossley-Holland, Laurie Lee, Peter Levi, Ogden Nash, John Updike and David Wright.

The editor for most of these books, and the person at André Deutsch with whom Hill had most of his dealings, was Diana Athill, who joined the firm as a founding director in 1952 and stayed until retirement in 1993 aged 75. In Athill's memoir, *Stet: An Editor's Life* (2000), she looked back at her career as an editor of poetry books with ambivalence. 'I was nervous in the world of poetry', she writes:

> I read the work carefully, tried to make the jacket blurb say what the author wanted it to say, was moved by some of the poems as wholes and by parts of other poems ... all that was all right. But I also felt a kind of nervous reverence which I now find tiresome, because it was what I supposed one *ought* to feel in the presence of a superior being; and poets, although they do have a twist to their nature which non-poets lack, which enables them to produce verbal artefacts of superior intensity, are not superior beings.[8]

Athill concludes her brief discussion of poetry publishing in a tone of slight bafflement about why André Deutsch spent so long publishing poetry at all, when its strengths were for the kind of prestige literary

---

[8] Diana Athill, *Stet: An Editor's Life* (London: Granta Books, 2000), pp. 65-6.

fiction (Mailer, Updike, Rhys, Naipaul, Atwood) which in the firm's heyday could sell many times more copies than poetry ever could:

> poetry was never easy to sell, and we were not among the houses that were best at it. I find it hard to understand why we stayed with it as long as we did. Certainly I loved some of the books on our poetry list, but given my prosaic nature I would not have minded if we had never developed such a list. ... Poetry may not have lost us money (we paid poets minuscule advances and designed their books very economically), but it certainly didn't make us any, and none of us minded: an attitude which fifty – forty – thirty years ago was not worthy of remark, and now has become almost unimaginable.[9]

André Deutsch's capacity not to mind about making no money from a whole class of books is bound up with the fact that it was one of the few independent publishing firms in London to resist the pressures of full conglomeration throughout the 1970s and '80s.[10] This allowed them to retain some attitudes carried forward from the era of the publisher as gentleman-amateur – bearing in mind that Deutsch, like so many of the great twentieth-century publishers in Britain, was a Jewish émigré whose relation to the English class-system was an outsider's. As Athill writes, one reason for maintaining a poetry list was that 'André simply thought that a proper publisher had a poetry list, rather as, in the past, an English country gentleman ... thought that a proper house had a library'.[11] The pressures of conglomeration also account for the decline of the firm during the 1980s, leading to its eventual sale to the Carlton Group; today André Deutsch leads a sad existence as a Carlton imprint specialising in military history books.

If she was 'nervous' around poetry, and doubtful about the reasons for publishing it, Athill nonetheless ranks Hill highest among the poets in the André Deutsch stable: 'it was Geoffrey Hill's dense and knotty poems which were, for me, the richest in sudden flashes and enduring

---

[9] Athill, *Stet*, p. 69.

[10] For an overview on the era of conglomeration, see Eric de Bellaigue, *British Book Publishing as a Business Since the 1960s* (London: British Library, 2004), Chapters One and Two.

[11] Athill, *Stet*, p. 69.

illuminations'.[12] Hill's dealings with André Deutsch began when he submitted a manuscript with the title *Poems 1952-1956* on 11 January 1957, with a short covering note listing his publication credits.[13] It is not clear why he chose André Deutsch to submit his book to; perhaps he was encouraged by the fact that they had recently published *A Way of Looking* (1955), the first book by Elizabeth Jennings, a fellow Fantasy Press pamphleteer and a poet similarly concerned with religion and reinvigorated traditional forms. In early March, Deutsch sent the manuscript to Laurie Lee, with the words 'Diana tells me that we have a rather good poetry manuscript, which I would very much like you to read'.[14] Lee had been engaged as the company's 'Literary Adviser' since 1954, to read manuscripts for them and take on a small number of other editorial duties.[15] He returned this reader's report:

> These are distinguished poems, distinguished by their clear warm use of words, the level solemnity of their thought, their modesty & lack of attitudes. If I had seen this book in print I would have gratefully recognized a true strong voice among the many new ones. 'Genesis' & 'An Ark on the Flood' are particularly fine, – 'minor Miltonic', in the modern idiom. Weaknesses include, in the earlier poems, an almost mesmeric monotony of rhythm, so that each poem, whatever its subject, seems to read straight on from the last. (He has, however, made attempts to vary his metres in some of the later poems.) There are lines, too, that have no flow, that come at you in sharp hard words chopped by colons & commas which give an effect too harsh & fragmentary for my taste. But the general effect of his book is one of care, skill, a respect for words. I would say that he is better than several dozen of his contemporaries.[16]

---

[12] Athill, *Stet*, p. 66.

[13] Letter from Geoffrey Hill to André Deutsch, 11 January 1957, held in the Andre Deutsch Collection (1950-1995), McFarlin Library, Department of Special Collections and University Archives, University of Tulsa, collection number 1988.013, box 175. Material from this archive collection is hereafter referred to by the abbreviation 'ADC' and the box number in which the document is held.

[14] Letter from André Deutsch to Laurie Lee, 7 March 1957, ADC 220.

[15] See the letter from André Deutsch to Laurie Lee, 25 June 1954, ADC 220, for details of Lee's Literary Advisership.

[16] Laurie Lee, undated reader report headed 'Poems 1952-1956 Geoffrey Hill', ADC 175.

Given that Lee was a writer of very considerable differences in style, temperament and literary taste to Hill, and given that Hill at this point was an unknown, with none of the accrued history of interpretations which helps readers today in confronting the challenges of his work for the first time, this is a report of impressive imaginative sympathy and judgement.

A letter communicating André Deutsch's desire to publish Hill's collection was sent by editor-director Nicholas Bentley on 3 April 1957, offering an advance of £25 and royalties of 10% on the first 1,500 copies sold, rising to 12.5% thereafter.[17] (In the event, *For the Unfallen* took until 1977 to sell its first 1,500 copies.)[18] Owing to the smallness of the Deutsch poetry list – it had already committed to publish four poetry books in the next fifteen months – they would not be able to publish the book for another 18 months, meaning that it should appear in Autumn 1958. The central reason for the long delay in publication was André Deutsch's policy of submitting every poetry book it published for consideration by the Poetry Book Society as its quarterly choice for members; the publisher did not want to put Hill's book up in competition with another Deutsch title. Hill wrote to accept these terms on in early April, and Bentley acknowledged his acceptance, while apologising for the 'economics of poetry publishing':

> Speaking at the moment in a purely personal capacity, I feel that some apology is due for the inadequate sum that we offer by way of an advance but the economics of poetry publishing, as we know only too well, really will not allow us to go above this. However, if the book goes as well as we have reason to believe it will, this is something that will sort itself out.[19]

(Bentley's blithe reassurance that Hill's tiny income from poetry 'would sort itself out' as his reputation increased was never really to come true: in one of the last letters from Hill in the André Deutsch archive, in June 1983, he complained wryly: 'If I had received £100 for every "wonderful" review sine 1959 I could have invested a tidy sum and retired on the interest' – whereas in fact his royalties for all books in

---

[17] Letter from Nicholas Bentley to Geoffrey Hill, 3 April 1957, ADC 175.

[18] Letter from Diana Athill to Geoffrey Hill, 8 July 1981, ADC 1975.

[19] Letter from Nicholas Bentley to Geoffrey Hill, 8 April 1957, ADC 175.

print for the second half of 1982 totalled £225.74.)[20]

In mid-November 1957 Bentley wrote to Hill to tell him of a further delay: the book could not now appear in 1958 at all, and was pushed back to Spring 1959.[21] But in Spring it was still not forthcoming. The delays understandably agitated Hill, who twice sought reassurance about when he could expect to receive an advance copy, first in late May 1959:

> You must forgive me if I appear to be a little broody about my book. So near and yet so far – these weeks are not an enjoyable limbo.[22]

— and again in late August: 'It seems that I am to exude the last scruple of blood tears and sweat over this book. Any opportunity for hope would be most welcome'.[23] Finally it was confirmed that the book would appear on 14 October 1959, almost three years after the initial submission. The first print run was 750 copies.[24]

The delay between acceptance and publication gave Hill much time to revise the contents of the collection. First, in mid-June 1957, he wrote to Bentley that he would like to change the title of 'An Ark on the Flood' ('which has always seemed a little ingenuous'), to 'The Living and the Dead'.[25] On 29 September he proposed a larger change: he wanted to drop 'An Ark on the Flood' – 'a poem with which I have recently become increasingly dissatisfied' – altogether, and replace it with 'half-a-dozen short poems which I, and a few people whose opinions I value, think to be among the best I have done'. This change, he felt, would make the book 'much more of a "whole", and less a collection of disjointed pieces', and would also mean that when the book appeared, 'the most recent poems in it will only be twelve months old, instead of eighteen months, which is a big difference at my stage of development.'[26] These six poems were 'Little Apocalypse', 'Elegiac Stanzas', 'The Lowlands of Holland', 'After Cumae', 'The Death of

---

[20] Letter from Geoffrey Hill to Dieter Pevsner, 21 June 1983, ADC 175.

[21] Letter from Nicholas Bentley to Geoffrey Hill, 19 November 1957, ADC 175.

[22] Letter from Geoffrey Hill to Nicholas Bentley, 20 May 1959, ADC 175.

[23] Letter from Geoffrey Hill to Nicholas Bentley, 25 August 1959, ADC 175.

[24] Letter from Nicholas Bentley to Geoffrey Hill, 28 August 1959, ADC 175.

[25] Letter from Geoffrey Hill to Nicholas Bentley, 17 June 1957, ADC 175.

[26] Letter from Geoffrey Hill to Nicholas Bentley, 29 September 1957, ADC 175.

Shelley' and 'The Bibliographers'. On 15 October 1957 Hill included them at the end of the revised manuscript which he returned to Bentley. He also gave a title to the collection, which so far had only had the provisional title *Poems 1952-1956*: the book would be called *Of Commerce and Society*, and would have lines from Allen Tate's 'More Sonnets at Christmas' as an epigraph.[27]

The further postponement until Spring 1959 gave Hill time for further thoughts. On 30 January 1958 he told Bentley he wanted to add two new poems he had now completed, 'which strengthen very much the "European" key-note of the later part of the collection, poems, in fact, about commerce and society', and that he was close to finishing two more: 'I plan to group these poems under the heading of Of Commerce + Society – which would "justify" my giving the title to the book so far as I can tell'.[28] By 24 April he had changed his mind about the title again, but was now altogether unsure:

> Several friends have helped me to feel that there is something not wholly satisfactory in the title I chose for my book. I tried for something <u>deliberately</u> drab – (as opposed to, say, "Look! Look! Ergot!" or "The Too-Redolent Salamander") but I think, now, that I made it not so much drab as <u>mincing</u>. Could I beg you to bear with me while I try to cast round for something else? If all else fails, would <u>Poems, 1952-1958</u> be alright? This at least has a sense of weight, while <u>Poems</u> by itself is just a little too eager and virginal.[29]

Finally, on 9 September 1958, Hill wrote to Bentley with the news that 'I have at last hit upon a title I like very much: "<u>For the Unfallen</u>"', and added that the four-line epigraph he had given to the collection 'should give it the ironical "placing" I intend.'[30] This title was accepted, and the book eventually appeared as *For the Unfallen: Poems 1952-1958*, with four lines plucked from the poem 'Doctor Faustus' and set in italics for its epigraph: '*A beast is slain, a beast thrives. / Fat blood squeaks on the sand. / A blinded god believes / That he is not blind.*' (FTU 11). It may

---

[27] Letter from Geoffrey Hill to Nicholas Bentley, 15 October 1957, ADC 175.

[28] Letter from Geoffrey Hill to Nicholas Bentley, 30 January 1958, ADC 175.

[29] Letter from Geoffrey Hill to Nicholas Bentley, 24 April 1958, ADC 175.

[30] Letter from Geoffrey Hill to Nicholas Bentley, 9 September 1958, ADC 175.

be that Hill's intention of 'ironical "placing"' was too arch or subtle for readers of the book to grasp; in all subsequent reprints of the collection, in *Somewhere Is Such a Kingdom* (1975), *Collected Poems* (1985), *New and Collected Poems* (1994) and *Broken Hierarchies* (2013), it was omitted.

*For the Unfallen* was respectfully received, and it had one very notable review, by Al Alvarez in the *Observer*, headlined 'Enter a Myth-Maker', which did, as Laurie Lee had predicted would happen in his initial reader report, recognise the emergence of 'a true strong voice'.[31] Hill was launched as a poet, but his attitude towards the matter of public authorial self-presentation – the coalface of a writer's confrontation with 'the recalcitrance of the world' – remained awkward and at-odds. When asked to provide a biographical note ahead of the publication of *For the Unfallen*, he had returned a very sparse entry which, he claimed, 'includes just about every printable feature of my not very exciting life'; he was reluctant even to admit to the existence of his Fantasy Press pamphlet of 1952:

> I would much prefer it to be forgotten that I was ever a Young Oxford Poet; and am uneasy about the possibility of being dubbed an Academic Wit. It is true that I balance an awkward coffee-cup from time to time in the Staff Lounge, but I am not an Academic and have but small wit.[32]

In the same letter, he could barely bring himself to supply critical quotations about his work, claiming, not very credibly, that he was unable lay hands on any:

> Various people have said various pleasant things about my poetry from time to time; but these I have lost or put aside in the mistaken, though high-minded belief that I was not to be corrupted by worldly fame.

He then went back on this somewhat by suggesting that Anthony Thwaite's phrase 'powerful religious poet' would be acceptable, though he still took the chance to quibble with it a little: 'I don't honestly feel that I could now be called a religious poet. Powerful, yes!'

---

[31] Al Alvarez, 'Enter a myth-maker', *The Observer*, 25 October 1959, p. 23.

[32] Letter from Geoffrey Hill to Nicholas Bentley, 30 April 1959, ADC 175.

But time and custom go a considerable way to changing a writer's attitudes towards authorial persona; excessive personal shyness is the twin of egotistic outward self-esteem. By the end of 1973, Hill could decline Athill's invitation to take part in a 'Deutsch Evening' of poetry readings at the Mermaid Theatre, explaining his objection to group readings not because of any scruple about the corrupting influence of 'worldly fame', but because group readings are inadequate to the status of a writer of his merit:

> They seem to me to be ethically, aesthetically and tactically an error. A poet of merit deserves a full hour to himself. If he's not got merit what's he doing there anyway?[33]

And by 1977, in the run up to *Tenebrae*'s publication, writing to Sheila Murphy, the publicity director at André Deutsch who would subsequently leave the firm and act as Hill's literary agent, he could adopt an attitude of detached irony when supplying a generous sample of review quotations for use in pre-publication promotion of the book:

> If the farce has to be played, let us play it for all it's worth. I enclose a brief selection from other recent unsolicited testimonials.
>                mix and stir, ad nauseam.[34]

Perhaps here in this private letter we can see an early suggestion of the capacity that would enter Hill's poetry much later, in *Speech! Speech!* (2000) in particular, for 'tragic farce' (BH 323; SS 35) performed with clowning anarchic brio.

The same attitude – self-ironical weariness at the farce-like recalcitrance of circumstance, mixed with a game attempt to play it for the best one can – characterises Hill's dealings with the matter of US publication for his work. The Tulsa archive holds many letters concerned with this, which would be a topic of interest to several of his supporters in the US poetry world during the 1960s and 1970s. Hill wrote to Bentley in May 1959 that he had recently seen Allen Tate, 'who expressed great willingness to recommend my book to the University of Minnesota

---

[33] Letter from Geoffrey Hill to Diana Athill, 12 December 1973, ADC 176.

[34] Letter from Geoffrey Hill to Sheila Murphy, 13 March 1977, ADC 177.

Press', but nothing came of this.³⁵ On 11 December 1959 Deutsch wrote to Hill, then based in Ann Arbor, Michigan on a year's visiting professorship, to update him on efforts to find a US publisher for *For the Unfallen*: Rutgers were still considering the book, which had been with them for three months, while Dufour Editions of Chester Springs, Pennsylvania had expressed an interest in doing an American edition.³⁶ On the same day, a representative of the Mid-Century Book Society of New York wrote to Deutsch to say that W.H. Auden (part of the three-man editorial board with the intellectual historian Jacques Barzun and Lionel Trilling) had suggested that *For the Unfallen* would be a 'good companion' to Philip Larkin's *The Less Deceived* as one of their 1960 selections for members; the Society therefore wanted to know whether Deutsch had any arrangement with a US publisher for the book, or would be willing be make an arrangement directly with them.³⁷

On 18 January 1960 Hill replied to Deutsch from Ann Arbor, Michigan that he had sent a book to Dufour and was still unsure about the extent of the interest from the University Presses of Rutgers, Wesleyan (where his friend and early supporter Donald Hall had some involvement as a reader for the press) and Indiana: 'I find the caution of the American publishers a bit chilling', he wrote, 'particularly after the excellent press my book has (on the whole) received'. The letter ends with a joke on how Hill might increase his sales: 'I am calling my next book The Collected Poems of John Betjeman'.³⁸ Eventually Deutsch agreed to sell Dufour the sheets for 250 copies which would be issued with the Dufour imprint on the title page and jacket, and separately to sell the Mid-Century Book Society 1,000 copies as their October 1960 poetry selection, which would have the André Deutsch imprint on them but would also have added review quotations on the front flap of the dust wrapper and a US selling price of of $3.50.³⁹

By the time André Deutsch was trying to find a US publisher for *King Log*, Hill's attitude to the question had been toughened by a decade's experience of limited success. He wrote to Athill in early 1968:

---

³⁵ Letter from Geoffrey Hill to Nicholas Bentley, 20 May 1959, ADC 175.
³⁶ Letter from André Deutsch to Geoffrey Hill, 11 December 1959, ADC 175.
³⁷ Letter from Patricia Day Bennett to André Deutsch, 11 December 1959, ADC 175.
³⁸ Letter from Geoffrey Hill to André Deutsch, 18 January 1960, ADC 175.
³⁹ Letter from André Deutsch to Paul Dufour, 21 July 1960, ADC 175.

> The quest for the American publisher is not to become a quest for the chimaera. My reputation is such that my work will be taken and known without that. If they are not interested now, they'll discover their cultural obtuseness eventually. And, personally, I don't care all that much for appearing in the States.[40]

– and a month later than this, with no progress made on the matter, he added, 'The Americans can stew in their obtuseness'.[41] Eventually, Dufour Editions took a small number of sheets of *King Log* in a similar arrangement to the deal struck for *For the Unfallen*, but it seems to have resulted in very little circulation and recognition of Hill's work in the US at this stage.

As well as Allen Tate, other supporters of Hill's work took a close, disinterested concern in the fate of his poetry across the Atlantic. In late summer 1972 John Hollander wrote to Hill in words which Hill transcribed in a note to Athill: 'You <u>really must</u> have a good American publisher, and when I return I'll try and do something about this, if I have your permission' (at the same time, however, Hollander noted that 'transatlantic reputations are even more problematic than cis-ones').[42] Likewise, Michael Schmidt of Carcanet Press corresponded with Athill in August 1972 with suggestions for possible avenues of approach to editors of US publishing houses; Schmidt had recently written an article in strong praise of Hill's work for *Poetry* (Chicago), and ended his letter to Athill with the words, 'Mr. Hill does deserve an American hearing!'[43] And Donald Hall, Hill's friend since Oxford days, wrote to Athill in summer 1973 with can-do determination to change Hill's situation as to US publishers:

> I have been following with great delight the rise in Geoffrey Hill's fortunes, in England. When I saw him last October, he told me that nothing was doing about getting printed in the United States. I know that the first two books were "printed" by Dufour, but that is the same as not being distributed at all. Have you had any luck with the Mercian Hymns? ... I

---

[40] Letter from Geoffrey Hill to Diana Athill, 29 February 1968, ADC 175.

[41] Letter from Geoffrey Hill to Diana Athill, 11 March 1968, ADC 175.

[42] Letter from Geoffrey Hill to Diane Athill, undated [?August 1972], ADC 175.

[43] Letter from Michael Schmidt to Diana Athill, 24 August 1972, ADC 176.

> would very much like to get hard to work as an unofficial agent in this country. Unofficial, and, I need hardly add, unpaid. I have already sent the 3 books to Harper and Row. And they would be good, and I hope it will work out, and I advise them. However, things are not good there for poetry right now, and it may be that if Alfred, Lord Tennyson walked in off the street, beard and all, they would show him the door.[44]

Athill was most grateful for Hall's proposal, writing in reply, 'I know that our foreign rights department have been flogging the poems about but I do think it makes a great difference if they come in from somebody like you'.[45]

Yet none of this, for the moment, resulted in success, and in the period following UK publication of *Mercian Hymns* Hill wrote to Athill:

> It was a bit vertiginous to meditate on the descending spiral of American publishers who don't want to know me. The 'Overlook Press' was a name to conjure with. ... As you know, in my present mood, I'm quite content not to be published in America and wouldn't want you to waste any time and effort on pursuing the matter unless some prospect seemed to be splendidly to our mutual advantage: which is not likely.[46]

Eventually, perhaps partly by accumulated weight of all this effort, in 1975 Houghton Mifflin – a name which had not appeared as a possible publication venue in any of this various correspondence – issued *Somewhere Is Such a Kingdom: Poems 1952-1971*, a volume which brought together Hill's first three books in hardback with an introduction by Harold Bloom, whose endorsement doubtless helped a great deal to get the book accepted.

The successor to *For the Unfallen* would not appear for another nine years after that book. On 8 March 1962, two and a half years after his debut had been published, Hill responded to an inquiry from Deutsch about his progress in terms which were not encouraging, even while they made clear his steady and patient confidence in his own powers:

---

[44] Letter from Donald Hall to Diana Athill, 20 June 1973, ADC 176.

[45] Letter from Diana Athill to Donald Hall, 29 June 1973, ADC 176.

[46] Letter from Geoffrey Hill to Diana Athill, 24 August 1972, ADC 176.

It is impossible to think in terms of another collection at present. Every poem has to be dragged out of darkness, hewn from quarries of silence. I have a handful of fine things; but the second book will have to be better than the first, and I set my sights very high with *For the Unfallen*.[47]

Hill eventually sent the typescript of *King Log* on 26 June 1967, more than five years after writing this letter.[48] Diana Athill acknowledged receipt on 29 June 1967, remarking that she was 'delighted' to see another volume from Hill, and promising to have 'a long discussion with André' about the manuscript, while keeping expectations fairly damp: 'I hope very much that we shall be able to overcome the problems – they increase every year – which have been making us cut back so severely on the publication of poetry'.[49]

Having read the manuscript, she penned a handwritten note headed 'Geoffrey Hill's poems', probably intended for Deutsch:

We should decide about these. They are difficult to understand, because they are full of oblique academic allusions and are altogether rather laboriously knotty, but they are impressive (or so it seemed to me in so far as I did understand them), and he is the most highly esteemed of our poets by the pundits. Alavarez & co will sit up & take notice at his uttering again after such a long gap. I think we should publish them, if we are going to continue publishing poetry at all.[50]

On 24 July 1967 Athill wrote to Hill to tell him that although she was still waiting to have a detailed editorial conversation about the poems with Deutsch, she wanted to convey her thoughts to him:

I admire the poems, particularly Funeral Music and the Arrurruz poems. The allusions often escape me – I feel I'd need to know you well before I got the full meaning of the poems. It's probably because of having the essay on Funeral Music that

---

[47] Letter from Geoffrey Hill to André Deutsch, 8 March 1962, ADC 175.

[48] Letter from Geoffrey Hill to André Deutsch, 26 June 1967, ADC 175.

[49] Letter from Diana Athill to Geoffrey Hill, 29 June 1967, ADC 175.

[50] Diana Athill, undated note headed 'Geoffrey Hill's poems', ADC 175.

> those poems are the ones I enjoyed most, and this worries me a
> bit – a degree of condensation which makes one depend on an
> explanation always makes me feel rather frustrated (I'm not a
> good poetry reader!). But the images, colour, tone throughout
> the whole book – very austere and frightening. Each time I
> read the poems I'm more moved, groping nearer them.[51]

Notwithstanding Athill's only partial confidence in her understanding of the poems, the book was soon accepted for publication. On 11 March 1968, after requesting a publication date as soon as possible, Hill makes an unusual request:

> it would please me to have as small an edition as is economically
> feasible and reasonable. The idea of the book as physical entity
> is very exciting: for the rest, the repercussive power of the
> printed word seems savage and daunting.[52]

Such a request must only have increased Athill's feelings of confused nervousness around poetry, poets and their strange ways.

The question of submitting *King Log* for consideration by the Poetry Book Society once again caused some delay in publication. This time it also caused some tension between author and editor. When Hill had learnt back in 1959 that *For the Unfallen* was not to be the quarterly choice of the PBS, he wrote to Nicholas Bentley on 30 April that while he was sorry to hear it, 'if anything my faith in my own powers is strengthened':

> John Berryman's Homage to Mistress Bradstreet has appeared
> ungarlanded, and, after Lowell, he is about the finest younger
> American poet (he may well be better than Lowell, certainly
> than Wilbur).[53]

This is the earliest evidence of Hill's attraction to Berryman's writing. A few years later, in the poetry notebook dating from 1964-5, he wrote out a phrase from Berryman's poem 'The Song of the Demented Priest' in capital letters: 'THE VIOLENT & FORMAL DANCERS', and next to

---

[51] Letter from Diana Athill to Geoffrey Hill, 24 July 1967, ADC 175.
[52] Letter from Geoffrey Hill to Diana Athill, 11 March 1968, ADC 175.
[53] Letter from Geoffrey Hill to Nicholas Bentley, 30 April 1959, ADC 175.

it, 'TITLE FOR A BOOK' – and thereafter this was the working title for what became 'Funeral Music'.[54]

If being ignored by the PBS was Berryman's fate, it was okay for Hill too, in 1959. Nine years later, for his second book, he could not react so coolly to having his publication date delayed for PBS submission. On 6 March 1968 Hill wrote to Athill following a telephone conversation about the postponement of *King Log*'s publication until July, to lay out the reasons why he was so strongly opposed to this postponement, in a list worked up with underlinings and capitalizations:

> a) This is not a first book. I am not an unknown quantity. This is a book which has been eagerly awaited, by a whole number of people, for several years. Now that the 'grapevine' has heard that a new book is due, I am receiving various enquiries and, already, I have been able to send the name of editors who are requesting review-copies.
>
> b) I would point out that <u>For the Unfallen</u> was NOT a Poetry Book Society choice, in 1959. I forget what was. The reception of my work was influenced as much as anything by Alvarez's laudatory review in <u>The Observer</u>.
>
> c) If the book is delayed until July it will, in my opinion, fall into the doldrums <u>so far as the important weekly and Sunday</u> reviewing is concerned. The summer months are bad months, with regular reviewers and readers away on holiday. To me, the REAL danger in this <u>far outweighs</u> the tenuous advantages of a mere possibility that the book <u>might</u> be chosen by the P.B.S.[55]

When Athill's reply came on 13 March 1968 it was characteristically formidable in its measured tone and careful accuracy:

> I am sorry we have to argue, but must persist in doing so – having, indeed, more reason to do so than I gave you when talking on the telephone, when I believe I said that the Poetry Book Society take a couple of hundred copies of a choice. They

---

[54] Poetry Notebook 5, held in the Brotherton Collection at BC MS 20c Hill/2/1/5 (n.p.).
[55] Letter from Geoffrey Hill to Diana Athill, 6 March 1968, ADC 175.

> take 750. ... From our point of view it is distinctly worth while to hope for this, and I should have thought it was from yours too – though of course I can't tell you what you think or feel, considering that I rather resented your doing that to me when you said that Deutsch publishes poetry as a charity, so to speak, so can't mind about how soon they sell how much of it. I know better than you do what our attitude is; you know better than I do what yours is; all either of us can do is to state our own. ...
> Your points a) and b) seem to me – I'm sorry – irrelevant.[56]

As a compromise, Athill suggested bringing publication forward by one month to June, and requesting a speedy decision from the PBS. Hill accepted both the importance of trying for a PBS selection and the June date.[57]

In the event, *King Log* was not selected by the PBS as their quarterly Choice, which would have resulted in the 750 guaranteed sales to members of the Society, but was selected as their Recommendation. Hill wrote the required statement for their bulletin with almost comical brevity and evasiveness, setting his tone with an opening quotation from Dryden: "'Tis not my intention to make an Apology for my Poem'.[58] He was willing to have the fact of the PBS Recommendation acknowledged for promotional purposes on the book's cover, but still held back some reservations about the manner in which it would intrude upon the design:

> If this is done, may I beg that the words should not be bold-printed across the face of the utterly lovely woodcut, which would destroy the whole aesthetic purpose and defeat my cherishing. Could it be printed on a loose slip?[59]

Athill confirmed that the words 'Poetry Book Society Recommendation' would only be printed 'very small, at the top of the front flap, and not on the front of the jacket.[60] Contrast this with the attitude of Laurie

---

[56] Letter from Diana Athill to Geoffrey Hill, 13 March 1968, ADC 175.

[57] Letter from Geoffrey Hill to Diana Athill, 17 March 1968, ADC 175.

[58] Geoffrey Hill, untitled statement for Poetry Book Society Bulletin (1968), reprinted in *Don't Ask Me What I Mean: Poets in the Own Words*, ed. Clare Brown and Don Paterson (London: Picador, 2003), p. 115.

[59] Letter from Geoffrey Hill to Diana Athill, 12 June 1968, ADC 175.

[60] Letter from Diana Athill to Geoffrey Hill, 14 June 1968, ADC 175.

Lee who, when his book *My Many-Coated Man* was chosen by the PBS in 1955, wrote to his publisher to request that 'our little pointed boast' be printed so prominently on the cover and spine that it would 'stand out immediately'.[61]

Hill was abashed at the confrontational tone of his earlier letter to Athill about the potential postponement: 'I am more sorry than I can say that a pleasant acquaintanceship should have become clouded in this way and I can only hope that in retrospect it will appear as an episode unhappy but ephemeral'.[62] When Hill wrote this letter he and Athill had never met, but since, as he suggested, 'letters prolong difficulties and misunderstandings that a few moments direct discussion could resolve', and she agreed, 'it's far easier to give the proper weight to people's words when one is better acquainted with them', they soon met for lunch, and subsequently their correspondence avoided any such difficulties, with Athill serving as a sympathetic, patient, witty and supportive editor. In *Stet*, she looked back on the relationship:

> Geoffrey was a difficult writer to work with because of his anxiety: he was bedevilled by premonitions of disaster, and had to be patiently and repeatedly reassured although my own nerves, worked on by his, would be fraying even as I spoke or wrote my soothing words. ... Whatever it may be that causes a poet to know himself one, Geoffrey was walking evidence of his own sense of vocation. Living seemed to be more difficult for him than for most people.[63]

Athill goes on to tell a story of Hill's high anxiety about the printing of the copyright acknowledgements for *Mercian Hymns* – which, she says, were eventually printed wrongly even so. A similar case arises in the archive when Hill notices that the text is printed on a slant in the paperback reprint of *King Log*; Athill gets her ruler out to confirm that there is a slant of a few millimetres, but then discovers that the original hardback had the same slant, without Hill or anyone else noticing. What had seemed 'very beautiful' now seemed 'an ugly book' to Hill, a matter compounded by his 'unhappy bias of temperament which homes in and

---

[61] Letter from Laurie Lee to André Deutsch, 14 May 1955, ADC 220.

[62] Letter from Geoffrey Hill to Diana Athill, 17 March 1968, ADC 175.

[63] Athill, *Stet*, pp. 66-7.

fastens like a remora on matters which others can shrug off.[64]

In the years following the writing of *Mercian Hymns*, Hill once again found the composition of new poetry severely difficult, a matter compounded by the circumstances of his personal life, and his editor was an important and sympathetic ear for discussion of his difficulties. On 18 June 1972 he wrote to Athill, thanking her for rescuing him from 'monologuists of various kinds' when she accompanied him to a prize-giving at the Royal Society of Literature, and ventured that she was unlikely to be 'subjected to any further ordeals on my behalf':

> They must have run out of prizes and I have run out of talent. I suppose in time this may become an equable numbness; at the moment it feels close to the abomination of desolation. I offer this by way of apologia for having been a rather boring monologuist myself on the subject.[65]

Three years later, as Hill begins to look towards what would become *Tenebrae*, on 11 Aug 1975, the situation has not improved much:

> I have been going through my post-1971 poems very searchingly and the result is not very cheering. There are several poems, good enough in themselves to appear without disgrace in periodicals, that would <u>not</u> be good in a book. They are poems written in the slip-stream of better things; they reveal themselves as such. They would introduce a note of dilute repetitiousness quite alien to my previous three books.
>
> My hypothetical <u>fourth</u> Deutsch book <u>must</u> be a stunner, when it comes, i.e. it must gather up things with the power of <u>Lachrimae</u>, <u>The Pentecost Castle</u>, etc., into a great storm. If I tried to cobble together a fourth BOOK now, it wouldn't work <u>as a book</u>. ...
>
> For better or worse, I feel, a major creative phase is over. Perhaps there will be nothing else. Perhaps whatever else emerges will be unrecognizably different.[66]

---

[64] Letter from Geoffrey Hill to Diana Athill, n.d., ADC 176.

[65] Letter from Geoffrey Hill to Diana Athill, 18 June 1972, ADC 176.

[66] Letter from Geoffrey Hill to Diana Athill, 11 August 1975, ADC 176.

At times Athill seems sympathetically to take on Hill's manner of neurotic worry for accuracy of detail; in 1981, writing to apologise for a miscalculation of royalty payments due to Hill since *For the Unfallen* had passed 1,500 sales in 1977, when Hill's rate should have risen to 12.5% but did not, she wrote 'there have often been times when I've felt guilt to be my proper element'.[67]

Anxious care for minute details serves well an author concerned with calibrating bibliographic codes for maximal effect. Hill's poetry books often show an intricate, elaborate deployment of paratext and peritext: in their multiple stratified divisions of title, section title, poem number or title; in their carapace of epigraphic and dedicatory text (the latter carefully distinguishing between poems 'for' someone, in memory of someone, 'after' someone); in their self-parodically scrupulous and enigmatic back-matter of notes and acknowledgements; in the thoughtfully chosen images on the front of the book. This was the case for the early books as much as for *Broken Hierarchies*, and in the archive we can witness these bibliographic decisions being reached and refined.

We have seen that Hill tried to pluck four lines from one of his own poems to make an epigraph which would give 'ironical "placing"' to his title in *For the Unfallen*; he also appended dates of composition to each poem in that book, as if awkwardly pointing up a debut poet's mixed pride and embarrassment at his own precociousness. In *King Log* he took things further by creating a two-part structure for the book. *King Log* appears to be the overall title for a book made up of two unequal units: a first section, gathering poems and poetic sequences under the title 'King Log', and a second section, marked by a new title page, named 'Postscript: King Stork'. When she first read the manuscript, Diane Athill was baffled:

> Why have you put IN MEMORY OF JANE FRASER where it is, in 'King Stork'? This is what I mean about being a bad reader – I recognize that her presence there must have a reason, but I fail to "get" it.[68]

It seems that Athill – who, in fairness, had not been Hill's editor on *For the Unfallen* – did not realise that 'In Memory of Jane Fraser' was a revised version of a poem from Hill's first book. It was surely this which caused

---

[67] Letter from Diana Athill to Geoffrey Hill, 8 July 1981, ADC 175.
[68] Letter from Diana Athill to Geoffrey Hill, 24 July 1967, ADC 175.

Hill to add the words 'An Attempted Reparation' as a sub-title, and to add the sentences which explain why he is printing, in his second book, a revised version of a poem from his first book: 'I dislike the poem very much and the publication of this amended version may be regarded as a necessary penitential exercise' (KL 70). Clearly, if the coining of a slightly awkward nonce-word in the line 'a few sprinkled leaves unshook' can be considered a wrongdoing worthy of penitence and reparation, Hill was in earnest when he wrote that 'the repercussive power of the printed word seems savage and daunting'. Hill clarified the relationship between 'King Log' and 'King Stork' for Athill in his letter of 7 February 1968:

> King Log would seem to be indolent and self-regarding poetry and King Stork the super-ego that devours the worshippers of this wooden and floating art.[69]

As well as 'In Memory of Jane Fraser: An Attempted Reparation', 'King Stork', the punitive devouring super-ego, was also going to contain a substantial biographical note on the fictional poet Sebastian Arrurruz. But on 6 December 1967 Hill wrote to Athill to change his mind about including it:

> It was sweet of whoever wrote it to play along with my 'in-game' about 'the Spaniard who wrote at the turn of the century' but I'm chickening out. My temperament, I regret to discover, is not sufficiently resilient to sustain Nabokovian flights and in short I have become jealous and resentful of my own creation. People keep telling me how terrific he is and ask 'how did you get on to him?'[70]

By such decisions a poet defines how he will be read. A version of *King Log* which included a 'Nabokovian' essay on Sebastian Arrurruz would have cast Hill as a more ludic, flamboyant, metapoetic, 'postmodern' poet than he has generally been thought.

In its design and conception as a book, *Mercian Hymns* was no less deliberated than its predecessor (with *King Log*, Hill wrote to Athill in December 1967, 'I brood obsessively over that SPINE').[71] Hill describes

---

[69] Letter from Geoffrey Hill to Diana Athill, 7 February 1968, ADC 175.

[70] Letter from Geoffrey Hill to Diana Athill, 6 December 1967, ADC 175.

[71] Letter from Geoffrey Hill to Diana Athill, 23 December 1967, ADC 175.

Thomas Kinsella's *Another September*, published by Dolmen Press in 1958, as 'one of the "models" for the Mercian Hymns format' in terms of the relatively square proportions of the page and the way in which the poems sit squarely in the middle of each page.[72] At the time when the book was being designed we find him closely in negotiations with Athill and the design team about the book's format.[73] In a letter to Michael George, the in-house designer at André Deutsch, on 14 October 1970, Hill expressed his desire to have *Mercian Hymns* set in the typeface Joanna, 'the favourite type of the poet and designer David Jones', remarking that 'Joanna seems especially attractive, particularly in its italic'.[74] Clearly Hill had been reading the 1969 Fulcrum Press edition of Jones's book *The Tribune's Visitation*, which states on its acknowledgements page, 'The book has been set throughout in the author's favourite type Joanna'.[75] Literary affinities extend beyond poetic influence to the whole business of how poets conceive of books as design objects. Jones is the patron saint of poet-bookmakers here, the poet whose handling of cadence is fully instinct with his mastery of lettering and inscription. Likewise, when the joint Agenda Editions / André Deutsch edition of *The Mystery of the Charity of Charles Péguy* was being planned, Hill wrote to William Cookson of *Agenda*, who took care of all production details, that he wanted it to resemble another David Jones book which Agenda Editions had recently published: 'it would give me great joy to appear in the same format as The Kensington Mass which is in every way one of the most beautiful books of poetry to have appeared in recent years'.[76] As Sheila Murphy, by then acting as Hill's agent, reported, Hill was 'absolutely opposed to dropping the acetate, and wishes the book to be in every respect exactly like The Kensington Mass'.[77]

In the course of correspondence about *Mercian Hymns*, Hill acknowledges the grinding minuteness of his care for the small details, apologises for it, then adds:

---

[72] Letter from Geoffrey Hill to Diana Athill, 15 February 1974, ADC 176.

[73] See the letters from Diana Athill to Geoffrey Hill, 24 July 1970, and from Geoffrey Hill to Diana Athill, 30 July 1970, ADC 176.

[74] Letter from Geoffrey Hill to Michael George, 14 October 1970, ADC 176.

[75] David Jones, *The Tribune's Visitation* (London: Fulcrum Press, 1969), p. [vii].

[76] Letter from Geoffrey Hill to William Cookson, 28 August 1982, ADC 176.

[77] Letter from Sheila Murphy to Dieter Pevsner, 6 December 1982, ADC 176.

> I don't ask for these things lightly, or indifferently or whimsically, you know. One feels immensely burdened by the THING-NESS of what one is doing: the ultimate impossibility of retraction.[78]

I began this essay by talking about some of Hill's post-publication revisions to poems, particularly in the texts in *Broken Hierarchies*. It seems that he became happier to revise poems post-publication in the last two decades of his life. 'Retractions', in the Augustinian sense of 'rehandlings', are precisely what the late revisions are at.[79] Hill quite freely altered, amended, undid previous revisions, even in poems which seemed utterly remote from his later ways and concerns. Before *Broken Hierarchies* had been published, Hill was comparing it to Whitman's 1892 'deathbed edition' of *Leaves of Grass* ('L. of G. *at last complete* – after 33 y'rs of hackling at it, all times & moods of my life…').[80] In the same way, Hill's six decades of writing have been strongly revised, sometimes with dramatic textual interventions, to find their 'definitive form', as the back cover of the dust wrapper proclaims. This makes a strong contrast with the frame of mind Hill was in when he made 'an attempted reparation', 'a necessary penitential exercise', of the revisions for 'In Memory of Jane Fraser', or when he felt burdened by 'the impossibility of retraction' in a published poem. His attitude may have changed, yet his sense of 'the recalcitrance of the world' with regard to publishing remained constant. In another letter to Athill at the time of *Mercian Hymns*, he apologised for 'the pernickety character of my original enquiry' concerning a rights issue around the Caedmon recording *The Poetry and Voice of Geoffrey Hill*, but added: 'It is the nature of the world, though, that makes one pernickety. The small print.'[81]

---

[78] Letter from Geoffrey Hill to Diana Athill, 23 December 1970, ADC 176.

[79] On Hill and retraction, see Matthew Sperling, *Visionary Philology: Geoffrey Hill and the Study of Words* (Oxford: Oxford University Press, 2014), p. 69.

[80] Hill's remark was made during a reading at the London Review Bookshop on 20 September 2007, of which a recording is held in the Brotherton Collection at BC MS 20c Hill/7/2/13; Whitman quotation from a letter to Richard Maurice Burke, 6 December 1891, in *Selected Letters of Walt Whitman*, ed. Edwin Haviland Miller (Iowa City, IA: University of Iowa Press, 1990), p. 292. Thanks to Carl Robert Anderson for his Whitman help.

[81] Letter from Geoffrey Hill to Diana Athill, 17 November 1976, ADC 176.

# Abbreviations

**Geoffrey Hill, Poetry**

BH   *Broken Hierarchies: Poems 1952-2012*, ed. Kenneth Haynes (Oxford: Oxford University Press, 2013)

**Volumes included in *Collected Poems* (Harmondsworth: Penguin, 1985), and subsequently in *Broken Hierarchies***

FTU   *For the Unfallen: Poems 1952–1958* (London: André Deutsch, 1959)

KL   *King Log* (London: André Deutsch, 1968)

MH   *Mercian Hymns* (London: André Deutsch, 1971)

T   *Tenebrae* (London: André Deutsch, 1978)

TM   *The Mystery of The Charity of Charles Péguy* (London: Agenda Editions and André Deutsch, 1983)

**Volumes included in *Broken Hierarchies: Poems 1952-2012*, ed. Kenneth Haynes (Oxford: Oxford University Press, 2013)**

C   *Canaan* (London: Penguin, 1996)

TL   *The Triumph of Love: A Poem* (1998; Harmondsworth: Penguin, 1999)

SS   *Speech! Speech!* (2000; London: Penguin, 2001)

OS   *The Orchards of Syon* (London: Penguin, 2002)

SC   *Scenes from Comus* (London: Penguin, 2005)

WT   *Without Title* (London: Penguin, 2006)

TCP   *A Treatise of Civil Power* (London: Penguin, 2007)

O   *Oraclau | Oracles* (Thame: Clutag Press, 2010)

CL   *Clavics* (London: Enitharmon Press, 2011)

OB   *Odi Barbare* (Thame: Clutag Press, 2012)

**Geoffrey Hill, Prose**

CCW   *Geoffrey Hill, Collected Critical Writings*, ed. Kenneth Haynes (Oxford: Oxford University Press, 2008)

LL   *The Lords of Limit: Essays on Literature and Ideas* (London: André Deutsch, 1984)

# Notes on Contributors

**Martin Dodsworth** is Emeritus Professor of English in the University of London and a former Chair of the English Association. He has written elsewhere on Geoffrey Hill, notably in Peter Robinson's *Geoffrey Hill: Essays on his Work* (1985).

**Stephen James** is a Senior Lecturer in English Literature at the University of Bristol and the author of *Shades of Authority: The Poetry of Lowell, Hill and Heaney* (2007). He has published articles on Hill in several journals, including Essays in Criticism and The Cambridge Quarterly. His next monograph will be *Geoffrey Hill and the Poetry of Nature*.

**Tom Jones** is a teacher and researcher in the School of English, University of St Andrews. His publications on the literary and intellectual history of eighteenth-century Britain and Ireland include *Pope and Berkeley: The Language of Poetry and Philosophy* (Palgrave, 2005), a study of the connections between the work of these friends; an annotated edition of Pope's *Essay on Man* (Princeton, 2016); and essays on the history of linguistic thought. His interest in poetics is expressed in *Poetic Language: Theory and Practice from the Renaissance to the Present* (Edinburgh, 2012) and essays on contemporary poets such as Andrea Brady and Thomas A. Clark.

**Edward Larrissy** is an Emeritus Professor of Queen's University, Belfast, where he is affiliated to the Seamus Heaney Centre for Poetry. He is the author of, among other books, *Reading Twentieth-Century Poetry: The Language of Gender and Objects* (1990), *Yeats the Poet: The Measures of Difference* (1994), *Blake and Modern Literature* (2006) and *The Blind and Blindness in Literature of the Romantic Period* (2007). He is the editor of, among other books, *Romanticism and Postmodernism* (1999), *W.B. Yeats: The Major Works* (2001) and *The Cambridge Companion to British Poetry, 1945-2010* (2016). He is a Member of the Royal Irish Academy.

**Steven Matthews** is Professor of Modernism at Reading University, UK. His books include *Irish Poetry: Politics, History, Negotiation. The Evolving Debate, 1969 to the Present* (Macmillan, 1997); *Yeats as Precursor* (Macmillan, 2000); *Les Murray* (Manchester U.P., 2001), and *Modernism: A Sourcebook* (Palgrave, 2008). His *T.S. Eliot and Early Modern Literature* appeared from O.U.P. in 2013, and *Ceaseless Music*, a critical-creative reflection on Wordsworth's *The Prelude*, in 2017 (Bloomsbury). He has published two poetry collections – *Skying* (Waterloo Press 2012) and *On Magnetism* (Two Rivers, 2017).

**Samira Nadkarni**'s publications trace her interest in postmodern poetry and performance, human rights, pop culture, hermeneutics, ethics, neo/colonial-ism, fan studies, and digital texts. She serves on the editorial board for the undergraduate journals, *Watcher Junior* and *Lumiere*; writes reviews for the speculative science fiction and fantasy magazine, *Strange Horizons*; contributed to the digital poetry project *i <3 e-poetry*; and has had her creative writing published in *New Writing Dundee, Grund Lit*, and *Causeway Magazine*. She is the co-editor of *War in the Whedonverses*, forthcoming with McFarland and Co in 2019. Apart from teaching undergraduate English literature, she is a working maritime journalist and sub-editor.

ALEX PESTELL is an occasional independent scholar living in Berlin. His book *Geoffrey Hill: The Drama of Reason* was published in 2016 by Peter Lang.

NATALIE POLLARD is the author of *Speaking to You: Contemporary Poetry and Public Address* (OUP, 2012), and of *Fugitive Pieces: Poetry, Publishing and Visual Culture from Late Modernism to the 21st Century* (OUP, 2019). Her current research connects contemporary literature with drawing, architecture and sculpture, the politics of design and of address, typographical innovation and avant-garde forms. Natalie has active research and teaching interests in ethical pedagogy and posthumanism, knowledge, wonder and play.

ANDREW MICHAEL ROBERTS is Professor of Modern Literature in the School of Humanities at the University of Dundee. His research interests are in modernist fiction and poetry, contemporary British poetry, digital poetry, literature and science, and literature and visual culture. He was Principal Investigator for the AHRC-funded project, 'Poetry Beyond Text: Vision, Text and Cognition' (2009-2011), www.poetrybeyondtext.org. His books include *Conrad and Masculinity* (Palgrave, 2000), *Geoffrey Hill* (Northcote House, 2004) and *Poetry & Ethics* (Liverpool University Press, forthcoming). He is Co-Director of the Centre for Poetic Innovation at the Universities of Dundee and St Andrews.

MATTHEW SPERLING is Lecturer in Literature in English from 1900 to the Present at University College London. He is the author of *Visionary Philology: Geoffrey Hill and the Study of Words* (2014); of numerous essays on poetry, publishing history, and visual art; and of a novel, *Astroturf* (2018), longlisted for the Wellcome Book Prize. His second novel will be published in 2020.

ELEANORE WIDGER received a doctorate from the University of Dundee in 2018, on contemporary British 'radical landscape poetry' and Romantic environmental aesthetics. She was the 2018 Doctoral Fellow at the Centre for Poetic Innovation and began her postdoctoral research with an NPIF Innovation Placement at the Scottish Poetry Library, Edinburgh. Her work has been published in *English* and *The Journal of British and Irish Innovative Poetry*.

# Bibliography

This bibliography lists Hill's principal volumes and collections of poetry and prose, along with a selection of individual prose writings and interviews. A detailed bibliography of Hill's works up to 2011, by Kenneth Haynes (from which this bibliography draws), can be found in *Geoffrey Hill: Essays on His Later Work*, ed. John Lyon and Peter McDonald (Oxford: OUP, 2012).

**Volumes of Poetry by Geoffrey Hill**

*For the Unfallen: Poems 1952-1958* (London: André Deutsch, 1959).

*King Log* (London: André Deutsch and Chester Springs, Pa: Dufour Editions, 1968).

*Mercian Hymns* (London: André Deutsch, 1971).

*Tenebrae* (London: André Deutsch, 1978).

*The Mystery of the Charity of Charles Péguy* (London: Agenda Editions and André Deutsch, 1983).

*Collected Poems* (Harmondsworth: Penguin, 1985; hardback edn, London: André Deutsch, and New York: Oxford University Press, 1986). Includes the five volumes listed above, with some minor revisions.

*New and Collected Poems, 1952-1992* (Boston, MA and New York, NY: Houghton Mifflin, 1994).

Includes the five individual volumes listed above, plus thirteen 'New Poems' (1992)', of which all but one were later included in *Canaan*.

*Canaan* (London: Penguin, 1996; Boston and New York, NY: Houghton Mifflin, 1997).

*The Triumph of Love* (Boston and New York: Houghton Mifflin, 1998; London: Penguin, 1999).

*Speech! Speech!* (Washington, DC: Counterpoint, 2000; London: Penguin, 2001).

*The Orchards of Syon* (Washington, DC: Counterpoint and London: Penguin, 2002).

*Scenes from Comus* (London: Penguin, 2005).

*A Treatise of Civil Power* (Thame: Clutag Press, 2005).

*Without Title* (London: Penguin, 2006; New Haven, CT: Yale University Press, 2007).

*Selected Poems* (London: Penguin, 2006). Selections from all of the above individual volumes (except *A Treatise of Civil Power*).

*A Treatise of Civil power* (London: Penguin and New Haven, CT: Yale University Press, 2007). Substantially different to Clutag Press volume.

*The Daybooks III: Oraclau | Oracles* (Thame: Clutag Press, 2010).

*The Daybooks IV: Clavics* (London: Enitharmon Press, 2011).

*The Daybooks II: Odi Barbare* (Thame: Clutag Press, 2012).

*Broken Hierarchies: Poems 1952-2012*, ed. Kenneth Haynes (Oxford: Oxford University Press, 2013). Includes the volumes listed above (including those previously included in *Collected Poems*), with some significant revisions. It adds *Pindarics (2005-12)* and *Ludo* (2011). It also adds three new volumes under the heading *The Daybooks* (2007-2012) to the three of the *Daybooks* already published separately, renumbered to give the following list:

> *The Daybooks* (2007-2012)
>
> I   *Expostulations on the Volcano*
>
> II  *Liber Illustrium Virorum*
>
> III *Oraclau | Oracles*
>
> IV  *Clavics*
>
> V   *Odi Barbare*
>
> VI  *Al Tempo De' Tremuoti*

*The Book of Baruch by the Gnostic Justin*, ed. Kenneth Haynes (Oxford: Oxford University Press, 2019).

### Hill's Dramatic Writing

*Brand: A Version for the Stage* (Geoffrey Hill's version of Henrik Ibsen's play *Brand*, based on an annotated literal prose translation by Inga-Stina Ewbank) (London: Heinemann, 1978; revised edition Minneapolis, MN: University of Minnesota Press, 1981).

*Peer Gynt and Brand*, versions by Geoffrey Hill (*Peer Gynt* based on a literal translation of Henrik Ibsen's play *Peer Gynt* by Janet Garton, ed. Kenneth Hayes) (London: Penguin, 2016).

### Hill's Prose Writings: Collections

*The Lords of Limit: Essays on Literature and Ideas* (London: André Deutsch, 1984).

*The Enemy's Country: Words, Contexture and Other Circumstances of Language* (Oxford: Clarendon Press, 1991).

*Style and Faith: Essays* (New York, NY: Counterpoint, 2003).

*Collected Critical Writings*, ed. Kenneth Haynes (Oxford and New York, NY: Oxford University Press, 2008). Includes the essays from the preceding three volumes (with some corrections and revisions), together with thirteen new essays, grouped into two collections, entitled *Inventions of Value* and *Alienated Majesty*. The Editorial Note states that Hill 'conceived of [these collections] as books'.

**Hill's Prose Writings: selected items not included in the above volumes**

'The Poetry of Allen Tate', *Geste*, 3.3 (Nov. 1958), 8-14.

'The Poetry of Jon Silkin', *Poetry & Audience*, 9.12 (26 Jan. 1962), 4-8.

'The Dream of Reason', *Essays in Criticism*, 14.1 (Jan. 1964), 91-101.

'"I in Another Place": Homage to Keith Douglas', *Stand*, 6.4 (n.d. pub 1964), 6-13.

'"The Conscious Mind's Intelligible Structure": A Debate', *Agenda* 9.4-10.1 (Autumn / Winter 1971-72), 14-23.

'Geoffrey Hill Writes...', *Poetry Book Society Bulletin*, no. 98 (Autumn 1978), 1.

'A Sermon Delivered at Great St Mary's University Church', Cambridge, 8 May 1983.

'C.H. Sisson', *PN Review* 39 11.1 (Mar. 1984), 11-15.

'"The Age Demanded" (Again)', *Agenda* 26.3 (Autumn 1988), 10-12.

'Acceptance Speech for the T.S. Eliot Prize', *Image: A Journal of the Arts and Religion*, no. 28 (Fall 2000), 72-6.

'Between Politics and Eternity', in *The Poets' Dante: Twentieth-Century Responses*, ed. Peter S. Hawkins and Rachel Jacoff (New York, NY: Farrar, Straus and Giroux, 2001), 319-32.

'Thought of a Conservative Modernist', in *Post-Modernisms: Origins, Consequences, Reconsiderations*, ed. Claudio Véliz (Boston, MA: The University Professors, Boston University, 2002), 96-104.

'Geoffrey Hill', in *Don't Ask Me What I Mean: Poets in Their Own Words*, ed. Claire Brown and Don Paterson (London: Picador, 2003), 115-8.

'R.S. Thomas's Welsh Pastoral' in *Echoes to the Amen: Essays after R.S. Thomas*, ed. Damian Walford Davies (Cardiff: University of Wales Press, 2003), 44-59.

'Sidney Keyes in Historical Perspective', in *The Oxford Handbook of British and Irish War Poetry*, ed. Tim Kendall (Oxford: Oxford University Press, 2007), 398-418.

'A Sermon Preached in Balliol College Chapel, 11 November 2007', *Balliol College Annual Record 2008*, 24-7.

'Civil Polity and the Confessing State', *Warwick Review*, 2.2 (June 2008), 7-20.

'Sermon for the Commemoration of Benefactors: Emmanuel College, 24 November 2010', *Emmanuel College Magazine*, 93 (2010-11), 34-9.

Professor Sir Geoffrey Hill Lectures, Faculty of English Language and Literature, University of Oxford (2010-15), podcast recordings, <http://www.english.ox.ac.uk/professor-sir-geoffrey-hill-lectures>.

Geoffrey Hill, 'Mightier and Darker': review of Grevel Lindop, *Charles Williams: The Third Inkling*, *Times Literary Supplement*, 23 March 2016.

**Interviews**

'Literature Comes to Life …', with Michael Dempsey, *Illustrated London News*, 249 (20 August 1966), 24-5.

'Out of Parenthesis', with Alan Page, *The Times Literary Supplement*, no. 3479 (31 October 1968), 1220.

'Under Judgment', with Blake Morrison, *New Statesman*, 8 February 1980, 212-14.

Interview with Hermione Lee, *Book Four*, 2 Oct 1985, Channel Four television.

'An Interview with Geoffrey Hill', with John Haffenden, *Quarto*, 15 (March 1981), 19-22, reprinted in *Viewpoints: Poets in Conversation with John Haffenden* (London: Faber and Faber, 1981), 76-99.

'Poetry: Interview: David Sexton Talks to Geoffrey Hill', *Literary Review*, 92 (Feb. 1986), 27-9.

'Of Letters, Learning and Louts', with Nigel Spivey, *Times Higher Education Supplement* (6 Sept. 1996), 20.

'The Art of Poetry LXXX: Geoffrey Hill', with Carl Phillips, *Paris Review*, No. 154 (Spring 2000), 272-99.

'The Praise Singer', with Robert Potts, *Guardian* (10 Aug. 2002), Features and Reviews, 16-19.

'A Growl in his Voice, a Twinkle in his Eye', with Nicholas Lezard, *Independent* (6 Feb. 2005), 28-9.

'Cambrian Readjustments: An Interview with Geoffrey Hill', with Damian Walford Davies and Richard Marggraf Turley, *Poetry Wales* 46.1 (Summer 2010), 10-13.

'Interview: Geoffrey Hill, a Ruskinian Tory', with Jessica Campbell, *Oxford Student* (26 May 2011), 31. Online: http://oxfordstudent.com/2011/05/26/interview-geoffrey-hill-oxford-professor-of-poetry/.

'"If I write about destruction it's because I'm terrified of it": An Interview with Geoffrey Hill', with Dominic Hand and Sofía Crespi de Valldaura, *Isis*, 27 April 2015.

'Translating and Recreating Ibsen: An Interview with Geoffrey Hill', with Kenneth Haynes, 'Afterword' to Henrik Ibsen, *Peer Gynt* and *Brand*, trans. by Geoffrey Hill (London: Penguin, 2016), pp. 343-51.

# Index

*Note: Locators in the form 10n refer to a footnote on that page.*

Abrams, M.H. 102
Adorno, Theodor 172, 210, 211n
*Agenda* (magazine) 11, 16–21, 116, 274
Agenda Editions 255, 274
Alvarez, Al 261, 266, 268
   *The New Poetry* anthology 11, 112
Anderson, Benedict 244
André Deutsch (company) 15, 255, 256, 257, 258, 262, 263, 271, 274
Arendt, Hannah 172
Arrowsmith, William 171
Athill, Diana 15, 255–6, 257, 262–75
   *Stet: An Editor's Life* 255–6, 270
Auden, W.H. 263
   'In Memory of W.B. Yeats' 8
Austin, J.L. 14, 71–2, 152–4, 156, 160, 168
   *How to Do Things with Words* 152

Bacon, Francis 118
Baker, Hylda 205
Barlach, Ernst 228, 229, 230
   *Schmerzensmutter* (*Mother of Sorrows*) 227
Barrell, John, *The Idea of Landscape and the Sense of Place* 56
Barthes, Roland 8
Barzun, Jacques 263
Bate, Jonathan 142
Bayley, John 186n
Belloc, Hilaire 107
Benjamin, Walter 172
Bennett, Charles 241
Bentley, Nicholas 258, 259, 260, 262, 267
Bergonzi, Bernard 183
Bergson, Henri 172
Berryman, John 252, 267, 268
   'The Song of the Demented Priest' 267
Bible 177, 178, 179, 245–6, 253
Birtwistle, Harrison 199
Blake, William 81, 88, 94
   'The Chimney Sweeper' 88
   *Jerusalem* 190
   *The Marriage of Heaven and Hell* 68
   'A Poison Tree' 79
   *Songs* 79
Bloom, Harold 265
Bonhoeffer, Dietrich 172, 176
Boulez, Pierre, '*Pli selon pli*' 145, 149
Bradley, F.H. 14, 151, 152, 167, 169, 170
Bradwardine, Thomas 161, 176
Brahms, Johannes 175, 176
Brewster, Scott 102n
Bromwich, David 209n, 217, 218–19
Brooks, Cleanth 88
Brown, Colin 244n
Browning, Robert 90
Brueghel, Pieter, *The Blind Leading the Blind* 155
Burke, Edmund 73n, 116, 117, 118, 172
Burrow, Colin 105
Butler, Joseph 12, 65, 66, 74–5, 84, 172
   *Fifteen Sermons* 74–5

Caedmon 275
Carcanet Press 264
Carducci, Giosuè, *Odi Barbare* (*Barbarous Odes*) 62, 233
Carew, Thomas 138, 240
   *Coelum Britannicum* 138
Cavalcanti, Guido 55n
Cayzer, Elizabeth 235
Celan, Paul 201
Chaplin, Charlie 205
Charles I 236, 237, 239, 241, 245, 246, 248, 250
Clare, John 12, 56
Clutag Press 27, 28, 29n, 227n, 231n, 232, 233, 234n, 252, 253
Coleridge, Samuel Taylor 14, 63, 116, 117, 152, 161–6, 189
   *Anima Poetae* 165
   *Biographia Literaria* 63, 162, 164
   'Conversation Poems' 92
   *Table Talk* 163, 164
Colonna, Vittoria, *Amaro Lagrimar* 35
Confucius 176

# Index

Conquest, Robert, *New Lines* anthology 112
Cookson, William 231n, 274
Cowley, Abraham 79
Cowper, William 66, 67, 81–3
   'The Castaway' 82, 83
Crossley-Holland, Kevin 255
Crozier, Andrew 99, 103, 112n
Cunningham, John 239n

Dallapiccola, Luigi 253
Dante Alighieri 9n, 30, 32, 36
   *Paradiso* 29
Daumier, Honoré, '*On dit que les Parisiens sont difficiles à satisfaire*' 208
Davie, Donald 67, 75, 76–7, 79–80, 83, 159
Davies, Damian Walford 45n
Derrida, Jacques 112
Descartes, René 126
Deutsch, André 15, 231n, 255, 256, 257, 263, 265, 266, 269
Diana, Princess of Wales 213–14, 215
Dodsworth, Martin 24
Dolmen Press 274
Dolmetsch, Arnold 198
Donne, John 12, 50, 88, 138, 198
   'A Nocturnal Upon S. Lucy's Day' 51
Dryden, John 66, 69, 72, 76, 80, 269
Dufour Editions 263, 264
Dutchske, Rudi 89n

Eberhardt, Richard 99n
Edwards, Michael 176n
Elgar, Edward 108
Eliot, T.S. 24–5, 26, 30, 32, 33, 36, 38, 94, 105, 112, 169, 170, 175, 176, 181, 186n, 188, 195, 196n, 198, 205, 208, 209, 217
   *Anabasis* 23, 24, 37
   *Ariel Poems* 23
   *Ash-Wednesday* 23, 29, 31, 32
   *Coriolan* 31, 32
   *East Coker* 35
   *Four Quartets* 31, 35, 37, 169
   'The Function of Criticism' 32
   *The Hollow Men* 23–4, 31
   'Imperfect Critics' 120
   *Little Gidding* 26, 35
   *The Love Song of J. Alfred Prufrock* 8
   *Marina* 24, 31, 32, 33–4, 170, 171, 172
   *Sweeney Agonistes* 31
   'The Three Voices of Poetry' 104
   'Tradition and the Individual Talent' 206–7, 210
   'Triumphal March' 31
   *The Waste Land* 23, 31, 169
   'What is Minor Poetry' 32
Emerson, Ralph Waldo 110n, 172
Empson, William 88, 94, 183–4, 185
   'Arachne' 183
   'Let It Go' 183
Enitharmon Press 134n, 227n, 232, 233, 241n

Faber 16
Fantasy Press 232n, 257, 261
Fisch, Harold, 'Alchemy and English Literature' 49
Fisher, Allen 99
Fisher, Roy 99n
Fitter, Chris 57–8
Foreman, Susan 241n
Forrest-Thomson, Veronica 99, 113
Fulcrum Press 274
Fuller, Roy 255

Gallagher, Kenneth T. 126
Gascoyne, David 255
George, Michael 274
Gervais, David 242
Gide, André 122, 126, 127
   *Les Nourritures Terrestres* (*Fruits of the Earth*) 122, 125
Goodwin, Mark 13
   'Borrowdale Details' 139, 140
Green, T.H. 116, 152, 153, 156, 167, 168, 169, 172
   'Popular Philosophy in its Relation to Life' 168
Grigson, Geoffrey 40
*Gringoire* (journal) 160
*The Ground Aslant* (Tarlo anthology) 13, 135, 139, 142, 146
Gurney, Ivor 25, 107

Haeften, Hans-Bernd von 194, 229, 230, 235
Haffenden, John 17, 143, 185, 189
Hall, Donald 264–5
Hampson, Robert 112n
Harper and Row 265
Harrison, Tony 86
   *V* 121–2
Hart, Henry 69n, 75–6, 79n, 242n
Hartman, Geoffrey 142
Haughton, Hugh 120, 123, 127
Haynes, Kenneth 231n, 254
Heaney, Seamus 103
   'Englands of the Mind' 242–4
   *North* 18n
Hegel, G.W.F. 151
Heidegger, Martin 100, 249–50
Henrietta Maria of France 237
Herbert, George 13, 62, 134, 137, 138, 148, 149, 198, 246, 247
   'The Altar' 143–4, 246, 248–9
   'The Church-Porch' 248
   'Easter-Wings' 54, 135–6, 137, 246, 247
   'Jordan II' 247n
   *The Temple* 247–8
Hernández, Miguel, 'Elegy' 143
Herrick, Robert 138
Higgins, David H. 62
Hill, Geoffrey
   DRAMA
      *Brand* 30, 98n
   POETRY
      'After Cumae' 259
      *Al Tempo De' Tremuoti* 34n, 200
      'Annunciations' 87–8, 93, 119n
      'An Apology For the Revival of Christian Architecture in England' 92, 165, 166, 179, 226n, 227, 243n, 244
      'The Argument of the Masque' 70–1
      'An Ark on the Flood' 257, 259
      'The Bibliographers' 260
      *The Book of Baruch by the Gnostic Justin* 10, 201–2
      *Broken Hierarchies* (collection) 10, 44n, 54n, 193n, 232–3, 253, 254, 261, 272, 275
      'Broken Hierarchies' (poem) 30
      *Canaan* 9, 30, 31, 135, 143, 145, 171, 173, 175, 180, 200
      'Citations' (I) and (II) 110, 128
      *Clavics* 13, 27n, 30, 34n, 54–9, 62, 134–42, 144–50, 226n, 227, 231, 232, 236–40, 241n, 245–7, 249, 250
      'Coda' 28–9, 35, 45, 191
      *Collected Poems* 9, 79n, 255, 261
      'Cycle' 171–2
      *The Daybooks* 10, 43, 44, 59, 61, 63, 107, 202, 227, 254
      'De Jure Belli ac Pacis' 31, 191
      'The Death of Shelley' 259–60
      'Discourse: For Stanley Rosen' 34, 88, 151, 165, 167
      'Doctor Faustus' 174, 260
      'Elegiac Stanzas' 174, 259
      *Expostulations on the Volcano* 27n
      'Ezekiel's Wheel' 176–9, 199
      'Fidelities' 179
      *For the Unfallen* 17, 78, 174, 255, 258–61, 263–7, 272
      'Four Poems Regarding the Endurance of Poets' 135, 143, 232n
      'From the Annals' 175
      'Funeral Music' 10n, 30, 86, 92–4, 119, 179, 186–7, 191, 197, 200, 266, 268
      'Genesis' 79n, 93, 257
      *Hymns to Our Lady of Chartres* 254
      'Improvisation on "O Welt ich muss dich lassen"' 181
      'Improvisation on "Warum ist uns das Licht gegeben?"' 175
      'In Memoriam: Ernst Barlach' 227–30
      'In Memoriam: Gillian Rose' 155–6, 157
      'In Memory of Jane Fraser' 272–3, 275
      'In the Valley of the Arrow' 34–5
      *King Log* 17, 26, 31, 135, 143, 158, 174, 179, 187, 232, 254,

255, 263, 264, 266–70, 272–3
'Lachrimae' 21, 179, 187, 271
'The Laurel Axe' 166
*Liber Illustrium Virorum* 27n
'Little Apocalypse' 259
'London Reading' (podcast of poetry reading) 43n, 54n, 61n
'The Lowlands of Holland' 259
*Mercian Hymns* 7n, 13, 17–19, 21, 22, 24, 30, 72n, 82, 105, 108, 134, 135, 142–3, 160, 174, 187, 188, 191, 200, 226, 227, 232, 242–4, 255, 264, 265, 271, 273–5
*The Mystery of the Charity of Charles Péguy* 13, 30, 45, 66, 134, 135, 139, 140, 154, 174–5, 200, 231n, 255, 274
*New and Collected Poems* 261
*Odi Barbare* 27n, 30, 59–63, 226n, 227, 232, 233–5, 244n, 250
'Of Commerce and Society' 121, 191
'On the Reality of the Symbol' 175
*Oraclau | Oracles* 18, 28, 32, 38, 43–7, 50–2, 61–2, 232
*The Orchards of Syon* 9, 30, 35, 37, 60, 95, 96–7, 106, 179, 184n, 199, 226
'Ovid in the Third Reich' 158, 159
'A Pastoral' 119
'The Pentecost Castle' 20–4, 78, 184, 187, 271
'Pindarics' 226n
*The Poetry and Voice of Geoffrey Hill* (recording) 275
'A Prayer to the Sun' 143, 232n
'A Précis or Memorandum of Civil Power' 98, 120–4, 127, 128–9, 130
*Preghiere* 232n
'Psalms of Assize' 231n
*Scenes from Comus* 9, 26–7, 70–1, 166, 189, 191, 192, 193, 244n
'Sei Madrigali' 200

'September Song' 78, 86–7, 88, 187, 199
'Sobieski's Shield' 200
'Soliloquies' 135, 187
'Solomon's Mines' 174
*Somewhere Is Such a Kingdom* 261, 265
'The Songbook of Sebastian Arrurruz' 30, 31, 94, 105, 108, 135, 187, 200, 232, 254, 266, 273
'Sorrel' 143
*Speech! Speech!* 9, 14, 30, 66, 67, 80–3, 87, 105, 108n, 124, 160, 168, 199, 203–22, 231, 262
'The Stone Man' 31, 187
'Summer Night' 119n
*Tenebrae* 20, 21, 78–9, 119n, 179, 200, 247n, 255, 262, 271
'Terribilis est locus iste' 191
'Three Mystical Songs' 19–21, 30
'To the Nieuport Scout' 145
*A Treatise of Civil Power* (collection) 9, 18, 27n, 28, 37n, 99–101, 120, 128, 185–6, 191, 200, 227, 231, 232, 250, 252–3
'A Treatise of Civil Power' (poem) 27, 28, 252
*The Triumph of Love* 9, 30, 37–8, 40, 44, 66–71, 80, 101, 106, 161, 186n, 189, 196, 199, 224–6, 231, 253
'The Troublesome Reign' 174
'T.S. Eliot in Swansea, 1944' 32, 33
'Two Chorale-Preludes' 30
'Two Formal Elegies: For the Jews in Europe' 78
*Without Title* 9, 30, 34, 40, 71, 200, 226n
PROSE
'The Absolute Reasonableness of Robert Southwell' 105
'Alienated Majesty: Gerard M. Hopkins' 110n, 120
'Alienated Majesty: Walt Whitman' 105, 110n, 120

'The Art of Poetry' (interview) 15n, 108n, 174n, 176n, 182n, 186n, 187n, 194, 196, 197, 199, 200n, 203, 207, 208, 212, 213, 221
'Between Politics and Eternity' 29
Clark lectures 118, 133n, 198
*Collected Critical Writings* 10, 14, 172, 254
'"The Conscious Mind's Intelligible Structure": A Debate' 116, 118, 160
'Dividing Legacies' 32
'Dryden's Prize-Song' 64, 65–6, 184, 197
*The Enemy's Country* 118n
'Envoi (1919)' 55n, 107, 123, 132, 133, 198
'Eros in F.H. Bradley and T.S. Eliot' 32, 98–9, 169
'Gurney's "Hobby"' 107
'Jonathan Swift: The Poetry of "Reaction"' 69, 70, 117
'Keeping to the Middle Way' 138–9, 149
'Language, Suffering, and Silence' 25
'Lines of Force' (lecture) 233n
*The Lords of Limit: Essays on Literature and Ideas* 152, 255
'Milton as Muse' (lecture) 155
'Of Diligence and Jeopardy' 77
'Our Word is Our Bond' 14, 72, 83, 116, 153, 154, 155, 156, 170, 189, 218
'"Perplexed Persistence": The Exemplary Failure of T.H. Green' 105, 117, 167, 168, 172
'A Pharisee to Pharisees' 52, 53, 57, 58n, 59
'Poetry as "Menace" and "Atonement"' 71, 72, 77, 113, 114, 115–16, 117, 152, 159, 185, 195, 218
'A Postscript on Modernist Poetics' 19, 30, 47–8, 53, 137, 175, 184, 187, 195, 196

'Redeeming the Time' 117, 162–3, 164, 166, 189, 200
'Rhetorics of Value and Intrinsic Value' 65, 74, 188
'R.S. Thomas's Welsh Pastoral' 37n, 52–4
'Tacit Pledges' 105
'The Tartar's Bow and the Bow of Ulysses' 65, 72, 105, 118n, 220, 221
'Thus my noblest capacity becomes my deepest perplexity' (*Sermon at Great St Mary's*) 102n, 117n, 194n
'Translating Value: Marginal Observations on a Central Question' 53
'Unhappy Circumstances' 80
'The Weight of the Word' 77, 80, 81, 136, 148, 149
'What Devil Has Got into John Ransom?' 187, 194
'Word Value in F.H. Bradley and T.S. Eliot' 31–2, 169
Hitler, Adolf 158n
Hobbes, Thomas 72, 172
Hollander, John 264
Homer 210
Hooker, Jeremy 44n, 46, 47, 172
Hoover, Paul 107–8
Hopkins, Gerard Manley 12, 46, 52, 53, 60, 94, 96, 116, 153, 200
    Sermons 53n
    'That Nature is a Heraclitean Fire and of the comfort of the Resurrection' 47, 48
    'The Windhover' 47
    'The Wreck of the Deutschland' 154
Hough, Graham 102n, 107
Houghton Mifflin 265
Howerd, Frankie 205
Hughes, Ted 103
Huk, Romana 208, 211n
    'Poetry of the Committed Individual' 85–6
Hume, David 65, 66, 73n

# Index

Ibsen, Henrik, *Brand* 30, 98n
Indiana University Press 263
*The Isis* (magazine) 11, 119
Izambard, Georges 175

Jacobs, Nicolas 19
Jakobson, Roman 115
James I 241
James, Henry 180
James, Stephen 101
James, William 172
Jenner, Simon 106
Jennings, Elizabeth 255
   *A Way of Looking* 257
Jerome, St. 177
Johnson, Robert Sherlaw 126
Johnson, Samuel 74, 183
Jones, David 11, 16–19, 25, 33, 38,
   175, 176, 188, 274
   *The Anathémata* 16, 22
   'Britannia and Germania Embracing'
      34n
   *Dai Greatcoat* 24n
   *Epoch and Artist* 20, 21
   'The Fatigue' 16
   *In Parenthesis* 16, 24–5, 29, 33
   *The Kensington Mass* 274
   'Petra Im Rosenhag' (painting) 34n
   *The Sleeping Lord* (collection) 16–17,
      19n, 22
   'The Sleeping Lord' (poem) 18n,
      22–3, 24
   *The Tribune's Visitation* (collection)
      274
   'The Tribune's Visitation' (poem)
      17n, 27
   'The Tutelar of the Place' 18–19, 37
Jones, Inigo 240, 241, 243–4n
Jonson, Ben 138, 240, 245
Joyce, James 24, 25
Jukes, Pryce 45

Kant, Immanuel 168
   *Critique of Judgement* 164
Keats, John 116, 117–18, 119, 195, 196
   'Ode to a Nightingale' 116, 117–18
Keyes, Sidney 25n
King, Henry 39, 42, 44n, 45n, 62n

Kinnahan, Linda 102, 103
Kinsella, Thomas, *Another September*
   274
Knottenbelt, E.M. 242n
Krook, Dorothea 172

Lacan, Jacques 100n
Langbaum, Robert, 'The New Nature
   Poetry' 40
Larkin, Philip, *The Less Deceived* 263
Lawes, William 54, 138, 139, 140, 141,
   237, 238, 239, 240
Lebowitz, Fran 115
Lee, Laurie 255, 257, 258, 261, 269–70
   *My Many-Coated Man* 270
Levi, Peter 255
Levin, Samuel 73n
Lindley, David 101–2, 104, 108
Lindop, Grevel 7
Locke, John 65, 172
Logan, William 39, 40
Lowell, Robert 112n, 267
Lyon, John 42, 188n, 205
Lyotard, Jean-François 94

MacKinnon, D.M. 172
Mallarmé, Stéphane 145, 146
Marcel, Gabriel 122, 126
Maritain, Jacques 160
Matthews, Steven 54, 101
Maurois, André 125
McDonald, Peter 120, 121
McNeillie, Andrew 15, 231n, 233, 252,
   253
Messiaen, Olivier 123
   *Quatuor pour la Fin du Temps*
      (*Quartet for the End of Time*) 122,
      125–6, 127
Mid-Century Book Society of New York
   263
Mill, John Stuart 102n
Miłosz, Czesław 126n
Milton, John 26, 27, 69, 81, 192, 253
   *Paradise Lost* 28, 128, 177
   *A Treatise of Civil Power in*
      *Ecclesiastical Causes* 120, 253
Mirren, Helen 100n
Monk, Geraldine 99

Morley, Lord (Henry Parker) 224, 225
Morrison, Blake 185
Mounic, Anne 195n
Mozley, J.B., *Eight Lectures on Miracles* 50
Mulford, Wendy 13
  'Salthouse, 1986' 136
Murdoch, Iris, *On 'God' and 'Good'* 152
Murphy, Kathryn 116
Murphy, Sheila 262, 274
Mustill, Edd 88n

Nash, Ogden 255
Nettleship, R.L. 167
*New Lines* (Conquest anthology) 112
*The New Poetry* (Alvarez anthology) 11, 112
Newman, John Henry 116, 188
  *Loss and Gain: The Story of a Convert* 165
Newton, John 82
Nichols, Roger 126
Nietzsche, Friedrich 187n

O'Hara, Frank 99n
Okigbo, Christopher 176, 177
Olson, Charles 103, 112n
Ong, Walter J. 53
  'Wit and Mystery' 52
Oppen, George 112n
Orpen, William 233, 234, 235–6
  *Leading Life in the West* 235
  *Self Portrait* 234
  *The Signing of Peace in the Hall of Mirrors, Versailles, 28 June 1919* 234, 235
Ovid 158
Owen, Wilfred 25
Oxford University Press 233, 254

Paret, Peter, *An Artist Against the Third Reich* 230
*Paris Review* 187, 197, 207
Parker, Henry (Lord Morley) 224, 225
Pärt, Arvo 123, 124n
Patterson, Ian 88n
Paulin, Tom 107n, 149–50, 244n
Pearson, Gabriel 179

Péguy, Charles 28, 29, 45, 154, 175
*The Penguin Book of Spanish Verse* 78
Penguin Books 27n, 28, 227n, 232, 252, 253, 255
Perloff, Marjorie 103, 112n
Perse, St-John 23, 188
  *Anabase* 24
Petrarch, *Trionfi* 224, 225, 226
Petronius, *Satyricon* 68
Pierre de Nolhac 226
Piggott, Stuart 18
Pitney, Gene 110
Plath, Sylvia 112n
Plato, *The Republic* 58
*Poetry* (magazine) 264
Poetry Book Society 258, 267, 268, 269, 270
*Poetry of the Committed Individual: A Stand Anthology of Poetry* 86
Pope, Alexander 69, 77, 167, 175
  *The Dunciad* 76
Pound, Ezra 24, 31, 66, 72, 76, 83, 112n, 116, 122, 123, 175, 176, 181
  *Cantos* 103, 105, 238
  'Envoi (1919)' 122, 123, 132, 133, 198
  *Hugh Selwyn Mauberley* 123
Powell, Michael, *The Man in Black* 175
Presley, Frances 13
  'April' 136–7
Prynne, J.H. 11, 12, 85, 88–92, 95–7, 99
  'Die a Millionaire' 89–90, 91
  'The Holy City' 90–1, 95–6
  'Sketch for a Financial Theory of the Self' 90
  'Thoughts on the Esterházy Court Uniform' 91
Pugin, Augustus
  *An Apology for the Revival of Christian Architecture in England* 165–6, 243n, 244n
  *The Present State of Ecclesiastical Architecture in England* 248n
"Pylons" (magazine) 30

Radcliffe, Sophie 26
Rahner, Karl 187

*Theological Investigations* 175
Ransom, John Crowe 183–4, 194
Ratcliffe, Sophie 253
Raworth, Tom 99, 111
Reemtsma, Hermann F. 230n
Ricks, Christopher 29n, 33, 118–19, 184n
Riley, Denise 11, 13, 99, 100–1, 103, 108–11, 113–15, 118, 120, 133
   'Dark Looks' 101
   *Impersonal Passion* 113
   'Linguistic Unease' 113–14, 115, 128
   'Lyric' 109–10
   'A Misremembered Lyric' 110
   *Mop Mop Georgette* 99, 101
   'Rayon' 101
   'A Shortened Set' 110, 129–32
   'Song' 100
   'Well All Right' 101
   'When It's Time to Go' 101
   *The Words of Selves* 113
Riley, Peter, 'Vertigo' 146, 147–9
Rimbaud, Arthur 154, 155, 175
Roberts, Andrew Michael 94, 138, 144, 188–9, 208–9, 213
Robinson, Peter 73n, 75, 164
Rockham, H. 29
Romer, Stephen 42
Rose, Gillian 14, 155–6, 157, 170
Rosenberg, Isaac 25, 254
Rowland, Anthony 100n
Royal Society of Literature 271
Ruddock, Margot 194
Ruskin, John 243n
   *Political Economy of Art* 223
Rutgers University Press 263

Sampson, Fiona, *Beyond the Lyric* 104
Sartre, Jean-Paul 86, 210, 211n
Schelling, F.W.J. 162, 164
Schlegel, Friedrich 113
Schmidt, Michael 264
Scotus, John Duns 53n
Searle, John 73n
Sexton, Anne 112n
Shaftesbury, Third Earl of (Anthony Ashley Cooper) 12, 66

'Soliloquy, or Advice to an Author' 70
Shakespeare, William 29, 34, 88
   *Love's Labour's Lost* 196
Sheppard, Robert 112n
Sherry, Vincent B. 72–3n, 242
Sidgwick, Henry 168
Sidney, Philip, *The Arcadia* 62n, 233
Sijé, Ramón 143
Silkin, Jon 11, 86, 87
   'A Daisy' 86
   'Death of a Bird' 86
   'Furnished Lives' 86
Simias of Rhodes, 'The Wings' 247n
Simms, Jacqueline 254
Skelton, John 219, 220, 221
   *Magnyfycence* 221
Smart, Christopher 79
Smith, Stevie 255
Sophocles 249
Southwell, Robert 194
Stallworthy, Jon 254
*Stand* (magazine) 11, 86
*Standpoint* (magazine) 234n
Stuart-Smith, Stephen 233
Swift, Jonathan 12, 66–70, 75, 76, 81, 117
   *A Tale of a Tub* 68

Tarlo, Harriet 140
   *The Ground Aslant* anthology 13, 135, 139, 142, 146
Tate, Allen 99n, 102, 260, 262, 264
   'More Sonnets at Christmas' 260
Tennyson, Alfred 175, 265
Thomas, R.S. 26, 32, 52–4
Thomson, James 12
   *The Seasons* 56
Thwaite, Anthony 261
Trilling, Lionel 263
Trotter, David 92, 93
Turley, Richard Marggraf 45n
Turner, J.M.W. 150

UK Arts and Humanities Research Council projects 144
University of Minnesota Press 262–3
Unwin, Mary 81

Updike, John 255

Valéry, Paul, 'Le Cimetière marin' 186n
Vaughan, Henry 12, 13, 50, 52, 57–8, 62, 134, 137, 138, 141, 198, 246, 247
   'The Evening-Watch: A Dialogue,' 137, 141
   'The Morning-Watch' 54, 57, 246
   'The Night' 52, 57
Vaughan, Thomas 141
   *Lumen de Lumine, or, a New Magicall Light* 52
Vendler, Helen 102, 105, 111, 123

Wainwright, Jeffrey 9n, 69, 78n, 80–1, 242
Watts, Carol 111, 129
Watts, Isaac 76, 77, 78
Webb, Robert 240
Webern, Anton 108
Weil, Simone 14, 22, 33, 76, 151, 152, 156–61, 170, 195
   *L'Enracinement* 19
   *Gravity and Grace* 156, 157, 159
   *The Need for Roots* 19n, 157, 160, 184
   Notebooks 20n
   *Waiting for God* 157n
Wesley, Charles 66, 77, 80
Wesley, John 66, 80, 81
Wesleyan University Press 263
Whitman, Walt 105
   *Leaves of Grass* 10n, 275
Wilbur, Richard 267
Williams, Charles 7
Williams, Raymond 88
Williams, William Carlos 103, 112n
Wittgenstein, Ludwig 26, 100, 161, 172
Wood, Hugh 193
Wordsworth, William 42, 66, 72, 105, 116, 117, 119, 130, 142, 168
   'Ode: Intimations of Immortality' 117, 163
   *The Prelude* 92
Wright, David 206n, 255
Wylie, Alex 9n

Yale University Press 27n, 28, 232, 252
Yeats, W.B. 8, 26, 30, 116, 118, 185, 194
   'Byzantium' 178
   *Letters* 20n
   'Nineteen Hundred and Nineteen' 229
   'The Statues' 30

Zukofsky, Louis 112n

www.ingramcontent.com/pod-product-compliance
Lightning Source LLC
Chambersburg PA
CBHW021137230426
43667CB00005B/154